SOCIAL PROBLEMS
AND
SOCIAL POLICY:
The American Experience

SOCIAL PROBLEMS AND SOCIAL POLICY: The American Experience

THE PROBLEM OF UNEMPLOYMENT

BY

PAUL H. DOUGLAS

AND

AARON DIRECTOR

ARNO PRESS

A New York Times Company

New York — 1976

Editorial Supervision: SHEILA MEHLMAN

———◆———

Reprint Edition 1976 by Arno Press Inc.

Reprinted from a copy in the University of Illinois Library

SOCIAL PROBLEMS AND SOCIAL POLICY: The American Experience
ISBN for complete set: 0-405-07474-3
See last pages of this volume for titles.

Manufactured in the United States of America

———◆———

Library of Congress Cataloging in Publication Data

Douglas, Paul Howard, 1892-
    The problem of unemployment.

    (Social problems and social policy--the American
experience)
    Reprint of the ed. published by Macmillan, New York.
    Bibliography: p.
    1. Unemployed. 2. Economic history--1918-1945.
I. Director, Aaron, joint author. II. Title.
III. Series.
HD5706.D6 1976   331.1'37   75-17217
ISBN 0-405-07488-3

THE PROBLEM OF UNEMPLOYMENT

THE MACMILLAN COMPANY
NEW YORK · BOSTON · CHICAGO · DALLAS
ATLANTA · SAN FRANCISCO

MACMILLAN & CO., LIMITED
LONDON · BOMBAY · CALCUTTA
MELBOURNE

THE MACMILLAN COMPANY
OF CANADA, LIMITED
TORONTO

THE PROBLEM OF UNEMPLOYMENT

BY

PAUL H. DOUGLAS

Professor of Economics, University of Chicago

AND

AARON DIRECTOR

Instructor in Economics, University of Chicago

PREFACE BY

FRANK AYDELOTTE

President, Swarthmore College

NEW YORK

THE MACMILLAN COMPANY

1931

Printed in the United States of America by
J. J. LITTLE & IVES COMPANY, NEW YORK

TO

FRANCES PERKINS
PAUL U. KELLOGG

AND

S. S. FELS

DEVOTED SERVANTS OF THE COMMON GOOD

ACKNOWLEDGMENTS

We are most of all indebted to Swarthmore College and to the Steering Committee of the Swarthmore Unemployment Study for the unfailing coöperation which they showed us. No association could have been more pleasant than was ours with them and our work was facilitated and aided at every turn by their friendly help and understanding. Our work has been improved by the material which was gathered when one of the authors served as technical adviser to the New York Committee on the Stabilization of Employment and as Secretary to the Pennsylvania Committee on Unemployment. The members of these committees have been of great aid to us and we wish to thank them and more particularly to acknowledge the help received from Henry Bruere, the Chairman of the New York Commission, Frances Perkins, the Industrial Commissioner of New York and Governor Gifford Pinchot of Pennsylvania. We wish also to thank a number of others who have been of great assistance and more particularly Professors Garfield Cox and Lloyd Mints of the University of Chicago, Professor Arnold Tolles of Mt. Holyoke College, Miss Aryness Joy of the staff of the Federal Reserve Board, Senator Robert F. Wagner, Mr. Bryce M. Stewart, Miss Mary Gilson and the Industrial Relations Counsellors, Inc.

We owe a debt of gratitude also to Mrs. Frances Slaugh, Miss Boon and Miss Agnes Jacques for the care with which they helped to prepare the manuscript for the press.

Finally we wish to thank the editors of the Survey, the

Annals of the American Academy of Political and Social Science, the American Federationist, and Current History for permission to reprint with adaptations some material which was originally prepared for these journals.

PAUL H. DOUGLAS
AARON DIRECTOR

Chicago, February 26, 1931.

PREFACE

This volume is the result of a suggestion made by a group of business men in Philadelphia and New York that there should be undertaken at Swarthmore College a comprehensive and continuing study of the problem of unemployment, including the results of economic research and of practical measures for regularization which were being undertaken in various industries.

The Board of Managers of the College quite reasonably felt that it would be unwise to embark on so far reaching and expensive a project, one which was out of the line of ordinary academic work, without a preliminary survey of the field. Funds for this survey were generously given by a donor who refuses to allow his name to be mentioned, and Professor Paul H. Douglas of the University of Chicago was invited to come to Swarthmore to undertake it.

The task which Professor Douglas was called upon to do was a difficult one, and he accomplished it with a success which far outran the expectations of all those connected with the study. It was nothing less than to analyze the vast amount of material which had been printed on the subject, to bring together fugitive reports of experiments in the regularization of employment in a hundred different industries, to summarize the experiences of other countries in the organization of employment exchanges and plans for unemployment insurance, and to organize all this material on the various aspects of the question in such a way as to indicate what are the most promising lines of inquiry and by what means definite results could best be reached. That achievement, of which this volume is the permanent record, constitutes the first and most important step in attacking the problem.

This book is the report which Professor Douglas and his assistant, Mr. Aaron Director, made to the authorities of Swarthmore College. It has been accepted by the Board of Managers as a program for further research which will be undertaken at Swarthmore, provided sufficient funds can be found for that purpose. If these funds are not available, the book will nevertheless constitute an important contribution to the subject.

The proposed study of unemployment at Swarthmore met a hearty response from leaders in economics and in industry from the moment that it was announced. During the time that he was in residence at the College Professor Douglas was called upon to act as technical adviser to the New York Commission on Reducing Unemployment and drafted their report; he served as secretary of Governor Pinchot's Pennsylvania Committee on Unemployment and wrote the report of that Committee; he assisted Miss Perkins, Industrial Commissioner of New York, in preparing for the Governor's Conference on Unemployment called by Governor Roosevelt, and was able to render useful service to the Conference during its sessions in New York, January 23rd and 24th. In addition he assisted in the drafting of unemployment insurance bills which are now proposed in various states, including Ohio, Illinois, and Michigan; and at the request of the Board of Arbitration of the Women's Clothing Industry in Cleveland he drew up the report upon which the final award of that body was based. Had time permitted and had it been possible to employ a sufficiently large staff, the number of these practical activities could have been largely increased.

Both the work which Professor Douglas did and the opportunities which he was compelled to refuse demonstrate the need for such a study as has been planned at Swarthmore. The unique feature of that plan was the proposal to bring the results of economic research directly to the service of industries which were seeking to regularize employment and of public agencies which were making plans for employment exchanges and for schemes of insurance against unemployment.

The whole question has much in common with many problems of public health which have been solved by the application of scientific research to methods of public administration. There is probably no disease which is the cause of more human misery than results directly or indirectly from unemployment. This fact is apparent to the general public in periods of industrial depression like the present, but it is not widely realized that irregularities of employment, "unemployment within employment," the prejudice against older workers and the introduction of labor saving machinery, cause acute misery to large sections of the laboring class in times of prosperity as well.

Unemployment is like disease furthermore in the complicated nature of its causes and in the vast amount of scientific knowledge and scientific research which must underlie any effective measures for its amelioration. In questions of public health this is well understood. There are many organizations for research into the causes and care of various diseases not merely of men but of plants and animals as well, but no similar effort has ever been made on an adequate scale to understand unemployment. Only by some such method is there any hope of controlling this disease of our economic system. It cannot be cured by muddling through. Our industrial organization is a vast and complicated machine which only the expert can understand and which has never yet run smoothly for any very long time, in any country, in any generation, since the Industrial Revolution. The difficulties are mainly caused not by lack of good-will on the part either of labor or of capital, but by lack of understanding of the complicated issues involved.

The failure of our industrial organization to function smoothly, the fact that men must starve because they have produced too much food, or go naked because they have produced too many clothes, or sleep in the parks because they have built too many houses—this failure is fraught with the gravest consequences to the security and well-being of all industrial states. It seems clear that our only hope of reducing unemployment lies in bringing the best brains in economics and in industry to a coöperative study of the problem. The economists can never solve it by theoretical methods alone, and it seems clearly futile to expect that the practical men will be able to solve it by rules of thumb. Only in some combination of the best ideas of both is there any hope of success.

It is precisely to effect that combination that the Swarthmore study was planned. Professor Douglas has stated in the following pages the elements of the problem. Bringing together a staff of the best men of the country to grapple with the questions involved would be expensive. But the cost would be only a tiny fraction of the immense sums that have been spent this winter in attempts to relieve the misery inevitable in the present situation.

The suffering of the millions who have been out of work during the last few months has appealed profoundly to the sympathies of thinking people throughout the country. A magnificent attempt has been made on an unprecedented scale to relieve this widespread destitution. But all this effort, splendid as it was, has done almost nothing to cure the disease. Only research jointly conducted by scholars in their libraries and by industrialists in their factories can do that.

Such a study would be useless unless it could be continued through a period of years. With that assurance there seems to be at least a hope of definite and practical results. If the necessary funds to support it are forthcoming, the research will be undertaken at Swarthmore; if they are not, it is our hope that Professor Douglas' incisive statement of the problem will stimulate the undertaking of a similar study elsewhere.

FRANK AYDELOTTE.

Swarthmore College
March 1931

CONTENTS

CONTENTS

LIST OF TABLES

PART ONE

THE EXTENT AND COSTS OF UNEMPLOYMENT

CHAPTER I

THE MEASUREMENT OF UNEMPLOYMENT AND THE UNEMPLOYMENT CENSUS OF 1930

1. THE NEED FOR MEASURING UNEMPLOYMENT

Unemployment is a familiar phenomenon. Most of us know that there are large groups of men not at work and that the number of these varies from season to season and year to year. The slightest acquaintance with the fact will indicate that the great majority of these workers are hunting for employment and unable to obtain it.

Since wage-earners receive an income only when employed, the loss of a job is followed by tragic consequences. So tragic are these consequences that many fine-spirited men and women are impatient of attempts to measure the extent of unemployment, regarding such efforts as a cold and heartless waste of energy which might better be devoted to the much needed work of prevention and relief. But the scientific mind knows that measurements are not obstacles to but essentials of any adequate program of reform.

There can be no appreciation of the seriousness of unemployment without a knowledge of its true extent. In the absence of information about the number unemployed, many people will drug themselves into the belief that but few of those seeking work are really unable to find it. The comfortable men and women of the ruling class do not like to admit unpleasant facts about a social system which has proved its worth by giving them—the deserving persons—its material rewards. Hence until the evidence is available they will continue to believe that there is little unemployment. Even then, some will continue to believe it—but not so many.

3

For this reason those who intentionally underestimate the extent of unemployment, as a means of applying mental healing to industry, are guilty of a cruel wrong. They provide for the conscience of the comfortable classes a salve which the latter are only too anxious to obtain and which facilitates the closing of their hearts to the necessity for reform. The higher the position in political and economic life which is occupied by these malpractitioners of statistics, the greater is the resulting harm.

But while those in power naturally tend to minimize the amount of unemployment, others by either temperament or design tend to exaggerate it. Belief in these highly colored estimates might lead people to adopt ill-considered programs of change. And so there is no remedy for unemployment without a quantitative analysis of its extent.

This analysis will advance the program of reform by helping to determine the relative importance of the various causes of unemployment. It will make possible an approximation of the amount caused by seasonal and by cyclical fluctuations and knowledge as to whether or not the amount is changing. Such measurements will help us to prepare a program with such a distribution of our energies as is in some proportion to the need for them.

Finally, a knowledge of the extent of unemployment is essential, not only for awakening a "consumer-demand" for reform measures, but is equally as necessary for their administration. It is impossible, for example, to use public works adequately to balance business depressions without knowing approximately the increases or decreases in unemployment; nor can a system of unemployment benefits and contributions be elaborated without a fairly good idea of the rate of unemployment.

2. How Can We Measure Unemployment?

Obtaining a measure of unemployment is not, however, a simple procedure. Not only is it difficult to discriminate between involuntary and other forms of idleness, but it is even more difficult to devise and put into effect the machinery for collecting this information.

It is customary to define unemployment as a situation in which workers able to work are unsuccessfully seeking employment. This at once excludes those not seeking work even though they be idle. Granting the desirability of this exclusion, there remain the difficulties of determining whether or not a particular individual is really seeking a job. It may also be asked whether it is proper to exclude all the disabled and mentally incompetent as is done above or to include those who, though normally able to work and who indeed may be on some company's payroll, are not able to work at any particular time because of illness.

Allied to this is the question whether to include old men and women who, after a lifetime of employment, are unsuccessfully seeking work, or whether to exclude them since they probably will never obtain employment. Having decided to exclude them, is it sufficient to use automatic age limits, or must we have more elaborate standards to separate the older workers who will probably not reënter industry from those who will again obtain employment?

If the aged present their difficulties, the young are no less troublesome. Are the boys and girls who have left school and who are seeking unsuccessfully for jobs "unemployed"? Or must they first get positions and lose them before we can classify them in this group?

Another difficulty is one which has troubled the moving spirits in our 1930 census of unemployment, and their method of dealing with it has not been wholly happy. This is whether any distinction should be drawn between: (1) those employees who are out of work because their employers have told them that they are not needed any longer and (2) those other employees who are no less out of work but who, when they were laid off, were told or allowed to infer that when business began to improve and more workers were added, they would be gradually reëmployed. Can the latter, though not employed, be said to have a "job" in any such significant sense as to merit their being distinguished from those who know that they must look elsewhere for employment? As we shall see, the Census Bureau and the Department of Commerce decided that such a distinction should be drawn and in their published announcements have emphasized primarily the first class or those who knew that they would not be reëmployed at the given plant. Whether or not this is a justifiable major distinction and whether it was handled properly by the Census Bureau is a matter which we must postpone for later treatment.

But even if we assume that lay-offs should be counted as unemployment, should we also include hours lost within a day or week, or should we count only those cases where the workers are laid off for whole days or weeks at a time? This, in brief, is a question as to whether unemployment may be partial as well as complete.

These are then some of the difficulties which inevitably arise in the attempt to define and measure unemployment. The definition which will be adopted in practice will depend in no small measure upon the type of method which is used to gather the data. If this could always be remembered, a great deal of somewhat fruitless discussion could be avoided.

In the mind of the authors the following five methods are the principal means of collecting these data, and we believe that their sequence represents the approximate degree of precision in grouping and accuracy of measurement which can be obtained from each:

(1) **Census of Unemployment.** This is by all odds the most inclusive way of collecting material since everyone not at work can be brought within it and then classified into a number of different groups. Such censuses of unemployment have been taken in the United States three times before the 1930 census, namely in 1890, 1900, and 1910. In these censuses, gainfully occupied workers were asked if they were out of work during the preceding year and, if so, for approximately how many months. The returns were published in the Censuses of 1890 [1] and 1900 [2] according to whether

---

[1] *Eleventh Census*, Vol. 2, pp. cxxxvii-cxliii; 448 ff.
[2] *Special Reports of Twelfth Census*, Volume on Occupations, pp. 76-77.

the workers lost from 0 to 3 months, from 3 to 6 months, and 6 to 12 months, but the returns for 1910 were never tabulated.

The very inclusiveness of the census method makes it so expensive that it can be used only infrequently. But even when it is impossible to take such a general census it is sometimes practicable to take a census for a given sample of the population in specific localities. The most inclusive of these smaller censuses was that conducted by the United States Bureau of Labor Statistics in 1915 for approximately 890,000 wage-earners in twenty-nine different cities.[3]

Since then, there have been a number of very good local censuses of unemployment. Among these may be mentioned the studies by Croxton of Columbus, Ohio, and Buffalo, New York; the Dewhurst-Willits censuses for Philadelphia of 1929 and 1930, the Cincinnati censuses for the same years and smaller studies in Bloomington, Indiana, and Champaign-Urbana, Illinois.

(2) Statistics Derived from Unemployment Insurance. Unemployment insurance generally brings as a by-product a distinct improvement in the statistics of those unemployed. The unemployment statistics which we have for England and Germany are, as a matter of fact, derived primarily from such sources and they are a big improvement over what was formerly available in these countries. In such cases, the definition of unemployment depends entirely upon the provisions of the unemployment insurance act. If the law aims to compensate only a certain portion of those who are out of work, such as those who have been unemployed for more than a given period in a year, then to that degree the numbers receiving benefits will be less than the real numbers. Similarly the rules governing the conditions under which benefits, if any, are to be paid to those who voluntarily quit their job or who are discharged for cause will also affect the numbers shown.

[3] *Bulletin 172* of the *U. S. Bureau of Labor Statistics,* Unemployment in New York City and *Bulletin 195, Ibid,* Unemployment in the United States.

The value of such figures over a period of time is, moreover, sometimes impaired by varying interpretations imposed either by law or by administrative authorities.

Less reliable figures are obtained in countries which subsidize voluntary unemployment insurance. The trade unions, which are generally the groups to take advantage of the subsidies, necessarily make reports on those of their numbers who are unemployed. This, as we shall see, is a better source than trade-union reports made independently of any insurance plan. But, because of the fact that these returns are confined to specific groups of workers, the statistics are less valuable than those collected under compulsory insurance systems.

(3) Statistics Derived from the Operation of Public Employment Offices. The out-of-work registers of the public employment offices sometimes furnish material from which statistics of unemployment can be derived. Its value depends upon the number of employment offices and whether registration of unemployed workers is compulsory, etc.

(4) Trade-Union Reports. Unless associated with the administration of out-of-work insurance schemes, these reports are likely to be made somewhat casually by the trade-union secretaries. It was the presence of these benefits which made the trade union reports in Great Britain before 1911 quite reliable, while their absence has helped to invalidate the trade union data which were collected by New York [4] and Massachusetts [5] and which are now being published by the American Federation of Labor.

In Russia where unionism is all-inclusive and where the discipline and the statistical work of the unions are both highly developed, the statistics on unemployment from union sources are the best in that country.

(5) By Subtracting the Probable Numbers Employed

[4] New York collected data for the years 1897-1916. For an analysis of these data see Paul H. Douglas, *Real Wages in the United States*, pp. 405-09.

[5] See *Labor Bulletin 140* of the *Massachusetts Department of Labor and Industry* 1923, pp. 20-21, The period covered was 1908-23. The Massachusetts Bureau recommenced gathering statistics on the unemployment of building trades unionists in 1926.

from the Probable Labor Supply. When other means are not available, an approach to the measurement of unemployment may be made by: (1) Determining the probable numbers seeking employment. These can primarily be based on the periodic censuses of occupations with interpolations for the intervening years according to the rate of population growth, etc. (2) Determining the probable number of persons employed. This can now be done with fair accuracy because of the improved indices of employment. (3) Subtracting the numbers employed from the probable labor supply. We thus obtain a residual which we may regard as an approximation to the amount of unemployment. This method was first used by Hornell Hart [6] and has since been further developed by King,[7] Givens and Wolman,[8] and by one of the present authors.[9] It has been criticized by a number of writers.[10] It is true that an error in the computation of either the labor supply or the numbers employed (unless compensatory) will give rise to a larger error in the residual. The nature of the materials is such that this method should not be used where there are other more reliable sources of data. When this other material is lacking, as has been the case in the United States, it is, however, better to compute such an index than not to have one at all. As we shall see in the next chapter, there are indications from other sources that the results obtained for this country are not far from the facts.

3. The Unemployment Census of 1930

Public interest in the subject of unemployment increased appreciably during 1928 and 1929, and as a result of many demands and Congressional action the Department of Com-

---

[6] Hornell Hart, *Fluctuations in Employment in Cities of the United States*, Trounstine Foundation, Cincinnati, 1917, pp. 47-59.

[7] W. I. King, *The National Income; Extent and Distribution.*

[8] *Recent Economic Changes*, Vol. II, pp. 469-78.

[9] Paul H. Douglas, *Real Wages in the United States*, pp. 430-449.

[10] Cf. W. A. Berridge, Cycles of Employment and Unemployment in the United States, *Journal American Statistical Association*, March, 1922, p. 43.

merce included questions on the subject of unemployment in the 1930 Census. It was decided to change the form of inquiry from that used in 1890, 1900, and 1910. It will be remembered that in those years the person interviewed was asked to estimate the probable amount of time during the preceding year which was lost by those in the family who were gainfully employed. This, it was thought with some reason, was subject to a considerable margin of error since it was at best difficult to remember the total amount of time lost during the whole preceding year, and this was especially so where the housewife furnished the information. Hence it was decided merely to ask whether or not those who customarily were gainfully employed had been at work on the last preceding working day. A separate schedule was devised for those not at work to show the main reasons for failure to work.[11] This separate unemployment schedule divided this group into two main classes—(1) those who "had a job" and (2) those who did not have a "job." Under each category the reasons for unemployment were asked according to the following scheme: [12]

I. *Those who "had jobs":*
   a. Those laid off but who expected to return to their former jobs.
   b. Those idle because of sickness or disability.
   c. Those voluntarily idle without pay.
   d. Those drawing pay though not at work (*i.e.,* those on vacation, etc.).
II. *Those who did not have jobs:*
   a. Those unable to work.
   b. Those unwilling to work.
   c. The remainder.

Still further information was called for under both of the main headings. Thus, those who "had jobs" were asked how

[11] See Charles E. Persons, Unemployment as a Census Problem, *Journal American Statistical Association, Papers and Proceedings, 91st Annual Meeting,* March, 1930, pp. 117-20.
[12] See the *Unemployment Schedule* and the *Instructions to Enumerators* (14th census), pp. 38-41; 42-47.

many days they had worked during the preceding week and how many days there were in their full-time weeks, while those who were without jobs were asked how long they had been in this condition.[13]

In the meantime the stock market crash of late October, 1929, gave evidence that a period of depression was at hand. It soon became apparent that this was, in fact, occurring although various high-placed governmental officials issued statements which were designed to reassure the country. But despite the efforts to induce prosperity by official utterances, it is no secret that administration leaders were greatly embarrassed during the winter, spring, and summer of 1930 by the depression, which instead of disappearing, spread persistently. Since the existence of prosperity had been claimed as the fruit of Republican policy, they were afraid with reason that, having identified themselves with the state of business, they would be taxed with responsibility for its decline.

Under these circumstances, it was only human that they should have been somewhat embarrassed by the Census of Unemployment which would publish to a waiting world the precise number of persons out of work during April. The Census Bureau at one time issued directions that the preliminary results of the unemployment census were not to be published locally, and it seemed that the material would be withheld pending the preparation of the complete report —a matter of probably two years at the least. So many inquiries were, however, received that this ruling was reversed in late May and the local supervisors were authorized to announce data on the "most significant class" of the unemployed, namely those "without a job, able to work, and looking for a job." [14]

---

[13] There was some criticism of this method directed chiefly at (1) the difficulty of defining and measuring unemployment among the self-employed such as farmers, professional people, small merchants, and handicraftsmen, and (2) the lack of provision for collecting information on the number of *hours* lost by all workers during the preceding week. See *Journal of the American Statistical Association;* Papers and Proceedings of 91st Annual Meeting, March, 1930, pp. 186-88.

[14] *New York Times,* May 27, 1930, p. 17.

On June 26 the Census Bureau and Secretary Lamont issued a preliminary statement [15] that "according to preliminary returns covering about one-fourth of the population of the country, the total number of persons usually having a gainful occupation who were reported at the time of the Census in April as having no job, although able to work and looking for a job, amounted to 574,647, or 2.0 per cent of the total population of the territory covered, which numbered 29,064,480."

This statement was elaborated on by some of the newspaper reporters as indicating that the number of the "unemployed" was approximately 2,300,000 [16] which was, of course, very much below the estimates of the critics of the administration. Although the general public undoubtedly believed that the Census Bureau was referring to the "unemployed," and although some of the column headings used by the Census Bureau might well have contributed to this impression, the figures really applied to only one of the seven classes which were not at work on the "day preceding" that on which the census questions were asked. They included only those who were "without a job, able to work, and looking for a job."

It was soon pointed out that these statistics did not include those who had been laid off but who thought they could return later to their jobs. The Census expert on unemployment, Dr. Charles E. Persons, had indeed resigned because this group was not included in the preliminary estimates. He urged that, since the "jobs" which these workers were supposed to hold yielded neither work nor income at the time of the Census enumerators' visit, they should be counted as among the unemployed in the preliminary estimates. In our opinion this criticism was well-founded. It is, as a matter of fact, a common practice of many industrial companies to tell their employees when they are being laid off for lack of work or even actually discharged that they will

---

[15] See mimeographed release, *Preliminary Returns from the Unemployment Schedule*, 3 pp., June 26, 1930.
[16] See *New York Times*, June 27, p. 23.

be reëmployed "if and when" employment rises again. This softens the blow of dismissal. But the possession of such a "job" on the part of men who are out of work is so rarefied as not to justify their being regarded as employed.

The reply of the Census Bureau to such criticisms was that figures for only the "jobless" were tabulated in order to expedite getting information to the public. It is true that, due to the form in which the Census schedule was arranged, it would have been more difficult for the local census offices to deduct from the total of those who were said to "have a job" those who were ill or on a vacation than it was to make the deductions in the "jobless" column which were actually made. It could, however, have been done. But further, the local offices could easily have supplied the total number who were entered as "not working," since the enumerators were paid a separate fee for each of these names. This total, to be sure, contains those on vacation and ill among those "with jobs" and also includes in the "jobless" column those who were adjudged to be ill or unwilling to work. But the figures given out were an appreciable understatement and probably erred almost as much on the other side.[17] It can at least be said that the Census Bureau, in issuing the statement, was not sufficiently careful to point out just how limited a group it was covering and did not devote enough attention to indicating qualitatively how the addition of the other groups would appreciably raise the number of the unemployed and quantitatively in not giving the total numbers who were not employed on the preceding day.[18]

[17] This is indicated by the census press release of December 13, which gave detailed tabulations for 25 states, the District of Columbia and three other cities, with a total population of 42.9 millions. The total number not working in all seven classes was 981,864 of which 567,540 were those "out of a job, able to work, and looking for a job" (i.e. Class A) and 188,870 were those listed as having "jobs" but "on layoff without pay excluding those sick or voluntarily idle" (or Class B). Class A thus included 58 per cent of the total not working and Class B slightly over 19 per cent. All other classes formed approximately 23 per cent or only very slightly more than Class B itself.

[18] That the statements of the Census Bureau and the Department of Commerce had the effect of making the public believe that the number unemployed was identical with those whom the Census labeled in Class

4. The Number of "Jobless" as Shown by the 1930 Census

Two months later, on August 23d, the Census Bureau issued another statement on the "jobless" for the United States as a whole. This time the Bureau was careful specifically to point out the six other groups which were to be tabulated later. The figures for the various geographic sections were as follows:

TABLE 1

Number of "Jobless" Who Were Willing and Able to Work
in April, 1930

Section of United States	Population 1930 (Preliminary) (000 omitted)	Persons Out of a Job, Able to Work, and Looking for a Job (000 omitted)	Per Cent of Population (3)÷(2)
(1)	(2)	(3)	(4)
Total	122,698	2,508.2	2.0
New England . .	8,170	197.5	2.4
Middle Atlantic .	26,288	704.1	2.7
East North Central	25,246	681.9	2.7
West North Central	13,287	179.9	1.4
South Atlantic .	15,774	190.0	1.2
East South Central	9,886	84.7	.9
West South Central	12,162	166.0	1.4
Mountain . . .	3,698	70.6	1.9
Pacific	8,187	233.5	2.9

It will be noticed that the percentages which have been computed for this class of "jobless" are in terms of the total population. A better basis would of course be the numbers who normally count themselves as gainfully occupied, while

A as "jobless but able and willing to work" is evidenced by a sentence in President Hoover's message to Congress in December, 1930, in which he declared that "the number of those wholly out of employment seeking for work was accurately determined by the census last April as almost 2,500,000." If the chief magistrate was confused about the meaning of the returns six months after the preliminary announcement was made, it is small wonder if the general public has likewise obtained a misleading impression.

a still better basis would be those who were employed by others for wages or salaries. The Census, however, did not have this material worked up so shortly after the collection of the schedules. While it will be impossible to give any precise computation of what the percentage of the jobless would be upon these bases until the final report of the Census Bureau is made, some approximation can be attempted.

In an address on August 31st, Director Steuart of the Census estimated the number of the gainfully employed at between 47 and 49 millions.[19] This would mean that the 2.5 million "jobless" who were able and willing to work formed between 5.1 and 5.3. per cent of the gainfully occupied. However, to get an accurate measurement of the ratio of the number out of work to those who were really exposed to unemployment, we should have to subtract the self-employed who, by the very fact that they own the land, the tools, the stores, etc., with which they work, cannot be out of a job. While we do not know the numbers in this group, we can make some estimates. Dr. Leo Wolman, in his study for the Committee on Recent Economic Changes, estimated that 32,695,000 or 74 per cent of the 43,943,000 persons whom he thought were gainfully occupied in 1927 were employees of one kind or another.[20] If we were to apply this percentage to the 47 million whom Director Steuart believes that the Census will show to have been gainfully employed in 1930, we would have a total of employees and salaried workers of approximately 34.8 millions. The 2.5 millions of the "jobless" who were "able and willing to work" would amount therefore to approximately 7.5 per cent of this group.

The question then presents itself as to how many were in the classes of: (1) Those who had been laid off for shorter or longer periods of time, and (2) those who were unable to work because of sickness or disability, and (3) juveniles who, seeking to enter industry for the first time, had not yet been able to find employment. Since these lat-

---

[19] *New York Times,* September 1, p. 15.
[20] *Recent Economic Changes,* Vol. II, p. 474.

ter had not been listed as normally being employed, they were not included on the unemployment schedule among those who had not been at work on the preceding day. They did, however, swell the numbers of those who were seeking work.

The tabulation of unemployment data for 25 states and the District of Columbia which was released by the Census Bureau on December 13, 1930,[21] together with subsequent announcements for 6 additional states and 13 cities not included in any of the above states showed 1,421,000 "jobless who were able and willing to work" (Class A) out of a total population in these states and cities of 71.3 million people. Class A therefore formed 2.0 per cent of this sample which was precisely the ratio to the population which had been shown by the August release for the country as a whole. The sample may therefore be considered as typical. The number in Class B [21a] in this sample was 376,971 or .53 per cent of the population. At this rate the probable number in Class B in the country as a whole would have been 650,000, or a total in Classes A and B together of 3,158,000, or approximately 9.1 per cent of the probable number of employees in the country. Classes C and D (those unable to work because of illness or disability) numbered 250,052 or .35 per cent of the total population in the sample. If this percentage holds for the country as a whole, the total number in this group would amount to 429,000. If this group is included with Classes A and B, the resulting total would be 3,587,000. This would be approximately 10.3 per cent of the most probable number of employees in the country.

It is of course almost impossible to estimate how many juveniles there were in the labor market who were unsuccessfully seeking work for the first time but a consideration of this class would somewhat swell these totals.

It should furthermore be borne in mind that the census

---

[21] See the mimeographed press releases by the Census Bureau for December 13, *Unemployment, By Classes,* and for later dates.

[21a] "Those laid off but who expected to return to their jobs" and who were able and willing to work.

enumerators undoubtedly did not obtain a record of all those who were absent from work on the preceding day. The taking of the census as a whole was greatly hampered by the difficulties which the enumerators had in finding families out at the time they were visited. Since the enumerators received only 2 cents for each schedule filled out for those who were not at work, it was but human for many enumerators to give up the attempt after several unsuccessful efforts to fill the schedule. The inclusion of this group would also increase the total figure.

It is therefore probably conservative to estimate the minimum number of those who were out of work in April (including those ill and disabled) at somewhere around 3,800,-000. If the ill and disabled were excluded, the total would be around 3,400,000.

5. THE DECLINE IN EMPLOYMENT, MAY, 1929–APRIL, 1930, AS A BASIS FOR AN ESTIMATE OF TOTAL UNEMPLOYMENT

In May, 1929, the index of employment for manufacturing which is compiled by the United States Bureau of Labor Statistics and which included approximately 3,900,000 workers was only eight-tenths of a per cent below the average for 1926. In April, 1930, it was 10.9 per cent below this average.[22] This decline from 99.2 to 89.1 was a fall of 10.1 per cent. Thus, within the space of 11 months the number of wage-earners employed in manufacturing declined by approximately one-tenth of the total number. Since the probable number of wage-earners who were employed in this branch of work in May, 1929, was approximately 8,600,-000,[23] a decline of 10.1 per cent in this number would amount to almost 870,000. This may, therefore, be accepted as the most probable number of wage-earners who were thrown out of work in manufacturing in this period.

[22] *Monthly Labor Review,* June, 1930, p. 207.
[23] The number of wage-earners in 1927 was 8,350,000 (1927 *Census of Manufactures,* p. 14). In May, 1929, the index of employment was 2.8 per cent above that of 1927. (*Federal Reserve Bulletin,* November, 1929, p. 711.) This increase would bring the probable number of manufacturing wage-earners up to 8,594,000.

On the Class I railroads, the fall of employment during these 11 months was one of 8.4 per cent.[24] This was equivalent to a decline of 132,000. The decline in a number of other industries, according to the statistics of employment collected by the Bureau of Labor Statistics, was as follows:[25]

TABLE 2

THE RELATIVE DECLINE IN EMPLOYMENT IN SELECTED INDUSTRIES, MAY, 1929–APRIL, 1930. (1929 = 100)

INDUSTRY	RELATIVE INDEX MAY, 1929 (1)	RELATIVE INDEX April, 1930 (2)	MOVEMENT IN POINTS (3) = (2) − (1)	MOVEMENT IN PER CENT (4) = (3) − (1)
1. Bituminous Coal	96.6	94.4	− 2.2	− 2.2
2. Anthracite Coal	103.7	84.1	− 19.6	− 18.9
3. Metalliferous Mining	100.8	89.3	− 11.5	− 11.5
4. Quarrying and Non-Metallic Mining	104.1	87.4	− 16.7	− 16.0
5. Telephone and Telegraph	100.4	98.9	− 1.5	− 1.5
6. Power, Light, and Water	98.4	100.7	− 2.3	− 2.3
7. Electric Railways	100.4	95.2	− 5.2	− 5.2
8. Wholesale Trade	99.0	97.3	− 1.7	− 1.7
9. Retail Trade	97.3	97.3	. . . .	. . . .
10. Hotels	98.1	100.1	+ 2.0	+ 2.0

It is difficult to estimate the probable number of persons who were employed in each of these industries in May, 1929, which is necessary if we are to approximate the actual number who were thrown out of work in these lines during the eleven months. No great error will be created if we take over the figures which W. I. King and Leo Wolman have worked out for 1927 and apply them to 1929. The change between the two years was not great, and in any case the

[24] *I.e.*, from a relative of 94.9 to one of 87.0 See monthly reports of Interstate Commerce Commission entitled *Wage Statistics*.
[25] *Monthly Labor Review*, July, 1930, p. 200.

error would only be the percentage of this difference by which employment dropped after May, 1929.

Using in the main the King-Wolman estimates [26] and applying the percentage changes in employment, we can obtain the following approximation to the numbers who were dropped from these lines of employment.

TABLE 3

ESTIMATED NUMBER DROPPED FROM PAYROLLS OF CERTAIN SELECTED
AMERICAN INDUSTRIES BETWEEN MAY, 1929, AND APRIL, 1930

INDUSTRY	ESTIMATED NUMBER EM-PLOYED MAY, 1929 (000 OMITTED)	PERCENTAGE CHANGE TO APRIL 1930	ESTIMATED CHANGE IN NUMBER EMPLOYED (000 OMITTED)
1. Bituminous Coal . . .	500	− 2.2	− 11
2. Anthracite Coal . . .	125	− 18.9	− 24
3. Metalliferous Mining . .	120	− 11.5	− 14
4. Quarrying and Non-Metallic Mining	92	− 16.0	− 15
5. Telephone and Telegraph .	470	− 1.5	− 7
6. Power, Light, and Water .	221	− 2.3	− 5
7. Electric Railways . . .	322	− 5.2	− 17
8. Wholesale Trade ⎫ 9. Retail Trade ⎭ . .	4,623	. . . .	. . . .
10. Hotels	1,000	− 2.0	− 20
TOTAL	7,473		− 80

It thus appears that in these industries employing approximately 7,500,000 workers, the decline in employment was approximately only 80,000.

If we add manufacturing and transportation to this group we find that industries with a total number of approximately 17.5 million wage-earners and salaried employees [27]

[26] *Recent Economic Changes,* Vol. ii, pp. 469-78. We have slightly altered their estimates for coal mining and have estimated that approximately only one-fifth of the total number of mercantile employees are in wholesale trades, and that one-half of the hotel and restaurant employees are in hotels.

[27] The salaried employees in manufacturing are not, however, included.

decreased their forces by approximately 1,075,000, or by about 6.1 per cent.

This does not take into account any decline in the numbers employed (1) in the building trades; (2) in domestic and personal service; or (3) in hired farm labor. Neither does it include (4) farmers who left the country to come to the towns and cities to seek work there; (5) juveniles seeking to enter employment for the first time, and who, if placed, would slightly swell the numbers employed by the excess of their numbers over those retiring; (6) immigrants who would normally have the same influence upon the size of the working force.

According to the Federal Reserve Board, the total volume of building contracts was 17 per cent less in April, 1930, than it had been eleven months before.[28] If employment dropped by a corresponding amount, which was probably not far from the truth, this would have meant a decrease of about 190,000 in the numbers employed.[29] This would have brought the total increase in unemployment which we could account for up to 1,265,000, or approximately 6.9 per cent of the total sample available.

It is virtually impossible to estimate by how much unemployment has increased among the other groups. It would certainly be most conservative to set this number at slightly over 400,000 and to bring the total decline up to approximately 1,700,000. There was of course a considerable amount of unemployment in May, 1929. There always is, and there had been signs for some time that, due to the displacement of labor from agriculture, manufacturing, mining, and transportation, unemployment had been on the increase. It is probably not far from the facts to estimate that there were approximately 2,000,000 unemployed at that time. The further decline would bring the numbers unemployed in April, 1930, to approximately 3,700,000. This is

[28] *Federal Reserve Bulletin*, August, 1930, p. 491. The relative indexes (1923-25 = 100) were May, 1929, = 143; April, 1930, = 118.
[29] W. I. King estimates the numbers employed in construction in 1927 (exclusive of highways) to have been 1,141,000, *Recent Economic Changes*, Vol. II, p. 477.

approximately the same number as that arrived at from a study of the census returns when the ill and disabled were included.

6. THE FURTHER INCREASE IN UNEMPLOYMENT FROM APRIL, 1930, TO THE BEGINNING OF 1931

Thus the index of manufacturing employment of the Bureau of Labor Statistics dropped from 89.1 in April to 76.5 in November, or a fall of 12.6 points and 14 per cent.[30] The further decline in the total number employed in manufacturing would at this rate have been slightly over 1,100,-000. The numbers employed on the Class I railroads decreased from 1,573,000 in April to 1,439,000 on October 15,[31] which was a fall of 124,000. The movement in a number of other industries was as follows: [32]

INDUSTRY	PERCENTAGE CHANGE FROM APRIL TO NOVEMBER	INDUSTRY	PERCENTAGE CHANGE FROM APRIL TO NOVEMBER
Anthracite Coal . . .	+ 17	Power, Light, and Water	+ 7
Bituminous Coal . . .	− 2	Electric Railways. . .	0
Metalliferous Mining. .	− 19	Wholesale Trade . . .	+ 5
Quarrying and Non-metallic Mining . . .	− 10	Retail Trade	+ 26
		Hotels	− 2
Telephone and Telegraph	+ 3	Canning and Preserving	+ 29

The increases and decreases in the various industries other than wholesale and retail trade virtually offset each other. While the two latter occupations showed an appreciable advance because of the Christmas trade, it is probable that the relative increase was by no means as great for all such establishments as for the larger units included in the sample of the Bureau of Labor Statistics. Against this seasonal increase in the numbers employed in trade should of course be set the seasonal decline in construction. Although the

[30] *Monthly Labor Review*, January, 1931, p. 205.
[31] *Ibid.*, pp. 55, 198.
[32] *Ibid.*, p. 221.

monthly volume of building permits is an imperfect measure of the relative amount of actual construction by months, it is interesting to note that the total value represented by such permits in over 280 cities was approximately a third less in November than it had been seven months before. It would seem probable that the actual decline was sufficient to offset the temporarily increased employment in trade. After the Christmas season virtually all of the added workers in retail trade were laid off.[33] The continued seasonal decline in the building trades still further increased the numbers of the unemployed and when taken in conjunction with the decrease since April of about 1,225,000 in manufacturing and transportation, it would seem conservative to estimate the total decline in the numbers employed in these three major industries to have been not far from 1,600,000. A minimum estimate of unemployment (excluding the ill and disabled) for the beginning of 1931 would seem therefore to be approximately 5,000,000 with the possibility that it might well be somewhat more. Were the ill and disabled also to be included, the total would probably run to at least 5,400,000. The former estimate of unemployment would amount to approximately 14.5 per cent of the wage-earners and the latter to approximately 16 per cent.

In addition to all this, there should also be included the factor of part-time. This has been widely resorted to by business during the present depression. The Bureau of Labor Statistics found for example in November, 1930, that 41 per cent of the 10,700 manufacturing establishments from which it received information were working on part time and the extent of such part time is also indicated by the fact that whereas the index of manufacturing employment was 22.6 per cent lower in November, 1930, than it had been in April, 1929, the total amount paid out in wages was 34.7 per cent less.[34]

[33] The numbers employed in wholesale and retail trade in Illinois dropped 10 per cent in January, 1931, as compared with December, 1930, and were approximately 4 per cent less than they had been in April, 1930. See the *Illinois Labor Bulletin*, Jan., 1931.

[34] *Ibid.*, p. 205.

7. How Shall We Continue the Index of Unemployment?

Once given a bench-mark figure of unemployment for April, 1930, periodic estimates of the amount of unemployment can be made by two methods, namely, (1) by adjusting the unemployment figures by the movements of the indices of employment, and (2) by censuses in selected cities. The Bureau of Labor Statistics now compiles indices of employment for manufacturing, coal mining, metalliferous mining, public utilities, electric railways, trade, hotels, etc., which now include about 5.1 million employees and which are a fairly good sample of the some 15 million workers who are employed in these industries. The Interstate Commerce Commission collects monthly data on the numbers employed on Class I railroads. By one of the Wagner bills, the Bureau has been directed [35] to collect statistics on the building industry which is virtually the only major industry which is not represented.

After the percentages of unemployment have been worked out for the various industrial groupings, it will then be possible to apply from time to time the changes in employment, and thus obtain an approximation to the amount of unemployment in the various lines.

The Wagner Act also called for the collection of statistics of man hours by the Bureau of Labor Statistics, and, if this is done, it will also be possible to measure fluctuations in part-time as well and consequently in the total volume of employment.

The second method is by taking periodical censuses of the unemployed in a number of cities and towns and tying these results on to those of the base period. As we have mentioned, such censuses have already been conducted in a number of cities. The Bureau of the Census has already carried out such a study for 20 cities in January, 1931, and could in the future work out coöperative relationships with local school attendance officers, colleges, and uni-

[35] It was not, however, furnished with the funds to do this.

versities, etc. It could thus get a fairly good sample at a minimum of expense. In this way there would always be direct evidence about the probable number of the unemployed

CHAPTER II

AN ESTIMATE OF THE AMOUNT OF UNEMPLOY-MENT IN THE UNITED STATES, 1890–1926

Since it is desirable not only to measure unemployment at a particular time, but also to obtain some idea of what its past extent has been, one of the authors has computed an index of unemployment covering the major industrial groups for the period 1890-1926. The method which is used for manufacturing and transportation is that of subtracting the probable number employed from the probable labor supply. This method has a certain margin of error, but as we shall see, there is a considerable amount of other evidence to indicate that the results are probably not far from the truth.

1. The Index of Unemployment for Manufacturing and Transportation, 1890-1926 [1]

By reclassifying the census data on occupations upon an industrial basis, we obtained estimates of the probable number of persons attached to manufacturing and transportation in the census years. Estimates for the intercensal years were made by assuming that the native-born workers increased at an even absolute rate and that the foreign-born workers increased according to the relative volume of immigration. But in years of prosperity, the labor supply is increased by an influx of workers from the farms, of women, and of juveniles. Hence for these years the labor supply was adjusted slightly so that there would be at least 3.5 per cent of unemployment resulting from sickness, dis-

---

[1] The methods followed are described in detail in Paul H. Douglas, *Real Wages in the United States, 1890-1926*, pp. 430-449.

ability, and the changing of jobs. This percentage seems to be established as the approximate minimum from the trade-union reports made in Massachusetts during the years 1908-23.

The numbers employed in manufacturing are obtained from the censuses of manufactures and interpolated for intercensal years according to the movement of the employment indices which we have constructed. Similar methods were used to obtain the probable numbers employed on the street railways, while the reports of the Interstate Commerce Commission give the numbers employed on the railroads.

From these data we obtained estimated percentages of the numbers unemployed which are shown in the following table:

TABLE 4

ESTIMATED PERCENTAGE OF UNEMPLOYMENT IN MANUFACTURING AND TRANSPORTATION, 1889–1927

Year	Estimated Percentage of Unemployment	Year	Estimated Percentage of Unemployment	Year	Estimated Percentage of Unemployment
1889	5.6	1902	3.5	1915	12.4
1890	5.1	1903	3.5	1916	3.5
1891	5.6	1904	7.1	1917	3.5
1892	3.7	1905	4.0	1918	3.5
1893	9.6	1906	3.5	1919	4.0
1894	16.7	1907	3.5	1920	4.3
1895	11.9	1908	12.0	1921	21.2
1896	15.3	1909	5.1	1922	15.4
1897	14.5	1910	3.7	1923	4.4
1898	13.9	1911	5.6	1924	8.3
1899	7.7	1912	4.0	1925	5.1
1900	6.3	1913	5.4	1926	4.5
1901	4.5	1914	12.9	1927	5.6

The average amount of unemployment for the period 1889-1926 was 7.5 per cent and for 1890-99, 10.4 per cent. But these percentages will be increased if we include building and mining.

2. Unemployment in the Building and Mining Industries

We have used for our index of unemployment in the building trades the percentages shown by trade union reports for New York and Massachusetts.[2] These are shown in the following table:

TABLE 5

Estimated Percentages of Unemployment in Building Trades, 1897–1926

Year	Estimated Percentage of Unemployment	Year	Estimated Percentage of Unemployment	Year	Estimated Percentage of Unemployment
1897	32.0	1907	20.8	1917	21.6
1898	28.3	1908	35.8	1918	17.7
1899	20.9	1909	22.5	1919	17.5
1900	26.7	1910	20.2	1920	23.8
1901	17.8	1911	25.7	1921	26.6
1902	15.9	1912	18.1	1922	19.2
1903	21.1	1913	21.5	1923	17.2
1904	17.7	1914	34.6	1924	25.9
1905	12.0	1915	31.5	1925	21.4
1906	8.7	1916	20.7	1926	17.6

The typical form of unemployment in coal mining is that of part time lost within the year. The annual reports of the Geological Survey give the average number of days on which mines are open in the bituminous and the anthracite fields during each year. By subtracting these from 306, the maximum number of days on which the mines could be open, we can obtain the average minimum number of days of unemployment. Percentages of unemployment for the bituminous and anthracite fields combined have been worked out and are given in Table 6 on the following page.

[2] See Douglas, *op. cit.*, pp. 450-56, for the adjustments made. The Wolman-Givens series was used for the years 1921-27.

TABLE 6

Unemployment in Coal Mining, 1897–1926

Year	Percentage Unemployed	Year	Percentage Unemployed	Year	Percentage Unemployed
1897	41.7	1907	25.0	1917	18.2
1898	39.8	1908	36.5	1918	16.1
1899	30.4	1909	32.2	1919	31.4
1900	31.0	1910	28.0	1920	24.8
1901	28.9	1911	28.5	1921	43.3
1902	35.7	1912	26.6	1922	53.5
1903	27.9	1913	22.1	1923	36.5
1904	34.3	1914	32.2	1924	37.1
1905	30.8	1915	31.7	1925	37.2
1906	31.4	1916	23.2	1926	27.8

3. A Combined Index for Manufacturing, Transportation, Building, and Mining

By combining these various series, we obtain the total shown in Table 7 and in Chart 1.

TABLE 7

Unemployment in Manufacturing, Transportation, Building Trades, and Mining, 1897–1926

Year	Percentage Unemployed	Year	Percentage Unemployed	Year	Percentage Unemployed
1897	18.0	1907	6.9	1917	6.0
1898	16.9	1908	16.4	1918	5.5
1899	10.5	1909	8.9	1919	6.9
1900	10.0	1910	7.2	1920	7.2
1901	7.5	1911	9.4	1921	23.1
1902	6.8	1912	7.0	1922	18.3
1903	7.0	1913	8.2	1923	7.9
1904	10.1	1914	16.4	1924	12.0
1905	6.7	1915	15.5	1925	8.9
1906	5.9	1916	6.3	1926	7.5

The average obtained by this method for the thirty years, 1897-1926, is 10.2 per cent. This percentage has been criticized by some as being too high. These critics declare, for example, that they do not see how unemployment in these industries can be as high as 5.5 or 6.0 per cent in such peak years as 1917 and 1918. But the following considerations should go far to justify the estimate.

1. The index does not cover all industries. It includes mining and building where, because of weather and other

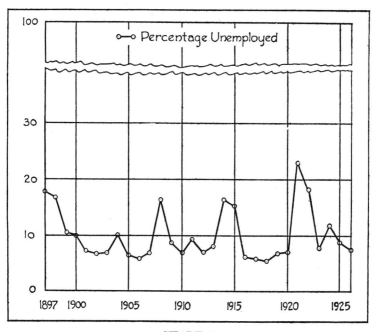

CHART 1

Estimated Percentages of Unemployment in Manufacturing, Mining, Transportation, and Construction in the United States, 1897-1926

factors, seasonal unemployment is always considerable. It does not include mercantile trade or public utilities where employment is relatively constant. The average is, therefore, undoubtedly somewhat more than it would be if all industries were included, but this does not discredit it for what it purports to cover.

2. The index includes not merely the unemployed who are able and willing to work, but the sick and disabled as

well. The inclusion of this group naturally swells the percentage.

4. Evidence Which Helps to Corroborate the Index of Unemployment

There are two sets of evidence to indicate that the estimates of unemployment which have been made are perhaps not far from the truth.

1. The first of these is the degree of agreement between the estimates and the percentages shown for 1889 and 1899 by the United States census and for 1915 by the census of the Bureau of Labor Statistics.

As we have stated, the census published data gathered in 1890 and 1900 on the number of people who lost a given number of months during the preceding year because of unemployment. By using the 1901 study of the United States Bureau of Labor [3] of the unemployment suffered by 25,000 heads of families, we can approximate the average length of time lost by the workers in each of the three categories into which they were classified. It was then possible to compute the total number of man weeks and the percentage of time which was lost through unemployment.

These are as follows:

	1889	1899
Manufacturing	4.8	6.0
Transportation	3.0	3.9
Building	8.8	12.0
Manufacturing and Transportation	4.5	5.6
All three groups	5.6	7.0

Now our unemployment percentage for manufacturing and transportation in 1889 was 5.6 per cent or 1.1 per cent more than the census average. In 1899 our average for the three industries combined was 9.3 per cent or 2.3 per cent more than the census average. For manufacturing and transportation alone, our average was 7.7 per cent or 2.1 per cent above the census average.

[3] *18th Annual Report,* United States Commissioner of Labor, pp. 248-49.

These are quite surprisingly close approximations when we remember the very different methods by which they were constructed.

Samples taken in twenty-nine cities in 1915 by the Bureau of Labor Statistics, when adjusted by indices of employment for the other months in that year, show an average unemployment of 10.9 per cent. This method, however, probably understates the amount of unemployment in the closing months of that year and the real average by this method would in consequence have been fairly close to 12 per cent.[4] The average which we have computed for manufacturing and transportation alone is 12.4 per cent and, if the building trades are included, 14.4 per cent. Since the Bureau of Labor Statistics investigation included industries such as trade, etc., where the volume of unemployment was less than that included in our analysis, these differences cannot be said to be appreciable.

It is to be hoped that the census data on unemployment in 1909 can be tabulated so that the census results for that year can be compared with ours. This will afford a still further check upon the relative reliability of our index.

2. The second set of evidence which tends to confirm our index is the fact that it agrees very closely with the movements of business conditions. If we compare the index with the description of various years given by Willard L. Thorpe in his *Business Annals,* we find that our index increases in years of depression and falls in years of prosperity to about the same relative degree which one would infer from the qualitative description which Thorpe gives. There are but two exceptions to this agreement. It is clear that in 1898, our index overstates the amount of unemployment which existed, while it is almost equally clear that Thorpe was in error in treating 1915 as a year of "revival and prosperity." Some improvement there certainly was in this year but, as the Bureau of Labor Statistics' own story shows, unemployment was indeed relatively high.

[4] For the reasons for this see Douglas, *op. cit.,* pp. 413-16.

5. Summary

We do not pretend that the index which has been computed for the years 1897-1926 is perfect. It could not be from the very nature of the materials which were available for its construction. Census data for isolated years give it, however, a considerable degree of corroboration and until better estimates are made, it is advanced as the closest approximation to the truth which it is at present possible to frame. To the degree to which it is accurate, it indicates the following generalizations:

1. The average percentage of unemployment, including illness and disability, for manufacturing, transportation, mining, and construction during the thirty years from 1897 to 1926 was approximately 10 per cent.
2. If other occupations, such as the public utilities, trade, domestic and professional services, government employment were included, this average would be lowered slightly. It is impossible to say precisely how much this reduction would be although we believe that it would probably be somewhere between 1 and 2 per cent. If the sick and disabled were excluded, the percentage would likewise be reduced slightly more. We believe therefore that the average for all industry would be approximately 8 per cent.
3. The minimum percentage of unemployment in these four sets of industries (except during the war) seems to have been about 6 per cent. This indicates that ill-health, chronic, and seasonal causes are responsible for approximately this amount or for about six-tenths of the total.
4. In periods of business depression, unemployment in these occupations rises as high as 20 per cent. On the average about 4 per cent of the time in these industries seems to have been lost through cyclical fluctuations, which were therefore responsible for about four-tenths of the total unemployment.

5. There has been no observable and pronounced tendency for the volume of unemployment either to diminish or increase. While the period of the 1890's had a somewhat higher relative volume of unemployment than the later years, it should be noted that the average of the four major groups of industries studied was approximately 11 per cent for the years 1920-27 inclusive, while the average for the entire thirty years from 1897 to 1926 was 10 per cent. Those who argue that unemployment is steadily growing worse over long periods of time have little substantial evidence. Similarly those who declare that unemployment is constantly getting better will be almost equally hard put to it, despite the black years of 1893-95, to defend their position.

6. So far as unemployment is concerned, it is seen that not all cycles are of equal importance and that the three and four-year cycles which have of late been emphasized are not as important as those of from 6 to 8 years' duration. Thus the depression years 1907-8, 1914-15, 1920-21, and 1929-30 caused far more hardship than did those of 1911, 1924, or 1927. We should, therefore, distinguish between major and minor cycles.

CHAPTER III

UNEMPLOYMENT IN OTHER COUNTRIES

Statistics of unemployment are among the least adequate of economic data. Only in the very recent years with the introduction of compulsory unemployment insurance are we getting figures which are at all comprehensive.[1] Previously —with the exception of Great Britain since 1912—the figures of unemployment were based on the returns of trade unions. Where these latter statistics are the result of the administration of unemployment benefits they are of course more reliable than the estimates given by trade union secretaries. The numbers reported as out-of-work even under the first system cannot, however, be used to indicate the total volume of unemployment. In this chapter we shall use the trade union percentages to indicate general fluctuations and to draw some general conclusions. But a word of caution must, however, be introduced even against this general use of the statistics. Within any one country the proportion of workers included in trade unions has varied from year to year, and in so far as the percentage of organized workers varies between industries we have a biased sample.[2] Comparisons between countries are made difficult by varying definitions of unemployment. "Exact information is not available as to the definitions adopted in the different countries, but it may be stated that invariably unemployment directly due to strike, lockout, and sickness is excluded. Generally also, the figures are limited to unemployment for a particular day. . . ."[3]

[1] For the data now being published see the current numbers of the *International Labour Review.*
[2] *International Labour Review,* January, 1921, pp. 115-120.
[3] *Ibid.,* p. 118.

In Table 8 on the following page are set out the available annual data to show the fluctuations in unemployment in a number of European countries. Explanatory notes for each country and for France and Russia which are not included here, will be found at the end of this chapter.

The data clearly indicate that in every country, with the possible exception of Belgium, the post-war average percentage of unemployment is substantially larger than the pre-war average. There is also less similarity of timing of fluctuations than there was before the war. While the depression years of 1920-21 and 1930 generally affected all countries as did the depression years of 1907-8 and of 1914 before the war, within each country other independent fluctuations were superimposed on these common fluctuations.

Bearing in mind the limitation of the data as regards comparisons between countries we can say that before the war Denmark had a very high percentage of unemployment due, in part we believe, to the great seasonal variations which characterize that country. Australia and Sweden likewise had a slightly higher percentage than the other countries. The United States, as we have indicated in a previous chapter, had probably the highest percentage of all countries.

Since the war Canada and Belgium have probably changed but little, the Australian percentage has risen somewhat, and the other countries have witnessed increases which are indeed challenging. A further point worth noting is the importance of partial unemployment in the two countries for which we have data. In Belgium it is indeed larger on the average than is the percentage of complete unemployment and in Germany it is about the same. While it is generally recognized that in periods of depression short time is resorted to, the extent has probably been underestimated.

In the succeeding chapter some analysis is made of the differences in unemployment between countries. But some interest attaches also to the monthly variations in the various countries. For the United States only the variations in

TABLE 8

Trade Union Percentages of Unemployment in Various European Countries [1]

Year	Great Britain			Germany [4]		Belgium [5]		Denmark [6]	Sweden [7]	Canada [5]	Australia [8]
	Trade Union Per-centages [2]	Compulsory Insurance [3]		Completely Un-employed	Partially Un-employed	Completely Un-employed	Partially Un-employed				
		No. Un-employed (1000)	Percentage of Those Insured								
1904	6.0	...	...	2.1	...	...	...	...	...	...	...
1905	5.0	...	...	1.6	...	...	...	...	...	...	...
1906	3.6	...	...	1.2	...	...	...	...	...	...	6.7
1907	3.7	...	...	1.6	...	...	...	...	...	...	5.7
1908	7.8	...	...	2.9	...	...	...	...	...	...	6.0
1909	7.7	...	...	2.8	...	...	...	...	...	...	5.8
1910	4.7	...	...	1.9	...	...	...	10.7	...	...	5.6
1911	3.0	...	...	1.9	...	...	...	9.5	5.3	...	4.7
1912	3.2	...	...	2.0	...	...	...	7.6	5.4	...	5.5
1913	2.1	...	...	2.9	...	...	...	7.5	4.5	...	6.5
1914	3.3	...	...	7.2	...	...	...	9.9	6.7	...	8.3
1915	1.1	...	...	3.2	...	...	...	7.7	7.8	8.0	9.3
1916	.4	...	...	2.2	...	...	...	4.9	4.2	1.9	5.8
1917	.6	...	...	1.0	...	...	...	9.2	3.9	1.9	7.1
1918	.8	...	...	1.2	...	...	...	17.4	4.4	1.4	5.8
1919	2.4	...	...	3.7	...	...	...	10.7	5.5	3.6	6.6
1920	...	...	...	3.8	...	...	...	5.8	5.4	4.6	6.5

	1	2	3	4	5	6	7	8	9	10
1921	1,650	13.7	2.8	5.4			19.7	26.6	12.5	11.2
1922	1,381	13.3	1.5	2.8	3.1	3.4	19.3	22.9	7.1	9.2
1923	1,320	11.5	9.6	26.8	1.0	1.7	12.7	12.5	4.9	7.1
1924	1,202	10.4	13.5	15.3	1.0	2.3	16.7	10.1	7.2	8.9
1925	1,347	11.4	6.7	8.6	1.5	4.1	14.7	11.0	7.0	8.8
1926	1,557	12.6	18.0	16.0	1.5	2.7	20.7	12.2	5.1	7.1
1927	1,179	9.7	8.7	3.4	1.8	3.9	22.5	12.0	4.9	7.0
1928	1,299	10.8	8.6	5.7	.9	3.5	18.5	10.6	4.5	10.7
1929	1,262	10.5	13.2	7.5	1.3	3.0	15.5	10.2	5.7	11.1
1930 ⁹ . . .	1,683	13.9	21.3	13.0	2.5	6.0	12.7	10.1	10.2	11.6
Pre-War Average through 1914—	4.6		2.6				9.0	5.5		6.1
Post-War Average		11.8	10.4	10.5	1.6	3.4	16.3	13.1	6.7	9.0

¹ For Great Britain the numbers and percentages of unemployed derived from the insurance system are also given.
² *19th Abstract of Labour Statistics* (cmd. 3140), p. 78.
³ We are indebted to Mr. Arnold Tolles for computing these yearly averages from the monthly returns published in the British Ministry of Labour Gazette.
⁴ *Statistisches Jahrbuch für das Deutsche Reich.*
⁵ Averages of the monthly reports in the *International Labour Review.*
⁶ *Statistisk Aarbog.*
⁷ *Statistisk Arsbok.*
⁸ *Official Year Book.*
⁹ Incomplete.

employment are available. These are therefore discussed separately in Chapter VI. The seasonal variations in some of the European countries are summarized in Table 9.

Unless otherwise noted the data on which the table is based are taken from the *International Labour Review*. In the case of Great Britain the percentages of unemployment are those derived from the insurance system and in-

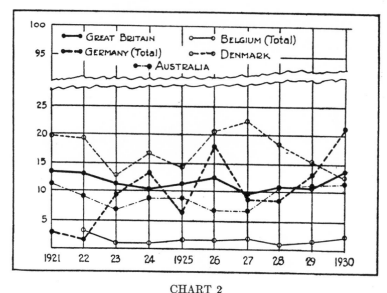

CHART 2

Comparative Percentages of Unemployment in Other Countries, 1921–1930

clude partial as well as complete unemployment. In the other countries the percentages are derived from trade union reports. Since there was no apparent trend during the period covered, the method of computing the seasonal factors consists simply of computing a general monthly average for the entire period, averages for all the January, February . . . percentages and subtracting the former from the latter. These are referred to as the deviations from the average. In each case these deviations represent the percentage of unemployment above or below the average

TABLE 9

SEASONAL VARIATIONS IN THE PERCENTAGES OF UNEMPLOYMENT IN VARIOUS EUROPEAN COUNTRIES

	JAN.	FEB.	MAR.	APR.	MAY	JUNE	JULY	AUG.	SEPT.	OCT.	NOV.	DEC.	YEARS INCLUDED	GENERAL MONTHLY AVERAGE
GREAT BRITAIN														
Deviations from Average	+1.1	+.5	−.4	−.7	−.3	−.1	..	+.1	..	+.1	+.2	−.3	1922–29[1]	11.4
Relatives	110	104	97	94	97	99	100	101	100	101	102	97	1922–99	11.4
Deviations from Average	+.35	+.05	−.15	.25	−.4	−.3	−.3	..	−.15	+.2	+.1	+.6	1900–13[2]	4.3
GERMANY														
Complete Unemployment														
Deviations from Average	+3.5	+3.4	+.9	−1.1	−1.9	−2.0	−1.8	−1.6	−2.0	−1.1	+.3	+3.4	1920–29	8.5
Relatives	141	139	111	87	78	77	79	81	77	86	102	140	1920–29	..
Partial Unemployment														
Deviation from Average	..	−.4	−.5	−1.0	−1.7	−1.3	−.5	+.5	+.9	+1.5	+1.5	+.5	1920–29	10.2
Relatives	100	96	95	90	83	87	95	105	109	115	115	115	1920–29	..
BELGIUM														
Complete Unemployment														
Deviations from Average	+1.3	+1.0	+.1	−.1	−.2	−.4	−.5	−.6	−.6	−.6	−.2	+.8	1922–29	1.5
Relatives	187	167	107	93	87	73	67	60	60	60	87	153	1922–29	..
Partial Unemployment														
Deviations from Average	+1.0	+.7	..	−.1	−.1	−.3	−.2	−.3	−.6	−.7	−.3	+.7	1922–29	3.1
Relatives	132	123	100	97	97	90	94	90	81	77	90	123	1922–29	..
DENMARK														
Deviations from Average	+8.1	+8.1	+4.1	−.7	−3.6	−4.9	−5.0	−5.0	−.2	−3.9	−.3	+8.3	1920–29	16.0
Relatives	151	151	126	96	77	70	69	69	67	75	98	152	1920–29	..
SWEDEN														
Deviations from Average	+3.9	+3.3	+2.6	+.9	−2.0	−2.2	−3.0	−3.4	−3.4	−2.1	−.3	+5.7	1920–29	13.4
Relatives	130	124	119	107	85	83	78	74	75	84	98	143	1920–29	..

[1] Based on monthly reports of the percentage of unemployed among insured workers of Great Britain and Northern Ireland, *Statistical Abstract for the United Kingdom* (1930), cmd. 3465, p. 81, and *International Labour Review* for 1929 figures.

[2] A. L. Bowley and K. C. Smith, *Seasonal Variation in Finance, Prices and Industry*, London and Cambridge Economic Service, Special Memorandum, No. 7, July, 1924, p. 15.

due to seasonal influences. The relatives are obtained by expressing the averages of all the January, February . . . percentages as percentages of the general monthly average.

In Great Britain since the war, as before, the variations in unemployment due to seasonal influences are relatively small. The greatest departure from the average takes place in January when on the average 1.1% or one eleventh of the unemployed is to be attributed to seasonal influences. From June to October inclusive, unemployment is at or near the average. December now shows a decline whereas before the war it was characterized by a seasonal increase in unemployment.[4]

The other countries show a distinct contrast. Thus in Germany in the months of December through February the percentage of unemployment is normally approximately 40% above the general average and in the case of Denmark approximately 50%. The severe winters in these countries undoubtedly are responsible for a substantial part of the variations.

The great seasonal variations in Belgium are quite surprising. But as the general average is quite small, any errors in the original data would greatly magnify the percentage variations. It is also worth noting that the variations in partial unemployment are relatively small, indicating that this is primarily a phenomenon of the business cycle.

In the past the interest has centered in the cyclical fluctuations of unemployment. It seems clear, however, that seasonal variations deserve much more attention than has been given them.

Note A

GREAT BRITAIN

Prior to 1912, when statistics began to be available from the unemployment insurance system, the only data on unemployment in Great Britain were those of a number of trade-unions who paid out-of-work benefits, and are much more reliable than mere

---

[4] For variations in some specific industries before the war see Bowley and Smith, *op. cit.*, pp. 14-15.

general estimates and reports such as were made by American unions to the New York and Massachusetts Departments of Labor. The statistical basis for these reports was at first very slender, the membership of unions covered being less than 100,000 from 1851 to 1872. By 1893, it amounted to approximately 300,000 and rose to over 500,000 by 1900, and to 800,000 by 1912.

Sir William Beveridge has recombined these figures by weighting the percentages for each industry by the relative number of persons employed, rather than by the relative trade union membership, and found the average for forty-eight years from 1860 to 1907 inclusive to be 4.4 per cent.[5] In years of prosperity, 2 per cent were generally out of work, although in 1872 apparently only 1 per cent was unemployed. In periods of severe depression, on the other hand, the percentage would rise to 8 or 9, and in 1879 was indeed 10.7.

It was thought for some time that these trade-union statistics somewhat understated the real amount of unemployment since they were drawn from the more skilled employees who presumably had steadier work, and because they excluded such casual occupations as dock and longshore work. On the other hand, they did include the building trades, where the seasonal fluctuations were greater than the average, and the engineering, shipbuilding, and metal trades which were more susceptible to cyclical fluctuations. On the basis of the fluctuation in the trade union as compared with the unemployment statistics since 1912, Mr. John Hilton, Director of Statistics for the British Ministry of Labour, has concluded [6] that in good times the trade-union figure "has approximated very closely to the general percentage unemployed," but that in depression years it is too high. If this were the case prior to 1912, as it seems probable, the average pre-war percentage of unemployment would be somewhat under 4.4.

From 1912 the numbers listed as unemployed under the Unemployment Insurance Acts of 1911 and 1916 as well as those under trade-union benefits, which increased in scope during this period, are available. The comparative percentages by these two methods are shown in the table on the following page.

Since 1920, the best source is that of the Unemployment Insurance System, which covers approximately 12 million workers. The number unemployed as published consists of the number of unemployment books "lodged" in the employment exchanges in making claims for benefits. While the number insured upon which

[5] Beveridge, *Unemployment—A Problem of Industry,* p. 39.

[6] John Hilton, Statistics of Unemployment Derived from the Working of the Unemployment Insurance Acts, *Journal of the Royal Statistical Society,* March, 1923 (vol. LXXXVI), p. 182.

PERCENTAGE UNEMPLOYED IN GREAT BRITAIN — 1912–1920

YEAR	PERCENTAGE UNEMPLOYED	
	Insurance Data	Trade-unions (adjusted weights)
1912	4.5[1]	3.3
1913	3.6	2.1
1914	4.1	3.4
1915	1.2	1.1
1916	.6	.4
1917	.7	.6
1918	2.8	.8
1919	[2]	2.1
1920	[2]	2.0[3]

[1] Insurance data only for last four months of year.
[2] Computation of insurance percentages is difficult because of out-of-work donations.
[3] For eleven months only.

the percentages are based is determined once a year when the books are renewed, revisions are made quarterly to take account of additions, withdrawals, and other changes. The published results refer to the last Friday of each month. While the British statistics of unemployment are the most comprehensive available, they do not include agriculture, private domestic service, and a few excepted occupations. Comparability between years is disturbed by the legal and administrative changes of the insurance system.

NOTE B

GERMANY

Until the passage of the German Unemployment Insurance Act of 1927, the most extensive records of unemployment were those compiled by the trade unions paying out-of-work benefits. The publication of these began in 1904 when the workers covered were 454,000. In 1913 the number increased to two million, and in 1920 to 5.5 million. By 1927 the number decreased to about three million, but at the beginning of 1930 it rose again to approximately 4.6 million. It should be recalled that the number covered by the insurance system is approximately 17 million.

One of the great advantages of the German statistics is the publication of the number of workers on short time. The importance of this form of unemployment can be seen by comparing the two percentages month by month. The trade union returns are published monthly in the *Reichsarbeitsblatt*.

Since 1920 there are also published statistics showing the number of workers receiving state relief.

The demand for labor as shown by the vacancies offered, and the supply of labor as shown by the number of workers registered each month at the employment exchanges are also important. But in the future the most important measure of unemployment will undoubtedly be the returns of the compulsory insurance system. For the number receiving benefits since October, 1927, see Chapter 26.

Note C

BELGIUM

The publication of the percentages of unemployed workers among Belgian trade unions dates from 1902. During the war, however, this was discontinued. In December, 1920, the publication of the unemployment statistics as derived from the Unemployment Funds was resumed.[7] The number covered in 1914 was only 77,000. It increased greatly at the end of 1920 and since then has remained over 600,000. Approximately one-half the industrial workers are thus covered. As in the case of the German trade union statistics, the numbers completely unemployed, and partially unemployed are published separately. The number of days lost and the number compensated by benefits are also published. Even for the workers covered the returns showing the number unemployed are not complete as they do not include those not qualifying for benefits and those who exhaust their claims. The monthly reports are published in the *Revue du Travail*.

Note D

DENMARK

The Danish figures are derived from the reports of the trade unions paying out-of-work benefits. While they are compiled for every Friday, those published in the *International Labour Review* refer to the last Friday in each month. The publication of the Danish figures did not begin until 1910. From 1904 to 1910 there were published, however, the number unemployed at the end of each month. From the annual figures of trade union membership a rough idea of the percentages can be obtained.[8] In 1912 the

---

[7] *International Labour Review*, January, 1921, p. 115.
[8] See *Statistisk Aarbog*, 1913, p. 124.

unions reporting had a membership of 106,000 [9] and in 1929, it increased to 276,000.[10] The number of days lost is also reported.

NOTE E

SWEDEN

The publication of the Swedish statistics was begun in 1911. Unlike the countries noted so far, the Swedish reports include those of unions not paying benefits. The figures published in the *International Labour Review* refer to the last day of each month. In March, 1911, the number of workers covered was 62,000,[11] in December, 1920, it increased to 146,000 [12] and in December, 1929, to 322,000.[13] In 1925 when the number of trade unionists covered was approximately 232,000 there were approximately 392,000 workers employed in manufacturing.[14]

NOTE F

CANADA

Canada did not begin publishing the percentages of unemployment among trade unionists until 1915. The reports include unions not paying out-of-work benefits, probably to a larger extent than in the case of Sweden. The figures as published in the *Labour Gazette* and in the *International Labour Review* refer to the last working day of each month. In 1915 the unions reporting had only 56,000 members.[15] Since then the number covered has increased and in July, 1930, the number was 201,000.[16]

NOTE G

AUSTRALIA

Very few of the Australian unions reporting on unemployment pay out-of-work benefits. But the majority of the larger organizations have permanent secretaries or organizers who are closely in touch with the members and with the state of trade. Further, many unions keep registers and provide for reduced subscriptions for numbers unemployed.[17] The Australian statistics differ from those previously noted in that from 1891 to 1913 they were gathered but once at the end of each year. Since 1913 they have been obtained quarterly. The results published in the *Labour Reports*

[9] *Ibid.*, p. 124.
[10] *Ibid.*, 1930, p. 122.
[11] *Statistisk Arsbok*, 1918, p. 210.
[15] *International Labour Review*, January, 1921, p. 116.
[16] *Ibid.*, November, 1930, p. 653.
[12] *Ibid.*, 1921, p. 213.
[13] *Ibid.*, 1930, p. 240.
[14] *Ibid.*, p. 132.

refer to the number unemployed for three days or more during a specified week. While those unemployed on account of strikes or lockouts are not included those unemployed on account of sickness or accidents are included. Unions of workers in permanent employment, such as railwaymen, are excluded from the returns. The Australian sample is, however, quite large. The number of workers covered was only 12,000 in 1906, but in 1913 it increased to 251,000, and in 1928 to 429,000.

NOTE H

FRANCE

The French records of unemployment among trade unions go back to 1894. They were, however, discontinued during the war and while some statistics are published in the *International Labour Review* for recent years, they are based on so small a sample as not to warrant their inclusion in Table 8. While the number of unemployment funds officially constituted amounted to 264 (of which 233 were communal funds in communes of more than 5,000 inhabitants and 31 departmental funds in localities of less than 5,000 inhabitants), the number actually in operation and sending returns regularly hardly reaches at the present time more than 25. The figures given each month are the number of men and women receiving benefit.[18]

The only other data consist of the number of applications and vacancies as reported by the employment exchanges in each department.[19]

NOTE I

RUSSIA

Even though there are no reliable statistics of unemployment in Russia, the available facts are worth noting because of the importance of Russia. The statistics derived from the insurance system cannot be used, for although theoretically it applies to the whole working population, in fact, "only a small number are actually covered. The resulting statistics are therefore very incomplete for they only cover the number of unemployed who have received benefit and their percentage to the total employed registered."[20]

---

[17] *Official Year Book*, 1927, pp. 549-50.

[18] International Labour Office, *Studies and Reports Series N. (Statistics)* No. 7. *Methods of Statistics of Unemployment*, 1925, p. 54.

[19] Cf. *post*, p. 310.

[20] International Labour Office, *Studies and Reports Series N (Statistics)* No. 7. *Methods of Statistics of Unemployment*, 1925, p. 54.

There are, however, statistics derived from the official labor offices through which the engagement of workers was made compulsory in 1924. Even these statistics cannot be considered complete. "A large number of workers prefer not to take advantage of these facilities. The figures published at irregular intervals are based on reports from 70 chief towns and show for each month the number of unemployed registered and the vacancies notified at the end of the month, as well as the number per 100 vacancies, distinguishing sex, the number of vacancies per 100 unemployed and the number actually placed without distinction of sex." [20a]

The numbers registered for work are shown in the following table: [21]

NUMBER UNEMPLOYED REMAINING ON LIVE REGISTER
(000 omitted)

END OF MONTH	1925	1926	1927	1928	1929	1930
March . . .	*	1,056	1,478	1,576	1,756	1,079
June	1,100	1,066	1,217	1,471	1,448	786
Sept.	1,055	1,071	1,041	1,365	1,242	..
Dec.	951	1,290	1,353	1,616	1,316	..

In the earlier years, there can be little question but that even these figures understated the real conditions. Thus according to a memorandum prepared by the All-Russian Council of Trade-Unions itself, in April, 1927, no less than 1,774,000 or 18% of their members were out of work.[22] The non-unionists, who then numbered about 750,000, were not included in this estimate. Because of the preference in hiring which is given to unionists, the percentage of the unemployed amongst non-unionists is undoubtedly appreciably greater than amongst the unionists. It seems difficult to believe that there could have been less than 2 million urban workers who were unemployed at this time. Nor did even this figure include the peasants who had recently come from the country to seek work in the towns and who at that time were not permitted to register at the exchanges.

When it is remembered that the employment exchanges showed only 1,055,000 to have been unemployed at this time, some idea can be gained of the degree to which the employment exchange figures then minimized the real problem.

[20a] Ibid.

[21] *International Labour Review.*

[22] Prepared by the Statistical Division of the All-Russian Council of Trade Unions, and printed in the description of unemployment in *Soviet Russia in the Second Decade* (edited by Chase, Dunn and Tugwell), p. 231.

It is probable that with the improvement of the statistical work of the employment exchanges, the margin of error has diminished. When one considers that the number of urban workers cannot greatly exceed 8 million, it is apparent that until recently the relative percentage of unemployment has probably been higher than that of any other European country.

CHAPTER IV

SOME EXPLANATIONS FOR THE COMPARATIVE DIFFERENCES IN UNEMPLOYMENT BETWEEN COUNTRIES.

1. Why Unemployment Is Apparently so High in the United States

The apparent fact that the relative volume of unemployment in the United States has been on the average nearly twice as great as the pre-war British average and has been only slightly less than the British average during the decade of deepest distress, seems at first thought to be surprising. But in the opinion of the authors, the following reasons go far to explain why the American average has been so high in comparison with the British.

(1) The Factor of the Weather. Most of the American population live in regions with hot summers and cold winters. In England, on the other hand, the winters are not very cold nor are the summers very warm. In consequence the demands of the American consumer change more sharply from season to season than do those of the English. Clothing, for example, is purchased in two main varieties, and these are bought during two rather closely concentrated seasons, in the fall and spring respectively. In England, on the contrary, there is not a great difference between winter and summer attire, and the purchase of clothing is much more evenly distributed from month to month.

What is true of clothing is almost equally true of other industries as well. We buy meat and carbohydrates, for example, during the winter and change our dietary during the summer to include more fresh vegetables and fruit. In the summer also the consumption of ice-cream and cold drinks multiplies apace. The English dietary, on the other hand, as American visitors to that country can bear eloquent testi-mony, has a uniformity and unalterableness which is much like the reputed grace of God.

Similarly, we buy skates and sleds for winter sports, and bathing suits, tennis racquets, and golf sticks for the sum-mer. In England where snow and ice are but infrequent, any given sport is practiced for a much longer season.

Because of the relative mildness of the English winters, the household consumption of coal, as American travellers can again testify, does not rise as sharply during the winter as here. Nor do English industrial plants need to burn as much coal to heat their work-rooms. Since more coal is burned in England during the summer than here because of the slight development of gas for cooking purposes, it fol-lows that the seasonal fluctuations in the demand for coal in England are far less than here. Were other things equal therefore, the English coal mines would, in consequence, normally work more days during the year than ours.

Since American roads are much less passable during the winter months than are the English, few automobiles are bought during this season, and the bulk of our purchases are instead concentrated between the months of March and June inclusive. Since irregularities of purchasing lead to irregularities of production and employment the sharp ex-tremes of climate create a considerable amount of unem-ployment in the clothing, coal, mining, and automobile industries.

Finally, building and road making can be carried on fairly steadily in England, "wet" rather than cold weather being their chief barrier. In the United States, while the advent of steel construction and of newer types of material has enabled more construction to be carried on during the win-ter than was formerly possible, there is still an appreciable diminution in the volume of construction during the winter months. The percentage of unemployment among the Amer-ican building trades-workers is consequently higher than among the British workers.

The variability of weather will thus account for the seasonal unemployment in clothing, automobile manufacturing, mining, and building—probably the four most irregular industries in the United States. The greater equableness of the temperature in England, on the other hand, leads to smaller seasonal fluctuations in these industries, and to less unemployment.

But the effects of the climate do not stop here. A large number of industries producing the raw material and some of the parts for these finished products also move in an erratic course in the wake of these industries. The irregular operation of the clothing industry leads to irregularity in the textile industries. The high degree of seasonal irregularity in the production of automobiles causes similar fluctuations in the production of tires, automobile parts, etc. The fact that little building is conducted during the winter months leads to a sharp falling off during the immediately preceding months in the manufacture of bricks, cement, glass, lumber, etc. Thus the seasonal effects of the weather fan out in a multitude of directions, creating irregularities and unemployment as they go.

(2) **Style and Fashion.** A second force producing irregularity is the greater sway of style and fashion in the United States than in England. This inevitably results from the much smaller influence which hereditary status has in our society as compared with that of England, and the much greater opportunity which men and women have here to rise in the economic and social scale. Although Englishmen dislike to admit it, England is in fact still largely a caste-ridden country. The middle and upper classes draw themselves sharply away from the workers, and in the main look down upon them because of their accent and because they are compelled to work with their hands. The upper classes maintain a separate system of schools for their own children. The upper positions in the Civil Service, in the professions, in banking and in business are in the main reserved for the socially dominant groups. Because of this relative closing of the gates of opportunity and because the "upper"

classes have been successful in giving to large sections of the "lower" classes, deep-seated inferiority complexes, members of the working classes have in general little hope of rising individually in the social and economic scale.

Within the upper classes in turn, prestige results either from birth or from attainments. The consequence is that men and women realize that they cannot improve their standing greatly by struggling. This causes them to place less emphasis upon dress, upon house furnishings, and upon all those articles of consumption which men and women frequently use as means of distinguishing themselves from the rest of mankind and of assisting them to rise in the social and consequently in the business world.

In the United States, on the other hand, the opportunities for the individual to rise are far greater. The public schools, combined with the state universities, give an education to large numbers of the children of the poorer classes which enables them to compete on much more equal terms with the children of the more privileged classes. In addition, the traditions of business tend to favor individual worth rather than social standing far more than is the case in England. Men, moreover, do not marry so closely within their own social class as in Great Britain, and the women of the less privileged classes have therefore a greater opportunity of moving upward by a "fortunate" match.

Both women and men are therefore much concerned about their personal appearance. The middle classes worry about whether the furnishings of their homes and other self-regarding expenditures are in style. Being in the mode enables those who are rising in the social scale to obtain more easily those social contacts which can be turned to business and professional use. The ability and desire of Americans to "get ahead" and to be up to the minute in the social and economic race makes them therefore peculiarly susceptible to style changes.

Styles of clothing, automobiles, furniture, sports, etc., change therefore more rapidly here than in a caste dominated society such as that of England. But since it is impossible to adapt production perfectly to these shifting styles, the inevitable consequence is a greater irregularity of employment.

The relative English stability of status is therefore one factor which causes the seasonal fluctuations in that country to be less than here. Their stability of employment may, however, be purchased in this case at too dear a price.

(3) **Geographical Shifts.** A third factor which leads in itself to a greater volume of unemployment is the fact that geographical shifts of population are greater here than in England. Our population shifts are truly extraordinary, as the rise of cities like Detroit, Chicago, and Los Angeles abundantly demonstrates. American city dwellers are, moreover, inclined to overestimate the rate at which their particular city will grow and there is a consequent tendency to overbuild beyond the needs of future population. Workers are therefore drawn into cities in the "boom" days. When a city fails to maintain its expected rate of growth, some time is required before the surplus workers can find employment elsewhere, and there is, in consequence, an intervening period of unemployment.

The fact that the comparative productive possibilities of various sections of the United States have not been as perfectly known as have those of the different regions of England has also led to a geographical displacement of labor and to attendant unemployment. Thus the textile industry has recently discovered that the South offers more advantages than had previously been thought, and in consequence there has been a movement away from its former seat in New England which has left large numbers unemployed in Lawrence, Lowell, Manchester, Fall River, and New Bedford. Similarly, the westward drift of the shoe industry to Cincinnati and St. Louis has left in its wake considerable unemployment in Lynn, Brockton, and Haverhill.

(4) **The Tempo of Industry.** Finally, the fact that the rate of industrial progress has been greater in the United

States than in Great Britain has by itself operated to increase the amount of unemployment. The British index of production increased by approximately 23 per cent between 1907 and 1924, and the output per employed worker by 4 per cent.[1] But this was a relatively slight advance when compared with the American increase of 80 per cent in the physical product of manufacturing during that time, with a gain of 45 per cent in output per employed wage-earner.[2]

This greater rate of industrial progress creates two rather closely interrelated sources of disturbance. (a) The industrial mechanism, gets more easily out of balance; (b) business men tend to become too optimistic about the future of their particular industries. Both of these forces operate to create unemployment.

When the production of various commodities is advancing rapidly but at uneven rates, the profit margins of specific industries are disturbed not only by changes in demand but by the fact that the increases in production in some of the industries may have caused the value per unit of product to fall by a so much greater relative share as to make those industries receive a smaller share of the national income than originally.[3] This will inevitably cause the wage rates in these industries to be below those for similar labor in industry as a whole, and will therefore necessarily lead to an expulsion of labor from those industries to others. But in the transitional period, as we shall see, much time is lost by labor. The consequence is that the very speed of industrial progress compels a much more accelerated shifting of labor and capital from industry to industry to conform to the principles of a normal and equalized rate of return on the margins of all industries. And in a period in

---

[1] N. A. Tolles and Paul H. Douglas, A Measurement of British Industrial Production, *Journal of Political Economy*, Vol. XXXVIII, pp. 1-28.

[2] See Paul H. Douglas, *Real Wages in the United States*, p. 547.

[3] This would be the case where their "flexibilities of value through time" were less than unity. For an elaboration of this point, see an article by Paul H. Douglas, Technological Unemployment, in the *Bulletin of the Taylor Society*, December, 1930, pp. 254-261. See also the article by Tolles and Douglas, *op. cit.*

which the rate of change is increasing, unemployment necessarily rises as well.

American business men have, moreover, been slow to grasp the fact that virtually no industry which starts out developing rapidly can maintain for long the same rate of growth.[4] In consequence, many American industries tend to be overbuilt, and to have capital equipment and a working force which have been assembled because the managers had assumed that the business would continue to grow in the future as it had in the past.[5] It becomes necessary, therefore, for labor to move out of these industries just as we have pointed out that building and construction workers have had to leave towns. Unemployment again results in this process of transition.

In a country like England where the rate of material progress is much slower, the value ratios of the various commodities are not altered so sharply and in consequence the transfer of labor is much more gradually accomplished. Similarly, since British business has not seen the material expansion during the last third of a century which American industry has witnessed, British enterprises are not so overoptimistic about the future of their particular enterprises. They, in consequence, do not expose themselves to the same danger of overbuilding and hence subsequently do not have to squeeze as much labor out of their particular industry as would be necessary in the United States. But here again, it is probable that the British have in the past purchased their greater stability at too dear a price.

2. Why Has Unemployment Been So High in Great Britain During the Last Decade?

As we have seen, the relative amount of unemployment in Great Britain has been over twice as great during the

---

[4] For a brilliant statistical proof that rates of growth lessen, see S. S. Kuznets, *Secular Movements in Production and Prices*, pp. 1-200.

[5] Fundamentally, the principle of diminishing incremental productivity would by itself tend to slow up the rate of growth.

decade 1920-1930 as it was in the forty years which preceded the Great War. Many fantastic explanations have
been offered to account for this increase, including the contention that capitalism in its maturity inevitably creates
a "surplus" population. The real causes seem, however, to
lie both in particular changes which have affected England's great exporting industries and in certain fundamental characteristics of her population and industrial
structure.

By no means all of England's industries are depressed.
On the contrary industry in the midlands and the south is
in excellent shape. The "depressed areas" of South Wales,
the Clyde, and the north are those where the four great
industries of coal, shipbuilding, textiles, and iron and steel
are located, and England's difficulties can largely be explained in terms of those industries. We turn, therefore, to
an analysis of the difficulties which have pursued these
four industries during most of the past decade.

Coal mining throughout the world has suffered greatly
from overcapacity and unemployment. The increasing use
of gas engines, the rise of the Diesel engine as motive
power for an increasing number of ships, and the development of hydro-electric power have all cut in upon coal.
In addition great economies have been effected in the burn-
ing of coal so that an appreciably smaller quantity is
required for the generation of a given quantity of power
or the creation of a given number of heat units. This has
caused a comparative shrinkage in the demand for coal
although the productive capacity of the European mines
has expanded because of the refitting of the French mines
and the development of mining in Poland and in other
countries. In such a condition, the burden of unemployment will largely be borne by those mines where costs are
highest. Since a large percentage of the British mines are
quite old and are operating with both antiquated equipment and higher wage scales, this has meant that English
coal in particular has found it difficult to compete in the
European market. This difficulty has been increased by

the German reparation payments of coal which have helped to supply the Mediterranean trade which formerly absorbed a considerable percentage of the English output.

Shipbuilding has declined because, although the world tonnage of ships is greater than before the war, the total volume of ocean trade has on the whole declined. The burden of idleness has been thrown upon the older ships which are in the main British. Such new ships as have been built in Europe are largely motorships equipped with Diesel engines and of a type of construction in which the Scandinavian and German yards, rather than the British, excel. The Clyde district has, in consequence, been largely idle.

The falling off in the export of textiles has been caused primarily by the rise of cotton manufacturing in the Orient and by the increased tariff barriers in Europe. The World War by shutting off English exports to the Far East stimulated the development of cotton mills in Japan and to a lesser extent in India and China as well and created new competitors for the post-war market. The growth of the Nationalistic movement in China and India during the post-war period has further operated to raise the tariff schedules against foreign cloth. The result has been a decrease in English sales and an increase in the unemployment of the textile operators. This tendency has been heightened by the higher tariffs which have been imposed by the newly created states in Central Europe and by the growth everywhere of the spirit of protection.

The decline of the English iron and steel industry was caused in part by the direct pressure of foreign competition and in part by the lessened domestic demand for steel which the decadence of shipbuilding and of textiles has necessarily involved. The diminution of smelting has in turn diminished the domestic demand for coal as has the increasing substitution of motor for railway transportation.

In addition to these specific industrial changes, certain general characteristics and policies of English industry have impeded its recovery. English machinery and production methods are in many cases hopelessly antiquated and are no match for the newer machines and methods which characterize countries which are not weighted down by accumulated tradition and by a heavy stock of obsolete equipment. English wages, while reduced in a great many industries, are probably still higher in comparison with those of foreign countries than is justified by the comparative efficiency of its workers. These factors would not in themselves create unemployment so far as the domestic market is concerned but they would and do operate to retard the sales of the great exporting industries.

A final factor which may have caused some unemployment was England's return to the gold standard in 1925. In order to effect this and to prevent the gold supply from being depleted, it was necessary that her price level should be reduced by 10 points. Such a decline occurred with the result that firms which had bought raw materials and labor at earlier and higher price levels were compelled to sell the finished goods at later and lower price levels. Such a shrinkage in monetary values has, as we shall see, an inevitably depressive effect upon business and leads many businesses to curtail production and therefore to increase unemployment. There seems to be little doubt that the fall in English prices in 1925, attendant upon the reëstablishment of the gold standard did interrupt the progress towards recovery which was then being made by English industry. The effects of such a fall might be expected to wear off after the price level was stabilized. The natural sluggishness of wage rates which has perhaps been somewhat reinforced by unemployment insurance has prevented a complete readjustment from being effected in this field of costs and has perhaps to that extent delayed the process of recovery.

3. Why Has Unemployment Been So Comparatively Low in France?

The French statistics for the last few years have shown only a few thousand at the most to be unemployed in that country and have frequently recorded the numbers at less than a thousand.[6] These statistics are, however, based upon the membership in the French voluntary unemployment insurance funds which have not included any considerable proportion of the French industrial workers. But while the official statistics do considerably understate the absolute number of Frenchmen who are unemployed, it is still nevertheless true that the percentage of French workers who are unemployed is very much less than in England, Germany, and the United States. Among the many alleged reasons which have been advanced to explain this phenomenon have been the facts that the French population is now virtually stationary and that mass production is less characteristic of France than of any other large country. We shall show in a subsequent chapter that the first of these assigned reasons is not in fact a cause and that the advance in the second creates transitional rather than permanent unemployment. The real factors which have kept the volume of unemployment at a comparatively low level seem, however, to have been the following: (1) The rising internal price level which continued in France until the stabilization of the franc in 1927. French prices rose steadily during the years from 1918 to 1927 and by the beginning of the latter year were more than double what they had been five years before.[7] This had a stimulating effect upon business since it meant that raw materials and labor which were purchased at an earlier and lower price level were combined into finished goods which were sold at a later and higher price level. The resulting accretion of money profits made businesses anxious to expand their operations and led amongst other results to a reduction in the numbers of the unemployed. (2) During the post-war period there has of course been an extensive rebuilding of the devastated areas. This work, largely paid for by the German indemnities, has given an abnormal stimulant to the construction industry and indirectly to manufacturing as well. This has helped to

---

[6] See *Bulletin du Ministère du Travail*, Volumes 28-35.
[7] *Bulletin du Ministère du Travail*. Oct., Nov., Dec., 1923, pp. 380-81; Jan., Feb., March, 1927.

reduce the volume of unemployment belów its natural level. (3) The third factor which has reduced the volume of unemployment for Frenchmen has been the French immigration policy. The National Council on Labor Supply advises on the numbers which should be admitted and these are regulated since 1926 according to the state of the labor market. Only workers who have a definite offer of employment are admitted and these immigrants are divided into two groups: (a) seasonal workers who are admitted for the peak months in agriculture and in other industries and who are compelled to leave the country immediately upon the termination of their work and (b) workers who are admitted for a period of two years but whose permit must be renewed by the labor authorities if they are to stay in the country beyond that date. It is thus possible for the French authorities in a year of business depression to send out of the country one-half of the total number of foreign laborers in the country and, if the depression continues over a period of two years, to expel all of the laborers from other countries and concentrate the available employment upon French citizens.

The degree to which French immigration policy has utilized these powers is evidenced by the fact that whereas the average annual number of immigrants who were admitted during the four years of 1923-1926 was 143.4 thousand for industry and 76.0 thousand for agriculture; this was cut in the recession year of 1927 to 18.8 and 43.5 thousand respectively. At the same time the number of workers who were repatriated was increased from a previous average of 52.6 thousand to 90.0 thousand. The comparison is made somewhat more striking if we compare the relation between the numbers admitted and repatriated, for whereas in 1926 the net balance of immigrants over those repatriated was 113.4 thousand, this relationship was reversed in 1927 when 25.6 thousand more workers were repatriated than were admitted.[8]

[8] L'Immigration Contrôlée des Travailleurs Étrangers en France de 1920 à 1927, *Bulletin du Ministère du Travail*, 1928, pp. 28, 31.

When business conditions revived in 1928, the number of immigrants admitted to enter agricultural and industrial pursuits were each raised by about 16,000 more than during the preceding year while the number repatriated was decreased by 36,000.[9] In this way, the net volume of immigration was increased by about 68,000. During the following year the number admitted to the country was still further increased.

The French immigration policy was therefore helpful in stabilizing employment in France by throwing part of the burden of fluctuations upon other countries.

4. Why Was Unemployment High in Russia and Why Has It Recently Decreased in the Face of an Opposite Movement in the Rest of the World?

The experience of Russia is particularly interesting since it is the only country in the world in which socialism is in operation on any considerable scale. For in that society 95 per cent of the manufacturing and 90 per cent of wholesale trade is in the hands of governmental or socialized agencies. The percentage of retail trade under the control of the coöperatives has moreover steadily increased until they and the governmental stores handle over three-quarters of the total turnover while there has been at the same time a distinct growth in the collective conduct of farming. The private reception of rent and interest has, therefore, been reduced to a minimum. If these sources of income or what the Marxists term "surplus value" are indeed the causes of unemployment, then unemployment should have been virtually non-existent.

But in fact the percentage of unemployment in Russia, until the last year, has been higher than in any other country. The fundamental cause for the large amount of unemployment in Russia has been the difference in the degree of gain which the urban and rural workers have obtained. By the spring of 1927, the manual workers of the towns and

[9] *Bulletin du Ministère du Travail*, 1929, p. 105.

cities could purchase with their incomes approximately 30 per cent more than they could have done in 1913.[10]

Since then their real wages have still further advanced. On the other hand, the peasants, while politically much freer than before the war, made little, if any improvement in their material condition. This increasing disparity between the condition of the rural and of the urban workers led large numbers of peasants, particularly those without draft animals and with only small plots of land, to leave the farms and to seek work in the cities. While the volume of manufacturing and the opportunities for employment in the cities expanded appreciably during the years from 1925 to 1928, the increase was not sufficiently rapid to absorb all of the migrants from the farms and the consequence was an increase in the relative amount of unemployment. In order to protect the urban workers from being inundated by this flow of peasants, it was provided that members of unions should be given preference in employment while the unions in turn ruled that only those who had previously been employed for wages were eligible for union membership. In this way, the newly arrived peasants were barred from union membership and consequently were virtually prevented from getting work in the state enterprises.

During the last year, however, the relative volume of unemployment has apparently been falling in Russia at the very time when, because of the world-wide depression, it has been rising appreciably in other countries. Thus whereas there were 1,242,000 unemployed on the "live" register in September, 1929, this number was reduced to 633,000 in July, 1930.[11] This figure has, in recent months, been still further reduced. It is now reported that the Russian employment exchanges have ceased to register further workers. This may mean either that there are now very few unemployed in Russia or that a large number of the unemployed

[10] See the chapter on Wages and the Material Condition of the Russia Workers in Chase, Dunn and Tugwell, *Soviet Russia in the Second Decade.*

[11] *International Labour Review,* November, 1930, p. 654.

are not allowed to register and hence do not appear in the official returns.

But although it is possible that the decrease in the volume of unemployment has not been as great as it seems, there is little doubt that there has been an appreciable improvement in the unemployment situation, while elsewhere it has steadily become more serious. The probable reasons for this favorable showing are:

1. Under the Five-Year Plan there has been an extraordinary increase in the tempo of industrialization. Under that plan, the total amount of the capital is expected to increase from approximately 70 billion roubles to 127 billions in 1932-33 or an increase of 82 per cent.[12] The construction of mills, power stations, machinery, etc., has been proceeding apace and this has helped to absorb a large number of the unemployed.

2. A planned economy managed for the social good may well have a greater capacity to prevent depressions and to keep the laboring force more steadily employed than an uncoördinated system of private establishments necessarily motivated by profit where the ultimate governor in the distribution of productive resources is the tendency of profits and wages to flow towards an equality. Under a planned economy industries can be given definite production quotas and assigned definite numbers of workers. It is thus much more possible immediately to provide every worker with a job than it is in private industry where no such general plan is set up. Employment is furthermore not contingent upon the maintenance of profit margins by the individual firms as is the case under private enterprise. Moreover since the investments of fixed capital are made at a scheduled rate, the heavy industries or those producing capital goods are not at the mercy of fluctuations in the demand for consumers' goods and hence employment in them can be continuous.

3. A third factor making for stability has been the control which the Russian authorities have been able to exercise

[12] *The Soviet Union Looks Ahead* (Liveright, New York, 1929), p. 229.

over their price level. Under the state monopoly of foreign trade, it has been possible to keep the Russian price level above that of the rest of the world and by an internal control of bank credit and monetary issue to know approximately what the future level of prices was going to be. The state trusts are therefore able to make their plans in advance to a far greater degree than private business in countries where the price level is uncertain.

The greater industrial stability which Russia has evidenced, as compared with the rest of the industrial world during the past year and a half, is of course not conclusive evidence of the superiority of a planned economy. This favorable record may not be maintained in the future and the fierce energy which now characterizes the program of industrial reconstruction may slacken to a very slow tempo. But the whole contrast should raise in the minds of openminded men the possibility at least of organizing the production forces of the western world and of extending to the industrial system as a whole some of those methods of setting standards, of planning, and of coördinating which have been so effective within establishments.[18]

[18] For a very suggestive statement of this problem see a paper by Dr. Harlow S. Person in the *Bulletin of the Taylor Society* for December, 1930.

CHAPTER V

THE HUMAN AND ECONOMIC COSTS OF UNEMPLOYMENT

We are becoming more aware of the great inroads which prolonged unemployment makes upon the lives of the workers and their families and the strain which it imposes upon charity. We need to realize the great misery which unemployment causes if for no other reason than to break down any smug complacency which we may have and to become imbued with the will to understand the problem and a readiness to help in coping with it. The best collection of individual case histories showing the effects of unemployment which has ever been made is that fathered by the National Federation of Settlements in 1929 under the direction of Miss Helen Hall and of which a popularized but accurate version has been prepared by Clinch Calkins in her *Some Folks Won't Work*.[1] When we remember that these cases were collected during years of supposed prosperity and covered only good workmen who lost their jobs through no fault of their own, we can appreciate something of the added suffering which a period of depression brings.

When unemployment strikes a family for any period, an impairment in the family's living standards very soon results. Much less milk is bought, as is evidenced by the fact that during the present depression there has been a decrease in the amount purchased in New York City alone of approximately one million quarts a week.[2] In the depression of 1920-21, the study of the Children's Bureau of 300 families when the chief breadwinners had been unemployed

---

[1] The full case histories edited by Miss Hall will soon be published by the University of Pennsylvania Press.

[2] *New York Times,* December 6, 1930.

for a long period showed that the consumption of milk had fallen to half.[3] Other foods, such as vegetables, are also purchased in much smaller quantity and in a considerable percentage of the cases, serious underfeeding results. The families also economize on clothes and fuel; the Children's Bureau found, for example, in its 1920-21 survey many cases where the children were unable to go to school because they did not have proper shoes or clothing. Many small children were compelled to go about their underheated houses barefoot on cold winter days while, at the same time, their fathers who were also inadequately fed and clothed had to stand in line for work in zero weather.

Housing accommodations are also curtailed. The families will move into smaller quarters or take others in with them. Those that have been buying their homes find themselves unable, in a large percentage of cases, to keep up the payments with the result that many lose the amounts which they have paid in the past.

The impairment of the food, clothing, and housing standards of the families leads in turn to an increase in illness. The Children's Bureau found that during the unemployment period of 1920-21, there had been some illness in two-thirds of the 300 families investigated. In Philadelphia, the Visiting Nurse Association was caring in December, 1921, for 5,165 cases or 61 per cent more than the 3,256 who were on its books in December, 1920.[4]

The studies by the Cleveland Nutrition Clinic of a group of children also show somewhat similar results. The weights of these children were carefully measured for seven consecutive months in 1920-21 and again in 1921-22. In the first period they gained an average of two pounds as compared with an average for the second of only three-quarters of a pound.[5] The report of the Association of Tuberculosis Clinics in New York City showed that during the first six months of 1930, the total number of new admissions to such

[3] *Bulletin 125*, United States Children's Bureau.
[4] Philip Klein, *The Burden of Unemployment*, pp. 35-36.
[5] *Ibid.*, p. 36.

clinics was 21,180.[6] This was an increase of 1,603 or 15 per
cent over the number admitted during the corresponding
period of the preceding year. Since the full effects of unemployment could not be felt within this period of time, it
is probable that the difference would be still greater during
the last half of the year and the first half of 1931.

The load upon the charities is of course greatly increased.
According to the study of Ralph G. Hurlin of the Russell
Sage Foundation, $2,813,000 was paid out by 237 agencies
during the month of October, 1930, to the needy in their
own homes, exclusive of the amounts paid out in mothers'
aid.[7] This was 118 per cent more than the amounts which
these same agencies had distributed for these purposes during the corresponding month of the previous year. The
United Charities of Chicago were, for example, distributing
relief to 13,667 families in December, 1930, as compared
with 3,837 in January.

In addition to all this, the lack of physical necessities
combined with the inevitable worry about the future frequently leads to a severe strain upon family relations and
happiness and, in many cases, to pronounced mental
disorders.

The economic pressure to which men and their families
are thus subjected necessarily causes an appreciable increase
in the volume of crimes against property. Dr. Blair Stewart
and Mrs. Eleanor Wheeler of Reed College have demonstrated this for Portland, Oregon.[8] They studied the movement for the years 1923-29 of (1) placements by public
employment agencies and (2) crimes against property as
recorded in the cases before the municipal court and found
the coefficient of correlation between them to be .811. Since
a high volume of placements was in general indicative of
a relatively low degree of unemployment, and vice versa,
this relatively high coefficient can be accepted as at least

[6] *New York Times,* November 11, 1930, p. 21.
[7] Russell Sage Foundation, Department of Statistics, *Relief Bulletin,*
October, 1930, p. 2.
[8] We are indebted to Dr. Stewart and Mrs. Wheeler for putting their
results at our disposal.

some indication of the effects' of unemployment upon crime.[9]

Unemployment has moreover its economic as well as its human costs, of which the following are the most important:

1. Loss in Wages to the Workers. We have estimated the probable average percentage of unemployment in manufacturing, transportation, construction, and coal mining (including that caused by personal disability) to be about 10 per cent. If this is reduced to 8 per cent for the non-agricultural workers, to allow for the lower rate in mercantile trade, etc., and for the amount caused by physical or mental unfitness, we would probably be about correct for industry as a whole.

The number of employees in the non-agricultural industries is about 34,800,000. An average unemployment figure of 8 per cent applied to this group would mean an average number unemployed of approximately 2,780,000. Studies by one of the authors indicate that the average annual earnings in 1928 of between 15,000,000 and 16,000,000 non-agricultural wage and salaried workers were $1,504.[10] This may probably be accepted as a fairly close approximation to the earnings of the group. Upon this basis, therefore, the most probable estimate of the average annual loss is approximately 4.2 billion dollars.

If unemployment could be completely eliminated, the workers would therefore have approximately [11] four billion more dollars in their pockets and consequently could buy many of the commodities which they and their families so badly need. Even if unemployment were reduced by only one-quarter, the workers' income would be increased annually by nearly a billion dollars.

All this does not take account of time which is lost

---

[9] For an expansion of the material upon this relationship see William A. Bonger, *Criminality and Economic Conditions.*

[10] Paul H. Douglas and F. T. Jennison, *The Movement of Money and Real Earnings in the United States, 1926-28,* p. 27. See also Paul H. Douglas, *Real Wages in the United States, 1890-1926.*

[11] We recognize that an increase in employment might operate to reduce the real hourly rate.

within employment, the reduction of which would still further swell the earnings.

2. Loss of Markets to Merchants and Manufacturers. The fact that unemployment diminishes the earnings of the workers by nearly four billion dollars a year means that merchants, manufacturers, and producers of all kinds are deprived of a potential market of that amount. If the workmen were employed steadily, they would, with their increased earnings, buy more milk and fruit, live in better homes, wear better clothes, send their children to school for longer periods, buy more electrical appliances to lighten the labors of their wives, and enjoy more recreation and outings. This would mean that the volume of sales in all of these lines and in others as well would increase. Manufacturers would be able to sell more of their products and the turnover of the retail merchants would also increase. Overhead costs per unit would in consequence diminish and business profits would rise.

By decreasing unemployment, business men will therefore be building up a larger market for their product. This latent market is indeed as great as our total export trade. We do not therefore have to look to foreign countries for an increase in demand to absorb the products of our industries. An even larger potential market lies within our own gates.

3. Losses from Unused Fixed Capital. Irregularities in production carry with them as a corollary a failure to use machinery and capital equipment of the country to full capacity. For industry must maintain at least sufficient equipment to keep its maximum forces employed and, when fewer workers are employed and less than the standard number of hours worked, the machinery and plant are as idle as are the men. One of the authors has estimated that in 1922 the total value at cost prices of the fixed capital in manufacturing alone amounted to approximately 24.4 billions of dollars. At the present time it is undoubtedly appreciably more. If we assume that the percentage of unemployment in manufacturing is on the average approximately 8 per cent, this would mean that approximately one-twelfth of this amount of capital, or at least two billion dollars, lies idle on the average because of unemployment.

Since interest, depreciation, taxes, and obsolescence must amount to at least 12 per cent per annum on this investment, this would mean a minimum annual loss of 250 million dollars in idle overhead for manufacturing alone. This is a most conservative estimate and the probabilities are that the costs are even higher.

Some industries have a particularly heavy cost because of their wide seasonal and cyclical fluctuations. Thus in the automobile industry, it is probable that if production could be carried on at an even rate, the industry could get along equally well with 20 per cent less capital.

4. Losses from Restriction of Output on Part of Workers Induced by Fear of Unemployment. Despite the introduction of moving conveyors and automatic machinery into American industry, which attempt, among other things, to remove the rate of production from the decision of the workers, it is possible for workers to slow down production and to restrict output. Such a restriction of output is widely practiced. The two chief causes for this are: (1) the fear on the part of those workers who are paid by piece-rates or bonus systems that, if they increase their output, their piece-rate will be cut; (2) the fear that, if they increase output, not all of the product can be sold and that, in consequence, many of the workers will be laid off. The fact of unemployment makes many workers, therefore, who are paid on a time basis anxious to protect their jobs by spinning the work out for as long as possible.

This is not inconsistent with the fact that the fear of unemployment sometimes makes workers increase their output lest they be discharged. This occurs when the employees know that though most of the force will be retained, their own tenure is not certain. This causes them to work harder in order to hold their jobs.[12]

---

[12] For a considerable amount of corroborative evidence see Douglas, Personnel Problems and the Business Cycle, *Administration*, July, 1922, pp. 15-27.

But when the workers know that they will probably be retained for as long as the work lasts and that the supply of the latter is limited, the fear of unemployment will make them loaf as much as they can without being detected. That is why the average output in many industries declines very noticeably as they begin to go into their dull seasons.

Both of these conflicting tendencies frequently struggle for supremacy within the worker. He is anxious to hold his job. If discipline is strict, output measurable, and the spirit of the workers individualistic, he is likely to seek protection by trying to win differential preference over his fellows with his employer by increasing his output. If, on the other hand, it is difficult to measure output, if discipline is not sharp and the workers have a collective spirit, they are likely to seek protection in lessened output.

Which of these motives has the more powerful influence, it is difficult to say. It would seem unwise, however, to rely too firmly upon the fear of unemployment as a stimulus to effort. In a very large percentage of the cases it has the opposite effect. Furthermore, modern psychology seems to indicate that while fear may have in some cases a very stimulating effect at the moment, the ultimate consequences are a diminished capacity to do work. Ultimately, therefore, fear is a psychologically debilitating force which should be minimized.

A sufficient stimulus to efficiency can probably be given to the workers through the fear of being discharged or disciplined for personal demerits without necessitating a permanent background of involuntary unemployment with which tacitly to menace the workers. It seems probable, therefore, that output per hour would rise if unemployment were appreciably reduced.

PART TWO

SEASONAL UNEMPLOYMENT

CHAPTER VI

SEASONAL FLUCTUATIONS IN EMPLOYMENT

1. The Measurement of Seasonal Variations in Employment

We have already pointed out how the consuming public buys many articles irregularly during the year. This, of course, means that the sales by retailers of these commodities are much less at some periods than at others. The retailers, in consequence, do not distribute their purchases from wholesalers, jobbers, and manufacturers evenly through the year but tend to bunch their orders to meet their busy seasons. The seasonal fluctuations in purchases by the ultimate consumers reflect themselves back, therefore, in almost corresponding fluctuations in sales by the manufacturers with the peaks of the latter naturally slightly preceding those of the former.

Now since many businesses produce only to order, these fluctuations in factory sales exert corresponding, if somewhat smaller, variations in the volume of production, and these in turn lead to fluctuations in the numbers employed.

Such facts as the above are a commonplace. But the amount of employment in any month is the result of many influences. The question then presents itself as to how much of the change from one month to the next is due to the change in trend, how much to the position of the month in the business cycle, and how much to the seasonal influences? Statistical methods have, however, been devised to break up any time series into these component parts.[1]

[1] Warren M. Persons, *Review of Economic Statistics*, Preliminary Volume I, 1919, and Chapter X in Rietz, *Handbook of Mathematical*

The best method seems to be that developed by Macaulay, which consists of computing a twelve month moving average—centered—expressing the actual observations as ratios of the corresponding moving average values, taking some average of all the January, February . . . ratios, and adjusting these averages so that their average equals 100. Two very capable studies of seasonal variation in employment have utilized this method. The first, by Dr. J. F. Dewhurst,[2] is for the state of Pennsylvania, and the other, by Miss Aryness Joy of the Federal Reserve Board, is based on the employment indices for the country as a whole.[3] These studies enable us to determine what the approximate normal seasonal variations are in a large number of industries and hence to determine the approximate seriousness of the problem. We shall first divide the various manufacturing industries into three groups according to the extent of their seasonal fluctuations and then discuss some of the non-manufacturing industries.

2. SEASONAL VARIATIONS IN EMPLOYMENT IN MANUFACTURING INDUSTRIES

The seasonal indices for the manufacturing industries are set out in Tables 10, 11, and 12.

The maximum and minimum variations in employment are shown in italics. As the average for each industry is equal to 100, the italicized figures show readily the maximum and minimum departures from the average for the year. These of course come in different months for dif-

Statistics; W. L. Hart, The Method of Monthly Means for Determination of a Seasonal Variation, Journal of the American Statistical Association, September, 1922; F. R. Macaulay, Index of Production in Selected Basic Industries, Federal Reserve Bulletin, December, 1922, pp. 1414-15; Helen D. Falkner, The Measurement of Seasonal Variation, Journal of the American Statistical Association, June, 1924; Lincoln W. Hall, Seasonal Variation as a Relative of Secular Trend, Ibid., June, 1924; W. I. King, An Improved Method for Measuring the Seasonal Factor, Ibid., September, 1924; A. L. Bowley and K. C. Smith, Seasonal Variations in Finance, Prices, and Industry, London and Cambridge Economic Service, Special Memorandum, No. 7, July, 1924.

[2] J. F. Dewhurst, Employment Fluctuations in Pennsylvania.

[3] Miss Joy has computed these seasonal indices after eliminating the downward bias of the employment index of the Bureau of Labor Statistics. See Federal Reserve Bulletin for November, 1929, pp. 706-716.

(i. e. where the maximum is over 12 per cent greater than the minimum)

Industry	Jan.	Feb.	Mar.	Apr.	May	June	July	Aug.	Sept.	Oct.	Nov.	Dec.	Maximum- Minimum / Minimum
Agricultural Implements	103	106	107	106	103	99	95	95	93	95	97	100	15
Automobiles [2]	95	102	105	106	109	102	100	103	103	100	89	88	24
Cement [2]	92	91	94	98	102	105	105	107	105	104	101	96	18
Cement [3]	98	98	97	99	101	101	102	102	101	101	101	99	5
Clothing, Women's	103	109	113	109	97	88	84	92	102	107	98	99	35
Confectionery	98	98	96	91	90	90	88	94	110	121	115	110	38
Fertilizer [2]	98	106	148	161	91	68	69	77	99	97	95	92	137
Furniture [2]	99	99	99	97	95	95	97	100	104	108	106	103	14
Furniture [3]	98	98	98	95	95	90	97	99	104	110	108	108	22
Ice Cream	86	87	89	96	105	115	121	117	109	98	90	88	41
Millinery [2]	95	98	113	117	108	98	71	84	107	110	104	97	65
Pianos and Organs	103	102	100	99	96	95	91	97	101	104	106	105	16
Rubber Boots and Shoes [2]	104	102	98	98	96	95	95	96	102	104	106	107	13
Shipbuilding	103	106	106	106	103	101	98	95	93	94	96	100	14
Stoves [2]	88	97	99	101	101	101	93	100	105	109	106	101	24
Stoves and Furnaces [3]	86	103	106	105	102	74	95	102	107	103	102	96	43
Sugar Refining Cane [2]	92	96	101	103	101	102	104	106	101	104	99	93	15
Sugar Refining Cane [3]	93	102	106	102	113	115	110	103	99	99	82	76	51
Tobacco — Cigars and Cigarettes [2]	92	98	99	98	99	100	98	100	104	106	106	102	15
Tobacco — Cigars and Cigarettes [3]	101	100	101	99	97	96	93	100	102	102	104	105	13
Tobacco — Chewing, Smoking and Snuff [2]	104	106	105	99	96	98	93	98	99	100	100	102	14

[1] Unless otherwise noted, the indices are taken from the *Federal Reserve Bulletin*, November, 1930.
[2] As there was evidence of progressive change in the seasonal movement from year to year, separate sets of seasonal factors were computed for each year. Those shown above are for the year 1929. Wherever possible these have been supplemented by the figures for Pennsylvania and are so noted.
[3] Pennsylvania figures, Dewhurst, *op. cit.*

ferent industries. In addition, the last column of the tables shows the differences between the maximum and minimum variations expressed as percentages of the minimum figures.

In the first group of industries shown in Table 10, the largest percentage variations are found in the fertilizer industry, millinery, ice cream, confectionery, and women's clothing, where the numbers employed in the busiest months exceeded the numbers employed in the slack months by 137%, 65%, 47%, 38%, and 35% respectively. If the table is analyzed in detail, it will be seen that, with few exceptions, the industries showing high seasonal variations produce consumers' goods. An explanation for the fluctuations in such industries as agricultural implements, fertilizer, cement, shipbuilding, and sugar refining can be found in the weather conditions which determine the period of production either directly as in the case of shipbuilding or indirectly as in the case of agricultural implements. In such industries as women's clothing and millinery, changes in fashion are the chief factors. In such industries as ice cream, confectionery, rubber boots and shoes, and possibly stoves, the weather conditions determine directly the fluctuations in demand. The variations in the furniture industry and partly in the stove industry are attributable both to changes in fashions and to the variations in the building industry. In each case the factors cannot be distinctly isolated. Thus the variations in the automobile industry are due not only to the fact that automobiles are luxury goods and hence influenced greatly by changes in styles, but also to the fact that road conditions lead to a greater use of automobiles in summer than in winter.

As the index of seasonal variation in the automobile industry is based on a single year, some additional data are worth noting. According to very complete Ohio figures,[4] the average percentage by which maximum employment has exceeded the minimum in that state for the years 1923-28 has been as follows:

[4] F. C. and F. E. Croxton, Fluctuations of Employment in Automobile Manufacturing and Related Industries in Ohio, 1923-1928, *Monthly Labor Review*, July, 1930, p. 45.

Year	Percentage by which Maximum Exceeded Minimum	Year	Percentage by which Maximum Exceeded Minimum
1923 . . .	50	1926 . .	11
1924 . . .	21	1927 . .	11
1925 . . .	19	1928 . .	10

The range of amplitude was therefore between 10 and 50 per cent with the average one of approximately 20 per cent.

Some idea of the fluctuations in employment can also be obtained by taking the crude indices of employment for the automobile industry for the various months in both 1925 and 1928 which were fairly prosperous years.

Index of Employment (1923–25 = 100)

Month	1925	1928	Month	1925	1928
January	89	90	July	105	111
February . . .	91	98	August . . .	107	118
March	97	103	September . .	112	122
April	105	105	October . . .	119	120
May	111	111	November . .	117	109
June	106	111	December . . .	112	108

In 1925, employment in the peak month, September, was therefore 23 points and 26 per cent more than it was in January, while in 1928 the difference was one of 32 points and 36 per cent. These are very great differences but they are fairly typical of the industry.

The second group of industries like the first consists primarily of consumers' goods. A combination of weather changes and fashion changes accounts for the variations in a great many of these industries such as men's clothing, hosiery and knit goods, shirts and collars, woolen and worsted goods, cotton goods, and boots and shoes. If boots and shoes were separated, the women's branch would probably fall in the first group. This indicates that the fashion

TABLE 11

INDICES OF SEASONAL VARIATIONS IN EMPLOYMENT IN INDUSTRIES WITH MODERATE SEASONAL FLUCTUATIONS

(i. e. where the maximum is from 6 to 12 per cent greater than the minimum)

INDUSTRY	JAN.	FEB.	MAR.	APR.	MAY	JUNE	JULY	AUG.	SEPT.	OCT.	NOV.	DEC.	MAXIMUM-MINIMUM / Minimum
Automobile Tires and Tubes	98	100	101	102	102	102	102	103	103	98	94	95	10
Boots and Shoes [2]	100	103	101	98	96	95	100	104	105	104	99	97	11
Boots and Shoes [3]	100	104	105	102	99	94	98	101	100	100	99	98	12
Carpets and Rugs	103	102	104	103	101	98	95	96	97	99	101	102	9
Carpets and Rugs [3]	104	106	105	104	102	99	89	91	97	97	102	104	19
Cast Iron Pipe	96	96	99	101	102	102	103	103	101	100	98	98	7
Clothing, Men's	100	103	102	97	95	100	101	103	102	101	97	98	8
Cotton Goods [2]	102	103	102	100	100	99	97	96	99	101	102	102	7
Dyeing and Finishing Textiles [2]	101	103	103	103	100	99	97	96	98	100	101	102	7
Flour [2]	100	100	99	96	98	96	100	102	104	105	103	101	9
Glass [2]	94	97	101	101	102	103	96	102	104	103	102	98	11
Hosiery and Knit Goods	99	101	102	102	101	100	96	97	99	101	101	100	6
Meat Packing and Slaughtering [2]	104	103	98	96	97	100	100	99	99	100	101	105	9
Meat Packing [3]	103	102	99	97	97	98	99	97	100	102	103	103	6
Paper Boxes	99	99	99	97	96	96	97	98	102	105	107	104	11
Shirts and Collars [2]	101	102	102	100	99	97	95	96	99	102	103	104	9
Stamped and Enameled Ware	96	103	107	105	104	102	98	96	97	98	98	104	11
Steam Fittings	97	101	101	101	101	101	98	101	102	98	100	95	7
Structural Iron Work	97	98	97	98	99	101	101	103	103	102	100	99	6
Woollen and Worsted Goods	102	102	100	98	98	98	95	98	99	102	104	103	9

[2] See note 2 to Table 10.   [3] See note 3 to Table 10.

TABLE 12

INDICES OF SEASONAL VARIATIONS IN EMPLOYMENT IN INDUSTRIES WITH LOW SEASONAL FLUCTUATIONS

(i. e. where the maximum is less than 6 per cent greater than the minimum)

INDUSTRY	JAN.	FEB.	MAR.	APR.	MAY	JUNE	JULY	AUG.	SEPT.	OCT.	NOV.	DEC.	MAXIMUM–MINIMUM / Minimum
Baking²	98	98	99	98	99	102	101	100	101	103	101	99	5
Brass, Bronze, and Copper	100	102	103	102	101	99	99	99	99	99	99	99	4
Car Building and Repairing—Steam	98	99	100	101	101	101	101	100	101	101	100	100	3
Chemicals and Drugs	101	102	101	101	99	98	97	98	100	101	102	102	5
Foundry, Machine-shop Products	98	101	102	102	101	101	101	100	100	99	98	98	4
Hardware²	101	102	102	99	101	101	98	98	101	100	101	100	4
Leather	102	103	102	99	98	97	98	100	101	100	98	100	5
Lumber — Millwork	98	99	100	101	101	101	101	102	99	100	98	98	4
Machine Tools	100	102	102	101	100	99	99	99	99	100	100	100	3
Petroleum Refining	98	99	99	100	100	101	102	102	102	100	99	99	4
Printing, Book and Job	102	101	101	99	99	99	99	98	99	99	101	103	5
Printing, Newspapers and Periodicals	100	100	100	100	100	100	99	98	99	100	101	102	4
Silk Manufactures	99	102	103	101	100	99	98	98	99	101	100	100	5
Steel Works and Rolling Mills	99	102	102	102	102	100	99	99	100	99	99	98	4

² See note 2 to Table 10.

changes are not as important in these industries as they are in those of the first group.

In a number of the industries, such as automobile tires, glass, steam-fitting, meat packing, and flour, the fluctuations are derivative. Thus the fluctuations in flour milling and meat packing result from the fluctuations in agricultural production, while the fluctuations in the glass industry result from fluctuations in the building industry as well as changes in fashion.

If the last group, shown in Table 12, is analyzed it will be seen to consist primarily of industries producing capital goods. These, as we shall show, experience much greater cyclical fluctuations than do other industries but they are at the same time relatively steady so far as seasonal fluctuations are concerned.

The presence of baking in the group of "steady" industries combined with the fact that meat packing has only a moderate seasonal variation suggests that standardized food necessities have little seasonal fluctuation.

3. TRADE

The volume of retail trade, as is well known, is much greater during the Christmas season than at other times of the year. This causes the curve of employment to rise appreciably during November and still more in December, only to fall sharply again in January. This is shown both by Dewhurst's index for Pennsylvania and Bureau of Labor Statistics index for 1929 [5] which are both given below:

MONTH	JAN.	FEB.	MAR.	APR.	MAY	JUNE	JULY	AUG.	SEPT.	OCT.	NOV.	DEC.
1929 B. L. S. .	99	95	96	95	97	97	94	94	98	103	105	120
Pennsylvania .	100	97	100	100	99	98	94	92	96	99	108	117

December is therefore shown by both of these indices to give employment to over 20 per cent more workers than February and to approximately 30 per cent more than

[5] *Monthly Labor Review*, July, 1920, p. 200.

July and August. November is also seen to afford from 10 to 15 per cent more employment than August.

The fluctuations in wholesale trade are not as great. Thus the Bureau of Labor Statistics Index for 1929 shows the following monthly variations:[6]

Month	Jan.	Feb.	Mar.	Apr.	May	June	July	Aug.	Sept.	Oct.	Nov.	Dec.
Relative Index of Employment . .	98	97	97	98	99	99	100	101	102	103	102	105

While cyclical and perhaps secular forces played their parts in helping to cause these fluctuations, employment in December was only 8 per cent more than in February as compared with the 28 per cent difference in retail trade.

4. Garage and Automobile Repair Shops

This comparatively new industry is estimated by the Committee on Recent Economic Changes to have given employment to 425,000 workers in 1927.[7] The Croxtons [8] found the following monthly variations to exist in Ohio during the six years 1923-28 and these are probably fairly typical:

Year	Percentage Maximum above Minimum	Year	Percentage Maximum above Minimum
1923 . . .	28	1926 . . .	15
1924 . . .	11	1927 . . .	12
1925 . . .	13	1928 . . .	12

The range was therefore between 11 and 28 per cent with an average of 15 per cent.

[6] Ibid.
[7] *Recent Economic Changes*, Vol. II, p. 473.
[8] F. C. and F. E. Croxton, *op. cit.*, p. 46.

5. Construction

The normal seasonal fluctuations in employment in construction have been measured by Watkins [9] for Ohio for the period 1914-24 and by Dewhurst [10] for Pennsylvania for the years 1921-27. These are shown in the following table:

Seasonal Fluctuations in Employment in Construction Industries

Month	Ohio 1914-24	Pennsylvania 1921-27	Month	Ohio 1914-24	Pennsylvania 1921-27
January . .	69	81	July . . .	119	113
February . .	66	72	August . .	123	111
March . .	74	81	September .	123	120
April . . .	90	94	October . .	120	115
May . . .	101	105	November .	110	109
June . . .	113	110	December .	92	89

While the fluctuations were somewhat less in Pennsylvania than in Ohio, which was doubtless caused by the milder winter in the eastern part of the former state, the seasonal variations were nevertheless striking. In Ohio 79 per cent more workers were normally employed in the peak month of September than in February while in Pennsylvania 67 per cent more were so employed. This indicates a very sharp seasonal fluctuation.

6. Coal

In the bituminous coal industry, differences in the rate of consumption of coal cause great seasonal irregularities in production and employment. Frederick G. Tryon has thus analyzed the problem of seasonal fluctuations.[11] "In a normal year, such as 1913, the rate of production is lowest in April and highest in November. If the average annual

---

[9] R. J. Watkins, *The Construction Industry in Ohio*, pp. 56-148, esp. p. 62.
[10] J. F. Dewhurst, *op. cit.*, p. 70.
[11] F. G. Tryon, Irregular Operation in the Bituminous Coal Industry, *Supplement, American Economic Review*, March, 1921, pp. 58-59.

rate be taken as 100, the rate in April in a normal year is about 83 and the rate in November about 115. The production capacity required during the month of maximum demand is thus from 35 to 40 per cent greater than in the month of minimum demand."

The seasonal fluctuations are appreciably less in the anthracite industry but there is still a certain amount of difference there between the spring and early summer and the late summer and fall.

7. SEASONAL UNEMPLOYMENT IN THE LARGE

The analysis which has been given shows a truly great seasonal fluctuation in employment in many industries, particularly among those producing consumers' goods of a nonstandardized comfort type and in industries directly affected by rhythm of the climate, such as building, mining, garage work, and the manufacture of agricultural implements. The full amount of unemployment which is caused by such fluctuations is indeed generally concealed by the fact that the dull seasons of various industries come at different times and consequently cause the index of employment for all manufacturing and for all industry as a whole to fluctuate by much less than the weighted average of the separate industries. Thus the Pennsylvania index for all manufacturing industries shows only a slight amplitude of variation amounting to but 4 per cent between the months of maximum and of minimum employment. These indices of normal seasonal variation by months were as follows:

MONTH	INDEX OF SEASONAL EMPLOYMENT	MONTH	INDEX OF SEASONAL EMPLOYMENT
January	100	July	98
February	101	August	98
March	102	September . . .	99
April	101	October	101
May	100	November . . .	100
June	99	December . . .	101

Even this fairly constant rate of employment would cause (assuming that there was no transfer of labor to agriculture, construction, etc.) about 2 per cent unemployment during the year.[12] The relative seasonal variation obtained by the Federal Reserve Board for manufacturing as a whole is substantially similar to this.[13] But this would only be the minimum amount of unemployment if there were a complete and instantaneous transfer of labor from the industries where at a given moment employment is declining to those where it is increasing. Such a complete mobility is very far from being effected. In many cases, the industries which are waxing are geographically distant from those that are waning. This by itself would make any general transfer unlikely. Secondly, a worker who has even moderate skill in one industry generally does not want to attach himself even in the slack seasons to another industry, both because of natural pride and because he is afraid that he may fail of employment in his own trade when the busy season begins again.

The amount of unemployment which is caused by seasonal fluctuations lies, therefore, between that indicated by (1) a weighted average of the normal seasonal variations of specific industries (disregarding signs) and (2) the index of employment for industry as a whole.

When the seasonal variations in manufacturing are combined with the large fluctuations in construction and mining, it seems probable that the estimate in Chapter II (which was made by a different method), that seasonal fluctuations cause approximately six per cent of unemployment in these industries is not far from the actual condition. If public utilities, trade, and domestic service are also included, the relative amount of unemployment resulting from this cause would of course be somewhat reduced.

[12] The sum of the points during the year by which employment falls below its maximum was 24 and this would be tantamount to an average unemployment of 2 per cent.

[13] See *Federal Reserve Bulletin*, November, 1930, pp. 661-663, and mimeographed bulletin of the Division of Research and Statistics, October, 1930.

CHAPTER VII

METHODS USED BY INDUSTRY TO REDUCE SEASONAL FLUCTUATIONS

The majority of managers still probably accept these fluctuations as forces with which they are powerless to cope, but there are several hundred employers scattered over many lines of business who are making an intelligent and relatively successful effort to produce regularly through the year and to keep their workers employed steadily. There are four principal methods by which they seek to obtain this stability:

1. SALES AND MARKET POLICIES DESIGNED TO OBTAIN A MORE EVEN RATE OF ORDERS

One way open to large organizations is advertising with a view to getting customers to buy more steadily. Such was the method adopted by the Sherwin-Williams Company of Cleveland. This method of stabilizing sales has been stated clearly by Mr. A. D. Joyce, the general manager of that company: [1]

"The time was when two-thirds of our business came to us during the spring of the year and the people had an idea that the only time to paint was in the spring. We launched a 'Paint in the Fall' campaign and brought out the fact that the old fashioned carpets were unsanitary—showed how old floors could be refinished with paint and varnish and rugs used. This made it possible and desirable for painting to be done in the winter. One season follows another until now the consumer paints and varnishes the year round, and our products instead of being seasonal ones, now have an all-the-year-round demand."

[1] Lewisohn, Draper, Commons and Lescohier, *Can Business Prevent Unemployment?* pp. 11-12.

Somewhat similar methods have been used in the mail order business. The National Cloak and Suit Company, which sells but does not manufacture women's and children's clothing, had at first only two heavy seasons of sales. The fall season lasted from the end of September until Christmas while the shorter spring season preceded Easter. They then introduced two additional catalogues, namely, one in January announcing a sale of white goods and another in June for a late spring sale. This brought substantial increases in sales during these months although it still left about four and a half months in which sales were at a low ebb. A somewhat similar method has also been employed by the Sears Roebuck Co.[2]

The C. F. Mueller Macaroni Company had been prevented for many years from selling much macaroni or noodles in the summer because of spoilage. It finally developed an air-tight package and by pushing sales and advertising managed to get consumers to buy substantial quantities during the warm months.[3] The Campbell Soup Company has also been able to increase its summer sales by its program of advertising.

Another more subtle way of getting the consumers' demand distributed more evenly over the year is to point out new uses for the old product. An excellent example of this method is that of Hills Brothers who pack *Dromedary Dates*. These had formerly been demanded primarily in the winter time but by advertising their use in salads, some demand was built up for them during the warmer months.[4] The Tao Tea Company, whose sales were formerly low during the summer, introduced the possibility of making tea with cold water from tea balls while retaining all the natural aroma. Increased advertising and demonstrations by salesmen were resorted to with the result that instead of sales decreasing 30 per cent during the summer months, they actually rose 6 per cent in July, 23 per cent in August, and 55 per cent in September.

[2] Feldman, *The Regularization of Production*, pp. 181-82.
[3] Feldman, *op. cit.*, p. 177.   [4] Feldman, *op. cit.*, p. 93.

Such advertising and sales policies frequently require an expenditure only possible for the largest concerns. But in some cases a combination of the concerns in an industry can carry on an advertising campaign which would be impossible for a single company. Thus the paint manufacturers combined to push a coöperative program of advertising and of sales promotion which would increase the total sales of paint and varnish and which would promote a greater volume of off-season purchases.[5]

Still another way of building up business in off seasons is to expand into territories where the seasonal fluctuations of the weather and of buying habits are different.[6] This has long been practised by many hotel managers who will take the most trusty members of their personnel south with them for the winter.

The S. C. Johnson Company, which manufactures floor wax, formerly suffered from the fact that their northern purchasers bought their floor wax during the period of spring house-cleaning. They found that house-cleaning is carried on in the South during the summer and winter and accordingly developed their business there.[7] Another classic case is that of the company manufacturing fireworks which helped to balance the northern Fourth of July by the southern Christmas, which is the time fire-crackers are chiefly touched off south of the Mason and Dixon line.

Sometimes extra pressure is put upon the sales force and the dealers to push the products during the slack season. Thus the Purina Mills of St. Louis put on sales and dealer contests which appreciably raised the valley of sales and of production during these months. Brown and Bigelow of St. Paul, who make calendars, also stimulated sales to dealers during the first part of the year by contests between salesmen. Two other companies whose demand tends to accumulate at the end of the year are the Ives Company,

[5] See Arthur M. East in *Marketing Policies and Sales Methods that Stabilize Business,* American Management Association, Sales Expenditures Series, No. 36, pp. 12-20.
[6] *System,* July, 1924, pp. 40-41, 101.
[7] Lewisohn et al., *op. cit.,* p. 10.

which manufactures toys, and the Dennison Company. The former has its salesmen try to get their dealers to order their toys for the next Christmas almost immediately after the preceding one on the ground that they will then know which ones have been most in demand during the holiday season which has just passed.[8] The work of the Dennison Company in getting advance orders from its dealers is of course well known.

But such attempts to level up the valleys by the process of blowing on one's hands and resorting to "ginger" methods of getting dealers to make advance orders have in recent years become far less effective. If the buying habits of the ultimate consumers are not altered, then even the efforts of high powered salesmen cannot overcome the reluctance of the dealers to stock up. The fear of changes in public taste, in business prosperity, and hence in sales, the possibility of price reductions, the cost of borrowing from the banks to meet the costs of holding the inventory, all make the merchants anxious to reduce their stock to the lowest possible figure. The greater rapidity of freight deliveries has in turn made it possible for firms to place their orders much closer to the time of delivery. Hand-to-mouth buying has in consequence come increasingly to characterize most branches of industry.[9] American businesses are in general, therefore, merely swimming against the tide when they simply try to get dealers to order in advance.

There are two means, however, by which the reluctance of the dealers to order in advance is sometimes lessened. The first of these is for the manufacturer, while getting the advance orders from the dealers, to hold the material until the proper season and bear the costs. This, for example, has been the policy followed by the Dennison Company. The second method is to protect the dealers against future fluctuations in price. This generally consists in giving to the dealer any savings which come from a reduction in prices between the time of ordering and of delivering goods, and of providing,

---

[8] Feldman. *Op. cit.*, p. 185.
[9] See L. S. Lyon, *Hand to Mouth Buying* (Brookings Institution, 1930).

on the other hand, that if prices increase during this period, the manufacturer will bear any loss from such price fluctuations.

This last method, it will be seen, really amounts to a price concession in favor of the dealer in order to stimulate advance sales and thus let the firm know what its volume of sales will be. The consequent stabilization of production and of employment is then the justification of what at first thought seems to be a "heads-I-lose-tails-you-win" policy.

An outright price concession is the other method of obtaining a more evenly distributed rate of orders. The demand for radiators, for example, is generally much greater during the fall months than during the late winter and spring. In order to help even out the flow of orders and of production, the American Radiator Company introduced a system of prices to its dealers which were graduated according to the season at which delivery was made. The prices for the months of February, March, and April were the lowest. These were increased at one time by 2½ per cent for shipments made during May, June, and July, and by a further 2½ per cent for the peak months of August, September, and October. During the next quarter, the price scale was then reduced by 2½ per cent to the level of May, June, and July, and the yearly rhythm was resumed by dropping prices back 2½ per cent more for February, March, and April shipments.

This price policy distinctly reduced the amplitude of the monthly fluctuations in sales and deliveries. Thus R. B. Flershem, the Sales Manager of the Company, stated that [10] "in the previous years the normal October was four times the normal February in the volume of deliveries. During 1923 (the year in which the plan was started) the volume of deliveries in October was only twice that of February."

Other companies which have frankly adopted a policy of price-differentials according to the season are the American Cast Iron Pipe Company of Birmingham, Alabama, and

[10] R. B. Flershem, *Sales Research Within the Company*, American Management Association (New York, 1924), p. 10.

the Continental Heater Corporation of Dunkirk, New York. It should perhaps be remarked at this point that the demand for furnaces, radiators, and steam pipes has been made somewhat more regular in recent years by the increasing practice of all-the-year-round building. Not all of the increased stability in these industries can therefore be ascribed to the seasonal price policy.

Perhaps the best known example of a seasonal price reduction to stimulate demand is that of the anthracite coal industry which, as early as 1900, announced lower prices for all purchases made during the summer months. These reductions have been passed on to the consumer and have led to an appreciable increase in the summer purchases. This has been one of the factors which has caused the amount of idle time in the anthracite industry to decrease greatly during these three decades. Thus during the four years 1897-1900, the average number of days worked per year in the anthracite field was only 160 while, if the strike year of 1925 is omitted, the average for the years 1923-26 was 261.[11]

Only a part of this great gain in the continuity of employment can of course be claimed for this policy, but its does seem to have been a substantial element.

2. A Planned Program for Sales and Production During the Year

Even though sales should continue to be distributed irregularly through the year, production need not be. The custom of most businesses is to produce only after a sale has been made. This makes production dependent upon sales and leads inevitably to irregularities in the rate of operation and of production. Within the business unit, moreover, the sales manager becomes the all important official and his policies come to sway those of the manufacturing departments.

[11] See P. H. Douglas, *Real Wages in the United States*, p. 456, and also the annual reports of the U. S. Geological Survey on the *Mineral Resources of the United States*.

Within recent years, a movement to introduce more order and more advance planning into business operations has gained ground. This is the movement for budgetary control. It involves as one of its features an advance estimate of the probable sales during the year and an effort to integrate the other branches of the business so that the goods may be produced as steadily as possible. This program of planned production seems to have been one of the many fertile ideas which Frederick W. Taylor developed and in which he envisaged accounting not merely as an attempt to make the columns of debits and credits balance, but as a means of controlling the operations of a business. This program has since been developed by many other accountants, production engineers, and business executives.

In its essence the program for advance planning and budgeting is based on the belief that future sales will not fluctuate chaotically from past averages and that they can be approximately predicted from past records and future probabilities. The method of carrying this out and the possible stabilization of employment resulting will be made evident from some of the examples which follow.

As is well known the automobile industry is one of the most irregular. From July until the following February or March the curve of production in the automobile factories declines, and with it the volume of employment. Some years ago, the Packard Motor Car Co. determined that it would try to stabilize its production. It, therefore, determined to produce in advance of orders by dealers and thus keep busy during the months when the other Detroit factories were laying off men and working part-time. This necessitated the six following steps:

(1) The company accurately estimated a year in advance the total production of cars. The method followed was, in brief, to take past sales, find the rate of growth in previous years, and then determine, in view of general market conditions, the situation in the automobile industries, changes in the Packard Car itself and the program of the company, whether this rate of growth could be expected to con-

tinue. In the preparation of this yearly quota, past experience was tinged with conservative optimism, but the company permitted itself no such orgy of hope as led the manager of another automobile company to believe that his already large concern could double its sales in one year. The yearly schedule was instead fixed at a point where it might be possible to increase production as sales outran the estimates, instead of at a point where the only readjustment which could be effected would be a decrease.

(2) Once the yearly standard had been set, monthly production quotas were fixed by dividing the total by twelve.

(3) An attempt was made to get the Packard dealers to take cars in advance of the time when they were usually ordered. Because of the fact that a Packard agency is generally a lucrative one which dealers wish to hold, and because a large amount of good-will has been built up between the company and its distributors, a considerable number of cars produced in the otherwise slack months was thus shipped to the dealers who helped in this way to absorb the slack.

(4) The aid of the dealers, however, not being sufficient to absorb the production of cars during the months from July to October, extra warehousing space was erected in Detroit and leased outside of New York and one other large city. The cars produced in excess of current sales were stored there in anticipation of the Spring rush to purchase.

(5) Along with the estimated sales and production budgets for the year, the probable sales by months were estimated on the basis of past experience. If 3 per cent of the average yearly production of cars during the preceding few years had been sold in January, then that figure would tend to be set as the probable percentage for that month in the quota of the coming year. On an estimated yearly basis of 36,000 this would be 1,080. This percentage was, of course, modified according to new developments which were expected to occur during the year.

The actual sales record was then closely compared from month to month with the budgetary estimates. If the former continued to fall appreciably below the latter, then the production budget was reviewed and revised downward. This would mean of course a reduction in the size of the force. If, on the other hand, it developed that the estimates had been too conservative and that sales were appreciably exceeding the productions, then production was increased to meet the new estimate which was made for the year. In other words, the budget was kept flexible and adapted to actual situations.

(6) If it developed that over the year as a whole production had been allowed to exceed sales, then an opportunity was afforded the public to become Packard owners at reduced prices. The cost of this reduction was borne entirely by the company and the dealers' commissions were untouched. This, naturally, made the dealers enthusiastic for the general policy, since the lower price stimulated total sales and hence raised their income. They consequently became even more willing to coöperate in the general program of stabilization by ordering more cars in advance.

Such a program of planned production and the storage of the excess could only have taken place in a car whose model was relatively standardized from year to year and upon which only minor changes were made. This has always been one of the outstanding characteristics of the Packard Car.

RATIO OF THOSE EMPLOYED IN PACKARD MOTOR CAR COMPANY[12] TO AVERAGE FOR THE YEAR

	1922	1928
January	60	94
February	65	96
March	77	97
. . . .	..	..
July	133	93
. . . .	..	..
October	103	112
November	98	109
December	97	..

[12] Compiled from statistics given in Unemployment in the United States, *Hearings 70th Congress, 2nd Session,* U. S. Res. 219, p. 71.

This stabilization program of the Packard Company was, on the whole, extraordinarily effective during the years preceding the depression of late 1929 and 1930. The preceding table showing the ratio of the numbers employed during months of the year to the average for the year during 1922 (which was before this plan went into effect), and during 1928 after it had been tried out, shows this increased regularization.

It will be seen from this that while in 1922 the numbers employed in the peak month of the year (July) were two and a fifth of those employed in January, in 1928 the peak month of October had only 19 per cent more workers [13] than January. The amplitude of fluctuation had been reduced to less than one-sixth of what it had been six years before. The level of employment during the whole first quarter of 1922 was in fact but one-half that of the peak month while in 1928 it was 86 per cent of this peak.

Part of the fluctuation in 1922 was due to the fact that in that year the recovery from the previous depression took place. But even in 1925 there were 45 per cent more workers employed during the peak month than during January and about 40 per cent more than during the first quarter of the year. This was an amplitude over twice as great as that of 1928.

The Gorham Silver Company is another concern which has adopted a program of budgeted and equalized production. This company manufactures most of the wedding silver which is sold in the United States. Since the major portions of the weddings in the middle and upper economic classes where silver is given as a present occur in the months of June and October, the Gorham Company found itself therefore with two sharp peaks of sales and with intervening low valleys. In the past, production and employment had followed a similar irregular course. The company decided that it would try to regulate production. It could not expect by advertising to change the marrying habits of the

[13] I.e. $\dfrac{112-94}{94}$

American middle class, but it discovered, that while there was a great fluctuation in the volume of its monthly sales there was a relative constancy in the yearly sales. It then decided to estimate in advance what the probable yearly sales would be and, like the Packard Company, to produce one-twelfth of this quota every month. This was done and the silver was stored to meet the June and October rush of weddings.[14]

A third interesting example is that of Procter and Gamble, the largest soap concern in the country. Prior to 1920, their sales and the production of soap fluctuated greatly from one season of the year to another. In 1919, for example, the maximum force employed in their Cincinnati plant was 3,195 as contrasted with a minimum force of 1,935. The maximum staff was, therefore, 65 per cent greater than the minimum. This high degree of contraction and expansion was not caused by corresponding irregularities in the rate at which consumers bought and used soap. Soap, as a necessity, is used at an approximately constant rate through the year, although there is something of an increase in the summer over the rate of use during the winter. The oscillations were caused by the fact that Procter and Gamble marketed their product through jobbers and these bought spasmodically. The company, after studying the situation, decided that the purchasing policies of the jobbers [15] "were based largely upon market conditions. The raw materials entering into our products are very well known, and the price of the finished product is governed largely by the raw material market. When a price advance in raw material was apparent to the jobbers, heavy purchasing naturally followed. Frequently, these orders covered their needs for months to come. Our factories operated at capacity, enrollment increased and our people were required to work overtime. After a period of full production, orders began to fall off, and the jobbers' stocks were more than adequate to meet

[14] We are indebted to Mr. E. S. Smith of the Committee on the Regularization of Industry for information about this case.
[15] This is a company memorandum printed in Dr. Herbert Feis' *Labor Relations*, pp. 98-99.

their normal sales' needs. Our production then continued until our depleted stocks were again replenished, when curtailment of output and reduction in enrollment of necessity followed."

In order to stabilize production therefore, William C. Procter, the President of the Company, decided that it was necessary to discontinue marketing through the jobbers, and to sell directly to the retailers. Because of the comparative steadiness in the purchases of the ultimate consumers, he believed this would lead to a more even flow of orders. In order to make this transition, however, many business changes had to be made. On the one hand an increased selling force trained in new methods and new types of approach adapted to the retail trade was needed. Since the jobbers formerly stored the soap pending its distribution to the retailers, Procter and Gamble now had to erect and lease large warehouses in different parts of the country. The cost of these and other changes necessitated by the new program has been estimated by L. J. Zoeller, the Personnel Manager of the Company, to have been well over two million dollars.[16]

Once this system of distribution had been perfected, the next step was to prepare an estimated sales budget for the following year, which is described by the company in the following terms:

"The first step necessary was to estimate the sales for the coming year. Approximate figures were supplied by the sales supervisors, each of whom is in charge of a group of ten to fifteen salesmen, covering a territory representing roughly two hundred thousand of population. These estimates were tabulated by the various district sales managers, and forwarded to the general sales department at Cincinnati, where they were reviewed, revised when necessary, and definite quotas prepared for each division of the sales department. The sales department agreed to stand by their estimate and to dispose of the products in a steady flow

---

[16] Beulah Amidon, Ivorydale, A Payroll That Floats, *The Survey Graphic,* April, 1923, p. 19.

throughout the year. The sales figures were then translated into a production schedule by the manufacturing department, covering the year's activities in the various plants.

"Supplementing the quota laid down at the beginning of each year by the sales department, very close contact is maintained between the manufacturing and the buying and sales Divisions, and on the twentieth of each month a revised production schedule is worked out, determining the various brands and sizes that will be required during the following month. As a whole, production based upon the yearly estimate is maintained, even when it becomes necessary for some of the finished products to enter the warehouses for a time, or when the sales exceed the production for the month. . . . In only one year did the actual sales, and estimate, fail of tally within a reasonable figure. In this particular year, the sales exceeded the estimate."

The new plan was begun in 1921 and after two years of experimentation, the Company felt justified in believing that it could thereafter guarantee at least 48 weeks of employment a year to all workers who had been employed for over six months and who had joined the stock-purchase profit-sharing plan. The Company had maintained a profit-sharing plan for over forty years which had gradually been changed from an outright distribution of cash to payments made to workmen who had bought stock of the Company. The guaranteed employment plan was confined to this group and did not include those workers who had been with the firm for less than six months, nor to those who, having been employed for more than this period, had nevertheless not bought stock. The first of these groups has amounted on the whole to approximately 25 per ecnt of the force, although their number has relatively diminished with time, while the second comprises about 10 per cent of the workers.

On the whole, the Company has been strikingly successful in diminishing the fluctuations from year to year as is indicated by the following table:

PROGRESS IN REGULARIZATION IN THE IVORYDALE PLANT OF
PROCTER AND GAMBLE, 1919–29 [17]

YEAR	MAXIMUM NUMBER EMPLOYED	MINIMUM NUMBER EMPLOYED	DIFFERENCE BE-TWEEN MAXIMUM AND MINIMUM	PERCENTAGE MAXIMUM WAS OF MINIMUM
1919 . .	3195	1935	1260	165
1920 . .	2846	1832	1034	157
1921 . .	2000	1459	641	144
1922 . .	1951	1516	435	129
1923 . .	2025	1731	294	117
1924 . .	2003	1740	265	115
1925 . .	2371	2252	119	105
1926 . .	2749	2341	408	118
. . . .	. . . .	. . . .	. . . .	. . . .
1929 . .	2652	2484	168	107

Instead of the maximum force being 65 per cent greater than the minimum as was the case in 1919, this difference had been diminished by 1929 to one of only 7 per cent. It will also be seen that the stabilization had been virtually attained by 1923 when the formal guarantee was put into effect. Col. Procter has spoken of the benefit which the plan has given to the company.[18] "Since the plan has been adopted our turnover after six months service in the company has been reduced three-fourths. The men are happier, better contented and more pleased with the guaranteed plan of employment than any other feature that the company has adopted for their benefit, and I might mention that the company has the profit-sharing, sick benefit, life insurance, accident insurance, and disability and old-age pension. The company has profited largely under the plan; it is difficult to estimate how much in dollars and cents, but the reduced cost of production secured through regularity of work with the same steady employee is very great. I think I am conservative in stating that it has reduced our cost of production from 3 to 5 per cent."

[17] These figures are taken from Feis, *op. cit.*, p. 108, and Miss Amidons' article in the *Survey Graphic*, April, 1930, p. 18.
[18] Unemployment in the United States, *70th Congress, 2nd Session, Hearings on S. Res.,* 219, p. 134.

In many other companies the probable sales are budgeted and the goods are produced at an even rate during the year. Among these may be mentioned such firms as Fels and Co., of Philadelphia, which guarantees 50 weeks of work a year to its employees; The Walworth Manufacturing Co.,[19] The J. F. McElwain Co.,[20] The American Radiator Co.,[21] Carter's Ink Co.,[22] Hills Bros.,[23] The Marion Steam Shovel Co.,[24] The Ault-Williamson Shoe Co.,[25] The National Cash Register Co.,[26] and The David Lupton Sons Co. of Philadelphia.[27] The New York Committee on the Stabilization of Employment which was appointed by Governor Roosevelt found a number of other companies in that state which were operating under a budgeted program and which had in consequence been able to stabilize their employment with a fair degree of success. Among these might be mentioned,[28] The Ithaca Gun Co., The Sterling Engine Co., The Remington-Rand Co., The Remington Typewriter Co., The Remington Arms Co., The Eastman Kodak Co., Bausch and Lomb, The Neptune Meter Co., W. and L. E. Gurley Co., Sheridan Iron Works, Otis Elevator Company, Richardson Boynton Co., International Harvester

[19] Howard Coonley, The Control of an Industry in the Business Cycle, *Harvard Business Review*, July, 1923; also Joseph H. Barber, Marketing Policies and Sales Methods That Stabilize Business, *Sales Executives Series, No. 36*, American Management Association, pp. 22-40.

[20] F. P. Murphy, *Profits through Production Control*, Executive Series Bulletin, Metropolitan Life Insurance Co., October, 1929, p. 5.

[21] R. B. Flershem, *Organization and Control of Production and Distribution*, American Management Association, 1927.

[22] *The Use of Research in Employment Stabilization*, Metropolitan Life Insurance Co., 1929, p. 10.

[23] Lewisohn, Draper, Commons and Lescohier, *Can Business Prevent Unemployment?* pp. 16-21; also Mr. Draper's testimony before the Senate Committee on Education and Labor. Unemployment in the United States, *70th Congress, 2nd Session, Hearings on S. Res.*, 219, p. 28.

[24] *Steadying Business;—The Metal Trades*, Metropolitan Life Insurance Co., No. 2, p. 4.

[25] *Executive Service Bulletin*, Metropolitan Life Insurance Co., May, 1929, p. 5.

[26] U. S. Senate, Unemployment in the United States, *op. cit.*, pp. 131-32.

[27] Clarke P. Pond, Marketing Policies and Sales Methods that Stabilize Business. *Sales Executive Series; No. 36*. American Management Association, 1926, pp. 40-43.

[28] Final Report of New York Committee on the Stabilization of Industry for the Prevention of Unemployment.

Co., The International Heater Co., The Utica Cutlery Co., The Ulster Knife Co., Griffin Manufacturing Co., Auto-Strop Razor Co., The Republic Metalware Co., The Union Fork and Hoe Co., The Oneida Community Limited, Kirkman and Sons, S. S. White Co., Elite Glove Co., The Columbia Mills, The Ocean Bathing Suit Co., and The Knox Hat Co. There are beyond doubt scores of other companies which have also adopted such a plan.

In general the firms which have attempted to budget production and steady employment have found it desirable, if they have previously produced a wide variety of goods, to reduce and standardize the number of these products. The Knox Hat Company, for example, found that it was making no less than 9,720 varieties of hats. Under such a system it was necessarily impossible to gauge how many of each variety would be demanded and production for stock was in the main impossible. By coöperation with the retailers, the number of varieties was reduced to 3,700 and more of each model was of course sold. It now became possible to plan in advance the probable sales and for some years at least to produce to stock during the slack seasons, thus giving practically all the year round employment to their workers.[29]

It is apparent, therefore, that the reduction of a previously unwieldy number of styles of the same product by decreasing the possibilities of errors increases the possibility of producing in advance rather than to order.

The program of advance planning can frequently be carried out in such a way that the parts for a finished product can be produced during the slack seasons and can then be assembled as orders come in during the busy periods. This is the practice, for example, of a New York firm manufacturing reflectors and lighting specialties, and is also followed by the National Cash Register Company of Dayton.[30]

This possibility of producing parts to stock makes it pos-

---

[29] *Factory*, February, 1924, pp. 153-56.
[30] Unemployment in the United States, *op. cit.*, p. 132.

sible to stabilize production in firms producing machinery to order when otherwise it would have to oscillate violently with the volume of orders. Thus the Allis-Chalmers Company of Milwaukee, while largely producing machinery on a special order basis, has nevertheless standardized most of the parts which make up these machines and can produce these during the season of slack orders.[31] A knife company in upper New York State also follows this policy of making the various parts during the off-seasons.

An interesting example in the field of publishing is the W. T. Hall Company of Chicago.[32] This latter concern in addition to printing monthly and weekly periodicals also published spring and fall catalogues. These had formerly greatly crowded the plant during these two rush seasons and at other times had left some departments operating at only 20 per cent of their capacity. By scheduling the catalogues and calling for copy, plates, cuts, and paper stock at specific dates in advance a large portion of this work was pushed farther back into the year and steadier work obtained. A somewhat similar practice is followed by the Wilmer Atkinson Company of Philadelphia which publishes the *Farm Journal*, a monthly with a circulation of 1,100,000.[33]

In addition to the concerns which definitely plan production in advance for periods of a year or a half-year and produce at an approximately even rate, there are large numbers of other firms which, while not working in terms of precise schedules will nevertheless manufacture to stock during the slack seasons in order to keep their workers employed and their plant occupied. The New York Committee on Stabilization of Employment indeed received letters from no less than thirty-six prominent manufacturers who used such more or less informal methods to balance production.

[31] U. S. Chamber of Commerce, *Balancing Production and Employment Through Management Control* (1930), p. 25.
[32] Feldman, *op. cit.*, pp. 221-22.
[33] For a description of the practices of this firm see Feldman, *op. cit.*, pp. 233-35.

3. The Development of "Side-Lines" and "Fillers" for the Slack Season

The classic example of such a dovetailing of seasonal products has, of course, been that of the combination of the coal and ice business. While this partnership has, however, been impaired in recent years by the development of electric refrigeration in the home, it still gives some relief to the coal dealers.

Perhaps the best known illustration is that of the Dennison Manufacturing Company whose chief product was formerly jewelry boxes. These were used primarily in the Christmas trade, so in order to even out production as well as for other purposes, the company took up the manufacture of crêpe paper, printed labels, tags, and other boxes.[34] Since business is a cumulative affair, new peaks of orders began to appear and, in order to insure continuity, still further products were taken on to fill up the valleys.

The canning and preserving industry has always been regarded as one of the most difficult to stabilize because of the relatively concentrated period during which the crops mature. At least three firms are making fairly successful efforts to cope with this problem by dovetailing products. The Beechnut Packing Company of Canajoharie, New York, has developed peanut butter and chewing gum as fillers for the winter months. The Welch Grape Juice Company formerly manufactured only grapejuice and a grape spread, and in consequence their workers suffered unemployment after grape-pressing time in the fall and before the demand for bottled grape-juice itself necessitated bottling it. Since then they have made jellies and a grape fountain syrup, which while not completely removing all of the lost time during this period, have lessened it appreciably. The Columbia Conserve Company of Indianapolis is so far as possible building up off-season business in non-tomato products and has developed a line of soups for winter and spring produc-

[34] See E. P. Hayes and Charlotte Heath, *History of the Dennison Manufacturing Co.* (1929).

tion including vegetable, green pea, consommé, beef, vegetable-beef, bean, oxtail, mock turtle, chicken, beef bouillon, etc. It also cans chicken à la King and chop suey during this period. Because of this and because its tomato soup period extended longer than that of most firms through its practice of reducing the tomatoes to pulp, it has been able to give almost steady work to its employees. It is indeed almost unique among American concerns in paying the vast majority of its workers on the basis of an annual salary equal to 52 times the standard weekly wage.[35]

A company which has practised a wide diversity of output is the Winchester Arms Company. The peace-time peak for firearms and ammunition comes in the fall and there is therefore always a necessity for some other product to utilize the unused capacity of plant and workers during other periods of the year. A still more powerful contributing force in this case was, however, the fact that the Company had necessarily expanded greatly in order to meet the war-time need for munitions and, like all munition plants the world over, was left with a plant which was apparently greatly in excess of peace-time needs. The Company set itself to develop a wide variety of products of which the following have been the most important: (1) cutlery; (2) flashlights and batteries; (3) roller and ice skates; (4) fishing tackle; (5) athletic equipment; (6) carpenters' tools.

Another interesting case is the A. C. Gilbert Company which originally manufactured toys chiefly sold in October and November. In 1914 the company launched a filler in the shape of a small electric fan at the low price of $5. This was a logical development since electric motors were manufactured for some of the toy products of the company. The fan was successful and the company came to believe that there was "a vast household market for moderate-priced, trade-marked electric appliances." Mr. Gilbert gradually followed up his successes with other products which contained small motors. The second to be developed was an electric mixer for drinks, mayonnaise, icings, etc., and this

[35] See Paul H. Douglas, *The Columbia Conserve Company* (1926).

was followed by "a vibrator, a hair dryer, and then a heater. After that came a ventilator for kitchen, bathroom or laundry"; later a juice extractor and a whisk broom. In addition to all this the price of the original fan has been reduced and somewhat larger ones added to the general line. By such tactics, the company has been able to utilize its plant to full capacity for twelve months of the year instead of two, to keep its workers busily employed throughout the year and to keep its toy salesmen "efficiently productive at all seasons." [36]

If side-lines and fillers are taken on, it of course follows that the workers on the main product should be transferred at the appropriate times to the auxiliary products. This will generally require a flexibility of training which the firm will have to provide.

If one examines the various cases in which developments of side-lines and fillers have been successful and where they have not, it is possible to lay down certain obvious but nevertheless important considerations governing the type of product which can be built up as a filler. In general it can be said that the new product should not be so dissimilar from the existing main product that it cannot be turned out with the same machinery, fabricated by the same workers, and marketed by the same selling organization. Thus when the S. L. Allen Company of Philadelphia, which manufactures agricultural implements, took on children's sleds to fill its pre-January trough, it could use virtually the same machinery for them as for the main products. Similarly, a New York firm which manufactures milk and ice cream cans for the summer trade, turns its attention with comparative ease to the manufacture of coal scuttles for the winter. A similar case is that of the A. C. Gilbert Company which has just been cited.

It should also be realized that the side-line should be one which can be made by the working force without too great difficulty. In the cases which have been cited, the skill of the workers could be carried over to the new products with

[36] *Printers' Ink,* November 1, 1928, pp. 17-20.

practically no loss. This is also virtually the case with the Welch Grape Juice Company, the Columbia Conserve Company, and the Beechnut Packing Company, and indeed in almost every instance where the experiment has been successful.

This adaptability of the working force should, however, be reckoned in terms of cost as well as of skill. It is a mistake in general to put highly paid workers at commodities which are produced elsewhere under a low wage scale. Thus the Columbia Conserve Company originally tried canning pork and beans as a means of filling its valleys but gave this up after a time, because, though the force turned out a good product, this article was produced in other canneries with unskilled and low paid labor. It became very difficult for the Columbia Company's pork and beans to stand its ground in the market, and the company then turned to higher priced products such as chop suey, chicken à la King, etc., where the high skill of the force could work to advantage and win its way in the competition of the market. Similarly, the failure of a number of clothing firms to keep on with some of the garments which they manufactured during the slack seasons was because operatives skilled on higher priced garments could not economically be transferred to cheaper garments where careful tailoring and workmanship were not required.

This should not be interpreted to mean that fillers should never be taken which cannot sell for a profit. As we shall see, the economies in the utilization of the overhead and the maintenance of a steady force of workers may be such that it would be better to produce these goods at a loss than not to produce them at all and to suffer a still greater loss. The point simply is that an ideal "filler" is a product which is adapted to the wage-scale and skill of the employers.

Finally, the product should be one which can be handled by the same sales force. This was one of the great advantages of the various side-lines which were taken on by the Winchester Arms Company. Its salesmen of firearms were already calling on hardware merchants and could sell to the same group, cutlery, flashlights, tools, skates, etc. Similarly, the same stores which bought agricultural implements from the S. L. Allen Company, could also buy sleds. Had it been necessary for these companies to develop a new sales force or to train the existing force to approach an entirely new set of customers, the added expense would, in most cases, have been so heavy as to have been impracticable.

Such considerations as these serve rather drastically to limit the field within which supplementary products may be chosen for development. Business men should look rather closely at home for such possibilities and not try exotic ventures.

A further caution should moreover be added. If side-lines and fillers should be chosen carefully, they should not be abandoned hastily. It will necessarily take time to build up confidence in the new product even though it be marketed to old customers. Managers will frequently be tempted to discard it and to try something else. But since such a product would also have to go through a period of trial it is better to stand by the original idea until it has been given an adequate trial. In addition if a company changes frequently, all of its products will suffer somewhat from the disrepute which such a fluctuating policy will inevitably cast upon them.

There is one further observation which should perhaps be noted. The process of "rationalization" within a large company with a number of plants frequently operates to make the dovetailing of side-lines more difficult. For such a program generally involves devoting each plant to a rather specialized use so that while the company may produce a wide variety of products, each plant will itself concentrate upon only one or at best upon a few. This is one of the advantages of specialization which a large company can obtain and has been practised, for example, by the General Electric Company. But the process of rationalization should not be carried too far and the various plants should each be given a group of products which so far as possible will dovetail into each other and permit steady employment through the year.

4. The Flexibility of Working Hours

If, for one reason or another, it is not possible to completely regularize production by the methods discussed, a fourth method has been adopted by some firms, namely to vary the hours of work in such a way that an approximately constant number of workers will be maintained, who will work more than the standard hours per week during the busy season and less than the standard during the off-seasons.

The Delaware and Hudson Railway is perhaps the most prominent exponent of this plan. That railroad works an elastic day which generally ranges from 8 to 10 hours. The understanding is that no one shall be laid off for lack of work until less than 48 hours per week is provided, and that no men will be hired until 60 hours of work is exceeded. In practice, the company has generally abstained from laying off men when the hours fell below 48 if the workers preferred to share the slack time, and on the other hand has seldom taken advantage of its opportunity to hire more men on those few occasions when the working hours have exceeded 60 per week. Over the period of time during which this policy of the elastic working day has been tried out, the hours of work for the men in the locomotive and rolling stock department have varied between 54 and 32. This policy combined with that of laying more rails during the wintertime has materially reduced the fluctuations in the numbers employed. Thus whereas the maximum number employed in the maintenance of ways and structures was in 1922 seventy-five per cent more than the minimum and fifty-three per cent more in 1920, in 1926 it was only sixteen per cent more and in 1928 only ten per cent more. In the maintenance of freight and passenger cars, the difference between minimum and maximum was reduced from 20 per cent in 1920 and 98 per cent in 1922 to only one per cent in 1926 and nine per cent in 1928. There has always been a greater degree of stability in the maintenance of locomotives but even here the difference of 33 per cent in 1922 was reduced to one of thirteen per cent in 1924 and 1928 and to three per cent for 1926.

Other firms which practise this custom of the flexible working week are the Columbia Conserve Co., the National Cloak and Suit Company of New York, the Wilmer Atkinson Company of Philadelphia, and Leeds and Northrup.

On the whole the practice has a great deal to recommend it. It is surely better that a constant number of men should work a varying number of hours than that a varying number of men should work a constant number of hours. There are however two safeguards which should be attached to any such plan: (1) If overtime is worked during the busy seasons, then during the dull period, the actual time worked should be correspondingly less than the standard. The method should not be used, in other words, to increase the total amount of time worked during the year. If the working week were only expanded upward, the advantages of stabilization would naturally be afforded to fewer workers. (2) The total number of hours worked during the busy season should not be so excessive as to fatigue the workers in such a manner that they can not fully recover during the periods of diminished employment. This means that it is much better for a plant with a moderate working week of 44 or 48 hours to adopt such a program than for one where the working week is approximately 60 hours.

CHAPTER VIII

THE GAINS AND COSTS OF REGULARIZATION

The average business man tends to cast a very doubting eye on such efforts to regularize as we have described in our last chapter and to believe that regularization is financially impracticable and that in a world where management must show profits to stockholders, there is little room for its application.

That there are financial costs connected with regularization cannot be questioned. To change consumers' buying habits is an expensive affair which can scarcely be afforded save by the largest companies or by extensive federations of smaller enterprises. Nor is success certain in any such undertaking, and the final result may often be an extensive waste of money on an advertising program with little to show for it at the end. Price discounts to dealers for early purchases and orders are in themselves of course, a reduction in the gross income of the company.

Furthermore, the program of planned and budgeted production itself costs money. In the first place, the office and administrative expenses connected with preparing such a sales and production budget are themselves frequently considerable. Even if we dismiss these as relatively unimportant, there are two more important costs involved in the policy of producing at an even weekly or monthly rate and of storing goods during slack seasons. These are the added costs of storage and of interest.

If the goods are to be stored, added space must be provided for them. Unless the company has previously had a considerable amount of warehouse space which was not used, it must build or lease these added facilities. The relative charges will be particularly heavy if the product is one with a low sales value per unit of bulk. Furthermore, if the goods are to be held for some time before they are finally sold, the company will have to pay the carrying charges upon the investment during this period of time.

The businesses which have made a success of regularization, however, are almost unanimous in believing that they have made savings which have more than offset the costs and that consequently regularization has paid them financially. These savings are of four main sorts.

(1) Regularization effects savings because it reduces the number of new workers needed to meet the seasonal peaks.

When the working force is allowed to fluctuate with the volume of sales, a great many new workers must of necessity be hired during the rush seasons to be laid off immediately afterward. They are therefore green workers, without any real interest in the firm and are, in addition, frequently overworked by the schedule of long hours. The inevitable result is that their average production is necessarily low while their rate of spoilage is high. This means a very much higher labor cost per unit than if the work were done by experienced hands. Regularization greatly lessens the costs resulting from labor turnover, since with the removal of that portion which is caused by the instability of jobs, only the portion caused by the instability of men would remain.

One New York firm, in stating to Governor Roosevelt's Committee on Stabilization of Employment why it believed regularization had paid, said: "New employees, even if they are what is known to the trade as skilled mechanics, are not even 40 per cent efficient for the first six months." Another company, in contrasting its policy of regularization with the fluctuating forces of other companies, said, "It is impossible to produce the goods as fast as they are sold during the season. If they are, it means overtime, high pressure and poor work with the consequent loss of sales by not having the goods ready when wanted; also a loss of customers on account of poor work due to high pressure and green help."

(2) Regularization reduces the amount of fixed capital needed per unit of output.

If the production of a business fluctuates appreciably during the year, then some of the machinery and capital overhead which is used during the peak period will necessarily be idle during the remainder of the year. The annual charges upon this idle capital, in the form of interest, depreciation, taxes, etc., will of course have to be met by the total volume of production with the result that prices will rise or profits be diminished.

If a firm regularizes by filling up the valleys with sidelines or fillers, these units can be produced without any appreciably greater capital costs. Unit costs will therefore be reduced and the firm placed in a much better financial position.

If a firm produces evenly through the year, it can, by thus leveling off the peaks, reduce the annual amount of capital which it needs. Since the total capital charges will be less, the unit costs, even with same volume of output, will be lower. One New York concern has indeed stated that because of its policy of regulation it is able to get along with 25 per cent less fixed capital than would otherwise be necessary.

It may be objected that since a company which begins to regularize will already have extra floor space and machinery which have been accumulated to help meet its peak load, and since these charges will continue, there will be no economies from regularization. But this contention ignores the fact that the company can in many instances contract its floor space and machinery, and either rent or sell that which has been given up. Furthermore it is possible for it to finance a considerable growth in its business with little or no addition of fixed capital. This can be done by having the increased production come from what would otherwise have been the unused capacity of the plant during the slack months. The Packard Motor Car Company, for example, was able to handle greatly increased sales after it introduced its policy of stabilization without adding appreciably to the size of its factory or to the number of its machines.

Regularization therefore means lower fixed capital charges for each unit of product. Though more space is needed in the warehouse, less is needed in the factory. And since factory space costs more than storage because of its being partly filled with costly machines, it follows that it is more economical to economize on it than on warehouse facilities.

(3) Regularization makes it possible to pay a lower than average hourly wage.

Another economy which regularization effects is that if a firm offers steady work, good employees will come to it, even though its hourly rate is below the general average. Workers are greatly concerned about having stable jobs, and if they are given these, will be content with somewhat lower hourly rates. Firms and industries with a high degree of seasonal irregularity are, as a matter of fact, compelled to pay appreciably above the average because workers know that the jobs will tend to be short-lived. In Detroit, for example, the hourly rate of the Packard workers is quite distinctly below the general Detroit average and yet the workmen are quite anxious to be employed there because of the steadier work.

Regularization thus enables the direct labor cost per unit to be reduced as well as the fixed capital charges. The fact that the employers gain from regularization in the form of a reduced wage-rate does not, however, mean that the workers lose. Yearly income is more important to them than hourly rates. The increase in the number of hours which each worker puts in during the year will in general more than outweigh any deficit in the wage rate. The yearly incomes of the workers can and generally will increase at the same time that unit labor costs are diminishing.

(4) Regularization, by insuring steady work, will reduce the tendency to restrict output.

As we have pointed out, when the workers see the busy period slackening, they tend to reduce their output in order to make the work last longer. This natural tendency may be checked in part under the piece-rates and "efficiency systems" of payment but it is nevertheless a powerful force which operates to lower production and increase costs. Where production and employment have been regularized, the workers are not exposed to this fear, and with its removal they will tend to increase their output. This will therefore reduce costs still further.

In summing up, therefore, it can be said that in many industries, and subject to the qualifications which will be shortly added, the economies from regularization will tend to exceed the cost. Regularization in general, therefore, is not philanthropy; it is good business. It is unfortunate that in the firms which have regularized, it has not been possible to draw up a balance sheet showing the respective losses and gains. The firms which have been successful seem, however, almost unanimously to feel that their policy has paid financially.

Despite the real advantages of regularization, however, we should beware of concluding that it can be applied in all industries and to all products. If one studies the companies which have succeeded in their policy of regularization, the five following factors are seen to determine the degree to which the policy does or does not pay:

1. THE DEGREE TO WHICH THE PRODUCT IS STANDARDIZED AND IMMUNE FROM STYLE FACTORS

Planned production to stock can only be successful if the product is as much in style when it is sold as when it is produced. Most of the firms which have made a success of regularization produce just this type of standard product. Thus Ivory Soap, the chief product of Procter and Gamble, is, like the eternal verities, the same yesterday, today and tomorrow. Procter and Gamble do not need to worry when they stock their warehouses with Ivory Soap in the winter lest it be out of style by the time the summer onrush of cleanliness arrives. So is it with Fels-Naptha Soap, Dromedary dates, Beechnut products, Welch's Grape Juice, Columbia Conserve soups, etc. It is significant that the Packard Company, the outstanding example of regularization in the automobile industry, is also one of the companies making few changes in the fundamental model for its car. Similarly, firms producing Gorham Silver, Community Plate (the product of the Oneida Community), radiators, typewriters, steam shovels, milk pails, filing cabinets, shoe-polish, etc., have been able to stabilize by this method for the same reason. Their goods can be stored without becoming outmoded.

It is far otherwise, however, in the case of commodities which are highly subject to changing styles. Women's clothing is, for example, almost as perishable as green groceries. Style follows style with great rapidity, and there is no surety that what seems to be in style now will really be desired by the consumer by the next month. In such a situation as this, it is as impossible for a manufacturer to produce to stock as it would be for a greengrocer to try to keep radishes and celery for long periods of time without ice. Nearly all forms of women's apparel are subject to this same fluctuation of styles. The women's shoe industry is especially chaotic. Paradoxically enough, part of the difficulty here has been caused by firms which, in attempting to regularize, introduced new models to attract the off-season trade. Other firms followed and after a time the industry discovered that the old seasons had been broken up and that a shifting succession of styles had taken their place.

Men's clothing and shoes are, of course, more standardized than women's and hence there can be somewhat greater regularity in production and employment. But even here it is difficult to produce much in advance of the season since it is not known what is going to catch on with the public taste. In the boot and shoe industry, the increasing importance of the style factor has compelled the abandonment of some previously successful attempts at regularization, notably those made by the International Shoe Company and by the Endicott-Johnson Company.

Whether the influence of style is becoming more or less important is still uncertain. In the men's underclothing and in the sheeting industries the increased use of colors has beyond doubt made these industries less stable. On the whole it is probable that in the industries producing consumers' goods, variety and style are playing a greater part than before but that in the industries producing capital goods the movement for standardization is reducing the number of separate varieties. In any event, the style factor serves as a distinct limit upon the program for regularization.

2. The Degree to Which the Product is Subject to Monopoly or Quasi-Monopoly

When a concern has a virtual monopoly on its product, it can stabilize much more easily than when there is a high degree of competition. The monopolist can, for example, resist the entreaties of the retailers to introduce variety into his products far more than a manufacturer in a highly competitive industry. He can also determine approximately how long a style will last and can more accurately forecast the probable demand for his product than where there is competition. He can therefore produce to stock far more readily than if he had a large number of competitors.

3. The Relative Cost of Storage

When commodities have large value in small bulk, such as silver, kodaks, films, optical products, measuring instruments, etc., storage costs are not heavy and regularization tends therefore to be a very practicable measure.

When goods are bulky, however, and have low value for each cubic yard of content, relative storage costs are naturally heavier. This will make it difficult to stabilize completely industries producing building materials such as cement, brick, stone, lumber, etc.

An interesting exemplification of this point is seen in

the case of automobiles. The Packard has a much higher value per cubic foot of space occupied than the Chevrolet, the Buick, the Hudson, or the Ford and storage costs are therefore relatively less for it. This is at least one reason, though it may not be a sufficient one, why some of the other automobile manufacturers have not followed the example of the Packard Co.

4. The Degree of Skill Required of the Workers

When a high degree of skill is required, the employers will naturally not wish to hire for the rush periods temporary workers who will botch the work. Nor will they want to lose tried and true employees whose replacement will cost a great deal of money. Such firms will naturally work for a policy of regularization which will keep their employees and give them continuous training. It is significant to note how many of the firms prominent in regularization work are of this type, among whom may be mentioned such measuring instrument firms as Leeds and Northrup; W. & L. E. Gurley, Consolidated Car Heating Company; Gorham Silver Company; Benedict Manufacturing Company; The Oneida Community; C. Kurtzmann & Company, piano makers; Bausch and Lomb, makers of optical products; Eastman Kodak Company; and Agfa-Ansco and various cutlery companies.

But where the workers are unskilled the losses from hiring new workers at the peak of sales and from losing the older workers, are not great. The advantages of regularization are therefore materially reduced.

5. The Relative Amount of Fixed Capital Required for Each Dollar of Product

Where the overhead charges are heavy, the pressure for regularization and for continuous employment is correspondingly great. Business men will try therefore to keep steel mills, rolling mills and machine shops, etc., running more steadily than they would flour mills, bakeries, and women's clothing factories, where the ratio of fixed capital to product is very much less.

Subject to the forces which have just been outlined, regularization can be made to pay in industries for which such policies are best adapted and could without doubt be much more extensively practiced than is at present the case.

In concluding our discussion of the gains and costs of regularization, we may perhaps turn from computing these in terms solely of their importance to the employer to a concluding query from the social point of view. It is this: The process of regularization tends to diminish the maximum number who are employed in an industry. It is very rarely that stabilization can be effected solely by filling up the valleys. Some levelling of the peaks seems almost invariably to occur. What then happens to the men who formerly obtained some work in the industry? Where can they find work? Is the net effect of regularization to throw these employees completely out of work and thus to obtain stabilization for some workers at the expense of others? These questions are very similar in nature to those which arise in connection with improvements in technical processes and in conjunction with the pooling of labor reserves by a system of public employment offices. A much fuller discussion of these points will be given later, but it can be said here that ultimately these apparently unemployed workers could find openings from one or more of the following causes: (1) the lower unit costs which an industry would realize through regularization would lead to some reduction in price. This in turn would cause more units to be demanded and would help absorb some of the workers. How many would be absorbed would depend not only on the relative reduction of costs and prices but also on the degree to which the quantity demanded responded to changes in price; (2) the surplus labor could be combined with the unemployed capital of which there is a considerable percentage in virtually all industries and thus find employment; (3) the surplus supply of labor could bid for work by taking lower wages, and with this general fall in wages, industry could absorb more workers so that the ratio of labor to capital would be greater than before. This would indeed probably happen and would bring to capital as a whole a consequent increase in the rate of interest which would be of still further advantage to it.

But the fact that the hourly rate of labor might be reduced by the workers who were squeezed out would not mean a diminished yearly income. This would in fact probably be larger since the national income would be increased (a) by the output of added workers who formerly were unemployed and (b) by the increased output of those who continued to be employed.

PART THREE

TECHNOLOGICAL UNEMPLOYMENT
AND THE
FEAR OF THE LIMITED MARKET

CHAPTER IX

THE FEAR OF TECHNOLOGICAL UNEMPLOYMENT

There is a widespread belief that the improvement in mechanical processes and in production is now throwing large numbers of men out of work, and a deep fear that it will continue increasingly to do so. If machinery is so improved that one man can manufacture twice as much of a product as before, will not only half as many workers be employed, and will not the remaining half be compelled to walk the streets as victims of technological unemployment? There are, moreover, many others who, while they do not claim that improvements in per capita production displace a corresponding proportion of the working force, nevertheless believe that some reduction in the numbers who can find employment will inevitably result.

If this view is true, then it will be relatively idle to hope to interest labor in increasing the effectiveness of work and in increasing daily output. In order to protect their jobs, the majority of the workers will instead naturally resist, either openly or covertly, all attempts to increase efficiency. Science and labor will thus be at war, and the reconciliation which many hope to effect between the two will be impossible. The unemployment problem will, moreover, become progressively more severe and will constitute an increasing tax upon the charity and the industries of the country.

Certainly the mechanical progress of the past thirty years and particularly of the last decade has been extraordinary, as illustrations from a few industries vividly demonstrate. One man operating a brick-making machine can now turn out 40,000 bricks an hour whereas the former output was approximately 55 per hour. The output per worker is therefore 720 times what it was. In the glass-bottle industry, one automatic glass-blower can turn out as many bottles in one hour as it formerly required 40 hand blowers to produce. In loading pig-iron, according to William Green, the president of the American Federation of Labor, two men can now do the work which formerly occupied 128.

If one turns from such individual cases to a survey of industry as a whole, we find that the physical productivity per worker in manufacturing, according to the indexes of the Federal Reserve Board, rose by 45 per cent between 1919 and 1929, while the per capita output in mining increased by an almost equal amount. Finally, owing to the increased use of the tractor and the combine and the better methods of feeding stock, the agricultural output per worker advanced by from 25 to 30 per cent during this time.

Those who believe in the menace of permanent technological unemployment will point to these very statistics as a proof of their contention. For while the output per worker has been increasing, the numbers employed in these lines of work have been diminishing. There were in 1929 approximately 500,000 or nearly 6 per cent fewer wage earners in manufacturing than there had been a decade before, while there were 300,000 or 15 per cent fewer workers on the railways. The number of miners was 200,000 less than it had been while during the period no less than 3,800,000 persons left the farms, of whom at least 1,500,000 were men and women eligible for employment. This decline of 2,500,000 workers occurred, of course, in the face of an increase of population which would normally have been expected to bring a gain of 2,000,000 workers into these industries. While the believers in permanent technological unemployment will freely admit that more workers are employed in other lines of employment such as garages and filling stations, hotels, and house-to-house canvassing than there were, and while they will grant that increased attendance in secondary schools and colleges has absorbed part of the slack, they nevertheless do not believe that these gains have been sufficient to make up for the losses in the major lines of employment. In consequence they believe that we are now suffering acutely from technological as well as cyclical unemployment, and they fear that worse is to come in the future.

If the contention that we are facing unemployment from such causes and on such a disastrous scale is correct, then the great mechanical improvements of the past would have resulted in such a proportionate displacement of labor that only a fraction of our present working force would be employed and the vast majority, even in times of prosperity, would be on the streets. This doctrine moreover carries with it as a corollary the principle that the real income of the working class cannot increase, inasmuch as the gains made by those who continue to be employed are counterbalanced by the losses of those who are dropped from their jobs.

Even the most superficial observer knows that neither of these consequences has been recorded. It seems to be true, according to the researches of Hurlin and Hansen,[1] that the real wages of the workers in the United States were in 1920 approximately three and one-half times what they were a century ago. The presence of unemployment in so highly civilized a society as our own is indeed a great shame, but even in the worst periods of depression from four-fifths to five-sixths of our workers are employed. There is indeed no evidence to indicate that the relative volume of unemployment has increased through the years. Our own index of unemployment for the period 1890-1926 seems to indicate that the percentage of unemployment was approximately the same for the years 1920-1926 as it had been on the average during the three previous decades. Since it has been precisely this period in which the greatest improvements in production have taken place, we may take some consolation in the failure of the consequences which were forecasted by the gloomy prophets to eventuate and to believe that they will not occur in that portentous future which the prophets survey with so much alarm.

---

[1] Hansen, Factors Affecting the Trend of Real Wages, *American Economic Review*, March, 1925, pp. 27-42.

But we need a more cogent analysis than a mere appeal to history to discover the fundamental economic reasons for believing that the increase in production will not permanently enlarge the volume of unemployment and that ultimately as large a proportion of the workers will be employed as before.

It is proposed to discuss this question under two main headings: (1) Will workers be thrown permanently out of employment by these improvements in machinery and in managerial efficiency? (2) Will many suffer temporary unemployment for shorter or longer periods of time, and if so, should they be protected against the losses which they experience and how?

CHAPTER X

DO TECHNICAL CHANGES CAUSE PERMANENT UNEMPLOYMENT?

1. IS PERMANENT TECHNOLOGICAL UNEMPLOYMENT IMPOSSIBLE?

The reasons by which economists in the past have generally tried to prove that the development of machinery and of improvements in production will not permanently displace labor are largely inconclusive to the modern mind. Following the French economist, J. B. Say, they have pointed out that the production of goods constitutes the demand for goods and that an increase in the quantity of one commodity is of itself an increase in the demand for all other commodities. Improvements, it is argued, create opportunities in the same or in other lines for the employment of labor.

But this analysis, couched as it is in terms of a barter economy, does not explain the processes by which an improvement in production in one industry in a money economy affects the employment of workers both in that industry and in others as well. It is well, therefore, to come to somewhat closer and more realistic grips with the problem.

We may begin by taking an industry where the productivity of labor has doubled within a given period, and which, for the sake of concreteness, we will assume to be that of book and job printing. We shall include under this heading all the other integrated arts and industries which help to turn out the end product of books and magazines. For the sake of further simplicity, we shall assume that this doubling in effectiveness takes place evenly throughout all the constituent branches. Not only are printers able to set twice as much type an hour as before, and pressmen run off twice as many pages, but proof-readers can and do read twice as much proof, papermakers produce twice as much paper, lumbermen cut twice as much lumber, and machinists turn out twice as many linotypes and octuple presses in a given time as before. Nor does the improvement stop here, for to make the picture complete, short-story writers are assumed to double their daily output as well.

Thus, whereas it formerly required the labors of 1000 men in all these lines of work to turn out the 600,000 copies of a weekly magazine which sold for ten cents, or an average rate of 100 per man day, (600,000 ÷ 6 ÷ 1000), let us assume that it would now require, when the average daily output per worker was 200, only 500 workers to turn out the former total daily product of 100,000. Will the remaining 500 workers be forced then to walk the streets? Let us see.

As output doubles, costs are reduced. If the workers are paid by the day, labor costs per magazine fall to one-half of what they formerly were. We can neglect for the moment other costs and assume that outlays for labor are all that is expended. This assumption is not so far from the truth, since, if we follow the raw material far enough back, we will find that probably three-fourths of the total expenditures are ultimately resolvable into payments for labor. If costs fall to one-half their former figure for all publishing firms and if there is free competition between the publishers, the latter will vie with each other in reducing prices in the effort to induce more people to buy copies of their particular magazine. If this competition is indeed full and complete, the price will fall in the same proportion as that by which costs were reduced, namely, by one-half. Under these conditions the new price will accordingly be 5 cents a copy instead of the former price of 10 cents. Now it is a truism that for virtually all commodities except certain luxury goods which are demanded because they are costly, a larger quantity will be demanded at a lower price than at a higher. The economist describes this in technical language by saying that the demand curve slopes downward and to the right. More than 600,000 copies of the magazine in question will in consequence be demanded and the sale of all the magazines whose prices were reduced will indeed be greater. This means that more than 500 workers will be required to turn out the magazine and that therefore, at the very worst, not all of the remaining 500 will be thrown out of work.

But, it will be queried, will not some of the workers, however, be thrown into the ranks of the unemployed, and if so, how many? That depends on the relative increase in the number of magazines demanded which is occasioned by the halving in the price, or upon what the economists term the elasticity of demand. There are here three main sets of possibilities, namely: (1) the quantity demanded may increase in the same proportion as that by which price was diminished, or double as price is halved; (2) the quantity demanded may increase in a greater proportion than that by which the price was reduced; and (3) the quantity demanded may increase in a smaller proportion than that by which price was decreased. The economist describes these three possibilities as examples where the elasticity of demand is respectively equal to unity, greater than unity, and less than unity. Let us trace the result in each case and see whether unemployment results.

If the quantity demanded increases in the same proportion as that by which price was reduced, then 1,200,000 copies of the magazine will now be sold at 5 cents. The daily production quota will now be 200,000 instead of 100,-000 as before and even though the average daily output is 200 instead of 100, a labor force of precisely 1000 will still be needed. There will not be, therefore, any unemployment under such a situation where the elasticity of demand is equal to unity.

What then about the situation in which the quantity demanded increases at a more rapid rate than that by which price was reduced, or in other words, where the sale of the magazine rose to more than 1,200,000 copies. Let us assume that sales triple instead of double, and that now 1,800,000 copies are sold weekly. This requires a daily output of 300,000 and this in turn requires the services not of 1000 men as before, but of 1500. The result in this case will not be any unemployment of existing workers, but rather an increase in the numbers needed in the paper and printing industry. The industry will thus recruit the 500 workers either from other industries or from those who had not previously been employed.

It has been just this elasticity of demand which has caused the number of persons employed in the automobile industry to increase, despite the increase in output per worker. At the present time, our automobile factories turn out approximately three times as many automobiles with a given number of work hours as they did in 1914. The price of automobiles has gone down although the general price level has risen, and this reduction in the exchange value of an automobile, together with the increased desire of the public for motion, has more than trebled the number of automobiles demanded, so that there were in 1927 approximately three times as many workers employed in the industry as in 1914. Up until 1919 most American manufacturing concerns had indeed similar experiences. An increase in production lowered both costs and prices but the increase in the quantity demanded more than made up for the increase in the average output, so that the relative number of persons employed in manufacturing increased with every decade. Because of this fundamental fact, nearly every American manufacturer maintained what Mr. Henry Ford now maintains, namely, that improvements in production do not cause unemployment, and that consequently the workers have nothing to fear from industrial progress.

But what if the demand is relatively inelastic, or if, as the price is reduced to 5 cents, the number of magazines demanded, though increasing, nevertheless does not double? Let us assume here that the reduction in price causes 900,000 copies to be demanded but not 1,200,000.

The daily production quota would then be 150,000. This would mean with an average output per worker of 200 copies, that only 750 men would now be needed in this industry, and that the remainder could no longer be employed there. There would be a similar contraction in the other publishing enterprises and the net result of the doubling in per capita output would not only be to increase the quantity of reading matter in this country by 50 per cent but also apparently to throw 25 per cent of the employees out of work.

We thus seem to have arrived at a point which apparently confirms the contention of those who urge that industrial advance causes technological unemployment. We seem to have discovered that it will inevitably result in the case of those commodities where the demand for the product is relatively inelastic. It has indeed been just this very inelasticity of demand which has caused the progressive decline in this country in the relative proportion of the population which is employed in agriculture. As the productive efficiency of the workers on the farms has increased, the values per unit have on the whole tended to decline to such a degree that the returns which the farmers could obtain were less than those enjoyed by corresponding workers in the urban industries. This has led to a migration from the farms to the cities with a consequent diminution in the relative proportion of the gainfully employed who are engaged in agriculture. This is indeed the logical consequence of the fact that as a man's income increases, he devotes a progressively smaller proportion of his added increments to purchasing food and the importance of food in his individual budget in consequence diminishes the higher up the income scale one goes. Similarly, as America has increased in prosperity, it has devoted less of its energies to raising food and more to producing other articles. In 1870, 47 out of every 100 workers were farmers, but in 1920 the percentage had fallen to 26 while the present census will probably show the percentage to be approximately 22. In other words, only half as many men are apparently needed to feed a population as was the case half a century ago. Allowance should of course be made for the fact that part of this relative decline is due to a decrease in the relative quantity of farm products which are exported while a still further portion has been caused by the transfer to the cities and to the towns of many operations such as slaughtering, butter-making, blacksmith work, etc., which formerly were performed largely on the farms. But even when all allowance is made for thse factors the relative decline is still probably appreciable.

Something of the same nature seems within the last decade to have overtaken the production of most standardized manufactured goods. The increase in the output per worker has not been accompanied by a corresponding increase in the quantity demanded with the result that the displacement of labor has been appreciable.[1]

But the real question is, however, whether these workers will be permanently unemployed, or whether new lines of work will open up for them. Here let us return to our example. Formerly when the price of the magazine was 10 cents, and when 600,000 copies were sold, the total weekly receipts were $60,000 or $60.00 for every worker employed. Now when the price is 5 cents, and 900,000 copies are being sold, the total receipts are but $45,000. The readers have 300,000 more copies of the magazine in their coat-pockets, but they also have 15,000 more dollars in their pocket-books which were formerly spent on reading matter. They will do one of two things with this $15,000:—namely, they will either spend it or save it. If they do the former, then they will buy more chewing gum, go to dance halls and movies more frequently, save up for a summer vacation, or buy one or more of a myriad of other articles which they desire. If they save the money, then the bank in which they de-

---

[1] From the standpoint of economic science, one of the most important tasks is to work out and apply a formula which will measure the flexibility of values through time of the various commodities. Such a study is at present being conducted by one of the authors and it is believed that the determination of these flexibilities will throw light on the changes in the occupational distribution which have occurred and help to predict the probable changes which will occur in the future.

posit the savings will invest it in the form of bonds, etc., which in conjunction with the savings of others will enable some railroads to double track their lines, steel companies to construct new blast furnaces, and public utilities to build new generating stations. The savings are in short expended upon capital goods—but expended they are.

The expenditure of these added sums increases the demand for the products upon which they are spent. It becomes necessary for these industries to take on more men, and they go into the labor market to obtain them. At the same time therefore that men are being squeezed out of the publishing business, purchasing power formerly expended upon the products of this industry is transferred to other industries and builds up added opportunities for work there. Nor is this all; the purchasing power transferred bears in the example given above, the same relation to the number of workers laid off as the total expenditures on magazines bore to the original working force. The number of workers laid off is 250 and the purchasing power transferred is $15,000 a week. This weekly average of $60 per worker is the same as that which originally prevailed in the industry when the ratio was one of $60,000 and 1000 men. It is indeed the same as that which still exists in the industry between the $45,000 of weekly receipts and the 750 men employed. Not only are new opportunities for employment built up as the old opportunities shrink, but they are built up to a degree equal to that by which the older opportunities decay. For every man laid off, a new job has been created somewhere, and the ratio between monetary purchases and employment is still the same as before.

The net result of these technological improvements is, therefore, not permanent unemployment, as at first seemed to be the case, but rather a transfer of labor from some lines to others. This tendency has been at work throughout the last decade. While agriculture, manufacturing, transportation, and mining have been on the wane so far as numbers are employed, the number of filling station operatives, hotel workers, entertainers, insurance salesmen, school teachers, etc., have been appreciably increasing. Young men who otherwise would have been farmers or clothing workers have in fact become movie ushers, saxophone players, and house-to-house canvassers.

From the reasoning outlined it is therefore clear that permanent technological unemployment is impossible. If the elasticity of demand for the commodity is equal to unity, or if the increase in quantity demanded is precisely proportional to the per capita increase in efficiency and the decrease in unit cost and in unit price, then there will be absolutely no change in employment. If the demand is elastic, or if the quantity demanded increases in a greater proportion than the increase in individual production and the fall in unit price, then actually more money will be spent on the industry than before, and more workers will have to be employed. There will then be a shift of labor from other industries to the one in question. If the demand is inelastic, or if the quantity demanded does not increase in as great a proportion as that by which individual efficiency rises and prices fall, then while some men will be squeezed out of this particular industry, an equal number of employment opportunities will be built up elsewhere from the transfer of purchasing power.

Improvements in industrial processes, like changes in demand, will produce, therefore, a shifting of labor and capital within the economy as workers and investors transfer themselves from industries where their return in terms of exchange value is less than the average to industries where the return is above or approaching the average.

These shifts are inevitable in a progressive society where there is a tendency towards an equalization of return. Those thrown out of work will not, however, be permanently unemployed, and to this degree therefore, the fears of permanent technological unemployment have been greatly exaggerated.

2. The Effect of Mergers, Piece-Rates, Regularization, and Shifts in Demand upon Unemployment

We have hitherto been considering the effect of technical progress upon employment. Let us now turn to improvements in managerial methods such as those effected by mergers, the introduction of piece-rates, and the regularization of employment and see whether similar results follow. After this, we shall consider the consequences of changes in demand.

Two of the economies which are frequently effected by mergers and consolidations are (1) the elimination of employees who are performing functions which in a combined organization are overlapping and superfluous, and (2) the closing down of the less efficient plants. Both of these economies, while they make large profits for the owners, do nevertheless throw some workers out of employment. But before concluding that these men are permanently eliminated from work, let us inquire what the owners will do with their increased profits. They have but two main sets of choices, namely, to spend these profits on themselves or to save them. In either case, they increase the demand for the new commodities upon which their increased profits have been spent and necessitate the employment of more labor in these lines of work. The final result is therefore the familiar one of transferring labor rather than of throwing it permanently out of a job.

Many workers mistrust the piece-rate and bonus systems because they believe that by inducing the workers to produce more than they would under time wages, the opportunities for employment are used up more rapidly and other workers are thus thrown out of work. Let us assume, for example, that the introduction of piece-rates causes the workers to double their output. Then if the piece-rate is not cut, and labor costs consequently remain the same as before, prices (under our assumption that labor costs are all) will not be reduced and no more units will in the total be sold. Certainly it would seem therefore, that with one-half of the former workers turning out this total, the remaining half would be forced out of employment. For while each worker employed will earn twice as much as before the total wage bill and hence the total demand for goods arising in this industry will remain unchanged. In such an event the displaced workers can be absorbed in this and other industries by accepting lower wage rates than they formerly obtained. This possibility of providing employment for workers displaced by technological changes has so far been ignored, but should be considered as supplementary to the previous analysis.

But, as anyone who has the most cursory knowledge of modern industry knows, employers will not be content if the employees double their daily earnings and, in non-unionized plants at least, a cut in the piece-rate will almost inevitably result. If the cut is proportional to the increase in output, so that the daily earnings of the workers are no greater than before, then the results will be the same as when the workers were presumed to have been paid on day rates. Labor costs will fall commensurately with the increase in average output, prices will be reduced correspondingly, and an increased quantity of the product will be demanded. The same principles will apply here as before. If the elasticity of demand is equal to unity, and the increase in the quantity demanded is proportional to the increase in average output and the reduction in price, then precisely the same number of workers will be employed in the given industry as before; if the elasticity of demand is greater than unity, then actually more persons will be employed in the industry than before. Only if the elasticity of demand is less than unity and the quantity demanded does not increase in as great a proportion as that by which individual output rose and prices fell, will the industry employ fewer men than before. But even here the fact that not as much money will be spent by the consumers on the product as before will mean that the unused purchasing power will be transferred to other commodities, which will, as we have seen, ultimately afford employment for those displaced from the industry where the increase in production originally occurred.

Finally, if the employers do not cut the piece-rate in the same proportion as that by which output rises, and therefore permit the workers to obtain higher daily earnings, a combination of these two sets of influences will operate to give employment to labor which at first flush would seem doomed to displacement. Thus, the lower wage rates accepted by the displaced workers will in part furnish additional employment in other lines while the lowered cost and price of the commodity will, by stimulating consumers to buy more, afford employment for workers within the industry. Finally, even if the market demand does not expand proportionately so that not all of the former workers will continue to be employed either within the industry or in making products for those who are still employed, then the purchasing power not expended on this product will be transferred by the consumers to other products and hence will give employment there.

The case is even clearer where there are shifts in demand. Americans have come, for example, to put a higher valuation on automobiles and radio sets than before, while they value cotton and woolen cloth and boots and shoes less highly than formerly. The result is that the former businesses have expanded while the latter have contracted. But while the numbers employed in the contracting industries naturally diminish, the numbers of those in the expanding industries naturally increase. Moreover, since every dollar not spent on some of the commodities is spent upon others, the opportunities for employment are built up in the same proportion as that in which they are torn down.

3. A More Detailed Analysis

The close reasoner may, however, legitimately object to the demonstration which has been given of the impossibility of permanent technological unemployment on the ground that our argument rests upon a number of assumptions of which the most important are:—(1) *That labor costs comprise all expenditures, and that a reduction in them consequently means a proportionate reduction in the total costs.* As a matter of fact, however, part of the expense of production is for interest on capital and rental payments on natural resources. These costs are not directly affected by an increase in productivity per worker, and consequently the reduction in total costs will not be as great as the reduction in labor costs. How then does this fact alter our general conclusion? (2) *That prices will be reduced in the same proportion as that by which costs are lowered.* This postulate is based on the still further underlying assumption that there is full and free competition between producers which will operate to lower price in the same degree as that by which the general cost curve is itself reduced. But in practice, competition is not perfect, and tendencies towards monopoly and price agreements are very common. Part of the gain in reduced costs may, therefore, not be passed on to the public in the form of lower prices but instead be intercepted by the owners in the form of higher profits. Under such conditions, it will be queried, may not permanent technological unemployment result? (3) Finally, in our illustration we have assumed *that the increase in per capita production has been general and uniform throughout all stages of the industry.* In practice, however, the technical improvement may be confined to one stage in the general sequence of operations, or if general, it may be much more characteristic of some stages than of others. Will the expansion in the quantity demanded be sufficient in this case, it is questioned, to absorb the large proportion of persons in these stages who would be thrown out of work if the production of the end product does not increase as fast as some of its elemetns.

Let us take up these three points in order:—

1. Does the fact that total costs per unit will not fall commensurately with labor costs invalidate the previous demonstration that permanent technological unemployment cannot occur? This situation may be illustrated by

supposing that wages formed two-thirds of the total cost, or $40,000, and that the other charges, such as interest and rent, comprised the remaining $20,000. A doubling in labor efficiency would reduce the labor cost from 6.67 cents ($40,-000 ÷ 600,000) a copy to 3.33 cents ($20,000 ÷ 600,000).

What then would happen to the payments for rent and interest? If no further investment in capital instruments and buildings were needed, then the capital charges per unit would be proportionately reduced. If no greater strain were put upon the land and ground rents were no higher, then rental charges would in consequence also fall in a proportionate degree. The cost per unit for these charges would then be 1.67 cents instead of 3.33 cents as before. The new total unit cost would therefore be 5 cents (3.33+1.67) instead of 10.0 cents as before.[1a] The reduction in total costs would therefore be proportional to the reduction in labor costs and the previous reasoning would be completely applicable.

But a doubling in output would, in fact, mean a greater strain upon natural resources and rents would in consequence rise. Furthermore, let us assume that the doubling of efficiency throughout the branches of the industry, including the machine-building trades, necessitated for each unit of final output twice as much "waiting" upon the part of savers as before. In short, we have now assumed that the expenditures for rent and interest would increase commensurately with output and that the unit costs for those services would be the same as before. The total costs would therefore fall, not to five cents per copy but to 6.67 cents (3.33+3.33). If the elasticity of demand were equal to unity, then the increase in quantity demanded (50 per cent) would indeed not be sufficient to absorb all of the workers in the same industry. For the quantity demanded daily would be 150,000 (or 900,000 on a weekly basis) and this would mean employment for 750 workers. But the remaining 250 workers would not be permanently unemployed,

[1a] Under the theory of infinitesimal changes, slightly different result would obtain.

since the capitalists and landowners would now have $30,-000 a week (900,000×3.33 cents) instead of $20,000 as before. With the added $10,000 they would be able to employ the 250 workers who would be squeezed out of the industry at the same rate of wages which they had formerly received, namely, $40 a week. While it might well be undesirable from the social standpoint that these 250 workers should now be engaged in producing luxuries for the wealthy rather than commodities for the great mass of the people, yet from the standpoint of employment, these people would not be thrown permanently out of work but would ultimately be employed.

There is of course the possibility that the strain upon natural resources and the amounts which were necessary to pay for the added waiting would not increase in the same proportion as output. In this event, the capital and rental charges per unit would be reduced with the increase in output. The price of the goods would in consequence be reduced by more than would be the case were interest and rental charges to increase proportionately with the output. The result would be that the increase in the quantity of the product which would be demanded would be greater than where interest and rental charges per unit remained the same as before, and a larger number of workers would in consequence be retained in the industry. For the rest of the workers, the expansion in the income of the capitalistic classes would be sufficient to keep them employed at some sort of a job even though at a different one.

2. We come next to the contention that a failure on the part of the producers to lower prices commensurately with the reduction in costs would prevent the workers from being absorbed in that industry or in any other. But this is quite palpably wrong, since the failure to reduce prices parallel with costs would inevitably occasion an increase in profits to the employers. The employers would then have the familiar choice of spending their added profits for luxuries or of investing them. In either case they would increase

the demand for the commodities upon which the added dollars were expended, and would draw into these occupations an additional quantity of labor sufficient to absorb those who were temporarily pushed out of printing and publishing.

3. Finally, is any serious qualification necessitated by the fact that the improvements may either be confined to or be concentrated upon a few stages in the production process rather than evenly distributed over all? Thus, let us say that in the men's clothing industry, the introduction of the multiple ply for cutting increases the amount of cloth which a cutter cuts during the day by no less than fivefold and that this is the only improvement which is effected. The reduction in cutting costs, even to one-fifth of what they were, would not apparently effect any appreciable relative reduction in the total cost or in the price of the garments manufactured. If the costs of cutting had been a dollar a suit, they would now be reduced to twenty cents. This reduction of eighty cents would, let us say, amount to only 2 per cent of the original price of the suit. If this saving were retained by the employers, then their increased profits expended either for consumers' or for capital goods would build up employment for the unemployed cutters or their equivalent elsewhere.

If the reduction in costs were passed on in the form of a lowered price, then while the increase in the quantity demanded would not be sufficient to re-employ many of the displaced cutters at their old jobs, it would, by increasing the total number of suits sold, increase the number of workers needed in other operations of the industry. If the elasticity of demand were equal to unity (and again assuming that labor comprises the total cost) then 2 per cent more workers would be needed in each and every one of the crafts. If the cutters formerly comprised 2.5 per cent of the force (which was the proportion of their costs to the total labor costs) or 50 out of a total force of 2000, then 40 cutters would have been released by the fivefold increase in output, and the increase in sales would only reabsorb one of these workers. But whereas 1950 workers were employed in the other crafts, the increase in sales of 2 per cent would call for 39 more workers in the other departments and hence absorb all of the remaining unemployed. All of the displaced workers could find an opening therefore in some branch of the industry itself and would not be compelled to seek opportunities in other industries. When the elasticity of demand is greater than unity then a slight reduction in price will cause an expansion in the quantities produced and in the number of workers needed in other occupations which will more than absorb the workers displaced from the particular operation.

Something perhaps of this tendency has been at work in recent years in the newspaper printing industry. The development of improved printing presses has materially reduced the number of press feeders but, as Dr. Elizabeth F. Baker has found,[2] the number of full-fledged pressmen who have been added to print the increased number of papers has more than offset this decline.

When, however, the elasticity of demand is less than unity, the expansion in the quantity demanded would not be enough to provide for all of the displaced cutters within the clothing industry itself. But since the quantity of clothes demanded would not increase in the same proportion as that by which the unit price was reduced, a smaller total amount would therefore be spent on clothes than was originally the case. Purchasing power would therefore be transferred to other occupations. This would ultimately build up in the familiar manner, employment opportunities for those cutters who could not be reabsorbed into the clothing industry as a whole.

Summing up therefore, we can say that the displacement of workers from their former occupations because of technological changes will be *greater*: (1) the less the quantity demanded of a commodity increases with a given reduction in price per unit; (2) the less is the proportion which labor

2 Elizabeth F. Baker, Unemployment and Technical Progress in Commercial Printing, *American Economic Review*, September, 1930, pp. 442-66.

costs form of the total expenditures; (3) the less is the degree to which a reduction in costs will reduce price, and (4) the less important is the operation to the whole industry.

In other words, therefore, the amount of displacement from former to other jobs will vary inversely with the elasticity of demand, the importance of labor in the final product, the degree of competition, and the relative importance of the operation or operations primarily affected by the technical changes.

In any event, however, employment opportunities are being built up elsewhere which will ultimately be adequate to provide for an added number of workers equal to these who under such conditions may have been eliminated from any given industry.

In the long run therefore the improvement of machinery in a given industry and the greater efficiency of management do not throw workers permanently out of employment nor create permanent technological unemployment. Instead they raise the national income and enable the level of earnings and of individual incomes to rise.

4. A QUALIFICATION

We have thus far been assuming that the improvement in production occurred in only one industry and we have found that the indestructibility of the purchasing power of the previous consumers would ultimately re-employ any displaced workers. But, as we shall see from the next chapter, there is likely to be a considerable intervening period of unemployment before all of the workers find employment. During this period, they will not be receiving wages and their purchasing power will in consequence be reduced. Some unemployment will tend to result elsewhere. This element of instability is multiplied if improvements are taking place simultaneously in a large number of industries and is particularly aggravated if the commodities are subject to an inelastic demand. If the rate of technical progress in a society is moreover accelerated, the number who are thrown out of employment temporarily is increased. The purchasing power of these workers is therefore temporarily reduced and their demand for goods curtailed. This transitional loss of employment has therefore a magnified effect and prevents the previous analysis from working out to the full extent and with the precision which has hitherto been implied.

We have also hitherto assumed in our discussion that the general price level remained constant while these technical improvements were occurring and that either the increase in the quantity of one commodity had an infinitesimal effect on the general price level or the increase in goods was matched by a corresponding increase in the effective supply of money and bank credit. But if these assumptions should not be true and if the general price level were to decline because the production of goods was proceeding at a faster pace than the available monetary supply, then, as we shall show in Chapter XIV, still further pressure would operate to produce a cumulative breakdown of production, employment and purchasing power.

CHAPTER XI

TEMPORARY TECHNOLOGICAL UNEMPLOYMENT

1. A REËXAMINATION OF THE EFFECTS OF TECHNICAL PROGRESS WITH REFERENCE TO THE CREATION OF TEMPORARY UNEMPLOYMENT

The preceding analysis has demonstrated that workers are not thrown permanently out of employment by improvements in technical production, and managerial efficiency, but that they are instead ultimately either employed in other industries or retained in the industry in which the improvement took place. But most of this analysis has ignored the question of time and has assumed that the consequences outlined follow immediately upon the initial causes. But in real life this is not so. It takes time for the readjustments to be made and during this period many individuals suffer. Economic science, in its praiseworthy zeal to establish long-time relationships, has all too often neglected the short-time factors which delay the working out of ultimate consequences. We shall not make much progress in dealing with the human results of technical change or in controlling it until we see fairly clearly that the ultimate benefit which flows to society in the form of higher real incomes is obtained only at the cost of great and undeserved hardship to many.

Let us begin by reëxamining the economic processes which we have traced and see why it is that the displaced workers are not immediately reëmployed.

(1) **Even in industries where more workers will ultimately be employed, there will be a transitional period of unemployment.** We have hitherto assumed that the reduction in cost and price by the manufacturer and the in-

crease in demand by the consumers were simultaneous. But consumers' goods produced in the factory generally go through the hands of wholesalers, jobbers, etc., before they finally reach the retailers' shelves. It takes some time therefore for the lower prices of goods at the factory to reach the consumer in the form of lower prices on the commodities which he buys. A still further period is needed before the buying public reacts to the reduced price by buying more. During this transitional period, therefore, production may have been carried on according to the old quantities or with an inadequate allowance for the future increase in the quantity demanded. Before the "pick-up" in demand occurs therefore, some of the firms may have reduced their staffs and many men have suffered temporary unemployment.

(2) Laborers who are squeezed out from the numerically contracting industries are not immediately absorbed into the expanding industries. We have hitherto tacitly assumed that the increase in the demand for labor in the expanding lines synchronized perfectly with the failure of the demand for the product where the improvement had taken place to expand sufficiently to keep all of the former workers employed. This is not realized in real life. The contraction of employment takes place, as we have seen, fairly quickly, and it may require some time before employment rises again even in that industry. Further time is required for the increased purchasing power which is now possessed either by those who are employed in the industry or by the consumers of the product whose price has been lowered to create elsewhere additional jobs, equal in number to those which have been destroyed in the given industry. Retail dealers, for example, have already existing stocks which in the case of most articles will absorb this increased demand for some time at least without necessitating any increase in their purchases from jobbers and from wholesalers. Even when the level of orders from the retailers does begin to rise, the stocks of jobbers and wholesalers will be able to meet this increase for a further period

before they in turn place larger orders with manufacturers. There will thus be an intervening space of time before increased purchases by the consumers translate themselves into increased orders from the factories. Nor will increased orders to individual factories cause an added staff immediately to be hired. The factories may for a time work more hours per week or improve their efficiency per worker and hence produce the added quantity with the original number of workers. Ultimately to be sure, the increased earnings of these factory workers and the higher profits of the firms will in turn give employment elsewhere. But this will require the passage of a still further period of time and the final effects may be fairly long delayed in coming. And yet during this transitional period, the displaced workers or an equal number of others will fail to be reabsorbed completely into industry.

(3) **The process by which the workers are reabsorbed involves a much larger number of separate shifts in which some time is lost at virtually every stage.** When one industry is growing and another declining the workers laid off from the latter are seldom transferred directly to the former. Thus, comparatively few of those who have left the clothing and textile industries have gone directly into the expanding automobile industry. What has instead tended to happen has been for them to enter other industries where they displace other workers who in turn find work elsewhere, displacing others in the process. This goes on until the numbers in the expanding industries such as automobiles are sufficient to meet the demands of the market. During this intermediate series of shiftings, some time will probably be lost at every stage. While the full burden will not be thrown exclusively upon the group originally displaced, the aggregate of unemployment which results will certainly not be measured by their losses but will in fact be considerably larger.

(4) **The decline in some of the industries involves changes of work and of residence which most workers are generally reluctant to undertake.** Workers are commonly

unwilling to recognize that their industry is declining, or prone to believe that even though the total numbers employed may be diminishing, there is nevertheless room in it for such able individuals as they believe themselves to be. For this reason, and because of the possession of skill which they can seldom exercise as effectively elsewhere, they are loth to get out of a sinking industry and tend to rely in a Micawberish fashion upon "something turning up." This very human combination of optimism and inertia of course very greatly prolongs the transitional period of unemployment.

This tendency to cling to old, even if decaying, industries is especially marked if the readjustment necessitates a change of residence. In England, the miners in the South Wales coal fields have been very reluctant to leave their desolate valleys where for the past six years employment has been very scanty, to seek employment in the expanding industries of the midland counties. Similarly in the United States, although there is a great deal of unemployment in the American coal fields, workers have been very slow to leave these regions for the city. Due both to the relative diminution of the demand for textiles and for boots and shoes, and to the shifting of these industries away from New England towards the south and middle-west respectively, unemployment in the New England towns of Lowell, Lawrence, Fall River, New Bedford, Lynn, and Haverhill has increased. While the population in these towns has on the whole shrunk since 1920, it has not done so commensurately with the shrinkage of employment.

The truth of the matter was very well summed up by Adam Smith when he pithily remarked that "of all kinds of baggage, man is the most difficult to be transported." Men become attached to localities and to a set of associations and friendships, and will make sacrifices rather than change them.

There are, moreover, two further forces which operate to hold men with families in their former localities. The first is the expense of moving, while the second is the fact of home ownership. Where there are several members of a family, the expenses of moving are appreciably greater than they would be for a single man. Aside from all matters of sentiment, it takes a much greater differential economic advantage therefore to induce the men with families to move than it does bachelors and those without dependents. A large percentage of workers in the United States, particularly in the smaller cities, are, moreover, saving towards owning their homes and substantial advertising pressure is being placed on an increasing number to act in this manner. To leave the locality therefore means a forced sale of whatever equity the worker may have and consequently generally entails a substantial loss. The homeowner will naturally try to avoid this as long as possible, and hence will be tied by his investments as well as by his emotions to his present dwelling place. It is in fact very doubtful whether, in view of the present uncertainties of industry, it is wise for most manual workers to attempt to own their own homes. If they are thrown out of work, they will find it extraordinarily difficult to maintain the rather heavy rates of payment which are required. Sometimes this is done but at altogether too heavy a cost. Sometimes the workers lose out completely and forfeit their back payments. Those who have to leave town almost invariably suffer heavy losses.

These two forces operate upon married men with families, and one portion of this group is particularly liable to be dropped when the working force is being curtailed, namely those over 45. The problems of job adjustment for these men, which are difficult enough anyway because of the nature of modern industry, are rendered even more distressing by the fact of dependents and attempts at home ownership.

From all of these causes therefore technological and business changes create a considerable amount of *temporary* unemployment which in the short run creates havoc. This is quite clearly demonstrated by three excellent recent studies by Lubin, Myers and Clague and by earlier studies by Professor George E. Barnett. Dr. Lubin and his associates [1] interviewed 754 workers in three cities who had been dropped from industry because of technological changes, in order to determine the relative ease with which they had found reëmployment. In order to eliminate unemployment which might be due to gross personal defects, no workers were considered who had been dropped for inefficiency or for insubordination. The results showed that 344, or 45.5 per cent of the 754 had not been able to find steady employment and were in consequence still unemployed.[2] Of this number in turn, 76 per cent had been unemployed for over two months, 65 per cent for over three months, 41 per cent for over six months, and 19 per cent for over nine months.

Nor had those who had finally succeeded in finding work had any easy time, for only 12 per cent had found work in less than a month, while 72 per cent had been unemployed for over two months before they were finally placed. Fifty-six per cent, or over one-half, had gone for over three months without work, while 41 per cent went for more than four months, 24 per cent for more than six months and 11 per cent for eight months.

R. J. Myers' study of 370 cutters who had been displaced from the men's clothing industry in Chicago because of the introduction of multiple plies in cutting and the elimination of the weaker firms showed somewhat similar results.[3] While only 42, or 11 per cent, had not found employment in the period of over a year from the time when they had been laid off, only 29 per cent of those who found work did so immediately.[4] One-third of the group which was ultimately placed lost six months or more of work, over half of whom in turn had taken a year or more before they could find a permanent job. The average amount of time which

[1] Isador Lubin, *The Absorption of the Unemployed by American Industry* (Brookings Institution, 1929), 36 pp.
[2] *Ibid.*, p. 4.
[3] R. J. Myers, Occupational Readjustment of Displaced Skilled Workmen, *Journal of Political Economy*, August, 1929 (Vol. XXXVII), pp. 473-89.
[4] *Ibid.*, pp. 477-79.

was thus lost in unemployment between the old and the new jobs was 5.6 months.[5] At the current rates of earnings, this was equivalent to an average loss of approximately $675. Ewan Clague's study of what happened to a group of over 700 rubber workers who had been laid off by the United States Rubber Company when it closed down its New Haven plant, also indicated a great deal of difficulty in finding new work, although the average amount of time lost by this group was probably less than for those studied by Lubin and Myers.[6] During the period of over a year which had elapsed since the workers lost their jobs, those over 45 years had lost, on the average, six months apiece, and 30 per cent of them had never found another job at all.

Since a considerable percentage of the workers in all three groups which were studied were still unemployed when the surveys were made, the real losses had not fully accrued during the period covered. Still further time would be lost before these men finally got work again. It is indeed probable that, because of the reluctance of industrial firms to hire men over 45 years, some of the older men would never be fully placed again. The technical and administrative changes might therefore serve to precipitate the latent discrimination against such older workers which otherwise would not have been exercised so immediately.

Finally, even if labor is ultimately transferred, it is frequently at a job which pays a lower wage and which is less satisfactory than the one which is left. Of the workers studied by Lubin and his associates, while 27 per cent received a wage equal to that which they had received before, and 19 per cent actually received more, 48 per cent nevertheless received less than before.[7] The group as a whole had, therefore, very distinctly lost ground. Myers' study gave very similar results. Twenty-three per cent were earning as much as before, 30 per cent were earning more, but 46 per cent were, on the other hand, earning less.[8] Myers found

---

[5] *Ibid.*, p. 479.
[6] A tentative report of progress was made by Mr. Clague at a meeting of the American Statistical Association in New York on May 23, 1930.
[7] Lubin, *op cit.*, p. 12.   [8] Myers, *op cit.*, p. 480.

indeed that 61 per cent of the displaced cutters wanted to return to the trade. In the New Haven study of the displaced rubber workers,. it was found that less than one-third were receiving either as much or more than before, and that such gains as there were amounted to but little. On the other hand, not only were over two-thirds of the workers receiving less on the new job than on the old, but the amounts of these losses were in some cases very great.

It follows therefore that, while a given set of workers may not be permanently unemployed because of technical progress, there is likely to be a transitional period of un-employment of considerable length and that most workers will be lower paid at the new jobs they find than they were at those they left. An increase in the rate of technical progress will therefore create an increase in the number of men who are temporarily unemployed. This may well have been one of the causes of the increase in unemployment in Germany during the years from 1926 to 1929. Moreover, as we have pointed out in the preceding chapter, the cur-tailment of the purchasing power of this increased number of the temporarily unemployed will tend to infect other industries and to intensify the danger of a cumulative breakdown of the processes of production.

In the past the sufferings of the displaced workers have been either ignored or accepted as inevitable. This we can-not permit in the future. It is but just that society, which benefits so greatly from these improvements, should take steps to lessen the loss which innocent workers suffer, and that adequate provision for these displaced workers should be one of the charges upon the net fruit of progress. A society which shows such extraordinary technical compe-tence should surely be able to devise the ways and means by which this loss may be minimized.

Unless this is done, it will be almost inevitable that labor will resist and oppose most attempts to raise the efficiency of industry. Even though they were to be convinced that in the long run they would be reëmployed somewhere even though displaced, yet the fear of the intervening period of unemployment and the prospect of reduced earnings in these new openings once they developed, would be sufficient in most cases to make them oppose improvements in industrial technique. If labor's support is to be enlisted in improving production, it will be necessary to work out some program which will protect the worker against as large a portion of these losses as possible. If such steps were to be taken, the amount of released and added effort which the workers would expend now that the fear of unemployment had been largely removed, might well be sufficient to meet the economic costs involved.

2. Reducing the Losses of Temporary Unemployment

By what concrete means then may this obligation of lessening the losses of those who are temporarily unemployed be realized? There are, of course, a number of possible methods of which the following are the most important:

1. *The forecasting by competent organizations of the industries and trades in which a displacement of labor is most likely to occur and the probable degree of displacement which may be expected.* Such a task may seem at first to be impossible. But if we knew (1) what were the probable elasticities of demand through time for the various commodities, and (2) what were the chief impending technical changes in various industries, it would be possible to estimate roughly the fraction of workers, if any, who would probably be displaced in the course of a decade [9] in the various major industries. It is not pretended, of course, that any precise prediction could be made, but on the basis of such information, a generalized judgment could nevertheless be given. This advice could then be given to the groups involved through trade papers, the schools, etc. If this were effectively done it would accelerate the movement of many

[9] One of the authors has devised a method for measuring these elasticities of demand through time, and is now carrying on an inductive investigation at the University of Chicago, to determine what these elasticities were for some 150 commodities during the years 1899-1929.

out of the declining industries and restrain others from entering. There would, in consequence, be a much more sensitive adjustment of the labor supply to the production needs of the industry, and the amount of temporary unemployment would be appreciably reduced.

2. *The planning and scheduling by management of technological change with a view to reducing the displacement of labor.* If management were to introduce technical improvements gradually instead of spasmodically, the amount of disturbance and of displacement would be appreciably lessened. Over a period of years, the adoption of such a policy need not result in less advance but the changes would be made at even rates of increment instead of coming in gusts, as is often the case at present. Some managers would also find it good business to introduce their improvements during periods of business prosperity when any displacement could be easily reabsorbed elsewhere rather than during periods of depression when reëmployment would be far more difficult.

It may be objected to all this that management should and will introduce these changes when it can save the most money and not when it will cause the least unemployment. This in many instances will call for thoroughgoing improvements being made at one time instead of carrying through a slow process of reorganization which would require a much longer period to effect. In some cases, technical advantages will be realized by changing machinery, etc., etc., all at once. It is better in many instances, however, to proceed more slowly and not disturb the current processes of production by too great a rate of alteration and reëquipment. There is, furthermore, an imponderable advantage to the slower but steadier rate of change which is commonly ignored. Since the workers will be less exposed to the dangers of unemployment, they will be more ready to coöperate wholeheartedly in the introduction of new methods and in consequence individual output is likely to be appreciably higher than it would be in the other case.

3. *In industries which are affected by the public interest,*

such as railroads, etc., mergers and consolidations might be permitted only on condition that men whose services were otherwise satisfactory should not, because of this fact, be dropped from the payrolls. Senator Couzens included such a clause in his 1930 bill on railway consolidation which gave to the Interstate Commerce Commission the duty of working out the precise method of adjustment.[10] One way which immediately suggests itself is that of not hiring new workers until, by the process of death and retirement, the working force has been reduced to its desired level without workers having been discharged or laid off by the employers. This practice should also be followed by private business to the fullest extent possible.

4. *An efficient system of public employment offices should be provided which will help to find a job for the displaced workers in other industries or occupations.* A common clearing-house for jobs and applicants helps to reduce the time which is lost from the workers traveling from plant to plant in pursuit of a job. Skilled employment work can, moreover, reduce this lost time still further by knowing whether the trade of the workers has rough equivalents in industries other than that from which they have been displaced. There are frequently very similar types of work performed in different industries which are called by different names. If these are known by the employment officials, they can frequently transfer men to similar work in very different industries and thus reduce the length of the transitional period.

When a city becomes distinctly overcrowded with labor, the employment offices could, moreover, serve as agencies to squeeze the surplus labor out of the city into localities where the chances for work are better. Such a policy as this would meet with the opposition of both employers and local merchants since the former would tend to want a surplus of labor in order to keep wages down below what they otherwise would be, while the latter would want a large labor force in order to have more purchasers of their goods.

[10] See the *United States Daily,* April 29, 1930, pp. 1 and 10.

But a coördinated system of exchanges under state or federal supervision rather than under exclusive local control, could help to meet this change by informing the local workers of opportunities elsewhere, and of facilitating their movement if and when they decided to leave the city. Not being subject to local control and pressure to the same degree as an exclusively municipal office would be, a state or national system could consider the general welfare to a degree impossible for a smaller body.

5. *The revamping of our systems of vocational training so that juveniles who are being trained may be given some preparation which will fit them for alternative industries and displaced adults prepared for new lines of work.* Because of the changes which have been described there is not as much surety now as there was that workers will follow the same trade all their lives. To prepare juveniles for this possibility of change, it would be well to avoid as great a specialization as was once contemplated in some of the earlier trade schools. Because of the possibility that a given set of trade skills may be rendered obsolete, another reason is given for making vocational training sufficiently broad to enable a worker later to transfer from one type of work to another with a minimum of loss. If specialized occupations are taught the young workers, it would be well that they should be taught a supplementary as well as a principal trade so that they might have another string to their bow in case they were displaced.

An adequate system of vocational retraining for displaced adults will also reduce the time lost between jobs and increase the earnings in the new occupations. At present, the displaced workers must make their own readjustments and try to pick up new trades by the painful process of working at them. But the absence of prior knowledge prevents them from being admitted to many trades which do need skilled or semi-skilled operatives and where, if they were once placed, they might be both happy and useful.

It is important, therefore, that those who either are or are about to be displaced, should be given every facility for retraining in some expanding occupation. Vocational schools could thus operate in coöperation with the employment offices. The coal-mining industry is, for example, a notorious instance of a relatively overcrowded industry. There are already at least 200,000 more miners than are needed to operate the mines fairly steadily, and with the development of mechanical loaders, this number will increase. If courses and training could be given in the mining districts in such subjects as automobile repairing, clerical work, selling, etc., it would be possible to drain off a large number from the industry and with the assistance of the employment service to place them fairly effectively. If the process of technical change in the industry is proceeding at a moderate tempo, the difficulties might also be reduced to a minimum by training for other trades the young people who would otherwise enter the industry and then by helping to transfer them. This movement would in itself lead to a natural contraction in the numbers employed in the industry since those who died or retired would not be replaced by the oncoming generation. This natural decline might be sufficient so that the industry could adapt itself to the new conditions without being compelled to lay off any workers, but even were this not the case, the number of workers who would be forcibly squeezed out would be less than if the younger persons who would have otherwise entered the industry were drained off elsewhere.

When adult workers are dropped from an industry because of technical changes, consolidations, or mergers, they should be furnished gratuitously with at least a short period of retraining. Here again the trades taught should not only be in the expanding industries but also for those types of work which will be most closely allied with the jobs which they have held in the past. To determine these vocational affinities would be a heavy burden for vocational education, but one which must be assumed if the problem is to be solved satisfactorily.

6. *The payment of a dismissal wage for those who are forced out of employment by such changes is also distinctly*

useful. Hart, Schaffner and Marx, for example, paid $500 apiece to nearly 300 cutters who either volunteered or were conscripted to leave the industry because the cutting of multiple plies of cloth diminished the number of cutters needed. Two other firms in the same industry, namely, the Arthur Nash Company and Ed. V. Price have also paid dismissal wages to small groups of workers who were no longer needed. The United States Rubber Company has also paid allowances amounting to one week's wages for each year of employment to the workers in the New Haven and Hartford factories which were permanently closed by the company in its efforts to concentrate production in low cost mills. Another firm which has adopted the dismissal wage system is the John A. Manning Company of Troy, New York.

The recognition of the social obligation by such firms without any legal compulsion is indeed most praiseworthy, and it is to be hoped that many other firms will follow their example.[11] Nevertheless, it is too much to hope that such voluntary action can adequately protect the displaced workers because of the following reasons: (a) Even in the case of the generous payment of Hart, Schaffner and Marx, the allowance was not quite enough to meet the loss in wages which the workers had already experienced because of unemployment, to say nothing of the losses which those who had not yet found work would suffer from unemployment in the future and the diminished earnings at other jobs which were received by nearly half the entire number. Where the payments were less adequate the loss would of course be correspondingly greater.

(b) As modern business is conducted to-day, it is highly improbable that the management of any very large percentage of prosperous firms would feel a sufficient obligation to their employees as to make voluntarily such payments. Modern management is to-day primarily responsible

---

[11] For a cogent plea for and a careful outline of a dismissal wage act by one of the most socially minded of American employers, see Ernest G. Draper's, A State Dismissal Wage Act, *The Survey*, Jan. 15, 1931, pp. 426-27.

to the stockholders for results, who in turn are inclined to measure the efficiency of the managerial staff by the relative amount of profits. Most modern managers would therefore find it difficult to justify their voluntarily incurring such an expenditure as would, immediately at least, diminish the profits of their clients, the stockholders.

Where the payment of the dismissal wage was necessary in order to get the consent of a strongly intrenched group of workers to the installation of improved machinery and to the use of more efficient methods of production, such a payment might be justified by the management as a necessary price for industrial and financial progress. But where the workers are relatively weak, few managers, even if disposed on humanitarian grounds to do so, will feel free to make payments which are not necessary to obtain the ends sought.

(c) If all this is true of prosperous firms in flourishing industries, it is far more applicable to hard pressed enterprises and to waning industries. Individual carriage plants which have been losing ground so rapidly because of the coming of the automobile, could scarcely afford to bear the added burden of maintaining the workers who were forced out of the industry until they could find other work. Similarly the coal industry, which is suffering in nearly all regions, could scarcely support the miners who increasingly will be squeezed out from the ranks. When it is remembered that it is the weak firms within an industry who fail first, the impracticability of relying upon individual employers to protect adequately the displaced worker should become still more evident. It indeed seems but proper that the expanding industries should help to pay at least some of the cost of temporarily maintaining the workers who have been squeezed out of the contracting industries. Since the growth of the automobile, hosiery, and radio industries has been at least partially at the expense of the cotton, woolen, boot and shoe, and phonograph industries, it would seem that there is an economic obligation upon the first set of industries and upon their users, to meet some of the losses which the workers in the other industries have experienced because of the change in tastes.

7. It would seem, therefore, to be relatively clear that some more general method of protection should be devised which would draw its funds from a wider source than the immediate plant or even the given industry where the workers were laid off. The only method of meeting these requirements would be by some form of insurance against unemployment. While this is still anathema to most American business men, it would seem inevitable that some such plan will be necessary if the workers are to be protected adequately against some of the inevitable consequences of industrial progress or change and thus released for constructive effort.

CHAPTER XII

SOME POPULAR THEORIES OF UNEMPLOYMENT: THE LIMITED MARKET

1. The belief in a limited market is what lies fundamentally behind the fear that technological unemployment will be permanent. If only a given quantity of goods and services will be consumed by society, it follows that an increase in output per worker must mean a proportionate decrease in the numbers employed. But this, as we have seen, is not the case. The increase in output operating through lower costs and either lower prices or higher profits ultimately causes either more of a given product or of other products to be demanded and produced.

It is this same fear of a limited market which causes most men and women to believe that even in normal times the opportunities for employment are limited and that consequently, if some persons obtain work, they can do so only by depriving others of the opportunity. Since the average man believes this to be so, he instinctively wishes to bar from employment those whom he thinks do not have as good an ethical claim for work as he and his kind. Since he believes that Americans should have the preference over foreigners, he accordingly thinks that those who are not citizens should be dropped from their jobs to make room for those who are. Upon the same assumption, the advocates of a protective tariff urge that when we buy foreign goods, we give employment to foreign labor and deprive native workers of that employment which would be theirs if we instead purchased domestic products. It is in large part because the great bulk of the people believe in this argument that the philosophy of protection is so strong the world over.

Similarly if work is limited, those who need it least should be barred, and preference given to those who need it most. It is thought unfair that in some families there should be two adult wage-earners since this is taken to mean that the heads of other families will be deprived of a job. It is this which in part causes the almost universal prejudice against the employment of married women. It is, for example, virtually impossible for married women to retain teaching jobs in England and the same is true in many sections of this country. Naturally also it is thought to be both ridiculous and unfair to have children employed at the assumed price of throwing adults out of work.

If unemployment still continues after all of these classes have been dropped, the believers in a limited market have still another unfailing remedy, namely, to reduce the number of hours and thus ration out the available employment among the needy claimants.

Some of these proposed changes are desirable in themselves without regard as to whether they are really remedies for unemployment. It is desirable, for example, that children under sixteen should be spared from the pressure of industry in order that they may have a better chance to develop, while a reduction of working hours in most occupations would make life more worth while to those who are employed.

But, for the moment, we are not discussing whether we should make such changes in our industrial life but merely whether it is necessary to adopt them in order to avert unemployment.

The belief that the available market, and consequently the available jobs, are limited, seems to find confirmation from the facts of everyday experience. Several applicants seek to obtain a desirable position. One is hired and the others are necessarily rejected. It is difficult to convince these men that they are not competitors and that the employment of the one does not mean the unemployment of at least one of the others. Similarly when a customer makes his purchases from one of a group of competing manufacturers or tradesmen, it is but natural for the others to conclude that what has given business to one enterprise has diminished either the actual or potential possibilities of its competitors.

But while this is immediately true in individual instances, it is not true in a larger sense. The married woman who is employed does not permanently drive others out of work but rather helps to create opportunities for employing others. For if she is employed, her wages will enable her and her family to buy more products than otherwise and thus to increase the demand for other goods. More labor will have to be employed in these other lines to satisfy the heightened demand. Similarly the earnings of the child or of the foreigner who comes to work do help to create an economic demand for more goods and consequently for more workers. If these classes are thrown out of work in the belief that they are taking the bread out of other mouths, they will still have to be supported. But there will be less with which to support them since the numbers of men in other lines of work are now necessarily less, because so many have been withdrawn to fill the places which have been vacated.

Similarly a barring of imports not only automatically cuts down exports, as every student of international trade well knows, and hence creates unemployment in the exporting industries, but it also means that a larger portion of the consumer's income is now spent on those goods which, because of their lower price, formerly were imported. There will be less to spend on other commodities produced at home and consequently the numbers employed in these other lines of work will shrink.

The truth of the matter is that the employment of any group of workers is normally not purchased at the expense of unemployment of others. Instead, by producing goods and adding purchasing power, these workers create opportunities for employment in other lines. To drop such workers from employment would normally decrease the national income, but it would not improve the employment situation.[1]

In a similar fashion, the relative amount of unemployment is normally not increased by a rise in the rate of population growth. The new workers coming into the labor market can normally find work there in producing needed commodities. If this number were to increase faster than the growth of capital and the progress of the industrial arts, their rate of wages would decrease but there would still be relatively as much employment as before. Birth-control is not therefore a remedy for unemployment, although it may be a desirable social policy.

The ultra-modern economist will tend perhaps to reject such an analysis as this because it is so closely similar to that of Bastiat and of the Manchester school whom he regards as being completely outmoded. It is, however, a basically sound interpretation of "normal" tendencies and is an adequate explanation of long-run forces.

2. The problem is complicated, however, by the business cycle and by the fact of industrial depressions. At such times the market is in a sense limited. Goods produced cannot be sold at a price which will give a profit and in a large percentage of cases must indeed be sold at an actual loss. There are large groups of unemployed men who in a barter and non-industrialized economy might be expected to go to work to produce the commodities which they reciprocally need. The tailor and shoemaker it would seem need not be unemployed, when each by producing his own product might thereby create a demand for the other.

But for some reasons, as yet imperfectly understood, it is impossible at present for them to do this and many in each group are unemployed although they each need badly the commodities which the others could produce. In such a situation, the reasoning which holds good for "normal"

---

[1] Historians and students of international affairs badly need to learn this lesson since they are accustomed to reason that an increase in the foreign trade of one nation is predominantly purchased at the expense of a diminution in that of others and that consequently the economic interests of various countries are basically in conflict.

times breaks down. Society then presents the tragic and absurd paradox of families being in grave distress for the lack of fundamental necessities at the very time when these industries are apparently unable to sell the products which are so badly needed. There is indeed no graver indictment of our industrial civilization than the spectacle of millions lacking food, clothing and shelter at the very time when there is said to be an "overproduction" of these very commodities.

There are indeed two almost contradictory systems of economics; the first is that which we have termed "normal" but which in fact, characterizes the upswing of the business cycle when the market is able to absorb the products of industry and thus provide employment for all save those temporarily out of work through the faulty organization of the labor market or from seasonal and technological causes. The second is that which characterizes the depression phase of the cycle when the employment opportunities are for the time limited. In this period it may well be socially desirable to ration work out to those who need it most, and a reduction in child labor, in the volume of immigration, and in the length of the working week would all be of material assistance. But such a program of rationing should be limited to periods of depression and should be abandoned when business again starts to improve. It is, in other words, a transitional rather than a permanent method of dealing with unemployment and if and when we are able to control and greatly reduce the oscillations of the business cycle, it will not be needed.

3. There is a very large school of thought which believes that the cause of business depressions lies in the fact that the workers do not receive the full product of industry.[2] Because of this, it is argued, they cannot buy back the goods which are produced and the accumulation of these unused stocks finally causes a stoppage of industry which continues until they are unloaded and new orders begin to flow.

[2] Sismondi, Rodbertus, and Marx of course all advanced this view and a modified version of it has been advanced in recent years by Henry Ford.

The chief error in this contention is that it treats the amounts which the workers receive in wages as being identical with the national income. This of course is not true. The owners of capital and land receive interest and rent, and business enterprises receive profits. These, together with wages, make up the national income. These groups, as we have previously pointed out, do not keep their incomes in idleness any more than the workers themselves. Instead they spend part of it on consumers' goods and save the remainder. In either case, they employ workers as surely as do the expenditures of the wage-earners themselves. An increase in the share which they receive and a consequent decrease in the share of labor does not mean, therefore, a permanent increase in unemployment but merely a transfer of workers from industries upon which the workers had spent their money to other industries upon or in which the capitalists are now spending or investing theirs. We are assuming of course in all this that the savings placed in banks are promptly reinvested by them. If a lag develops in this process of reinvestment, then there will be to that extent a decline in monetary purchasing power and probably an increase in unemployment.

PART FOUR

CYCLICAL UNEMPLOYMENT

CHAPTER XIII

BUSINESS CYCLES AND UNEMPLOYMENT

Thus far we have discussed causes of unemployment which operate in much the same fashion from year to year. They account for the presence of a considerable amount of unemployment in normally prosperous years but they do not account for the great changes in the amount of unemployment which occur between closely joined years. We have ignored in other words the business cycle which gives rise to annual fluctuations in production and employment, so that in years of revival and prosperity there is an appreciable decrease in the amount of unemployment, while in years of recession and depression there is an appreciable falling off in production and a great increase in unemployment.

In an economy where each family or minute group consumed what it produced there would be little scope for such fluctuation but the case is otherwise in a society characterized by large scale enterprise, the division of labor, and extensive markets.

Each unit in this intricate structure must estimate with the aid of previous experience, forecasting agencies, and current gossip, the quantities of goods which will be demanded, and at what prices, not at once, but at some future time. In such economies, the course of economic activity is not a smooth one. True, we can still determine statistically the long run normal situation. But an actual index of economic activity winds itself around this normal trend, in some years being below it, and in some above. These fluctuations seem inherent in what Professor Mitchell calls a "business economy." As each new country takes on these characteristics it also experiences these fluctuations.[1]

[1] See Thorpe, *Business Annals.*

1. The Cycle of Economic Activity[2]

A discussion of cyclical fluctuations in industrial activity can run in terms of (a) the initiatory impulses which lead business men to expect greater or smaller profits in the future and thus be encouraged to venture on a policy of expansion or contraction, and (b) the failure of equilibrating forces to bring about adjustments. This last involves a descriptive analysis of the process through which industrial activity runs, indicating the factors which lead to cumulative change in the same direction and then a similar process in the reverse direction, rather than to more immediate adjustments.

Professor Pigou has analyzed the initiating impulses in terms of (a) Real Causes, (b) Psychological Causes, and (c) Monetary Causes. Under the first heading are included variations in the yield of harvests which enable industrialists to trade with the agricultural community on better or worse terms; technical inventions which result in a new or larger product per unit of effort and which enable other groups to obtain better terms of exchange for their products; industrial disputes and their effects on production; net changes in taste or fashion leading to "increased keenness of desire" for some commodities. Under "Psychological Causes" Professor Pigou discusses the errors of optimism and pessimism which are the result of the real causes mentioned above, of monetary changes, and emotional factors. Finally, under monetary factors are the discoveries of gold mines, or improved ways of working existing mines for countries using gold as a monetary medium, and inflationary and deflationary policies in a country with a paper currency.[3]

[2] Cycles differ from each other in the amplitude of their movements. There is some dispute about the absence or presence of periodicity. However, there is sufficient general agreement regarding the main characteristics of these cycles, to justify us in speaking of a cycle of economic activity.

[3] Professor Pigou is usually classed in the Psychological or Emotional School of business cycle theory. But a careful study of his work, especially his recent book on *Industrial Fluctuations,* will show a very comprehensive analysis in which psychological elements play but a single, even though important, part.

Needless to say, there is no method of isolating these various impulses and arranging them in order of importance. In actual economic life they are inextricably mixed and tend to reinforce each other. Attempts to isolate these impulses have resulted in exaggerating the importance of any one—witness the weather theory of Jevons and Moore, or the monetary theory of Hawtrey and Fisher.

We begin, therefore, with any or all of the above factors leading business men to expect greater profits.[4] It will be best to begin when a period of depression has been running its course. Stocks of goods and raw materials have been depleted. The price level has fallen and is low compared with previous years. Costs have been reduced through the forcing out of inefficient business units, the elimination of less efficient workers, the acceptance of smaller margins of profit, and increased efficiency of the salaried and wage-earning staff.[5] Industrial strife is relatively small. The banks have accumulated large reserves and are as yet following conservative policies in granting credit. Technical improvements have accumulated during the depression period.

The accumulated stocks of clothing, furniture, etc., in the hands of consumers begin to get seriously depleted and they commence to buy more. Since retailers' stocks have run low, they are compelled to place larger orders with the wholesalers who in turn must purchase more from the manufacturing concerns which produce consumers' goods. The stocks of these factories have also been virtually exhausted and in order to meet the orders they must hire additional workers. This increases the income in the hands of the

[4] It will be obvious that our description is modeled in many respects upon that of Professor Mitchell in his monumental *Business Cycles*.
[5] It should be pointed out that this last factor has not been fully investigated. The argument runs somewhat as follows. In good times when work is plenty managers and workers become careless. Overtime leads to greater fatigue and less output per hour. Less efficient workers are taken on. On the other hand it is pointed out that in bad times workers are afraid of losing their jobs and are tempted to stretch the work out as long as possible. The whole subject needs further investigation. With it could be studied the social costs in terms of accident rates, demoralization, effects of varying incomes, etc.

workers and leads to a further increase in the demand for consumers' goods. This results in more orders from retail and wholesale establishments and consequently in more orders to the factories and in the employment of still more workers. This still further swells consumer purchasing power and cumulatively expands purchases, orders, production, and employment. The economic mechanism indeed gathers headway in the same cumulative fashion in which it slows up during the recession and depression phases of the cycle.

As orders continue to increase, it becomes necessary to increase the orders for capital equipment and supplies of raw materials. The index of employment rises still further and the volume of goods produced increases. Even though the volume of bank credit begins to increase, there is at first no increase in wholesale prices. When the index of wholesale prices does begin to rise, it at first rises at a relatively lower rate than the employment index. But there are real limits to increases in the employment index. Gradually the employable workers are all absorbed, and the employment index must remain stationary while the wholesale price index continues to go upward.

Instead of receiving a check the revived activity is diffused throughout the economic structure. An increased labor force at the same or higher wage rates means a larger aggregate wage expenditure. This means a further increase in the quantity of consumers' goods demanded. Business men become more optimistic regarding future prospects. To quote Professor Mitchell: "The improving state of trade will produce a more cheerful state of mind among business men and the more cheerful state of mind will give fresh impetus to the improvement in trade." [6] Enterprises faced with increasing orders which can only be filled by buying

---

[6] *Business Cycles and Unemployment*, p. 8. In Professor Mitchell's analysis of the business cycle, the whole process is more or less automatic, and is accelerated or retarded by outside events such as harvests, political events, etc. Professor Pigou on the other hand emphasizes these outside events and impulses from within which alter the business men's expectations of profits and so lead fluctuations above or below normal. He recognizes, of course, the reinforcing factors which come from the economic process once the business man begins to act in response to these impulses.

new equipment and hiring additional untrained help, hold out for higher prices. And as the banks increase their loans, and as there is not a corresponding increase in the volume of goods produced and sold, the price level begins and continues to go up.

At once a complicating factor is introduced. Once prices begin to increase, there is a general expectancy of their continued rise. Merchants become anxious to increase their stocks of goods which are now at low prices and sell them at higher prices. Producers become anxious to increase their stocks of raw materials. This leads to a greater demand for credit from the banks and a further increase in the price level.

It has often been noted that the price system does not rise and fall at the same rate throughout its various branches. Thus wholesale prices of raw materials rise sooner and fluctuate more violently than prices of finished goods. This factor alone, aside from elements of cost other than raw materials, would act as a check to expansion. There are, however, two further considerations. The productive process takes time. Hence in a period of rising prices when further increases are expected, business men expect both the prices of raw materials and finished goods to be higher than they now are. There is haste, therefore, to buy large stocks of raw materials at existing prices and sell the finished products at a later time at still higher prices.

If the various elements of the price level rose at the same time and at the same rates, there would clearly be no advantage to any group. But a great many of the economic transactions are in the form of contracts for more or less long periods of time. Under rising prices there results a bounty to the business interests at the expense of other groups. Thus enterprises having loans at a certain rate of interest will pay less in real terms for interest and principal under a rising price level.[7] The same sort of gain results

[7] This is true only if both sides to the transactions did not correctly anticipate the price increase. Professor Pigou stresses the fact that both sides underestimate price increases and overestimate price falls.

from the fact that wage rates are fairly sluggish and often fixed by contracts for fairly long periods of time.[8]

Even were there no real gains to business men as a result of rising prices, the fact that people think in terms of money and not in ultimate terms of goods, would lead them to attempt an anticipation of price increases, and the very anticipation would bring them about.

The gains resulting from the divergence of price movements noted above, and the increased volume of goods turned out means increased profits leading to further expansion of investments. Gradually the revival in business activity is turned into a period of prosperity. In the words of Professor Mitchell: "Not only does every increase in the physical volume of trade cause other increases, every convert to optimism make new converts, and every advance of price furnish an incentive for fresh advances, but the growth of trade helps to spread optimism and to raise prices, while optimism and rising prices both support each other and stimulate the growth of trade. Finally, as has just been said, the changes going forward in these three factors swell profits and encourage investments, while high profits and heavy investments react by augumenting trade, justifying optimism, and raising prices." [9]

How far can such a process continue? Sooner or later, there appear certain tendencies which impede further expansion and start a downward movement. First is the cost element. Once existing plants are operated to capacity any further expansion means new equipment at a higher price level. Very often marginal equipment is brought into use. Labor costs also are increased because of increased wage rates for normal hours and because of increased overtime with resulting high hourly rates. At the same time the average efficiency of labor—for reasons noted elsewhere—declines.

Another check is to be found in the credit situation. The

---

[8] This is a practice which is spreading in the organized trades in the United States.

[9] *Business Cycles and Unemployment*, p. 10.

demand for bank credit increases with the increased volume of goods and with the advance in prices.[10] But the volume of bank credit is not an unlimited quantity. The existing reserves, and the legal and customary restrictions, soon lead to increased discount rates and to a check of further expansion.

It was noted earlier that, after a period of expansion when the available working force is employed, the index of production ceases to rise. Any further expansion is, therefore, purely speculative in character. Orders are given for goods which will not be purchased by consumers within any normal period. Prices continue to rise. Just as soon as there is a check to the increased quantity of consumers' goods demanded, there is a real decline in the producers' goods industries. As orders decline, and profits are threatened, there is the beginning of recognition that prosperity may not last forever. Business men become cautious in granting additional credit to their customers and press for payment of outstanding obligations. Any weak members of the series are caught and their fortunes affect the fortunes of others. Once begun the process of liquidation spreads over the entire economic machine, because of the interdependence of enterprises and industries. The spirit of pessimism spreads as rapidly as did that of optimism. Existing orders are worked off and a part of the working force is laid off. The anxiety to sell in order to maintain solvency leads to a fall in the price of commodities. At times this passing of the peak in economic activity is spectacular with bank and business failures in newspaper headlines. More recently, reforms in banking policy have resulted in liquidation in a quieter manner, but with equally severe effects on the work-

[10] Mr. Carl Snyder has suggested and offered statistical evidence to show that the increased velocity of bank deposits just about takes care of the increased volume of trade and that fluctuations in prices are equal to fluctuations in the volume of credit. See New Measures in the Equation of Exchange, *American Economic Review*, December, 1924; *Business Cycles and Business Measurements*, Ch. VII, pp. 144-54. Professor Edie and Mr. Donald Weaver have recently produced additional evidence that this is also probably true for England despite the contrary position of Professor Pigou. Velocity of Bank Deposits in England, *Journal of Political Economy*, August, 1930, pp. 373-403.

ing population. The period of depression covers the entire business field, just as did that of expansion. The discharge of workers in some industries, reduces the aggregate wage bill and hence the demand for goods in other industries. This in turn leads to a contraction in the demand for raw materials. At each step in the decline more workers are laid off and there is further contraction of the demand for goods. As the physical volume of trade declines, there is great competition for new orders to utilize existing equipment. This leads to a reduction in prices accentuated by a reduction in the volume of credit. Declining prices lead to expectation of further declines. Just as there was a gain from past contracts, during a period of rising prices, so is there a loss during periods of falling prices.

Very gradually existing stocks of goods are exhausted, inefficient firms are squeezed out, the efficiency of labor is increased, other costs are reduced. Any new impulses which lead business men to expect greater profits will again begin a period of revival for which the surrounding circumstances are again favorable.

2. The Magnified Fluctuations of Industries Producing Capital Goods

Thus far we have made no distinction between the various industries. But one of the characteristics of cyclical fluctuations is that while they affect the entire economy at the same time, they do not affect the various industries to the same extent. It used to be the custom to plot series of pig iron production, remove the trend, and take the resulting fluctuations as measures of general fluctuations. The accumulation of statistical material has pointed out that the fluctuations in the entire economy are not as great, and that the amplitude of fluctuation varies from industry to industry.[11]

---

[11] An antidote to the exaggerated idea of general fluuctuations will be found in Mr. Carl Snyder's recent book, *Business Cycles and Business Measurements.*

A distinction which has always been recognized is the difference between producers' goods industries and consumers' goods industries. The fact that the former expand first, fluctuate more violently, and recede first, has been the occasion for theories of the business cycle in terms of causes originating in these industries.[12] Professor J. M. Clark has, however, demonstrated that because of the technical character of production inherent in our economic structure, the initiating causes can come from consumers' goods industries and still be consistent with the actual facts noted above.[13] The increase in the equipment industries is a function of the rate of increase of demand in the consumers' goods industries. It is, therefore, possible for the demand for consumers' goods to increase but at a decreasing rate and for the equipment industries to show an actual decrease at the same time. The result would, therefore, appear to be its own cause. Professor Mitchell has worked out an arithmetical illustration which is worth reproducing. Suppose the physical quantity of any product varies as follows:

First Year	100,000 tons
Second Year	95,000 tons
Third Year	100,000 tons
Fourth Year	110,000 tons
Fifth Year	115,000 tons

This product is turned out by machines each of which turns out one hundred tons a year. The number of machines in operation will, therefore, be as follows:

First Year	1000 Machines
Second Year	950 Machines
Third Year	1000 Machines
Fourth Year	1100 Machines
Fifth Year	1150 Machines

If one-tenth of the machines wear out each year, the replacement demand is as follows:

[12] For a consideration of the untenable nature of this view, see Pigou, *Industrial Fluctuations*, Ch. IX.
[13] Business Acceleration and the Law of Demand, *Journal of Political Economy*, March, 1917.

First Year . . . . 100 Machines
Second Year . . . . 95 Machines
Third Year . . . . 100 Machines
Fourth Year . . . . 110 Machines
Fifth Year . . . . 115 Machines

But the demand for additional machines was far more variable as shown by the following:

First Year . . . . no data
Second Year . . . . none
Third Year . . . . none
Fourth Year . . . . 100 machines
Fifth Year . . . . 50 machines

Adding the two together we get

First Year . . . . no data
Second Year . . . . 95 machines
Third Year 100   "
Fourth Year 210   "
Fifth Year 165   "

Hence small fluctuations in the demand for final goods are accompanied by large fluctuations in the demand for equipment.[14]

The differences in the extent of fluctuations can be seen in the table on the opposite page, showing changes in employment during the recent depression.[15] Thus whether the comparison be on the basis of the numbers employed, or the amounts of the payroll, the decline is very great in the equipment industries, such as lumber, stone, clay, iron and steel, etc., and least in food, leather, paper and printing, etc. Exceptions there are, but additional information would no doubt disclose the reason as in the case of textiles which have been in an unusually depressed state for some time.

These differences in the incidence of unemployment are especially significant for a policy directed at reduction of cyclical fluctuations or maintenance of the unemployed through unemployment insurance.

[14] *Business Cycles and Unemployment*, pp. 12-13.
[15] *Monthly Labor Review*, August, 1930, p. 190.

PER CENT OF CHANGE JUNE, 1930, COMPARED WITH JUNE, 1929

	NUMBER ON PAYROLL	AMOUNT OF PAYROLL
Food and Kindred Products	− 3.6	− 3.0
Textiles and their Products	− 13.5	− 20.2
Lumber and its Products	− 20.3	− 22.8
Leather and its Products	− 5.5	− 17.7
Paper and Printing	− 1.6	− 1.5
Chemicals and Allied Products	− 4.9	− 4.4
Stone, Clay and Glass Products	− 14.1	− 17.7
Metal Products other than Iron and Steel . .	− 18.3	− 24.8
Tobacco Products	− 2.5	− 4.6
Vehicles for land transportation	− 19.8	− 24.3
Miscellaneous	− 16.8	− 18.0
Agricultural Implements	− 27.9	− 38.1
Electrical Machinery, Apparatus and Supplies	− 16.9	− 15.9
Pianos and Organs	− 29.6	− 37.2
Rubber Boots and Shoes	− 20.1	− 28.1
Automobile Tires	− 24.4	− 26.5
Shipbuilding	+ 9.2	+ 5.1
All Industries	− 13.5	− 18.2

As a corollary of the differences in the fluctuations between industries are the differences between various areas within a country. The following table indicates the extent of these differences in the recent depression in the United States.[16]

PER CENT OF CHANGE JUNE, 1930, COMPARED WITH JUNE, 1929

	NUMBER ON PAYROLL	AMOUNT OF PAYROLL
New England	− 13.7	− 20.9
Middle Atlantic	− 11.9	− 16.2
East North Central	− 18.5	− 24.1
West North Central	− 9.6	− 11.9
South Atlantic	− 8.4	− 11.3
West South Central	− 10.5	− 7.8
Mountain	− 12.3	− 11.6
Pacific	− 14.6	− 13.4
UNITED STATES	− 13.5	− 18.2

[16] *Ibid.*, p. 190.

These differences are especially significant for a policy of planned public work, as the provision of work must not only be allocated to satisfy time requirements, but also place requirements.

3. Some Current Theories of the Business Cycle

While the current theories of business cycles are many, they are not as divergent as the literature would imply. What usually happens is that each writer in addition to pointing out the various processes involved singles out some one as the predominant and critical factor.[17]

From the very beginning of the discussion on business cycles, weather has held a very important position as a causal factor. The distinguished American economist who has developed this view is Professor Henry L. Moore, who finds main cycles of thirty-three years and secondary cycles of eight years in rainfall and hence in yield per acre. He then finds a high degree of correlation between these fluctuations and those of business activity. Setting aside the question of whether changes in harvests are the initiating causes of industrial fluctuation, there is little doubt that they can affect the behavior of business men.

The other theories fall into two main groups. There are those who find the source of industrial fluctuations in the existing institutions of production and consumption—some emphasizing the one and some the other. Others seek the causes in the existing monetary and banking institutions. There are many variations of each, and a few examples will suffice.

One of the theories which emphasizes the productive process is that of Professor Schumpeter who finds in the innovations of the enterprising business man an explanation of the business cycle. Any condition of equilibrium is disturbed by a process of expansion initiated by the few ener-

[17] Summaries of Business Cycle Theories will be found in Edward D. Jones, *Economic Crises* (1910); Alvin H. Hansen, *Business Cycle Theory* (1927); Wesley C. Mitchell, *Business Cycles, The Problem and Its Setting*, (National Bureau of Economic Research, 1927).

getic business men who apply existing and new scientific discoveries, work out new forms of organization, press upon the old markets new products, and extend existing markets. The period of expansion thus initiated ends in increased prices and costs and sooner or later a break takes place. The succeeding period of depression again leads to a condition of equilibrium which is again disturbed. The periodicity of the innovations is explained by the fact that, while the quality characteristic of the innovator is rare, imitation is fairly simple and the few carry the many with them.

A variation of the explanation in terms of the productive process is that which finds the source of fluctuations in recurring periods of general overproduction. Professor Albert Aftalion is a leading exponent of this position. Any rise in the price level after a period of depression leads business men to the view that the demand for consumers' goods is larger than the current supply at the former prices. They are therefore encouraged to increase their orders for equipment which in turn leads to an increase in employment, a stimulation of demand for consumers' goods and further increases in orders for equipment. But the construction of these takes much time. During the interval the period of expansion reigns supreme. When, however, the orders for equipment are filled and these begin to add to the stream of final goods, the quantity of these cannot be sold at prevailing prices. It then becomes apparent that general overproduction prevails.[18] Prices fall and there is no inducement to buy new equipment. As the demand for consumers' goods continues to grow the whole process is repeated.

Another variation of the theory is that which explains fluctuations in terms of savings and investments. Professor Tugan-Baranovsky and John A. Hobson are among the leading exponents of this view. According to the latter there is always an exact proportion between the income which is necessary for new capital and that for current con-

---

[18] This is overproduction, however, in terms of a given price level. The goods can be sold but only at a lower price level.

sumption. If this proportion were constantly retained there would be no occasion for fluctuations. But the existing distribution of wealth means that the income of the few who own a very large proportion of the wealth increases much faster than does their consumption. The excess is saved and invested. This leads to a further increase in the income of the few and further savings and investments. As the supply of goods increases the markets are flooded and prices must fall. Hence the incomes of the wealthy few are now reduced. savings fall below the correct proportion, and the markets are cleared. In time there is improvement and the whole process is repeated.

The other outstanding group of explanations of business cycles runs in terms of monetary and banking institutions, especially the latter. The expansion of credit leads to a rise in prices and a redistribution of purchasing power in favor of the business class. This in turn leads to increased activity and a further expansion of bank credit. There comes a time, however, when banks, looking to their reserves, must deny any further extension of credit and actually must contract the existing volume. This leads to a fall in the price level, and a contraction in the demand for bank credit. With a fall in the volume of trade there is a further decline in the demand for credit and a further fall in the price level. In either case the process is cumulative both upward and downward.

It is apparent that the emphasis on monetary factors lends itself the more readily to remedies than does the emphasis on the productive process. To approach remedies in terms of the latter explanation would involve some form of reorganization in the whole economy. Before, however, we turn to monetary remedies it is well to review both the influences of long-time price movements on cyclical fluctuations and the possible ways of counteracting the effects of cyclical fluctuations on unemployment.

CHAPTER XIV

PRODUCTION, THE GOLD SUPPLY, LONG-TIME PRICE MOVEMENTS AND UNEMPLOYMENT

1. There is one way in which technical improvements and savings do at times help to cause and to prolong business depressions and consequently to create unemployment. This is when they cause the volume of goods produced in society as a whole to increase faster than the supply of money and credit and therefore cause an inevitable fall in the general price level.

Such a fall in the price level has until recently been regarded by economists as having little effect upon business. But this ignores the fact that production takes time and that in a period of falling prices, businesses will be buying raw materials and hiring labor at an earlier and higher price level to be sold as finished commodities at a later and lower price level. There will thus be a shrinkage of monetary values during the process of production. This will be particularly serious for the industrialists since they will normally borrow money from banks to pay for their purchases of raw material and labor and will be compelled to pay this back from a shrinking sales price. Such a shrinkage of prices causes a greatly magnified relative decline in profits. For if the costs of production of an article which formerly sold for $1.04 are $1.00, then a fall of 4 per cent in prices will eliminate all profits.

In such a period, businesses will be producing more goods than before but profit margins will be rapidly shrinking and, in an increasing percentage of the cases, losses will result. Industrialists will, in consequence, be reluctant to go forward in the face of this continuous fall in values during the process of manufacture. They will instead tend to hold back until they believe commodity prices have reached the bottom when they can purchase large quantities of raw material with safety. But holding back and curtailing operations means that they must lay off men and work a smaller total number of hours. This in turn means that the workers with diminished earnings cannot buy as much from retail stores. The retail stores in consequence will not be able to purchase as much from wholesalers. The purchases of the retailers will, as a matter of fact, decline at an even greater ratio than their sales, since they will be living off their stocks. Wholesalers will sharply reduce their orders to manufacturing concerns and these hard-pressed enterprises will be forced to lay off more men. The diminished purchasing power of the workers will still further reduce the sales of merchants and will start a new cumulative decline of sales, employment, and purchasing power.

In such a condition there is a progressive breakdown of business, which in its cumulative process is essentially similar to that of a forest fire. Such a fire heats the immediate atmosphere, causing the hot air to rise. Colder air rushes in to fill the vacuum and creates a wind which fans the flames. This creates more of wind and this in turn heightens the fire until other forces may check its further expansion.

It is not pretended that this is the sole cause of business depressions but it is a factor which can initiate a period of depression and accentuate one initiated by other factors. One way of testing it is to measure the relative duration of business depressions in periods of falling prices as compared with periods of rising prices. The twenty-four years from 1873 to 1896 were ones in which the American wholesale price level fell by approximately 45 per cent. According to Dr. Willard Thorpe's excellent study, fourteen of these years or 60 per cent of the total were depression or recession years.[1] During the next twenty-four years, from 1897 to 1920 inclusive, the depression and recession years numbered six, only 25 per cent of the total.[2] These great differences

[1] Willard L. Thorpe, *Business Annals*, pp. 131-37.
[2] *Ibid.*, pp. 137-43.

should be proof of the depressive influence of a downward tendency in the price level and of the stimulation given by a rise in general prices.

The effect of deflation in most of the European countries during the last decade furnishes further corroboration of this thesis. When England's return to the gold standard in 1925 necessitated a fall of 10 per cent in her price level, the result was an appreciable increase in unemployment,[3] and the same result followed when Czecho-Slovakia deflated its currency and caused its price level to fall.[4]

If the supply of money and credit were to increase commensurately with the increase in production, the price level would be held constant and the goods produced would be sold at prices which would permit industry to go on with undiminished profits and without curtailment of activity.

But unfortunately an increase in the supply of goods does not necessarily give rise to a corresponding increase in the quantity of money and credit. The supply of the latter is controlled by other forces, namely the rate of increase in the world's gold supply and the banking structure and policies of the various countries.

It was because the world's supply of gold was increasing less rapidly during the period from 1873 to 1896 than was the production of goods that the secular fall occurred in the price level; while the rapid increase in gold production during the years from 1896 to 1915,[5] together with the improvement of world banking facilities which permitted more credit to be created from a given gold base, caused prices to increase by approximately 46 per cent.[6]

While the rate of gold production slackened during the war, the issuance of irredeemable paper money by the governments and the expansion of bank credit caused prices to rise greatly. After the war, inflation in Austria, Germany,

[3] See J. M. Keynes, *The Economic Consequences of Mr. Churchill.*
[4] H. G. Moulton, Economic Conditions in Europe, *American Economic Review*, March, 1923, pp. 48–49.
[5] In 1915, the world's production of gold was 470.0 millions of dollars or approximately 22.8 million ounces as opposed to 111.0 millions of dollars and 5.3 million ounces in 1890.
[6] Carl Snyder, *Business Cycles and Business Measurements*, p. 286.

and France caused still further rises in prices but by the present time virtually all of the countries have returned to either the gold or the gold-exchange standard.

2. The question is then squarely raised whether the probable future gold supply will be adequate to maintain the present world price level. Prof. Cassel has computed that the average annual increase in the quantity of gold from 1850 to 1910 was 2.8 per cent. Since the price level was approximately the same in these two years, he estimated that this was the "normal" rate of increase in the gold supply which was needed to maintain prices at a constant level.[7] This estimate rested on two assumptions, (1) that the increase in the volume of production would remain the same and (2) that the rate of economizing in the use of gold and of building more credit upon a given gold base would also remain the same.

Let us now turn to the question whether the present increase in the monetary stock of gold is sufficient to balance the probable increase in production and thus keep the price level constant. According to the estimates of L. D. Edie, the total stock of gold in the world in 1928 which was used for monetary purposes was 10.7 billions of dollars,[8] or approximately 520 millions of ounces.

If we assume that an increase of 2.8 per cent in the stock of gold is needed annually as from 1850 to 1910 to balance the increase in production, this would necessitate an addition at the present time of almost precisely 300 million dollars to the monetary supply of gold or approximately 14.6 million ounces of gold a year.

The production of gold in the world during the four years 1924-27 was at the average rate of approximately 19.3 million ounces or 399 million dollars a year.[9] This at first

[7] Cassel, *The Theory of Social Economy*, pp. 441-54.
[8] L. D. Edie, *Capital, the Money Market and Gold*, p. 39. The non-monetary stock of gold was estimated at 8.9 billions of dollars. For Edie's methods see his *Gold Production and Prices Before and After the World War* (University of Indiana Studies, 1928).
[9] *Official Yearbook of South Africa*, 1927-28, p. 502. The production by years was:

| 1924 | 19.0 mill. oz. | 1926 | 19.5 mill. oz. |
| 1925 | 19.1 " " | 1927 | 19.6 " " |

thought would seem to be amply sufficient, unless production were to rise much more rapidly than its long-time average. But this ignores the demand for gold in the arts and the hoarding of gold by Indians and other Orientals. The average consumption of gold in the arts for the five years, 1920-24, has been estimated at approximately 85 millions of dollars or 4.1 million ounces. This was approximately 30 per cent less than the average for the five years, 1909-1914, when it amounted to approximately 118 million dollars or 5.7 million ounces. The maintenance of the 1920-24 rate of consumption would in itself leave the remainder barely sufficient to meet the assumed requirement of around 14.6 million ounces, and the return to pre-war standards of consumption would bring the annual increment down below this figure.

In addition to all this, however, should be set the hoarding of gold in India. This averaged approximately 100 millions of dollars a year or 4.9 million ounces during the years 1919-24.[10] This left only from 8.7 to 10.3 million ounces (from 180 to 214 millions of dollars) of gold available annually for monetary purposes, and caused an increase in the monetary supply of only 1.7 or 2.0 per cent a year.

Many economists, including J. M. Keynes and Sir Henry Strakosch, attribute the world-wide depression, which began in 1929 and which is still continuing, to the fact that the world's monetary stock of gold increased at only this rate during the last few years while the world's production of food and raw materials, as shown by the index of the League of Nations, increased at between three and four per cent a year. In addition to this, the effect of the large gold movements to our Federal Reserve Banks and to the Bank of France resulted in large quantities being sterilized and caused a still further reduction in the price level. It is probable that these factors hastened the depression and deepened its intensity. It cannot be considered the sole cause of the depression, however, since periods of

[10] L. D. Edie, *Money, Bank Credit and Prices,* p. 258.

rising prices also have some, although fewer, depression years.

If the present rates of increase of gold and of goods continue, and if other factors do not change, it would seem that we may expect for the near future a decline in the price level of between one and two per cent a year.

Does such a prediction, however, rest upon so many highly dubious assumptions as to render any conclusion ridiculous? Prophecy is extremely hazardous, but we can make some progress towards understanding probable future trends if we consider each of the possibilities in turn.

First, is there any likelihood that the future production of gold will appreciably increase? The Rand mines outside of Johannesburg in the Transvaal are the center of the industry and now produce slightly over half of the world's gold. These mines are rapidly being depleted and the Government Mining Engineer in 1927 [11] estimated their probable annual crushing capacity for the succeeding fifteen years as follows:

Year	Crushing Capacity of Mines (in million tons)	Relative Capacity (1926 = 100)
1926	28.8	100
1931	25.8	90
1936	14.5	50
1941	6.3	22

According to this estimate, therefore, the producing capacity of the existing African mines would diminish by approximately one-half within the next five years, and in ten years, their output would be less than a quarter of that of 1927.

In a subsequent memorandum, the Government Mining Engineer estimated that the various mines would last for from three to four years longer than had been predicted and that the serious falling off in the production of gold

[11] *Official Yearbook of South Africa*, 1927-28, p. 505. This estimate was based on the then existing price level.

would be postponed until 1935 with the approximate low point being reached in 1946.[12]

Nor is it probable that an adequate number of new mines can be opened in the Rand to make good this ultimate depletion. The mining possibilities of this territory are now fairly well known and the efficiency of mining has been carried to such a point that it is difficult to conceive how ores of any appreciably lower grade could be mined profitably. The average amount of gold contained in each ton of ore mined in 1927 was only $6.95, almost precisely one-third of an ounce.[13] It would seem dubious that profitable mining can be pushed much beyond the point where the gold content of ore is only 1 to 80,000. It is therefore unwise to expect a permanent increase in supply from the Transvaal while the probabilities are that there will be an actual decrease.

The quantity of gold mined in other regions of the world has already decreased from 14.4 million ounces in 1913 to 9.5 million ounces in 1927, a relative decline of about one-third.[14] While it is always possible that new and large deposits may be discovered, this becomes more unlikely as the amount of unexplored territory diminishes. While mining engineers have by no means mapped the earth's surface, there would seem to be less possibility for new finds than existed during the last half of the nineteenth century when California, Australia, the Klondike, and South Africa were being opened up.

The probabilities are, therefore, that the annual increase of the world's gold supply will tend to slacken in the future. In view of the fact that the amount of the total gold supply will be increasing, this will mean a still further reduction in the *rate* of growth below the 2.8 or 3.0 per cent which

[12] See memorandum by Dr. H. Pirow in the *Interim Report of the Gold Delegation of the Financial Committee of the League of Nations* (1930), pp. 23-24. These estimates were based upon 1929 costs of production. A fall in the general price level and hence in the costs of production would prolong the life of the mines.

[13] These are average gold contents. The ratio is slightly less than this on the Old Rand and about 30 per cent more on the New Rand.

[14] *Official Yearbook of South Africa*, 1927-28, p. 502.

was needed from 1850 to 1910 to keep the price level constant.

Three further possibilities remain. First, will the general increase in production during the next decade or so be as great as during the sixty years preceding the World War? The rate of population growth, one factor in this increase, is, of course, appreciably slackening, but the index of production itself shows no sign of a secular slowing up. The increase in output during the years 1921-24 was, in fact, particularly marked. The pressure for an increased monetary supply is therefore likely to be as great in the future as it has been in the past.

Secondly, will any fall in the world price level be ultimately and automatically compensatory in its nature by stimulating the production of gold and by reducing its commercial use? That some such balancing will result is undeniable. Lower prices mean lower costs and lower costs permit the profitable mining of still lower grade ores.[15] The result would be that the production of gold would tend to rise above what it otherwise would have been and the rate of reduction in the price level would at the very least be dampened. Similarly, since gold is the only commodity whose price is fixed and constant, the fall in the general price level would mean a rise in its value per unit. This would normally cause a reduction in the relative quantity demanded in the arts and hence would release for monetary purposes a larger proportion of the annual increment which is mined. But it is extremely doubtful whether the elasticity of supply of gold together with the elasticity of the commercial demand for gold are such as to keep the annual rate of increase in the monetary stock of gold at a constant percentage. It should moreover be remembered that even the present rate of increase has apparently been insufficient to maintain a stable level of prices.

Thirdly, will the increasing development of our banking

[15] Dr. H. Pirow has estimated that a fall of 50 cents a ton in the cost of production would permit South African mines to keep output on its present level for about ten or twelve years. *Interim Report of the Gold Delegation, op. cit.*, p. 23.

institutions and their ability to create an ever increasing amount of credit upon a given gold base offset these tendencies for prices to fall? It should be borne in mind, however, that as a result of the war virtually all of the monetary gold has now passed out of circulation and is already used as a reserve for credit operations. While the use of checks will doubtless spread, it is difficult to see how the growth of this practice can be any more rapid than it was during the sixty years before the war. And during that period it required the expansion of credit as well as the "normal" increase of gold to keep prices constant.

The Gold Delegation of the League of Nations in its Interim Report [16] has drawn up estimates of the probable future production of gold, the probable demand for nonmonetary uses, and the quantities which will be needed to keep the price level constant under assumptions of (1) reserve ratios of 33 and 40 per cent respectively of gold for bank notes and liabilities payable at sight, (2) annual rates of increase in the production of goods of 2 and 3 per cent respectively. We choose the illustration of a 40 per cent reserve since that approximates the requirements and practices of modern banking.

It is thus apparent that according to this method of estimation there will be an appreciable deficit of gold during the decade which is to come.

Dangerous as prophecies are, therefore, the probabilities seem to indicate a slow secular decline in the price level during at least the next decade. If this is the case, the average amount of unemployment, for the reasons which we have already developed, bids fair to increase during the coming ten years.

If such are the probabilities, what, if anything, can be done to prevent them from taking their course? One suggestion that has been advanced is that the nations of the world should impose a heavy tax upon the commercial uses of gold. This, it is argued, would lead to a decrease in the quantity consumed in the arts and would release a larger

[16] Interim Report of the Gold Delegation, *op. cit.*, p. 16.

TABLE 13

ESTIMATES BY GOLD DELEGATION OF THE LEAGUE OF NATIONS OF RELATIVE
ADEQUACY OF FUTURE MONETARY SUPPLY OF GOLD IF NO ECONOMY IS
MADE IN ITS USE.

(In millions of dollars)

YEAR	ESTI-MATED GOLD PRODUC-TION (1)	ESTI-MATED NON-MONE-TARY DEMAND[1] (2)	AVAIL-ABLE FOR MONE-TARY PUR-POSES (3) = (1) − (2)	INCREMENTS REQUIRED TO PROVIDE 40% RESERVE FOR NOTES AND SIGHT LIA-BILITIES IF WORLD IN-CREASE IN OUTPUT EQUALS		EXCESS ON DEFICIT IN AMOUNT OF NEW MONE-TARY GOLD ON BASIS OF 40% COVERAGE IF WORLD INCREASE IN OUTPUT EQUALS	
				2% Annual-ly (4A)	3% Annual-ly (4B)	2 Per Cent (5A) = (3) − (4A)	3 Per Cent (5B) = 3 − (4B)
1930	404	180	224	200	303	+ 24	− 79
1931	402	182	220	204	313	+ 16	− 93
1932	410	184	226	209	323	+ 17	− 97
1933	407	186	221	213	332	+ 8	− 111
1934	403	188	215	217	341	− 2	− 126
1935	398	190	208	221	352	− 13	− 144
1936	397	192	205	226	363	− 21	− 158
1937	392	194	198	230	373	− 32	− 175
1938	384	196	188	235	385	− 47	− 197
1939	370	198	172	240	396	− 68	− 224
1940	370	200	170	244	408	− 74	− 238

[1] On the assumption that the non-monetary demand for gold increases at the rate of 1 per
cent a year.

amount for monetary use. While this proposal seems plausible, it would lead to gold having a higher price as a commercial commodity than as money. A tax of 100 per cent,
for example, would raise the price of fresh gold to the consumers from $20.67 to $41.34 an ounce. This would inevitably cause speculators to present gold certificates and
bank-notes for redemption in gold and then have these
coins made up surreptitiously for the various commercial
uses. While the government might try to control the
situation by a licensing system and by heavy penalties,
considerable "bootlegging" of gold would occur. This, by
diminishing the gold reserves, would go far to nullify the
results which the advocates of this increase hope to obtain.

In a subsequent chapter, we shall describe the alternative
methods which we propose for stabilizing the price level,

but since these involve controlling the cyclical as well as the secular fluctuations in prices, we must postpone our analysis until after we have discussed the more immediate remedies for cyclical fluctuations.

CHAPTER XV

PUBLIC WORKS AND CYCLICAL FLUCTUATIONS IN UNEMPLOYMENT [1]

1. The Proposal

The nineteenth century was replete with attempts on the part of public authorities to provide work for the unemployed. The Poor Law Commission (1908) exhaustively reviewed the British experience and condemned it in no uncertain terms on the grounds that the provision of relief works at no time succeeded in putting to work a significant percentage of the unemployed, the policy of payment demoralized the workers, the cost was extremely great, the work done was generally worthless.

But Professor Bowley in his testimony before the Commission outlined a general policy of allocating expenditures on public works which would be subject to none of the above objections and suggested four principles which would eliminate the unsatisfactory aspects of previous experience:

"(a) The work concerned would be started before Unemployment became acute, say, when the Percentage Unemployed Index reached 4 per cent.

(b) There would be no artificial demand made for labor, only an adjustment in time of ordinary demand.

(c) The Unemployed as a class would not be attracted, for the demand would come through ordinary trade sources, and before there was any considerable dearth of employment.

(d) The wages paid would be measured only by the work

---

[1] The discussion which follows is limited to unemployment resulting from cyclical fluctuations. Custom and the vagaries of the weather have made a seasonal industry out of public construction, synchronizing with general construction. Hence at present the proposal of a flexible system of public works cannot be used to reduce seasonal fluctuations.

done being contracted out on the ordinary commercial basis." [2]

This proposal of Professor Bowley was endorsed by the Minority Members of the Poor Law Commission and "Regularization of demand" became one of the major reforms in the Minority Report. The enthusiastic description has never been excelled and is worth quoting at length: "We think that there can be no doubt that, out of the 150 millions sterling annually expended by the national and local authorities on works and services, it would be possible to earmark at least four millions a year, as not to be undertaken equally, year by year, as a matter of course; but to be undertaken, out of loan, on a ten years' programme, at unequal annual rates, to the extent even of ten or fifteen millions in a single year, at those periods when the National Labor Exchange reported that the number of able-bodied applicants, for whom no places could be found anywhere within the United Kingdom, was rising above the normal level." When this report was made the ten year program would be invoked: "the Admiralty would put in hand a special battleship, and augment its stock of guns and projectiles; the War Office would give orders for some of the additional barracks that are always being needed, and would further replenish its multifarious stores; the Office of Works would get on more quickly with its perpetual task of erecting new post offices and other Government buildings, and of renewing the worn-out furniture; the Post Office would proceed at three or four times its accustomed rate with the extension of the telegraph and telephone to every village and kingdom, even the Stationery Office would get on two or three times as fast as usual with the printing of the volumes of the Historical Manuscripts Commission, and the publication of national archives. But much more could be done. It is plain that many millions have to be spent in the next few decades in rebuilding the

[2] Sidney and Beatrice Webb (editors), *The Public Organization of the Labour Market, Being Part Two of the Minority Report of the Poor Law Commission*, p. 283.

worst of the elementary schools, greatly adding to the number of the secondary schools, multiplying the technical institutes and training colleges, and doubling and trebling the accommodation and equipment of our fifteen universities. All this building and furnishing work, on which alone we might usefully spend the forty millions per decade that are in question, is not in fact and need not be for efficiency, due in equal annual installments. There might well be a ten years' programme of capital Grants-in-aid of the local expenditure on educational buildings and equipment. . . . At the same time the local authorities could be incited to undertake their ordinary municipal undertakings of a capital nature, whether tramways or waterworks, public baths or electric power stations, artisan dwellings or Town Halls, drainage works or street improvements, to a greater extent in the years of slackness than in the years of good trade." [3]

In recent years the proposal has been widely discussed. It was endorsed by the President's Conference on Unemployment (1921), it formed part of Lloyd George's election program of 1928, and more recently President Hoover urged both public authorities and private industry to speed their construction work in order to alleviate the present depression.[4] It is thus passing out of the period of discussion into that of action. It is our opinion that current hopes are greatly exaggerated and that the possibilities of using public expenditures to smooth out the fluctuations of private industry are subject to serious limitations.[5]

[3] Webb, *op. cit.*, pp. 282-83.

[4] There is at present a bill before Congress to establish a reserve fund of 150 million dollars to be used in periods of depression for public works planned in advance.

[5] On the whole, the writers discussing public works and cyclical fluctuations have been extremely optimistic. This was true not only of Professor Bowley in his testimony before the Poor Law Commission (1908) and of the Minority Report of that Commission (1909) but also of Professor Bowley and Mr. F. D. Stuart in a more recent examination of the problem, *Is Unemployment Inevitable?* pp. 366-82. See also Otto T. Mallery in *Business Cycles and Unemployment,* pp. 231-61; Vernon Arthur Mund. Prosperity Reserves of Public Works, *Annals of the American Academy of Political and Social Science,* Vol. CXLIX, Part II. Professor Dickinson has also expressed sanguine hopes: "In conclusion, it is repeated: that the

2. The Argument

At the present time public authorities follow the practice of individual enterprises in constructing works as the occasion arises. This means that in times of business prosperity, when the existing facilities are heavily taxed and when public officials are imbued with the same optimistic expectations of the future as the average business man, expenditures for public construction are greatly increased. And it is in times of depression that such expenditures are reduced. Hence not only do the public authorities do nothing to alleviate the unemployment situation, but actually aggravate the problem by bidding for labor in times of expansion and reducing the demand for labor in times of contraction. In other words, the demand of public authorities for labor is fluctuating, thus contributing to cyclical unemployment and at the same time reinforcing the fluctuations of private enterprise.[6]

volume of public construction was sufficient to have prevented the *major portion* of factory unemployment if this construction had been properly allocated; that this shifting of construction would not have materially affected the cost of construction for the whole period; that the political obstacles are forbidding, but not insurmountable if enlightened public opinion wholeheartedly desires to partly eliminate the evil of unemployment." Public Construction and Cyclical Unemployment, *Annals of the American Academy of Social and Political Science*, Vol. CXXXIX, p. 208.

A more balanced view will be found in Professor Pigou's discussion of the problem in *Industrial Fluctuations*, Part II, Ch. XII. A note of warning is struck by Mr. Georg Bielschowsky in an excellent article, Business Fluctuations and Public Works, *Quarterly Journal of Economics*, Vol. XLIV, February, 1930, pp. 286-319: "In short, the less is expected of a flexible distribution of public construction the more it will achieve. It is not 'The Road to Plenty,' it is not even a first rate device for reducing business fluctuations; it must rather be conceived of as the last finishing touch which a highly competent government may put upon a smoothly working business economy." (p. 318) Similar notes of warning will be found in Mr. Ronald C. Davison's recent book, *The Unemployed*, and in Dr. Leo Wolman's recent book, *Planning and Control of Public Works* (National Bureau of Economic Research).

[6] This was the general opinion of the Committee of the President's Conference on Unemployment, *Business Cycles and Unemployment*, pp. XXVII-XXIX; of Professor Bowley and Mr. Stuart. *Is Unemployment Inevitable?*, Part 4; of Professor Dickinson, Public Construction and Cyclical Unemployment, *Annals of the American Academy of Political and Social Science* (CXXXIX).

But Dr. Wolman in his recent study, *Planning and Control of Public Works*, points out that expenditures on public works are not very sensitive

Now since the expenditures of public authorities are on a non-profit basis, it is argued, there is no reason why the above procedure should be followed. Rather, government should follow an opposite policy. When private business is very active and the available suppy of labor fully employed, government should contract its own expenditures; when, on the other hand, private business is depressed, government should expand its own expenditures. Thus by timing its peaks to synchronize with the troughs of private economic activity, the "major portion" of cyclical fluctuations, to quote Mr. Dickinson, will be removed. And this will be a desirable policy from a purely economic view of public expenditures. At present the government spends more, so it is argued, in times of prosperity. At such times interest rates are high, cost of materials excessive, and wage rates inflated. By concentrating its expenditures in times of depression, government will get the benefit of low interest rates, reduced prices of materials, and deflated wage rates.

In examining this argument we shall first analyze the statistical material indicating the magnitude of public expenditures so as to get a general idea of the amounts to be manipulated. We shall then go on to examine the theoretical consequences of attempted shifts in public expenditures. Finally, we shall come to the practical obstacles inherent in the technical character of, and in the administrative agencies responsible for, construction of public works.

But before we proceed with this analysis it will be well to follow the practice of sketching briefly the historical experiences with supplying work to the unemployed in the form of relief work. This should enable us to make the necessary comparisons and see the pitfalls common to both relief work and a flexible system of public construction.[7]

to general fluctuations in private employment. What happens is that in periods of prosperity when it is difficult to float bonds, and when labor is scarce, public authorities do not press their new projects. Projects once begun, however, are not immediately abandoned. The result, it seems, is that public expenditures are by no means uniform or progressing at a constant rate but increase in times of prosperity, do not fall below the previous level in times of depression and then increase again.

[7] There is not as much difference between a planned policy of public

3. RELIEF WORK IN GREAT BRITAIN

Throughout the nineteenth century the provision of relief work in Great Britain was a device frequently used in periods of depression. The most important of its many forms were the hiring out of poor people at low wages, the workhouse, and the labor yard. These differed from current proposals in that back of them all lay the prevailing prejudice that unemployment was an individual and not an industrial problem, and that any aid should be so arranged as to deter application for it.[8]

The first attempt on a fairly large scale to provide local relief work was in Lancashire during the American Civil War when the textile workers were thrown out of work because of the cutting off of the cotton supply. After two years of out-relief and private charity, Parliament granted a loan to Lancashire for the creation of public works on which the unemployed were put to work. As there was need of local improvements there was no difficulty in finding work. The scheme was well administered, but during a period of three years only about 8,000 were provided with employment.[9]

The Lancashire experiment pointed the way for the relief of unemployment resulting from the changing fortunes of industry. Mr. Joseph Chamberlain urged a similar policy on Birmingham and, when he came to the Local Government Board, incorporated the principles of relief works in the Circular of 1886. The procedure outlined was to employ men whom, upon the Guardians' recommendation,

construction and the emergency provision of relief work in times of depression as is often implied. In so far as the latter consists of useful work it automatically involves a contraction of construction in periods of prosperity. The construction of additional roads, ships, and public buildings will automatically decrease the demand for these at a later date. In so far as the emergency relief works are economically carried out there is also no distinction to be made. The real difference consists in the delay involved in a program of emergency relief works and hence the possibility of greater shifts under a planned program. See Pigou, *Industrial Fluctuations*, Part II, Ch. XVI.

[8] For an account and evaluation of relief work in Great Britain in the nineteenth century see Webb, *op. cit.*

[9] Davison, *op. cit.*, pp. 28-32.

it was considered undesirable to send to the workhouse and to pay lower wages than those regularly paid.[10] This circular was issued in succeeding periods of depression, and while many localities had difficulty in finding suitable relief works, some followed the advice of the Local Government Board. The principle of lower wages had to be abandoned. Where men were added to the regular staff it was difficult to make any discrimination. Where they were employed separately, the work was the most unskilled, and the current rates were none too high. The trade unions were also in a position to raise objections against the undermining of the current rates. As there were more workers than could be employed, they were taken in rotation. Consequently there was little selection of workers and employment was intermittent.

The Unemployed Workmen's Act of 1905 was the last official pre-war attempt to provide work for the unemployed. It grew out of a voluntary organization in some of the London Boroughs (1903) which aimed at raising a fund to organize work on a better system for the unemployed. Under this act the committee received official sanction, and soon "Distress Committees," joint committees of the Local Authority, the Board of Guardians, and certain coöpted members experienced in the relief of distress, were set up in many parts of England. These committees could draw on the local rates for their current expenses but were to provide work out of the voluntary funds which in practice had to be supplemented by the state. Other functions of the committees were paying the cost of migration and emigration, establishing farm colonies, and organizing registration schemes for workers needing jobs and employers needing workers.

The numbers employed were never very large. Even though there was specific provision that casual workers were not to be included, many of their applications were granted. The summary of the work of these committees made by the Minority Report of the Poor Law Commission

[10] Webb, *op. cit.*, p. 117.

is, in a sense, a judgment on all attempts of a similar variety which had been made.[11] Work could not be provided continuously for any one man. The list of applicants was swamped by casual workers who were glad to receive odd days of work at current rates. Excessive cost of every work resulted. This was due in part "to the inevitable inefficiency of the unemployed men at the work to which they were set" and "to the difficulties inherent in working with heterogeneous groups of men" and in part to the expenditures for materials, plant, and supervision. There was a tendency "to a shrinkage of the ordinary staffs of the Municipal Departments and to a throwing out of employment of the regular hands of the Municipal Contractors," because the work on which they would ordinarily have been employed had been given to the Distress Committees.

In spite of the general condemnation of relief works before the War, the post-war period witnessed a revival of the old remedy. Mr. Davison suggests that governments were impressed with some economists' claims that such relief works would act as a stimulus to trade and that the whole scheme was a political device for subsidizing the financial needs of the badly depressed areas.[12] While this post-war experience is significant because of its magnitude, it has its limitations in that the policy of increasing the public demand for labor was applied as a remedy for the chronic unemployment to which Great Britain has been a victim and in the neglect of the time when public demand for labor must be contracted. A logical justification must run therefore either in terms of these relief works being in addition to the long time normal needs or else in terms of a stimulus to trade which the policy has failed to attain.

The Unemployment Grants Committee, composed mainly of business men, was set up toward the end of 1920, and local authorities having serious unemployment situations were invited to apply for subsidies with which to build public works. The terms offered were gradually improved so that by 1926 the central government was paying about

---

[11] Webb, *op. cit.*   [12] Ibid., p. 46.

half of the necessary capital and interest on non-revenue-producing works such as roads and sewers and about 25% on revenue producing works such as docks and electricity.

There at once arose the difficulty of deciding which localities were confronted with "serious" situations. Some of these could not always offer satisfactory schemes, and others, like the depressed mining and textile areas, were obviously not the ones to be urged to anticipate future needs. The old problem of the utility of anticipated public works thus came to the fore.

Labor was to be hired through the exchanges except that private contractors could choose about ten per cent of their staffs—and sometimes more—through other sources. For a while ex-service men were given preference but this had to be dropped. There at once emerged the old conflict between need and suitability as a basis of employment. Some authorities, recognizing the importance of good work, followed the latter principle. Others, confronted with too many applicants, fell into the old device of spreading work and thus introduced an encouragement to casual labor. A few went to the extreme of stamping the insurance books of those employed on public works for the required period and then returning them to the unemployment funds, thus relieving their local rates.

The number employed on the various schemes reached 95,000 on October 31, 1925. But not all these were employed through the aid given by the Unemployment Grants Committee, as large numbers were employed on arterial roads under the Ministry of Transport, and on land reclamation under the Ministry of Agriculture. But even the larger number is insignificant when it is recalled that in these years the unemployed varied from one to two millions. Since that time the number has greatly decreased and by 1927 no more than two or three thousand were employed on works aided by the Unemployment Grants Committee.

It is difficult to make a judgment on the costs. The largest part of the £105,000,000 spent up to January, 1927, went for non-revenue producing works. This was probably about four times the amount which would have been spent had the same workers received unemployment insurance. The problem hinges therefore on the utility of the public works which remain. Some undoubtedly were marginal expenditures which would not have been undertaken otherwise. Others were probably undertaken under mistaken forecasts of future needs. The net balance can never be definitely measured.

The outstanding conclusion, however, is that this was no solution of the unemployment situation. And yet the hope is not abandoned that larger and better schemes will somehow succeed in doing what they have so far failed to do. Thus Mr. Lloyd George in the election of 1928 offered the attractive slogan "We can conquer Unemployment." [13] A five-year program financed by loans and costing nothing to the taxpayer—except taxes—would at once absorb some 700,000 unemployed, and prepare the day for the time when private industry, rejuvenated by this scheme, would return to the old level. Mr. G. D. H. Cole has embodied this program as part of his policy for a labor government in the next ten years in his advocacy of a National Labour Corps to make England both a more productive country and a pleasanter one. Mr. Cole, however, does not offer details of expenditures and consequences which would follow from such a policy.[14]

4. RELIEF WORK IN GERMANY [15]

Before the war a number of German cities attempted to relieve the distress resulting from the recurring periods of depression by providing relief works. The post-war situa-

---

[13] See the *Manchester Guardian Weekly*, March 15, 1929, p. 210.

[14] *The Next Ten Years in British Social and Economic Policy*, Ch. III. See especially pp. 66-7 where Mr. Cole defends his hope that the previous difficulties associated with relief works can be eliminated.

[15] Carroll, *Unemployment Insurance in Germany*, Chs. III and IV, and Public Works and Unemployment, *American Economic Review, Supplement*, March, 1930, pp. 20-23. See also R. C. Davison Unemployment Relief in Germany, *Economic Journal*, March, 1930, pp. 140-46.

tion became much too serious to be left to the resources of the local authorities. But Germany, like Great Britain of an earlier period, was not yet ready to abandon the nineteenth century dogma that relief should be offered on the principles of need and the work-test. In 1919 when the number unemployed greatly increased, the federal government appropriated funds for the various localities to be used in starting relief works. In 1920 a more elaborate system, which came to be known as "productive unemployment relief," was worked out and the administration turned over to the agencies in charge of unemployment relief. This meant subsidizing private and semi-private bodies. Under the regulations laid down, jobs were to be given at current wage rates.

As most public work construction in Germany had been suspended during the war, abundant work was available for a while and at times some three-fifths of the unemployed were assisted in this way. Each worker was given a substantial amount of employment lasting four or five months. The funds for these expenditures were provided by the federal government, the states, and the local governments. But the inflation of 1922-23 greatly embarrassed the government bodies and much of the work had to be discontinued. Fortunately, however, unemployment also declined in the earlier period of inflation.

Unemployment increased again as 1923 wore on, and in November of that year the federal government worked out a system of loans and subsidies to be granted "for public, mixed public and private, and private relief work." While the object was to "increase the national output of foodstuffs, raw materials, or commodities essential to further production" only the expenditures on public works proved at all successful.

The various public bodies were to be given loans at low rates of interest and, where that was not sufficient inducement, were to be granted outright subsidies to push those works which they would not otherwise immediately undertake. The public bodies were not expected to carry out their own projects but to allow contracts, which were to be publicly advertised, and to see that the profits of the contractors were a minimum. While the hiring was to be on the basis of merit, only the unemployed could be taken on and these through the employment exchanges. Preference was to be given to those longest out of work; short time employment was permitted, and a maximum of three months was fixed except under very special circumstances. The pay was reduced to below the prevailing rate as a result of which the workers stayed on the job and performed their tasks only if they were paid a bonus.

Financial assistance to increase employment was granted to the railways, the postal service, for canal building, land reclamation, construction of dwelling houses, road building, and, in some cases, for factory buildings. Dr. Carroll gives some idea of the amount of work provided: "During the three-quarters of the year preceding the inauguration of the law of 1927, over six million days of work were provided in land reclamation projects, seven and one-half million on road building, one million on electric power development and six and one-half million on miscellaneous underground work." [16] In addition there were some 40,000 houses built. The number of workers employed varied from 66,000 to 149,000 per month.

It was the aim of the federal government, however, not to limit its financial assistance to public bodies but to stimulate private industry and thus provide "productive relief work" in still another form. Loans were to be made to private industries to continue employing people whom they otherwise were compelled to lay off or to employ people in new undertakings. These loans were to be made at low rates of interest and to be repaid in ten years. In actual practice, however, it was difficult to know whether a factory was closing down legitimately or in order to get a loan at the low rate, whether the new undertakings would prove productive, and also to choose between various applicants. This part of the program was much criticized and was abandoned

[16] *Op. cit.*, p. 39.

when the whole unemployment problem was overhauled in 1927.

Even the Public Welfare Agencies went in for providing employment as a condition of granting aid, although not on an important scale. The recipients looked upon this as a punishment for poverty, and other workers opposed it as interfering with their regular employment and undermining their standards.

In 1927 Germany went the way of Great Britain, recognizing that recurring periods of unemployment were beyond the control of either workers or employers, abandoning the work test, and adopting a system of Unemployment Insurance. It retained the principle of providing employment when possible on public works which were known as "value creating unemployment relief." As a result a person applying for financial aid might be given employment on public works to be financed by the various relief funds and by loans granted by the federal and state governments. As before 1927, the most successful undertakings have been in connection with land reclamation and improvements on roads and waterways. This means that the work is limited both in amount and in kind. In recent months no more than about five per cent of all persons in receipt of benefits have been supplied with work.[17]

It is difficult to pass judgment upon these ten years in Germany because of the unusual circumstances. In no sense was it a planned system. We have no way of judging the value of the works constructed, or their cost. Dr. Carroll is of the opinion that the cost was no greater than would be the case under usual circumstances.[18] She is also of the opinion that this whole program was a factor in the revival of 1926. It seems, however, that Germany has reached a point where her immediate needs, neglected during the war have been met, and in the future suitable employment may be hard to find. From now on the successful use of public works in times of depression may hinge on the ability to

[17] See post., p. 458.
[18] *Op. cit.,* p. 80.

find projects which are essential but which can also be postponed in the years of full economic activity.[19]

5. An Adjusted Policy of Public Construction

Recent studies have provided some, though not altogether adequate, statistical material, giving a general idea of the quantitative shifts in public construction which are necessary. The estimates of anticipation and postponement are made on the assumption that aggregate demand for labor would, in a time of depression, be larger than it would otherwise be, by the number put to work directly on public construction and on the materials necessary. No account is taken of the possible contraction in private demand or of the indirect expansion of demand. We shall examine shortly the validity of this assumption. In reviewing the data for Great Britain and the United States, we shall disregard this qualification for the time being.

Great Britain. Professor Bowley and Mr. Stuart have made a study of expenditures on public works in Great Britain to illustrate the thesis advanced by Professor Bowley in 1908.[20] The pre-war average percentage of unemployment was about five per cent. Taking a ten-year period, assuming that 80 per cent of the total cost of public expenditures goes for wages and that the annual wage bill was as that of 1911, or about £800 millions, the shifts indicated in the table on the following page would have been necessary to have a uniform average unemployment of five per cent.

This means that to have leveled the pre-war unemployment to five per cent it was necessary that £36 millions in wages (or £45 millions in expenditure) be held over during the first three years and spent in the next three and that £16 millions in wages (or £20 millions in total expenditures)

---

[19] Mr. Davison is of the opinion that "it was never possible to provide relief works for more than a small minority of the applicants, and that only at great cost." Unemployment Relief in Germany, *Economic Journal*, March, 1930, pp. 140-1.

[20] *Is Unemployment Inevitable?* pp. 366-377.

Unemployed (Per Cent)	Relation to Average	Variation in Wage Bill (Millions Sterling)
2½	− 2½	+ 20
3½	− 1½	+ 12
4½	− ½	+ 4
5½	+ ½	− 4
6½	+ 1½	− 12
7½	+ 2½	− 20
6½	+ 1½	− 12
5½	+ ½	− 4
4½	− ½	+ 4
3½	− 1½	+ 12

be advanced in the seventh and eighth years from the ninth and tenth. If a decade were taken to make the adjustments it would mean that the period of postponement be one of four years and that of advancement one of two and one-half years.[21]

What this would mean in terms of actual shifts of expenditures can be seen by a comparison of the actual expenditures, the percentages of unemployment, and the required adjustments. This the authors have set out for the years 1906-1913.[22]

	Actual Expenditures (Millions Sterling)	Relation to Average	Unemployment Per Cent	Relation to 5% Average	Expenditure Required by Policy (Millions Sterling)
1906 . .	40.7	+ 10.5	3.8	− 1.2	22
1907 . .	32.1	+ 1.9	3.8	− 1.2	22
1908 . .	37.5	+ 7.3	7.9	+ 2.9	63
1909 . .	24.1	− 6.1	7.7	+ 2.7	61
1910 . .	24.5	− 5.7	4.7	− .3	31
1911 . .	25.3	− 4.9	3.0	− 2.0	14
1912 . .	30.8	.6	3.2	− 1.8	16
1913 . .	26.5	− 3.7	3.1	− 1.9	15
Average	30.2				30.5

[21] Changes in the size of population and wage rates would necessitate larger absolute advances and postponements.
[22] Op. cit., p. 371.

Such transfers would probably leave in each year a sufficient amount for those expenditures which cannot be put off, and we can conclude that disregarding the administrative difficulties and cost to the government of increasing the fluctuations of its expenditures, substantial additions to the demand for labor can be made in times of depression. As we shall see later some deductions must be made for contraction in private demand which will follow, and some additions for indirect effects. Except for those who believe that public works alone can *eliminate* the cyclical fluctuations of private industry, the precise magnitude of the changes in demand is of no great consequence.

United States. A similar study for the United States but with less satisfactory material was made by Professor Dickinson.[23]

There are reproduced here the final results as to total public construction and necessary shifts to get stability in private employment.

[23] Public Construction and Cyclical Unemployment, *Annals of the American Academy of Political and Social Science*, CXXXIX, pp. 175-209. The most recent and comprehensive study is that of Dr. Leo Wolman, *Planning and Control of Public Works*. Dr. Wolman makes no attempt to calculate the necessary shifts. He is on the whole skeptical of the possibilities which public works have in eliminating cyclical fluctuations. The nature of the estimates on which fine calculations are based can be seen by comparing those of Mr. Dickinson with those of Dr. Wolman for the years when both give estimates:

	Wolman's Estimate		*Dickinson's Estimate*	
	TOTAL CONSTRUCTION (MILLIONS)	PUBLIC CONSTRUCTION	TOTAL CONSTRUCTION (MILLIONS)	PUBLIC CONSTRUCTION
1923 .	6,368	1,993	4,768	1,022
1924 .	7,305	2,500	5,237	1,111
1925 .	8,911	2,594	6,600	1,283

Dr. Wolman concluded that no reliable estimates could be made for years prior to 1923, and that his estimates probably underestimate the totals because of the difficulty in estimating costs of repairs and small expenditures which in the aggregate must be quite large. As Dr. Dickinson's figures are for a longer period they are here used, but only for purposes of general exposition. It is unnecessary to go into any discussion of the best measures of the amounts which must be transferred. For illustrative purposes one guess is as good as another.

	Total Factory Wages (Millions)[1]	Factory Employment Index Average 1919–25 = 100[2]	Public Construction (Millions)	Best Allocation (Millions)	Best Allocation. By Shifting ½ of Expenditures (Millions)[3]
1919	10,461	105	674	20	338
1920	12,153	108	852	25	426
1921	8,202	86	859	2,527	1,972
1922	8,759	94	1,034	1,732	1,194
1923	11,009	108	1,022	19	511
1924	10,109	99	1,111	1,229	1,111
1925	10,409	100	1,283	1,283	1,283
			Av. 976		

[1] Based upon census returns for 1919, 1921, 1923, and estimates for intervening years with the aid of the Federal Reserve Payroll Index.

[2] The Federal Reserve Index of Employment with the base shifted from 1919 = 100 to 1919 − 25 = 100.

[3] To make Index of Employment = 100 in every year.

6. Some Theoretic Objections

The critics of the principle of shifting the demand for labor assert that the whole procedure is futile even if there were no administrative and technical obstacles. Any attempt of government to increase the demand for labor, say the critics, will lead to an automatic and corresponding contraction on the part of private industry. This is actually an appeal to one form of the old wage fund doctrine. But, as Professor Pigou pointed out,[24] the stream of consumable goods at any one time has three branches: (1) that which is consumed by entrepreneurs and capitalists, (2) that which goes to labor, (3) that which is stored. It is clear therefore that a diversion of goods from the first and third branches will augment that of the second. Actually in times of depression the stock of stored goods is larger than usual and so there is a real possibility of increasing the quantity of wage goods going to labor. Hence even though a part of the new demand will be satisfied by diversion from the branch going to labor it will not all come out of that source. There is thus a possibility of increasing the net demand for

[24] *Industrial Fluctuations*, p. 316.

labor. The possibilities are further increased by the inclusion of amounts devoted to unemployment insurance and charity and finally, in the case of any one country alone, loans from abroad.

Objections have, however, been raised to the analysis in barter terms and it is argued that in an economy where money and banking exist the case is otherwise. If public authorities decide to employ more labor than they actually do, they must either borrow from the banks or sell bonds or increase taxes. It is therefore argued that what the public authorities spend, individuals cannot, the net result of which is that the aggregate demand for labor remains unchanged.

The activities of the public authorities can be carried out under two main sets of possibilities: (1) The price level may not be increased above what it would otherwise have been and will therefore be left at a point below the level which prevailed before the depression set in. (2) The price level may, because of the expansion of bank credit or the issuance of money, be increased above what it would otherwise have been with the result that prices would more nearly approach their original level.

When the price level is not raised the government can increase its demand for labor by levying a tax or floating bonds. If the tax or loan comes from funds which would otherwise be devoted to the employment of labor there will be a contraction in the demand for labor equal to the expansion caused by the government action. In so far as the tax or loan comes from funds which would otherwise be spent on consumers' goods, the demand for labor caused by government action is a net addition to the aggregate demand. While it is true that a reduction of expenditures on the part of those who would otherwise purchase consumers' goods would mean a reduction in the demand for labor producing these goods, the people set to work by the government will purchase these goods and thus counteract the contraction.[25] In actual practice the funds will come

---

[25] Mr. Hawtrey's contention that "if the funds raised by the Government had been left in the hands of the investors to be applied to some other

from both sources and there will thus be some contraction but a net addition to the demand for labor. This will be increased to the extent that funds otherwise used for unemployment insurance or poor relief are devoted to the payment of wages and employment of labor. It is conceivable of course that, if government expenditures came from bank credits and the banks followed a policy of price stabilization, they would have so to increase the discount rate as to contract the borrowings of private enterprises by an amount equal to the government borrowings.

Where the funds for government expenditures come directly or indirectly from an increase in the total supply of bank credits, even Mr. Hawtrey has admitted the possibility of increasing the demand for labor by the construction of public works. The attraction of government securities will lead individuals to transfer balances which they would otherwise have used for their own consumption and thus, as in the first case noted above, lead to a net addition to employment. The transfer of idle bank balances, which in periods of depression are said to be relatively large, and the additional bank credit will of course lead to a rise in the price level of wage goods.[26] But this would mean not only that the quantity bought by other workers would decrease but also the quantity bought by other classes, and hence an increase in the aggregate going to wage earners.

We can conclude therefore that it is possible for government to increase the demand for labor without a corresponding contraction of private demand,[27] and that this is

enterprises, there would be just as much reason to expect that these alternative enterprises would have given additional employment," disregards the demand side for funds.

[26] The rise will in part be counteracted in so far as stocks of goods otherwise withheld because of falling prices are put on the market.

[27] Mr. Hawtrey has contended that a creation of credit unaccompanied by any expenditure on public works would be equally effective in giving employment. "The public works are merely a piece of ritual, convenient to people who want to be able to say that they are doing something, but otherwise irrelevant." *Economica*, March, 1925, p. 44. But Professor Pigou has pointed out that the method of public works brings about the same result without a lowering of the discount rate which would be neces-

particularly the case when fresh monetary purchasing power is created to finance the construction work.

There are many who consider the indirect effects as even more significant. These are of two kinds. The psychological effects of increased government expenditures will lead business men to expect a revival, which will, therefore, tend to shorten the period of depression. The demand for wage goods on the part of those workers put to work will stimulate the demand for labor in those industries, and the effects of the original impulse will thus become cumulative. Some caution is, however, necessary because of the demand of the unemployed workers for wage goods effected through charity or savings or unemployment insurance which such a policy would reduce.

7. Technical Limitations to a Policy of Flexible Allocation of Public Works

The shifts contemplated by Professor Bowley and Mr. Stuart for Great Britain seem, in the main, feasible. Can the same be said of Professor Dickinson's sanguine conclusion "that the volume of public construction was sufficient to have prevented the major portion of factory unemployment if this construction had been properly allocated; that this shifting of construction would not have materially affected the cost of construction for the whole period." A glance at the table on p. 208 will show that under actual conditions of expenditure there was not in any year a decrease from the previous year. The adjusted expenditures postulate violent fluctuations from year to year. In terms of an average for the period 1919-25 the maximum departure from the average of actual expenditures was $\dfrac{1283}{976}$

sary to expand borrowings from the banks, and that the lowering of the discount rate may lead to foreign borrowings and thus counteract the internal expansion of credit. For the discussion between Mr. Hawtrey and Professor Pigou see *ibid.*, pp. 38-48; *Economic Journal,* June, 1929, pp. 183-94; *ibid.,* December, 1929, pp. 136-43.

or 132% and the minimum departure was $\frac{674}{976}$ or 69%. Under the contemplated shift the maximum departure would be $\frac{2527}{976}$ or 259% and the minimum departure $\frac{19}{976}$ or 2%. Even with a contemplated shift of one-half, the maximum departure would be $\frac{1972}{976}$ or 202% and the minimum $\frac{338}{976}$ or 35%.

It is impossible to conceive that out of an expenditure of $674,000,000 in 1919, $852,000,000 in 1920, and $1,022,000,000 in 1923, the costs of maintenance, which could not possibly be avoided, were no more than $20,000,000, $25,000,000, and $19,000,000 respectively.

Nor is this all. There are substantial changes in costs other than those resulting from changes in interest rates and wages, which must be taken into account. If it were merely transforming the fluctuations of government expenditures by changing their dates, the criticism advanced would not be valid. But contrary to the usual view the expenditures on public works are not very sensitive to business fluctuations—the rates of growth change as seen by the check for the United States in 1921 when expenditures were the same as those of 1920. If this period is at all representative and if the statistics indicate at least the general course of public works expenditures, it means transforming a halting trend with 674 millions in 1919, 852 millions in 1920, remaining stationary at 859 in 1924, increasing to 1,034 millions in 1922, remaining virtually stationary at 1,022 millions in 1923, increasing very slightly to 1,111 in 1924 and again slightly to 1,283 in 1925 to an oscillating curve with a magnitude of 20 in 1919, 25 in 1920, shooting up to 2,527 in 1921, coming down to 1,732 in 1922, and then shooting down to 19 millions in 1923 and up again to 1,229 millions in 1924.

Now any account of the saving which will result from carrying out a large part of the construction in times of low prices (although account must be taken of the effect of increased orders on prices, and the interest charges in anticipating works) must also take account of the costs of fluctuations involved in keeping idle a large part of equipment and organization.[28] This is especially serious when a community handles its own construction, and even where private contractors perform the work, it is still a problem where the equipment is at all specialized.[29]

When it is recalled further that in the United States about one-half of the expenditures on public works is for roads and the others on projects closely allied to building trades, a further check will be seen. The characteristic nature of a business depression is that it throws men out of work in all industries as well as in the construction trades. Training workers will be both costly and dangerous for the normal development of the labor market. Hence, only for the unskilled accustomed to such heavy work and the craftsman in the construction industries, will there be room for direct employment. Nor should we lose sight of the fact that public construction is as yet a seasonal industry, thus providing a further check to direct employment.

Disregarding for the time being the problem of the proper time when public works are to be expanded, it should never-

[28] It may be argued, however, that the present policy takes little account of immediate community needs, and that we would be merely substituting one haphazard system for another.

[29] The physical possibility of increasing specialized equipment will often be an essential consideration. The reply of the U. S. War Secretary on this point is worth quoting: "The public works under the charge of this office which would be affected by the proposed legislation are those for the improvement of rivers and harbors and for flood control. For carrying the bulk of river and harbor work special equipment is necessary, the amount of this equipment available throughout the country, including that privately owned, is not a great deal more than is necessary for work under the present scale of appropriation. If the appropriation should be doubled for a short period, it would be necessary, before it could be spent, for the Government or Contractors to acquire a large amount of additional equipment. When the appropriation reverted to its normal size, this additional equipment would be idle with heavy carrying charges." . . . Quoted from Calendar 862, U. S. Senate, *70th Congress, 1st Session,* Report No. 836, p. 3, in Wolman, *op. cit.,* note pp. 172-73.

theless be pointed out that large projects which will be most suitable for manipulation take time and cannot be abandoned in the middle. In fact the possibilities of employment increase as the work advances, and the chief addition to the labor demand may not come until the depression period is well over. Not only will this be serious if we have varying periods of depression, but also if these intervals come more often and are shorter.

It is Mr. Dickinson's opinion that the whole problem of forecasting the correct time at which public works are to be speeded up is of little importance. "It would be necessary for some agency to advise public officials when they ought to sell bonds and let contracts. It seems possible to fasten this apparently onerous burden upon a first-class clerk in the Bureau of Labor Statistics at Washington. His duty would be to watch the index of employment and immediately inform the numerous public officials throughout the country whenever the index approached 5 per cent above or below the average of the preceding years." [30] In a general way this is no doubt true. Forecasting, per se, is important only if the object of allocating public works is to anticipate a depression,[31] rather than to "melt" it. The former is an extremely doubtful procedure. Wages would still be high, prices of materials inflated, and the money market tight. Public authorities might, therefore, merely compete with private business for loans, labor, and materials. If public authorities are to wait until the "stresses" are removed, costs reduced, and inefficient enterprises pushed out, then it will be clear enough when unemployment is serious. In actual practice, however, this will prove a real obstacle to increased employment. Different localities will have varying amounts of unemployment and there will not always be a direct correlation between extent of unemployment and the need of public works. In some communities cyclical unemployment will be aggravated by that due to shifts in indus-

[30] Dickinson, *op cit.*, p. 200.
[31] This was the view of Professor J. M. Clark in his discussion before the American Economic Association, Public Works and Unemployment, *American Economic Review, Supplement*, March, 1930, pp. 15-20.

trial activity. Mining communities should hardly be the ones to anticipate public construction, when their index of unemployment is even much above normal.

Nor can we disregard the difficulties involved in forecasting the needs of a vast number of communities. We have already noted the difficulty in the case of communities which will probably decline industrially and where local pride in alleviating unemployment would lead to uneconomical expenditures. Other communities will overreach themselves in anticipating future needs. Nor is the problem of postponing a much easier one to solve. When the time comes to fill in the gap, needs may have changed; those which were planned will no longer be urgent, and others not planned will be essential. This applies not only as to choice between various projects, but also as to various technical methods in creating a particular project. Anticipated works may be constructed under technical conditions which soon become superseded and will hence be more costly. Risk in planning public works is always great and to do so with regard to fluctuations in business conditions as well as needs, may substantially increase this risk.[32]

8. Some Administrative Obstacles and Suggestions for Their Reduction.

A system of planned public works on a national scale would be greatly facilitated by centralization. In the United States any very large degree of centralization is inconceivable. The most important spending agencies are the municipalities, and the federal government is least important, responsible for no more than about ten per cent of the total.[33] While the expenditures of the federal government may be substantially increased, the municipalities and states will probably always remain the chief agencies. Of course the influence of the federal government which has recently shown some inclination to adjust its public con-

---

[32] See Georg Bielschowsky, *op. cit.*, pp. 309-13.
[33] Wolman, *op. cit.*, p. 2.

struction expenditures to fluctuations in private industry, can be greater than indicated by its fraction of the total expenditures. It can by example and by a system of grants-in-aid influence the expenditures of municipalities and states. Such influence, however, has its limitations. If the grants-in-aid are a very small portion of total outlay, the municipalities and states will not be attracted to spending much more than they would otherwise spend. Should the grants-in-aid be a very significant portion of the total outlay, the municipalities and states may be tempted to undertake unnecessary expenditures.

The lack of centralized authority within the municipalities, states, and federal government is even more serious than that between them. Thus the public works constructed by the federal government are in the hands of "thirty-nine federal agencies, four of which are independent and unattached and the remaining thirty-five are each a part of some one of nine of the ten national departments. Sixteen federal agencies are authorized to build roads, nineteen to do hydraulic construction, sixteen to work on rivers, and twenty-two on engineering and research." [34]

The situation in so far as the National government is concerned, however, bids fair to be improved by the recent enactment of the Wagner bill providing for the advance planning of public works and for the setting up of an agency (which is to be under the Department of Commerce) charged with the responsibility for the preparation of such plans.

The situation within the municipalities is of course much worse. Thus to quote an extreme example: "Within the City of Chicago there are some thirty-one distinct and independent local governments. In addition there are at least six semi-independent tax levying agencies, the tax levies of which are spread by some of these local governing bodies.

"In Cook County outside of the City of Chicago, there are approximately 380 additional local independent and semi-governmental agencies. . . .

[34] Mitchell, *Business Cycles and Unemployment*, pp. 246-7.

"The planning, design, and construction and maintenance of extensive public works and of surface and underground improvements are similarly diffused. Annual expeditures now totaling a million dollars for these purposes are made with little or no coördinated planning. Separate engineering, designing and construction and repair forces are maintained by the independent agencies." [35]

It is difficult to conceive of any substantial unification in the very near future. Hence whatever is to be done in the way of allocating public works will for some time have to be done primarily within the present framework of administration. This points to the emphasis which must be placed on studies of local expenditures and local variations in employment. Some help is to be looked for in the constant pressure of increased per capita indebtedness and tax rates. This is compelling communities interested merely in looking for economical expenditures of their funds, to increased research, planning, and budgeting. Some progress has already been made either by the local authorities or independent bodies of citizens as in Philadelphia and Detroit. It is to be expected, therefore, that those interested in the larger social issue of using public expenditures to moderate cyclical fluctuations of private business will be reinforced by those interested solely in their local economies.

The problem of planning has two other aspects. The first is the urgent need of getting a large administrative bureaucracy to act quickly. The vast majority of the officials are more interested in the immediate practical details than in the larger social issues. A canvass of many of these brought replies of which the following are typical: "We build and repair as needed. We think any other reason unbusinesslike. We do not believe it would be more than a drop in the bucket in solving unemployment conditions." [36]

Nor can we neglect the fact that these officials are imbued with the same spirit of optimism in a period of prosperity,

[35] Wolman, *op. cit.*, p. 162. Quoted from *Report of the J. L. Jacobs Company for the Advisory Board of Estimate and Apportionment*, Chicago, January, 1929.
[36] Wolman, *op. cit.*, p. 160.

and pessimism in depression, as are the business men of their communities. There will be great reluctance to go against the current beliefs. Nor can we disregard the use of public expenditures in a great many communities as rewards for political service. Many an administration will be reluctant to postpone expenditures when it is in office to a time when it will be out of office.

The other obstacle lies in the gradually built up system of checks and balances in American communities, partly the result of political theory, partly of accident, and partly to prevent extravagance for which American communities are notorious. Whatever the origin, there is at present, great delay involved in the making of plans and their approval, voting and selling of bonds, the awards of contracts and actual construction.[37] Speedy action is, however, the very essence of a planned policy of public construction. Hence a much more flexible fiscal policy will have to be elaborated, guarding, however, against the consequence of hasty action.

The whole problem would be greatly simplified if the various states were to set up State Planning Boards similar to that proposed for Pennsylvania by Governor Pinchot's Committee on Unemployment.[38] This plan calls for a board composed of representatives of the state government, of some of the municipalities and counties, and of the construction industry and its allied professions of architecture and engineering. It would have a full time executive officer and it would prepare a six-year plan of projected public construction for the state and the local bodies. This construction could perhaps be divided into three groups: Group A would consist of the pieces of work which must be immediately undertaken and which could not be delayed. A definite schedule should be set for these. Group B would consist of the work which should be undertaken sometime during the six year period but which need not be carried

---

[37] An extreme illustration is the Catskill Mountain Water Supply project for New York, which was first considered in 1897; work was begun in 1907 and stretched out through 1928. Wolman, *op. cit.*, pp. 209-11.

[38] See *Report Governor Pinchot's Comittee on Unemployment* (Harrisburg, 1931), pp. 16-17.

through by any specific time. Group C would consist of the work which would be desirable at a future time but for which funds would normally not be adequate within the existing period or for which the public need would not be great.

The engineering and architectural plans for all of this work should be drawn up in advance and kept up to date while the plan itself should always be revised every two years and projected ahead for the ensuing six years.

The work in Group B should be held in reserve for periods of depression. Should business conditions be especially severe, some of the more important projects in Group C might even be launched.

The bond issues for Class B should in general be authorized in advance so that this source of delay would be minimized. In many cases, where there are low constitutional debt limits against which localities or states may be pressing closely, it would be desirable to provide, subject to proper safeguards, flexible bonding powers and to permit additional bonds to be issued when the state planning board declared an emergency to exist.

A greater degree of control could be obtained over local works if it were provided that this flexible provision could only be used for purposes approved by the State Planning Board. It should also be provided that these extra bonds must be amortized within ten years so that there would be available an approximately equal amount of added credit when the next major depression occurred.

9. THE LONG-RUN EFFECT OF PLANNED PUBLIC WORKS

Our analysis so far, indefinite as it is, permits us to conclude that over a period of time it is possible, through the use of public expenditures, to reduce somewhat the extreme fluctuations in employment.

In the long run, however, we may expect more than this. We may actually expect a reduction in the average level of unemployment. An examination of present fluctuations in employment will point out that in times of great business activity the numbers employed are larger than the long run supply would indicate.[38] In such times the normal supply is augmented by accessions from agriculture, women, lower age groups, and, in the United States before the War, by immigration. When a depression sets in, these are not all thrown out of employment and those that are do not always return to their former positions. Had these not been attracted in the first instance, the fluctuations would be substantially reduced.[39]

Nor is this all. It is a well-known fact that wage rates are fairly rigid, being slow to change upward and even slower to change downward. This rigidity prevents the absorption of a portion of the unemployed at a lower wage rate. Now any reduction of the peaks and troughs of fluctuations in employment would level out some of the fluctuations in wages and would thus make possible over a long period of time the adjustment of a larger labor force than is now the case.

An effect of the opposite kind to that discussed here has recently been raised by Mr. Georg Bielchowsky.[41] If, he argues, an expansion of the government demand for labor is partly offset by a contraction in the private demand "the same process of reasoning would also lead us to infer that the decline in employment due to the withholding of public contracts in times of prosperity will likewise be counteracted, this time by an enlargement in the scale of private operations. Funds set free by the reduction in public building are likely to be transferred to private borrowers. Moreover, since the competition of would-be borrowers for loans is very keen in times of expanding business activity, we may expect that all of the funds thus released will find their way into private use and that, consequently, the amount of private employment thereby created will be as large as, or larger than, the amount by which public em-

[39] See Paul H. Douglas, *Real Wages in the United States*, Ch. 24.
[40] See Cassel, *Theory of Social Economy*, pp. 537-547.
[41] Business Fluctuations and Public Works, *Quarterly Journal of Economics*, February, 1930, pp. 286-319.

ployment has been diminished." (p. 297.) This extreme view can only be defended by those who ascribe to credit supply the sole factor of fluctuating economic activity. It is valid only if regard be had for the supply side of transactions. Credit cannot be looked upon as a fixed pool which is emptied by one if not another. Hence to argue that the demand for credit for public works in times of expansion [42] acts as a check on private over-expansion, is to disregard the fact that the public works industry is itself an important branch of the general construction industry. To that extent, it forms a part of the general demand for credit on one side, which, along with banks desiring to make the most profitable use of their resources on the supply side, brings about a given situation of expansion along with a multitude of other factors. Hence there is no reason for assuming that contraction of public demand will be offset by increase of private demand, and that a policy of adjusted public works will itself contribute to exaggerate private fluctuations. Just as there is some offsetting in time of expansion of public works, so there may be some offsetting in time of contraction.[43]

[42] There is some doubt whether this is a correct statement of fact. As the money market becomes tight and interest rates rise, municipalities seem to slow up in their bond issues.

[43] We have disregarded the fact that one check to expansion in time of great business activity is the exhaustion of the available labor supply. With a contraction of public works there would be released an additional number who could be absorbed in private industry and so be a factor to expansion. On the other hand a contraction of public works will also involve a contraction for materials, and in so far as workers are not at first employed, a contraction in demand for wage goods and so act as a counteracting factor.

CHAPTER XVI

THE INDIVIDUAL ENTERPRISE AND INDUSTRIAL FLUCTUATIONS

In the chapter on planned public works we pointed out the rôle of government in transferring the demand for labor from periods of business prosperity to those of depression. A similar policy is often urged on the individual entrepreneur and quantitatively the possibilities of transferring demand are even greater. In the United States the amounts annually expended on private construction are, for example, twice as large as the amounts annually expended on public construction. Private construction also fluctuates much more directly with, although somewhat in advance of, general industrial fluctuations and, as we have suggested in the chapter on public works, it is on the whole more economical to remove irregularities than to create irregularities in order to balance out existing fluctuations. Increased construction during depression periods would result in real economies in the form of lower wage rates, lower material costs, and lower interest rates.

These economies cannot, however, be realized unless the processes of depression have already been allowed to run their course. Hence we cannot expect private business to lessen appreciably the depth of the depression but merely to hasten the process of recovery. It should also be remembered that an offsetting cost would be the carrying charges involved in keeping the new construction idle until demand revived.

Of course it is not to be expected that thousands of individual house builders can be persuaded completely to take account of the industrial fluctuations in their demand for houses in the way we indicated. But there is some presumption for the hope that railroads, public utilities, and commercial builders, as well as large manufacturing enterprises can do something to add to the demand for labor in times of depression by planning their construction work over a long period of time. The prosperous position of the Union Pacific Railroad was, as a matter of fact, largely stimulated by the practice of Mr. E. H. Harriman and Kuhn-Loeb in putting large amounts of capital into it during the depression years of the nineties to prepare for the great increase in business which they correctly estimated would come with the turn of the century.[1]

The period of low costs is also favorable to the construction of office buildings, factories, and apartment houses which give prospect of being rented or used during later periods when price levels and rents will be higher. This is probably the reason why construction tends to be one of the first industries to emerge out of a depression and to lead the upward march of business, as it progresses into periods of revival and prosperity.

The fact that the individual entrepreneur is motivated by his own profit and cannot consider the social advantages of an increased aggregate demand resulting from a less fluctuating economy, to the same extent as government can, puts some limitations on the policy in question. In the words of Professor Pigou: "For any one debating whether or not to transfer a part of his demand from good times to bad cannot reckon to reap for himself the equivalent of more than a very small part of the social benefit that this involves. Such action as he takes to steady aggregate demand will, no doubt, cause the things he purchases to fall a little in real price, because labour, being employed more regularly, will be content with a smaller day-wage. But his purchases will only constitute a trifling proportion of the whole, and the bulk of the gain will go elsewhere. In other words, the marginal private net product of individual efforts to stabilize demand is substantially less than the

---

[1] See George Kennan, *Life of E. H. Harriman,* and for a somewhat fictionalized dramatization, Garett Garett, *The Driver.*

marginal social net product; and therefore, when self-interest alone is at work, these efforts are pushed far less than the general interest of society demands." [2]

Another suggestion occasionally made is that enterprises manufacture goods to stock, refrain from putting them on the market during the period of depression, and thus steady their employment. This, as we have pointed out in a previous chapter, is clearly impossible where fashion changes are important. Nor can the policy be followed by those making perishable goods. Because of the longer periods of time involved, storage and interest charges will be far heavier than where such a policy is pursued during the off-seasons of a normal year.

A final and even more conclusive consideration is that in a period of depression the price level continues to fall. We can hardly expect enterprises to continue manufacturing at high money costs when by holding off they can manufacture at lower money costs. Since one of the great financial losses of the depression periods is the shrinkage in inventories which takes place when the price level falls, we cannot hope that enterprises will add to their stock of goods when it is shrinking in money value.

A suggestion of a different order is to increase advertising and other selling expenses in a period of depression, instead of decreasing them, as is generally the case, and so succeed in marketing a larger quantity of goods than would otherwise be done.[3] To quote Mr. Henry S. Dennison: "We have found, for example, that customers who would not buy ordinary tags were willing to buy when we made up some new, attractive design which especially appealed." [4] But this quotation points to the limitations, as it is extremely doubtful whether the practice can be extended to other than special-

---

[2] Pigou, *Industrial Fluctuations*, p. 296.

[3] An interesting illustration where this policy is pursued is the case of the Dennison Manufacturing Company. To quote Mr. Dennison: "Our advertising appropriations are made on a five year basis, and the manager is supposed to reserve his advertising appropriations in good times and to spend freely in bad times." Edie (editor), *The Stabilization of Business*, p. 385.

[4] Mitchell and others, *Business Cycles and Unemployment*, p. 123.

ties. It cannot be used for standardized consumers' goods, nor for producers' goods.

An interesting bit of statistical information on the advantages of this method is to be found in a study of changes in the amounts expended on magazine advertising as compared with changes in sales in the depression of 1921 and the three subsequent years.[5] An analysis of the sales and advertising expenses of a fairly large sample of firms shows that those firms which did no magazine advertising at all during the period 1920-23 witnessed a decline of twenty per cent in their sales in 1921 as compared with 1920; that those firms which increased their magazine advertising witnessed a decline of twelve per cent; while those firms which decreased their magazine advertising witnessed a decline of twenty-six per cent in their sales.

There was thus a very high degree of positive correlation between changes in magazine advertising and changes in sales—the coefficient of correlation being .68 + .9. But we have no way of knowing whether the smaller decline in sales was purchased at too great an advertising cost nor hence of knowing whether this policy actually paid the firms which increased their advertising. But there is an even more important consideration. The interest of society as a whole noes not lie with the fortunes of individual firms, but in the demand for commodities in the aggregate. We are not concerned with the inroads which "fit-u-well" clothes made on "fit-u-better" clothes. And a subdivision of the firms analyzed into five categories,—personal items, house furnishings, clothing, automobile equipment, groceries, and building materials, throws some light on this point. One of Mr. Vaile's final conclusions is "That different classes of commodities respond in different degrees to advertising. In general, it may be said that these differences are in keeping with accepted statements concerning consumer's buying habits." [6] That is, the spread between increases and decreases for advertising and changes in sales is large in the

[5] Roland S. Vaile, The Use of Advertising During Depression, *Harvard Business Review*, April, 1927, pp. 323-30.   [6] *Ibid.*, p. 330.

case of personal items, such as tobacco and clothing, fairly large in the case of house furnishings and automobile equipment, very small in the case of automobiles and groceries, and practically nil in the case of building material. As Mr. Vaile points out, clothing, tobacco, etc., are bought chiefly by and for men who are influenced greatly by brands, which is not the case with groceries and building materials. Have we not, therefore, a mere shift in the demand for commodities from some firms to others and not an increase in aggregate demand? On theoretical grounds this seems the most likely conclusion. Little can, therefore, be expected in this direction.

Another alternative is for employers to reduce their prices. If all producers in a given line do this the result will be an ultimate increase in the quantity demanded and hence in the numbers employed. The amount by which production and employment will increase will naturally depend upon the elasticity of demand for the product—being appreciable if the demand is elastic but relatively slight if the demand is inelastic. If a single firm, however, adopts such a policy, its sales will naturally increase, but the gain will result from an almost equal contraction in the sales of other establishments.

In so far as fluctuations in business activity are the results of errors in estimating the future demand for commodities, and of ignorance regarding the activities of other enterprises, a regard for the information now available, and an improvement in the extent and reliability of that information will lead to some mitigation in the violence of fluctuations. The use of forecasting services [7] is as yet very limited, and an extension in their use and an improvement in their quality can supply the business community with information as to the changing course of economic activity regarding which it now remains in the dark. An improvement in these services must be directed toward forecasting the future of specific industries, increasing information regarding the

[7] For an appraisal of the merits of these services see Garfield Cox, *An Appraisal of American Business Forecasts*.

stock of raw materials and finished goods on hand, orders given, and state of the labor market. Within the enterprise itself, the utilization of well-developed accounting methods will put managers on their guard when inefficiency sets in and when further expansion becomes non-economical. It is not argued that individual enterprises can eliminate fluctuations, but in a situation as complex as it is, any mitigation of the consequences of trade cycles now obtaining merits consideration.

A proposal somewhat distinct from the above consists, not in an attempted mitigation of cyclical fluctuations, but in spreading their consequences in so far as the wage earners are concerned. It consists in a flexible policy of work in hours and in the substitution of partial unemployment among many for complete unemployment among the few. Thus if the labor supply is fully employed in times of good trade, a decrease in the hours from ten to nine, would, roughly, take care of a ten per cent decline in employment. A policy of spreading work can be carried out in either of two ways—reducing the number of hours worked, or reducing the number of days worked. Neither of these methods is new. In coal mining in both England and the United States the practice has long been a regular feature "organized and advised by the employers' association." [8] In the recent depression (1930) out of 598 firms reporting in New York, 292 had some plan for stabilizing employment; 157 of these with 62,899 employees used the method of part-time work.[9] But while this practice is now utilized, a wider extension upon a fixed policy is needed. If the practice were generalized, and a flexible policy of hours were adopted, it could also be utilized in times of good trade as a check to additions to the working force from other industries and age groups not otherwise employed.[10]

[8] Beveridge, *Unemployment,* p. 221.
[9] *The Industrial Bulletin of the Industrial Commissioner of New York State,* June, 1930, p. 251.
[10] This method is now (February, 1931) being proposed by the German Chancellor Bruening for the grave emergency which confronts that country.

While the consequences of these two methods are the same as far as the workers are concerned, a choice will depend upon the relative costs involved in keeping plants running every day or only a few days each week, depending on such factors as the size of the managerial staff, varying output per hour, etc.

The advantages of such a policy to the employers are by no means unimportant. Keeping together a trained labor force, accustomed to the work and peculiarities of the individual enterprise, removes the costs involved in hiring and training new workers in a later period. It will also tend to foster a greater amount of loyalty and coöperation than would otherwise be the case.

From the point of view of the workers, it will involve a smaller income for many and some provision for all, whereas now the income of some remains practically unaltered, and a few have no income at all during certain periods. On utility grounds this will lead to a greater aggregate of welfare.

But two points should be noted. There will be no alteration in the money demand for wage goods but merely a shift from some kinds of goods which the otherwise fully employed workers would buy, to goods which those who would otherwise be unemployed will buy. In fact, in so far as those who would otherwise be unemployed are supported through charity, there may be a diminution in the demand for wage goods. Under a system of unemployment insurance this is an even more important consideration. In either event the effect would not be great.

The second point has to do with the possible immobility of labor. If certain enterprises, or whole industries, have attached to themselves a larger labor supply during a period of prosperity than is justified by the long run trend, and—more important—than can be employed in a succeeding period of prosperity, a policy of partial employment will keep more workers attached who should be encouraged to place themselves elsewhere. The coal and clothing industries may well be cases in point. It is also somewhat significant in view of the accretions to the labor supply which take place from agricultural pursuits, women, and lower age groups. A policy of partial employment will encourage these to hang on to the industry when social policy may demand that they return to their former occupation or go completely out of employment. Some remedy can no doubt be worked out by taking these facts into account, but a policy of employment on other than grounds of suitability has its disadvantages.

But in spite of these difficulties and especially as long as unemployment insurance is not available, the policy of flexible hours of work ought to be greatly extended. This is especially the case if it is practiced in good and bad times alike.

CHAPTER XVII

THE STABILIZATION OF PRICES AND THE BUSINESS CYCLE

There is a general agreement among writers on business cycles that periods of rising prices are associated with increasing employment and periods of decreasing prices with increasing unemployment. There is general disagreement as to the definite causal connection between these phenomena. Thus on the one hand, Mr. Hawtrey regards the business cycle as a purely monetary phenomenon. "An expansion of credit and therefore of purchasing power stimulates sales, depletes stocks of commodities, increases orders to producers, raises prices, and altogether makes business at every stage more active and more profitable. Thereby the demand for bank credit is again intensified and a vicious circle of inflation is set up.[1] Professor Pigou, on the other hand, while granting the significance of the factor, places it as only one among many in the causal sequence of industrial fluctuations.[2] The other writers adhere to one or the other of these positions. It follows, therefore, that in coming to remedies for industrial fluctuations these writers place varying emphasis on the control of credit and the price level. Some, like Professor Fisher and Mr. Hawtrey, see in price stabilization and credit control the medium for eliminating all fluctuations. Others, however, look to these measures more as a method of lessening the violent character of the fluctuations. For practical purposes we need make

---

[1] Hawtrey, *Monetary Reconstruction*, p. 107. Professor Hansen was of a similar opinion when he stated that the "Cycle of prosperity and depression is at bottom a question of money, credit, and prices." *Cycles of Prosperity and Depression,* p. 110. In a more recent book Professor Hansen has somewhat tempered his views in this regard. See *Business Cycle Theory.*

[2] Pigou, *Industrial Fluctuations*, Part II, Chs. IV-VI.

no conclusion as to the merits of these opposing views. It is enough that there is a direct relationship between prices and employment and that a restriction of the volume of bank credit during periods of expansion which will check the rising prices, and an increase in the volume of bank credit during periods of depression which will check the falling prices will help to lessen, if not to remove, the fluctuations in production and tend to stabilize employment.

The method of direct stabilization of the price level through regulation of the quantity of money and the method of indirect stabilization through the control of bank credit are somewhat distinct and should be discussed first separately and then as to their relationships.

1. Direct Stabilization Through Regulating the Quantity of Money Under the Gold Standard

This method has become associated in the public mind with the name of Professor Fisher, who is its most ardent advocate. Professor Fisher's approach to the stabilization of the price level was influenced very largely by the injustices which result from price fluctuations in a society where so many of the economic transactions are in the form of contracts for more or less long periods of time, as well as by the importance which he attaches to price fluctuations as causes of business fluctuations.[3] In consequence while his proposal for the compensated dollar is still conspicuous, he also realizes the difficulty of carrying through the proposal in the face of credit manipulation acting to nullify stabilization. Credit control is, therefore, embodied in his proposals. But to this other aspect we shall return shortly. First advanced in 1911 in his book on The Purchasing Power of Money, it has since been discussed at great length.[4] Its essential features are the retention of the gold standard and the variation of the quantity of gold in a

[3] *The Purchasing Power of Money* (1911) and our Unstable Dollar and the So-called Business Cycle, *Journal American Statistical Association,* June, 1925.

[4] For a bibliography from 1911 to 1920 see Fisher, *Stabilizing the Dollar,* pp. 294-6.

dollar in accordance with the variations in a general price index. The proposal is to abolish the actual circulation of gold—which has practically been achieved in the United States—and to rely only on its circulation in the form of paper certificates. It will then be easy from a practical point of view to vary from month to month the quantity of gold bullion which the government will exchange for a paper dollar. "Today the Government will give 25.8 grains of gold bullion to the jeweler or exporter for each dollar of certificates he pays in, next month it might give 26 grains or only 24 grains." [5]

The basis for changing the weight from month to month is not to be left to the discretion of any government official, but is to be an automatic process determined by the variations in the index number of wholesale prices. Just as soon as the index rises by one per cent it will become imperative to increase the weight of the gold dollar by one per cent. The scheme does not hinge on a direct and immediate counteraction. The agency having charge of changing the weight of the dollar might find that the one per cent increase resulted in an insufficient check to prices or in too great a check. Another correction can then be made in the following month. Thus a trial and error process from month to month, while it will involve slight fluctuations around the level at which prices have been stabilized, will remove the kind of fluctuations which now exist. [6] The number of dollars in circulation would be regulated not only by controlling the rate at which the annual flow of fresh gold was converted into money but also by readjusting the outstanding stock of money to the new gold equivalents of the dollar. Thus if prices rose by 5 per cent, the mint would give only $19.64 in certificates in return for an ounce of gold instead of as originally $26.67. This in a closed econ-

---

[5] Fisher, Stabilizing the Dollar, in, Lionel D. Edie (editor), *The Stabilization of Business*, p. 95.

[6] "To avoid speculation in gold at the expense of the Government, a small fee, corresponding to what used to be called 'brassage' should be charged to depositors of gold and no single change in the dollar's weight should exceed that fee." *Ibid.*, p. 100.

omy would diminish the annual accretion to the monetary supply by 5 per cent from what it would otherwise have been. But since the annual addition of money forms but a small fraction of the total supply, it is necessary to control the quantity of the latter as well as the former. The chief means by which Professor Fisher aimed to accomplish this was by providing that, if the price level rose, gold certificates up to the proportionate amount received for taxes would be retired. When prices fell, additional quantities of gold certificates would be issued by the government in payment for salaries, services, etc. In this way the supply of gold certificates would be adjusted to the number of dollars which the supply of gold in the reserves represented. When prices were rising, the government would suffer a loss by the amount of certificates retired but, when prices were falling, they would gain according to the number of new certificates paid out. Although Professor Fisher's plan provided that these latter payments should merely be a substitute for other taxes and should not constitute a fresh addition to governmental expenditures, it is obvious that this is not essential. In periods of falling prices, the issuance of additional money by the government might be used to finance projects which otherwise would not be undertaken and to build up additional social capital in the form of public buildings, roads, parks, and housing for the poor. Although Professor Fisher's plan rests somewhat too heavily upon the assumption that an alteration in the relative amount of money will effect a proportionate alteration in the amount of bank credit, it would be a thoroughly effective method of stabilization if the United States were a closed economy and were not part of a world economic system. As it is, it would be impossible for us to stabilize our internal price level in the face of changing world prices if we insisted at the same time, as some of the proponents of the plan do, in redeeming our certificates in gold and in maintaining our foreign exchanges at par. For if prices began to fall over the world and were only maintained in this country by lessening the gold content of the dollar, which, however, was still kept at its former ratio with other currencies in foreign exchange, then it would follow that gold would have greater value abroad than here and that it would be drawn out of the treasury reserve and leave the country. Thus if the decrease in world prices were to be 10 per cent and the gold content of the dollar in this country were diminished correspondingly by 10 per cent from 23.22 to 20.90 grains, then if the foreign exchanges were maintained at this former parity, there would be a 10 per cent difference between the internal and external value of gold. For while a dollar would be the equal of 20.90 grains in this country it could be changed into 23.22 grains in foreign currencies. The first result would accordingly be speculative selling of American money into foreign currencies. Not only would fresh gold be taken to the American mint to be exchanged for certificates which would then be sold for foreign money but a large part of the outstanding stock of paper money would similarly be sold. This would mean that Europe would have large volumes of claims against our currency which, if it was to be maintained at the previous parity, would have to be redeemed not at the rate of 20.90 grains to the dollar but rather at the rate of 23.22 grains. Our gold reserves would in consequence be depleted, our price level would fall, and in order to maintain it, the gold content of the dollar would have to be still further reduced. But this would widen the disparity between the internal and external value of our gold and would lead to a cumulative speculation in our currency and to the progressive movement of gold abroad.

This in itself would seem to demonstrate the impossibility of maintaining both (1) a stable price level in one country and (2) stable foreign exchange ratios, in the face of world-fluctuations. There are two other forces which would, however, still further aggravate this tendency. Since a "dollar" would purchase more abroad because of the fall in the foreign price-level, than it would internally, then foreign travel would increase and more people with fixed incomes would go to live abroad. Imports of foreign goods into the

United States would moreover increase. While the continued flow of gold abroad would exercise a compensating influence by raising the foreign price level, this would be distributed over a wide economic system and would in all likelihood be insufficient to prevent the ultimate virtual disappearance of gold from the United States and with it the breakdown of the stabilization plan.[7] As long indeed as the currencies of the world are tied together at any fixed ratio, it will be impossible for any one country to stabilize its price level by itself. As we shall abundantly see, if the stability of the exchanges is to be insisted upon, only a world program of monetary control and price stabilization can be effective.

On the whole, Professor Fisher's proposal has the merit of being automatic and not depending on the discretion of government or banking officials. It is, however, subject to the cost of retaining large stocks of gold which might otherwise be lent at interest and it is tied up with the consequences of the future gold production of the world. Even more is it doubtful whether in spite of its distinguished advocates, there is any chance of governments being inveigled into its adoption. It would seem indeed as though the chances of introducing a paper currency wholly divorced from gold are better. To this we shall return later and now we turn to the considerations involving credit control as a means of reducing the fluctuations of business activity.

2. INDIRECT STABILIZATION THROUGH CREDIT CONTROL

Although the stabilization of the price level through credit control has recently received a great deal of attention because of the violent price fluctuations of the past fifteen years, it is not a new thing. Thus since the Bank Act of 1844 the Bank of England has so controlled its credit policy

---

[7] Professor Fisher has pointed out that under his plan the exchange rates would adjust themselves to changes in the gold content of the dollar. See his Stabilizing the Dollar, pp. 172-79.

as to eliminate the financial panics which formerly accompanied every business expansion. A similar policy has been followed in the United States since the establishment of the Federal Reserve Board. The basis of contr   followed has been the ratio of reserves to deposits. In both countries when the ratio of deposits to reserves approaches the maximum, it has been taken as a sign that the discount rate should be increased and hence act as a check on the demand for credit. Similarly, when the ratio falls away from the maximum, it becomes a sign that loans should be expanded and hence the discount rate is lowered.

But such control has thus far proved inadequate to do anything more than to prevent a financial panic. Much more is now required, and it is realized that the ratio of reserves to deposits is no longer an adequate guide if the object is to achieve a stabilization of business. Some other criterion is essential. Those in favor of such stabilization fall into two groups: (1) a few, who would like the banks so to exercise their control over credit as to keep prices stable, and (2) the majority, who would like to see merely an extension of the present policy of control which would be more effective in checking the expansion of business activity and thereby lessen the subsequent contraction.

The latter is at once the simpler of the two and in some degree is actually being practiced. It is capable of much extension. For this purpose we need make no decision as to the validity of a rigid form of the Quantity Theory of Money—which is now much disputed. All we need to assume is that an increase in the quantity of monetary purchasing power—whether in the form of gold, bank credit, or increase in the velocity of circulation—will lead to an increase in the general price level, or a decrease in the value of money, and that on the other hand, a decrease in the quantity of monetary purchasing power will lead to a decrease in the general price level or to an increase in the value of money. As bank credit is today the most important and flexible element of purchasing power, it follows that a contraction in bank credit will check an increase in a rising price level and that an expansion of bank credit will check a decline.

Now there are two distinct ways of controlling the volume of bank credit. It can be done either by changing the quantity directly through rationing or by changing its quantity indirectly by controlling its price, *i.e.*, the discount rate. As the first depends on the arbitrary control by many individual bankers it is not likely to receive very serious consideration. The second is not only receiving serious consideration but is actually being practiced in a limited way. Thus Mr. Keynes points out that the pre-war convention by which the Bank of England varied its extension of credit in accordance with the flow of gold has already been destroyed. "The war broke down the convention; for the withdrawal of gold from actual circulation destroyed one of the elements of reality lying behind the convention, and the suspension of convertibility destroyed the other. It would have been absurd to regulate the bank rate by reference to a 'proportion' which had lost all its significance; and in the course of the past ten years a new policy has been evolved. The bank rate is now employed, however, incompletely and experimentally, to regulate the expansion and deflation of credit in the interests of business stability and the steadiness of prices. Insofar as it is employed to procure stability of the dollar exchange, where this is inconsistent with stability of internal prices, we have a relic of pre-war policy and a compromise between discrepant aims." [8] A similar abandonment of the convention is seen in the United States where the Federal Reserve Board has impounded a great deal of the gold which has flowed in during and since the war, thus preventing an expansion of the reserves and a corresponding expansion of credit.

It is therefore not a new policy which needs to be advocated, but the extension of an experimental one now in vogue. How much can be expected in this direction?

Before the debacle of 1921 the Federal Reserve Board apparently realized the need of putting the brakes on credit expansion. In 1919 it wrote in its report: "The expansion

[8] Keynes, *Monetary Reform*, pp. 185-6.

of credit set in motion by the war must be checked. Credit must be brought under effective control and its flow be once more regulated and governed with careful regard to the economic welfare of the country and need of its producing industries." [9] While nothing was done to check the speculation of 1920, the collapse of 1921 brought additional testimony on the part of both officials and economists as to the merits of control. Thus former Governor Strong before the Joint Commission of Agricultural Inquiry in August, 1921, stated his opinion as follows: "I believe if it had been possible it would have been desirable for the Federal Reserve System to have advanced its rates at some point in the period between January and March, 1919." [1] This was also the view of Mr. A. C. Miller of the Federal Reserve Board. After pointing out that the credit situation in 1919 needed restraint, he goes on to say: "It would have been of the greatest advantage to the country if such restraint had been exercised by the Federal Reserve System in the year 1919, and the development of the runaway and speculative markets which developed in the second half of the year been measurably prevented." [11]

Similarly, Professor Sprague, speaking of the same period declared that: "Liberal credit was no longer as at the beginning of a period of activity, serving to stimulate and direct industry into promising channels. It was rather tending to disorganize industry, subjecting it to an increasing extent to speculative influences, to wage disputes and to numberless other strains. . . . A check on further credit expansion followed by some contraction was the one sure remedy. . . ." [12]

The fact that this policy of contraction was not exercised because of the financial policy of the United States Treasury is of no import for long-run considerations. The real significance lies in the general agreement that credit con

---

[9] *Annual Report for 1919*, p. 71.
[10] Hearing before the Joint Commission of Agricultural Inquiry, *67th Congress, First Session, Part 13*, p. 763.
[11] *American Economic Review*, June, 1921, p. 188.
[12] *Ibid.*, March, 1921, p. 23.

trol at the proper time would tend to reduce the expansion
of business activity and at the same time prevent as great
a contraction as is otherwise the case. But to what extent
may we rely on a future use of the discount rate based upon
considerations other than the reserve ratio, and how effective will such a tool prove to be?

The first objection which is commonly raised lies in the
existing strength of the reserves as a regulator of discount
rates, the lack of justification in the Reserve Act for a departure from that policy, and the prevailing public sentiment as distinct from expert opinion, which would disap-
prove such a departure. To quote Mr. A. C. Miller, a member of the Federal Reserve Board who was in favor of some
control of credit in 1919: "The proposals often made in
recent months to abandon the reserve ratio as an indicator
of discount policy and to base discount policy hereafter on
the observed effects of credit on prices, have therefore, the
character of academic proposals, even in present circumstances, which it must candidly be admitted, are less favorable, than was ordinarily true in the past, to quick respon-
siveness on the part of the reserve ratio to changing business, credit, and price conditions." [13] But we are inclined to
the view that while tradition is an important factor, it is
not a permanent obstacle—even under the assumption
that legislative action is necessary. The establishment of
the Federal Reserve System was itself a departure from
tradition much sharper than is involved in the proposal we
are considering.

But there are other more fundamental objections. Mr.
Miller in the same article raises the adequacy of price
changes as the sole criterion of discount policy for the
United States: "A great variety of factors enter into the
determination of appropriate discount policy. Among these
may be mentioned the state of business, industry, and trade
(both domestic and foreign), the state of money markets
(both domestic and foreign), international gold movements, seasonal conditions and needs, accidental economic

[13] *Ibid.*, June, 1921, p. 192.

disturbances, sometimes political conditions and the international situation, the stage of the business cycle, price movements, and the state of banking reserves. No one of these by itself can be conclusive of action to be taken. . . . But when all this is said, it may yet be added that ordinarily there is no one indicator which is more suggestive of the occasion of considering action on the part of a reserve bank than a change in its reserve ratio." [14] And this indicator has so far proved anything but effective. But for the limited control we are now considering, the multiplicity of factors cannot prevent a greater consideration being given to the state of the business cycle.

substitute criterion for the reserve ratio is not difficult to establish as long as we are content with the modest aim, not of influencing changes in prices connected with variations in the world's gold supply, or with changes in demand for commodities entering into international trade. but rather of influencing price fluctuations within a business cycle, so as to check the upward movement and at the same time lessen the violence of the rebound. For such a purpose it is merely necessary to adopt a discount policy designed to check the rapid expansion of credit in a period of great economic expansion. Professor Sprague has proposed the use of indices of production as a substitute criterion of reserve ratios. When a revival in business first takes place the expansion of credit is utilized to increase the flow of income. It is actually used to launch new enterprises and intensify the use of existing capital equipment. There comes a time, however, when the expansion of credit is used merely as a means of speculation. The existing labor supply is fully utilized. Additional loans are used to bid for labor already employed and to attract it from agriculture and from groups not otherwise employed. It is used to increase orders which are never expected to be filled and to boost prices. Hence when the index of production ceases to advance it is a sure sign that the limit of economic expansion in the form of increased income has been reached.

[14] *Ibid.*, p. 195.

At such times the discount rates should be so increased as to check any further demand for credit and if necessary to contract it.

We must now inquire how effective an increase in the discount rate will be on the demand for credit. The first limitation is to be sought in the fact that interest costs form but one of many, and not always the most important, element of cost.[15] A rise of one or two or three points may therefore not be a sufficient deterrent to the demand for credit. Further, the response to an increase in the discount rate is very slow. The rise in the short-time rate of interest may moreover well attract a much larger quantity of capital to the short-time market and make available an increased rather than a decreased amount of credit for borrowers. On the one hand, men within the given country will be attracted by the high rates of interest on commercial loans and in some cases will spend less and in others will invest a smaller amount in bonds, etc. In either case, they will bring more deposits to the short-time market. Nor is this all. If the rates of interest have been raised in one country above the level in others, the inevitable result will be a transfer of bank funds to the country which has increased its rate and which will go far to nullify the intended effect of the heightened rate. The increase of the rediscount rate in 1929 by the Federal Reserve Board in its effort to check stock speculation had such consequences. European banks, particularly the English, deposited large amounts on call with the American banks and thus enabled the speculative practices to go on.

Thus far we have been speaking of the ability of banks to check cyclical price rises by increases in the discount rate. It is doubtful whether these measures by themselves would completely remove them and still more doubtful whether such a policy could prevent a secular increase in

---

[15] It should be pointed out, however, that in the case of merchants demanding bank credit in order to carry stocks of goods, the interest rate is a very important element of costs. An increase in the discount rate will affect substantially their demand, and therefore indirectly the demand on the part of producers.

the price level, such as occurred during the period 1897-1914, from taking effect.

The difficulties in the way of checking a cyclical fall in prices through the rediscount policy are even greater. When prices fall during the depression phase of the business cycle, interest rates fall also, with the rates on short-time loans of course decreasing more rapidly than the long-time interest rate. In such periods of depression, the banks, because of their high reserve ratios of money to outstanding credit, have already large potential supplies of unused credit which they would like to loan out. They are unable to do so because businesses as a whole do not wish to expand their output and hence do not care to borrow these additional sums. Business men are afraid that prices will fall still further and that the monetary value of their goods will shrink in the process of manufacture. The demand for capital goods, as we have pointed out, shrinks moreover at an accelerated rate and with a declining sales volume, business does not want to increase its borrowings.

Since banks have therefore virtually no need to rediscount their loans in order to obtain more credit, a lowering of the rediscount rate will in itself be of little or no assistance in reviving activity. Ultimately, to be sure, the lower interest rate will furnish one of the conditions which are favorable for revival but before this occurs much misery is suffered during the period of depression.

Some of these same difficulties, although in an attenuated form, would continue to exist where the decline in prices was slow and gradual rather than catastrophic. There would be a tendency for business to borrow smaller sums, in the face of gradually shrinking prices and profits. The pressure for rediscounting would appreciably abate and with it the power to stimulate loans by a reduction of the rediscount rate. The lowering of costs through a reduction in the interest rates would be of some stimulus to business but would probably not be sufficient to lead business men to pursue a policy of expansion while prices were falling.

It is therefore much more difficult to check decreases in the price level, whether these be cyclical or secular in their nature, through altering the rediscount rate than it is to check increases in prices.

3. CONTROL THROUGH OPEN-MARKET OPERATIONS

Another means of controlling the volume of credit issued by banks, and hence the price-level, is that of open-market operations by the central banking agencies. By selling, during periods of prosperity and price increases, government bonds, bankers' acceptances, and other first-class paper to the banks, the central banking authority can absorb some of the lending power of the banks and thus reduce the amount of fresh credit which they can advance to business. An indirect method of restricting credit and reducing price advances is thus effected. In periods of recession, the central banking agencies conversely can buy government bonds, etc., from the banks and thus increase their power of creating credit and of expanding loans. But whether this will result in a corresponding increase in the amount of fresh bank loans which are made to business is somewhat doubtful since, as we have pointed out, it is necessary that business men want to borrow these sums of credit as well as for the sums to be available. And while business men will be attracted by the lower rate of interest which results from the abundance of credit, they will also be deterred by the general shrinkage in prices and the declining volume of sales.

The possibilities of checking a cyclical increase in prices are greater therefore than those of arresting a cyclical decline.

In so far as a slow secular fall in price is concerned, some relief would be given to the banks in gradually making available increased supplies of credit, but here again the difficulty comes from the demand side as to whether business, exposed to such difficulties, would wish to borrow more.

4. INTERNATIONAL INFLUENCES AND THE RELATIVE EFFECTIVENESS OF PRESENT METHODS

We should not moreover neglect the interconnection of the price systems of the various nations of the world which make even the lessening of cyclical swings difficult for any one country to effect. For if by credit control, the upward cyclical movement in prices in our country is checked while in other countries the price level rises, the result will be: (1) that foreign currencies will be sold for American exchange and gold will move into this country with a consequent increase in our bank reserves and a partial undoing of all that our Federal Reserve authorities had sought to accomplish through the manipulation of the rediscount rate and the sale of securities, (2) that our exports will be stimulated and our imports reduced, which will cause a further movement of gold into the country.

The opposite results would of course occur should we be able to lessen the fall in our price level at a time when world prices were sagging. The imports would increase and our dealers in foreign exchange would buy foreign currency. Gold would flow out and our price level would fall:

The truth of the matter is that under the gold standard, the web of international prices is such that aside from the disturbing influences of tariffs, transportation costs, and the inertia of individuals to move, there is a powerful tendency for the price levels of commodities which enter into international trade to approximate each other in all countries. It is difficult for the banking officials of any one country to stabilize or greatly to mitigate any appreciable fluctuation of prices which is worldwide in nature.

It seems safe to conclude therefore,—(1) that the possibilities of lessening cyclical fluctuations in business through credit control are greater for lessening the price advances during the prosperity periods than for arresting the price declines in the phases of recession and depression; (2) that under the gold standard even the former purpose cannot be worked out with full effectiveness by the banking officials of any one country alone. Some concerted action by the banking officials of the leading industrial nations is needed to realize the full advantages. (3) while it is probable that the depressive effects of a slow secular fall in the world price level can be mitigated by a cheapening of bank credit or a lowering of reserve ratios, it is not certain that this reduction in cost will be sufficient to induce business men to take full advantage of it in view of the increasing unprofitableness of business; (4) there would seem to be a necessity for governments to adopt more direct methods for seeing to it that the increased potential credit is actually put into circulation so that it can buoy up prices.

It would seem probable that if the nations are to stabilize their price levels, they must not tie themselves so implicitly to gold and to existing reserve ratios as is now the case. It is only a coincidence if the production of gold increases at the same rate as the production of goods, and therefore only a fortunate accident if the price level under present conditions is stabilized. If governments could be trusted to issue money and banks to issue credit in accordance with the movement of production, then a much closer approximation to stability would be obtained. This would seem to be a more rational basis for a currency than gold itself. But gold in the past has retained its position for reasons other than mere sentiment and inertia. Its chief advantage has been that it is more limited in quantity than man's foolishness and that when governments have broken away from a gold and adopted a paper currency, they have generally increased the quantity of money much more rapidly than production. The consequent result has generally been inflation with all its attendant injustices and disturbances. A gold standard will not fluctuate as much as this and if governments in the future can no more be trusted than governments in the past, then it would be much better to retain the gold standard with all of its attendant evils than to fly to others which would be far greater.

If, however, governments and banks in their financial power could be guided by economists and statisticians, who would be for the modern nation what Plato wanted his philosopher-kings to be for the Greek city-states, then it would be possible to issue only such quantities of money and credit as would keep the general price level approximately constant. There are perhaps four ways in which this might be done.

(1) By gradually lowering the present reserve ratios of central banks. The amount of credit which banks can create is fundamentally limited by the minimum ratios of gold which they are required by law to keep in reserve for the purpose of redemption against their note issues and sight liabilities. These minimum ratios average for the various countries of the world somewhere between 29 and 34 per cent.[16] In practice banks of issue generally find it necessary to keep a margin of safety of some 7 to 10 per cent above this legal minimum so that at present the quantity of bank-notes and sight liabilities in the world as a whole cannot normally be expanded above two and one-half times the quantity of gold. It is interesting to observe that this was the precise ratio which existed in 1928 since in that year the aggregate of bank-notes and sight liabilities was 24.5 billions of dollars as compared with the 10.0 billions of gold reserves.

If, as we have predicted, the world price level should in the future slowly decline because of the dimnishing rate of gold production, then one method of meeting the situation would be for the various nations and central banks gradually to reduce their reserve requirements so that the bank-note issue could expand sufficiently to compensate for the deficiency in gold. As the Gold Delegation of the League of Nations remarks,[17] "The minimum reserves which are required by law today are to a large extent the outcome of past tradition, of convention and habit, of the natural fear which each individual legislature has that a departure from general practice may impair confidence in the currency."

---

[16] *Interim Report of the Gold Delegation of the League of Nations,* *op. cit.,* p. 14.
[17] *Ibid.,* p. 19.

Since these ratios are conventional, "a considerable economy could quite certainly be accomplished were the current accepted minima reduced."

Individual nations might be reluctant to reduce their ratios because of their fear that it might be interpreted as a sign of weakness and thus operate to impair their credit. Furthermore, action by any one nation alone would have only a partial effect upon the world price level. But were a number of the most important nations to agree on such a policy no prestige would be lost and relief would be afforded.

These reserve ratios should not be suddenly and sharply reduced since this would permit a great expansion of credit which would in turn cause the price level to rise appreciably and would result in inflation. The reduction should instead proceed gradually by small percentages to offset a slow decline in the price level and should be subject to review if the price level did not continue to fall. The manipulation of the reserve ratio should be used for the stabilization of the long-time or secular price-level. It cannot and should not be used to prevent cyclical fluctuations in prices which should be controlled in other ways. Its function would, in other words, be comparable to raising the height of the monetary and credit ceiling gradually so that the normal increase of production and business could proceed without pressing too severely against it, but it should not move violently up and down in the effort to follow the fluctuations of business.

(2) By increasing the discount rate and resorting to open market operations on the up-swing in the business cycle. By the use of these methods, the rise in the price level which generally characterizes periods of prosperity can, as we have pointed out, be somewhat reduced and the consequent swings of the business cycle mitigated.

(3) By transforming the present gold standard into the gold exchange standard. Under such a plan, there would be a managed internal currency not redeemable in gold but the foreign exchanges of the various countries would be kept

at a parity with each other. An international gold settlement fund would be set up in some center, preferably with the International Bank of Settlements at Basel and balances of claims would be cleared here daily and the debits and credits of the various countries adjusted by transferring claims for gold from one to another. This international fund would therefore be used in a manner analogous to the gold settlement fund which is used in this country by the Federal Reserve Board to balance the checking claims of the various Federal Reserve Districts against each other.

Internally, however, each country would regulate its currency according to the movement of trade and production and with a view to stabilizing prices as completely as possible. More money would be issued during periods of depression in payment for government services. As we have pointed out, such financing might be compensated for by corresponding reductions in the amount of taxes levied or additional public projects might be embarked upon. In this latter way society might get some needed social capital such as housing for the urban unskilled workers who are unable at present to get decent accommodations, out of what would otherwise be working time lost through unemployment.

This would not be a completely costless creation of commodities, as is claimed by some, since the fact that the fall in prices would partially be arrested would mean that recipients of fixed incomes would not be able to buy as much as they otherwise would. But, as we have pointed out, there would be a net social gain.

The financing of such public works should, as we have pointed out, preferably be conducted by the floating of bonds, or by the issuance of added money by the government rather than by taxes. The first two methods enable the work to be financed by the creation of fresh monetary purchasing power instead of by transferring some purchasing power from the taxpayers. To the average man who by the experience of the past and by the admonitions of "hard-money" economists, has been taught to fear the issuance of paper money by the government, the method of bond issues undoubtedly seems preferable. But bond issues must be repaid with interest and this is not the case with an issue of paper money. The most that could occur would be a future retirement of money if the price level should move upward above the level at which it is to be stabilized. The issuance of money for such purposes bids fair therefore to cost the government and the taxpayers less than would the issuance of bonds.

It may be asked how such a system furnishes any safeguard against inflation. Since the monetary units are no longer subject to redemption in gold, it might seem as though there would be no protection against the possibility that the government, urged on by debtors and industrialists who benefit from rising prices, might increase the supply of money much more rapidly than was justified by the increase in production. But such a policy would cause an inevitable increase of imports into the country with the result that our gold balance would be seriously threatened. The desire to protect these balances and to keep the exchanges constant would therefore be a restraining influence against inflation. Even should other countries inflate their currency with the result that our exports to them and consequently our gold balance would increase, there would be no necessary rise in our price level. For our added gold would neither enter into circulation nor swell our internal bank reserves but would instead be sterilized in our account at the International Bank.

Such a plan would be economically practicable were the chief nations of the world only willing to transfer their gold reserves to such a center. But this in the present disturbed state of world affairs is politically impracticable. The nations would be afraid that in the event of a general war, their gold reserves would either be confiscated or else shut off from them. Until the nations feel assured of world peace, therefore, this reform must wait. This is merely another instance of how the threat of war impedes the economic development of the world by failure to adopt policies, which, were it not for war, would be eminently sensible for the nations to adopt.

Probably the most that can be hoped for is that such a policy may be adopted by groups of countries between the members of which there is little likelihood of war. Thus the British commonwealth of nations, including Canada, Australia, and South Africa, might adopt the gold exchange standard with the central reserve maintained in London. India of course had an almost precisely similar arrangement from 1893, when she was the first country to adopt the gold exchange standard, to 1927. Another possible nucleus would be France, Belgium, and Switzerland which are all nations which were once joined together in a common policy through the Latin monetary union. The Scandinavian countries are another natural combination, and there are other possibilities as well. If the United States and Great Britain could go so far as to forget their rivalries and pool their gold reserves, it would of course greatly increase the economies which any such program might effect.

(4) If the nations of the world do not choose to pool their gold reserves and effect a world-wide stabilization of prices through internally managed currencies and the gold exchange standard, it is still possible for individual nations to maintain internally stable price levels. They can do so, however, only if they abandon the gold standard not only for their internal currency but also for their foreign exchange. For then as they increase the issuance of money as the index of production rises and stabilize their prices as the world price level falls, there will be no corresponding flow of gold out of the country to drag the national price level down to the world's basis. For gold will not be exported or imported as a monetary unit and the adjustments of international balances will take place through the fluctuations in the exchange ratios of the various currencies. If prices were to remain up in the United States, because of its system of managed currency, while prices elsewhere were sagging, then so long as the old exchange rates of $4.866=£1 prevailed, American dollars when con-

verted into English pounds could purchase more in England, for example, than they could in the United States. The result would be that dealers in foreign exchange would sell American currency into the British and with the latter buy English goods for export into the United States. At the same time because of the economies, American travel in England would be stimulated. But while we would have to settle for these claims against us, nevertheless, because of the lower price level, they would not aggregate as much as the volume of American currency which was initially sold or exchanged. The result would be that with this surplus of our claims against England, which could not be settled in gold, American exchange would necessarily fall. It would tend to fall by an amount equal to the proportionate decline in the world price level. The exchange of goods and services between nations would then take place on approximately the same terms as before but with different exchange ratios for the currencies.

It is thus possible for one nation to stabilize its price level in the midst of a general world movement if it is willing to go off the gold exchange standard and allow its exchanges to fluctuate.

We should like to emphasize however that this program for a controlled price level and a managed system of currency and credit is conditional upon the exercise of sound economic judgment on the part of responsible officials and that it is based upon the assumption that stabilization rather than inflation would be the end sought. If this cannot be achieved, then it would be better to stick to the present gold standard. In any event, it will probably be wise to wait for several years to determine whether the recent fall in the price level will give a sufficient stimulus to the production of gold and to the monetary uses of that metal so that any further appreciable fall in the price level will be averted. If it is not, and if a shortage of gold continues, the world should move carefully towards some such program of stabilization as has been suggested.

PART FIVE

THE PLACEMENT OF LABOR

CHAPTER XVIII

THE FUNCTIONS AND PROBLEMS OF PUBLIC EMPLOYMENT OFFICES

A coördinated system of public employment offices can, by promoting a more efficient distribution of labor, reduce to some degree the amount of unemployment and be of service to both workers and employers:

(1) By providing a central place to which both jobs and applicants are referred, it can lessen the time lost by the workers in hunting for jobs and the expense which the employers suffer in unnecessary interviewing of the applicants they do not hire.

(2) By providing a central labor reserve, it can remove the necessity for individual enterprises maintaining separate and distinct reserves of labor to meet their peak loads. This is especially significant in industries employing large groups of casual workers.

(3) It can protect the workers from the exactions of private employment agencies which in many cases have charged excessively high fees for inadequate service and have been guilty of many unfair practices.

(4) It can provide special services to particular groups of workers such as juveniles, women workers, the aged, and those who have been forced out of an industry or locality by industrial shifts and who otherwise would be inadequately protected.

(5) It can furnish information about the state of the labor market not only as a whole but also in relation to specific industries and lines of work.

(6) If public unemployment insurance were to be established, a system of employment offices would be essential to the efficient administration of the measure.

1. The Reduction of Time Lost in the Seeking of Employment

The amount of unnecessary time which the unemployed lose in hunting for work from establishment to establishment is in its aggregate very large. Innumerable cases have been found of men who have actively but unsuccessfully sought work for long periods of time when there were suitable jobs close at hand which they did not know about. Even more cruel instances of waste occur when men will leave their homes, and lured on by false rumors of possible employment go to other cities to seek work unsuccessfully there. This may be and frequently is accompanied by some workers leaving these very cities into which labor is pouring and seeking work in the cities from whence these other workers are coming.

What is clearly needed therefore is some organized market for labor whereby the information about the jobs which are available on the one hand, and the men who are available upon the other may be made available to workers and employers.

We have already developed such organized markets for almost every variety of commodity except labor. Cotton, wheat, corn, oats, barley, rye, beef, pork, copper, tin, and scores of other products all have more or less highly organized markets to which buyers and sellers may go and where local surpluses and deficits are correspondingly adjusted by means of purchase and sale with a consequent transfer. But there is no such central clearing house for labor.

The labor market while disorganized, is not, however, quite the chaos which it is sometimes pictured as being. Agencies have developed to help bridge the gap between workers and jobs. In addition to personal services of friends and acquaintances, help wanted columns of newspapers, private employment agencies, and those conducted by some employers' associations and by some trade unions also help to place large numbers. These agencies are incomplete in that they cover only a small section of the field and have many incidental defects which mar the service they render. They have come into being in default of something better. They are not logically adequate substitutes for an all-inclusive, impartial, and non-profitmaking clearing house.

Such a clearing house would not only be of service to laborers in acquainting them with suitable available jobs but it would also be of service to employers by carrying through at least the first rough siftings of applicants and hence would reduce their employment costs. Not only do men lose time tramping from job to job but employers also lose time interviewing them. One large company in Chicago which employs on the average 40,000 men, interviews 250,-000 applicants a year in order to fill 25,000 jobs. It interviews, in other words, 10 men for every 1 it finally hires, and despite this apparently rigid selection, it has a labor turnover of approximately 60 per cent. Now, if the first sifting of labor could be done by public employment offices, it might easily be possible to reduce this ratio from 10 to 1 to 4 to 1. Even this reduction would save the company in question 150,000 interviews a year, which would probably amount to several hundred thousand dollars.

It should, however, be admitted that during periods of appreciable unemployment, men out of work will not content themselves solely with applying at the employment offices and waiting there for work. They will be afraid that not all of the jobs will be reported to these offices and may moreover suspect, however unjustly, that favoritism is being used in referring men to the available jobs. In addition to applying at the public offices, they will therefore almost inevitably tramp from one work place to another, in the hope that they may find a job for themselves. Under such circumstances therefore the public exchanges cannot be expected to abolish the tramping for work, nor is it perhaps desirable that they should completely do so. But at the very least, even at such times they lessen the amount of time which those whom they place would otherwise have lost.

2. The Economies of a Pooled Labor Reserve

A system of public employment offices can reduce the separate labor reserves maintained by individual businesses and by establishing a common pool of labor can release for other occupations men who otherwise would be unemployed or underemployed.

There are few establishments which need the same number of men throughout the year. Their business fluctuates from season to season and in some cases even within a month or a week. It is important for them therefore to have a reserve of labor somewhere upon which they can draw to meet the needs of these periods. Failing a general reservoir of labor from which they can draw, they feel compelled in self-defense to build up their own. They therefore tend to hold about them sufficient labor to meet their own peak load. But since not all businesses have their peaks at the same time, it follows that to the degree that each enterprise maintains its own reserve, there will be workers unemployed even at the busiest point for society as a whole. In modern times, this tendency of separate labor reserves to create more idleness than that necessitated by the general fluctuations of business as a whole, was first clearly pointed out by Sir W. H. Beveridge in his classic work on *Unemployment*. It can be illustrated most clearly by examples drawn either from longshore work or the loading of grain elevators.

Let us asume that there are ten wharves in a given port to each of which vessels naturally come somewhat irregularly. The needs of each wharf for men to unload and load the ships varies within a week from a minimum of 40 to a maximum of 100. The relatively busy and idle days of the various wharves do not, however, precisely coincide. While one wharf on a given day will need only 40 men, another will need 60 and another perhaps 100 and so on. Similarly when the first wharf is at its busiest with 100 men at work, some of the other wharves will have employment for only 40, or 50, or 70. In consequence, the number of workers needed in the harbor as a whole will not vary during a week from 400 to 1000 but rather from such a figure as 500 to one, let us say, of 700.

But if each wharf maintains its own labor reserve and holds workers outside of its gates to care for its own maximum needs, then each wharf will have attached to it 100 men and the supply for the harbor as a whole will be 1000. On the busiest day therefore under these circumstances, there will be 300 unemployed men in the harbor. The fluctuation of work within the harbor as a whole from 500 to 700 will account for the fluctuations in employment of 200 workers. But this excess loading of the labor market with 300 men is directly chargeable to the practice of maintaining separate labor reserves.

But, it may be asked, why will these men attach themselves to one particular wharf and not seek employment at other wharves when their own cannot offer them employment? The answer is of course that it is something of a fiction to postulate labor reserves for each plant which are totally and completely distinct from those of others. There is naturally some overlapping. But a complete pooling is prevented by a number of reasons. Ignorance is one of these. The workers do not fully know what the employment opportunities are elsewhere, and to this degree are not able to offer themselves for employment where it is ready. They are afraid in some measure that if they temporarily seek work elsewhere because their "own" firm cannot offer it to them at the moment, they will not be so readily hired by their own employer when he has need for them again. This fear as a matter of fact is effectively fostered by the practices of many employers who, in their anxiety to have a sufficient force to meet their own peak, will frown upon and punish those workers among their usual entourage who stray away to take work elsewhere when it cannot be given to them at the usual spot. This practice is naturally at its worst in casual employment where men are hired for only a few hours' or a few days' labor, and where it may seem scarcely worth while to hunt for work elsewhere lest possible employment should open up at the original place.

But the same evil principle is at work in other industries as well. To the degree that men are ignorant of opportunities elsewhere, then separate labor reserves are in fact maintained. To the degree that employers try to maintain their own floating supply of labor which can be brought in during rush times, this excess burden of unemployment is in fact created.

This tendency is also strikingly evidenced at times in various localities. During the winter of 1929-30, the Chamber of Commerce and the principal employers in a large automobile town of the Middle West made strenuous efforts to retain in their city large groups of unemployed men (large numbers of whom they had drawn into the city only a few months before) in order that there might be a sufficient supply of labor ready should business improve. Statements about the extent of unemployment were rigorously discouraged and, though the business prospects were bad, the workers were encouraged to keep applying for work at the factory gates where they were given soft words but little else.

In a somewhat similar fashion it has been the general practice for southern mill owners to bring into their villages not only enough workers to man the factories in the busiest season and to fill the ranks of absentees but in many cases to provide a still further surplus.

Through such methods as well as from ignorance, idle pools of labor are built up within separate communities at times when men may be needed elsewhere.

In order, however, for a plant to keep the excess numbers attached to them, it is necessary to dole out sufficient employment to keep them in line. If the minimum number of men needed by a plant in a week is 40, the maximum 100, and the average 60, then to hire 40 of the men for full-time would leave only an average of one-third for the remaining 60 men. Since this would generally not be enough employment to tie these men to the firm, a more likely distribution would be to have around 20 men on full-time, and then for the remaining 80 to work approximately half of their time. The ratio might indeed go even lower so as to have only 10 on full-time, and to have the other 90 work approximately 55 per cent of the working week. There would thus be a large percentage of underemployment, and the majority of the workers and their families would suffer greatly.

This situation could be cleared up were the full coöperation of the employers given to a central employment exchange which would pool the fluctuating demands for men upon only the number needed for the port as a whole and which would squeeze out the surplus drawn in by separate labor reserves. In the illustration which has been given, each firm would maintain only the 40 men which it needed as a minimum. There would therefore be 400 men attached to the separate wharves. The central employment office would then maintain the reserve of 300 men which would be needed to fill up the difference between the numbers specifically attached to the wharves and the 700 men needed to man the port on the busiest day. Since the average number employed in the harbor was assumed to be 600, these 300 men could be given on the average two-thirds employment. This could either be distributed (1) evenly among all the 300, or (2) since 500 men were needed in the port on the least busy day, 100 of the reserve force would be employed steadily though moved about from place to place, and the remaining 200 given half-time employment.

Virtually all of this program, however, would be conditional upon the exchange squeezing out from the industry 300 of the original 1000 workers in order to concentrate the employment upon the remaining 700. In practice, some of the dock stabilization programs which have been actually attempted have not had the courage to carry out rigorously such a program.[1] Thus the Liverpool plan has retained in

---

[1] Max Gottschalk, Employment and Unemployment in Some Great European Ports, *International Labour Review*, April, 1930, pp. 519-39.

the industry 5000 more workers than the port can employ on even its busiest day.[2]

All practices making information about other jobs more readily accessible or furnishing central facilities for recruiting, help to diminish this idle reserve. For even when the surplus in a given industry is not formally squeezed out nor explicitly denied an opportunity to work in those enterprises, the slow movement of economic forces operates in the same direction. Some of the workers take advantage of the facilities offered and go to other and expanding industries. Some of the firms, on the other hand, when they come to know that there is a central pool of labor from which they can draw to meet their needs, will voluntarily begin to concentrate their available employment upon fewer people. The squeezing-out process will therefore take place gradually but nevertheless appreciably.

It should also be realized that a system of employment offices can be extremely useful in pooling reserves of labor *between* as well as *within* industries.

The economies which result from the pooled reserve of workers are indeed almost precisely analogous to those resulting from the establishment of a unified High Command for the Allied Armies in 1918, under the direction of Marshal Foch. Prior to that time, the French and British had maintained separate sections of the front, and each sought to provide in its rear sufficient reserves to sustain an attack by the whole available German Army. And yet it was an impossibility for the whole German Army to strike at two widely separate sectors at the same time. One of the reserve armies of the Allies would therefore be unused at the most crucial moments of fighting, and was therefore, for all practical purposes, wasted. With the coming of the American Army, the wastage would have been still greater. The Allies therefore very tardily adopted the principle of unified command, of which the chief advantage was the pooling of reserves. The establishment of a common reserve there-

---

[2] See *ibid.*, and Lascelles and Bullock, *Dock Labor and Decasualization,* pp. 84-91, and pp. 179-87.

fore increased the effective strength of the armies as a whole. So would it be in industry as well as in war.'

"But," the question will naturally be raised, "what will happen to the men who are thus squeezed out? Unlike the situation in time of war, no immediate opportunities will present themselves. Will they not therefore be permanently unemployed, and will not the final result therefore be worse than the original situation?" To this, two adequate replies can be made. The first is that even if they were to be unemployed for a considerable period of time, it would be better for society to pay this price than to have the entire group of workers in an industry depressed and degraded through part-time casual employment. While it is better in a period of acute business depression for all of the workers to work part-time than for part of the workers to be employed full-time and the remainder thrown completely out of work,[3] yet this policy is not healthy as a permanent method of conducting business. It is better to squeeze out the excess and provide steady work for those who remain. This makes it possible for some of the workers to stabilize their lives and lifts them up out of the morass of casual and underemployed labor.

Moreover, it should not be thought that the excess workers who have been thus squeezed out will permanently be unemployed. There will be new opportunities for them elsewhere to which the employment offices can help to adjust them. If any of them have become unemployable, they should be given the medical, psychiatric, or other type of treatment which is needed to rehabilitate them. And finally, industry and society should see to it that the displaced

[3] This follows from the principle of diminishing utility derived from successive units of money. If 100 men are paid on the average $30 a week, and if business is reduced to one-half of its former level, less unhappiness is caused by giving all of the workers half-time and a consequent income of $15 a week, than to lay off 50 of the men outright and employ the remaining 50 for full-time and pay them $30 a week. The reduction of income from $30 to $15 per week which the practice of sharing work imposes upon those who would otherwise be employed, deprives them of less utility than the 50 who would be discharged outright would lose by having no income at all instead of the $15 which would be theirs under a system of shared employment.

worker should receive some form of insurance benefit which will help to maintain him until he finds employment again.

But at this point it is likely to be asked, "Where will the new demand come from to set these displaced casuals once again at work?"

(1) The steadier work which is given to those who remain in the original industry may enable the employers to pay them a somewhat reduced hourly rate. These reduced costs will in time make possible either lower prices for the product itself or higher profits for the owners of the industry. In the first case, the lower price will, as we have previously pointed out, cause more units to be demanded, and in consequence some of the displaced workers will be reëmployed to turn out this increased quantity. If it is the employer's profits, on the other hand, which are increased, then their direct expenditure or investment will create a demand for added labor in other industries.

(2) There is a large amount of unemployed capital in other industries with which these workers who have been squeezed out can be combined. Taken as a whole, a larger proportion of capital is probably unused than of labor. Furthermore, the fresh annual savings of capital will generally be sufficient to absorb any labor displaced in this fashion. Various investigations seem to indicate that the supply of fixed capital is growing at the rate of from 3 to 5 per cent a year. This is of course a much higher rate than that of the labor supply which now is not increasing by more than 1 per cent a year. These fresh increments of capital therefore will be used in part to give employment to those who have been displaced. To this extent therefore, the remaining workers will be furnished with a smaller additional amount of capital per laborer than would otherwise be the case. Since the ratio of the quantity of capital to that of employed labor will be somewhat less than it would otherwise have been, the rate of interest will be higher and the rate of wages lower than would have been the case.

But the workers will, however, ultimately be employed. Society will gain in the form of the steadied lives of the workers and the increased production which the released workers will create in other lines. The workers will gain through an increased volume of employment and a higher annual real income.

It might seem at first that the employers would lose from this program of stabilization since they would no longer have a surplus labor reserve with which to play one worker against another and hence to reduce the wage rate. Such a program of decasualization through a pooling of reserves would nevertheless be of distinct benefit to most employers. It would, for example, enable them to have a steadier working force and hence lessen the costs of training and reduced production which comes from having more or less casual help. Perhaps more important still would be the fact that since the basic force of workers would be assured of relatively steady work, they would not be so tempted "to go slowly" in order to prolong the period during which they would be employed. The removal of this fear would increase output and consequently lower costs.

In the second place, moreover, the mere fact of irregularity of employment compels a higher hourly wage than would otherwise be needed and this may be more than sufficient to offset the weaker bargaining power of labor. Finally, as we have pointed out, the rate of interest itself would probably be raised.

On the whole, therefore, the large majority of employers, as well as the workers and the general public stand to gain from a program of pooling the labor reserve.

There are two warnings, however, which cannot be too strongly uttered: (1) the employers, workers, and employment offices must have the courage resolutely to squeeze out during "normal" periods as much of the surplus labor in an industry as possible. This is always hard to do but ultimately it is beneficial. If a surplus over and above that which is needed to handle the days of busiest employment is allowed to accumulate and to be maintained, then to that extent the full possibilities of the public employment offices are not realized. (2) While the displaced workers will ultimately be again employed it may take some time for this readjustment to be effected. The displaced workers should be at least partially protected by some form of unemployment compensation during the intervening period and those who need it should be given educational and medical care.

3. PROTECTION AGAINST THE ABUSES OF THE PRIVATE EMPLOYMENT OFFICES

A system of public employment offices can help to protect the workers against the exactions of the numerous private employment agencies. There are a large number of fee-charging private employment agencies in the country. In the cities of New York State there were no less than 1149 such offices in 1930, nearly all of which were of course in New York City itself.[4] In Chicago in 1927 there were 387 licensed private agencies and probably a considerable number of unlicensed ones,[5] while the total number of licensed offices in Pennsylvania at the present time is approximately 275.[6] In Ohio there are about 100 private agencies.[7] If there are at least 2000 private fee charging agencies in these four major industrial states, it is probably a conservative estimate that there are somewhere between 3000 and 4000 such offices in the country as a whole.

These groups make a large number of placements. It has been estimated that the licensed private agencies of Chicago place between 375,000 and 475,000 workers a year.[8] In Pennsylvania, the licensed agencies reported their total placements in 1928 to have been 128,000. The number of placements in New York is unknown, but it would seem that they must on the whole be well over a million.

[4] *Report of New York Advisory Committee on Employment Problems,* 1930, p. 13.

[5] Theodore T. Cowgill, *The Employment Agencies of Chicago* (Unpublished M. A. Thesis, Univ. of Chicago), pp. 10-11; Letter from J. S. McKenna, Division of Private Employment Agencies (Illinois), July 15, 1930.

[6] Letter of Director of Employment, S. S. Riddle, July 9, 1930.

[7] Letter of Geo. F. Miles, Division of Labor Statistics, Ohio Department of Labor, July 12, 1930.

[8] Cowgill, *op. cit.,* p. 12.

Many of these offices perform highly valuable functions but unfortunately many others have been and are guilty of great abuses against the workers. Among these abuses, the following are perhaps the most important:

(1) *High Fees.* In 1915, the Federal Commission on Industrial Relations reported [9] that it knew "of cases where $5, $9, $10, and even $16 has been paid for jobs at common labor. In one city the fees paid by scrubwomen are at the rate of $24 a year for their poorly paid work." In Chicago the most common charge for unskilled labor in 1928 seems to have been from $2 to $3.[10] In Cincinnati in the same year, the usual fee for an unskilled worker was $2 and in one case was $5. These fees moreover had to be paid by the worker *before* he applied for the job.[11] The fees for semi-skilled or skilled work in the same city amounted to from $4 to $10, while for domestic workers the charges were around $5.[12]

In the field of clerical work, the fees charged in Cincinnati [13] were:

Monthly Salary	Fee
Less than $75	30% of first month's salary
$75–$100	40% of first month's salary
$100–$150	50% of first month's salary
$150–$300	60% of first month's salary

Thus a girl receiving a clerical position at $15 a week would have to pay $19.50 to the agencies in fees.

In Philadelphia, the average scales of the private agencies for clerical jobs were:

Positions Paying Weekly Salary	Average Agency Charges
$18	$19.74
20	21.94
25	29.92
30	41.37
35	56.88
40	65.00

[9] *Report Commission on Industrial Relations,* Vol. I, p. 109. For further details see *ibid.,* Vol. II, pp. 1165-1362.

[10] Cowgill, *op. cit.,* p. 27.

[11] Cincinnati Consumers' League, *Employment Agencies of Cincinnati,* pp. 11-12.   [12] *Ibid.,* p. 17.   [13] *Ibid.,* p. 24.

(2) *Fee-splitting.* It is quite a common practice for fore-men and, in some cases, personnel managers to hire workers from given employment agencies on condition that they be paid one-third to one-half of the fee collected. This practice makes the foremen anxious to have as many hired as possible. They therefore tend to discharge the men freely in order that the latter may be replaced by new workers who in turn will meet the same fate. In testimony before the Industrial Survey Committee of New York State, one witness testified that he was sent to a job where the foreman would discharge for no apparent good reason one-third of his men every week.[14] One expert in employment work testified that he had worked on one case in Buffalo and obtained affidavits showing "there was a working agreement between the foreman and a fee-charging agency whereby they were splitting fees. There were 500 men working in this plant in a period of six weeks and they were charged a fee of $5. At that time there were complaints by men that they paid a fee of $5 and they were allowed to work a week and then they were laid off and a new bunch put in and the fee was split between the agency and the employer of that firm. That was proven by affidavits of the men who saw the actual payment of money by the fee-charging agent to the employer of that firm." [15]

An investigation by the Camden, New Jersey, Chamber of Commerce disclosed that in certain industries in that city men could not obtain employment unless they were referred by specific agencies.[16] The fees charged by these agencies were high, amounting in some cases to $12 and in other cases to two weeks' wages, and the workers were, in an extraordinarily large number of cases, discharged as soon as the fees were deducted from their wages. No less than 22 men were sent successively to fill one vacancy, all of whom had been discharged within the space of sixty days.[17] This

[14] See summary of testimony in the pamphlet of the American Association for Labor Legislation, *Employment Agencies Officially Exposed* (1930).

[15] *Ibid.,* p. 13.   [16] *Philadelphia Bulletin,* February 3, 1930.

[17] *Camden Post* (New Jersey), January 31, 1930.

meant that the average amount of time spent on the job was less than three days. Fee-splitting seems also to be a quite common practice in the hotel and restaurant business. One of the trade journals in that industry reports the case of a hotel executive who offered to place an order for 80 men with a given employment agency if he were given half of the $1000 in fees which could be collected [18] and the same magazine has published a number of similar instances.

(3) *Failure to make adequate refund if the worker does not receive the job or obtains only temporary employment.* It is a common practice for some employment agencies to levy advance charges upon the workers and then send them out to jobs for which there is no surety that they will be employed. If the worker does not get the job, the firm is often reluctant to give the money back. Sometimes indeed the workers are sent to plants which have made no application for men. In such cases as these, only the most persistent workers who know how to apply to public authorities are able to recover their deposit. The firms who choose can generally tire out the worker by referring them to a series of successive possibilities instead of returning their money. Sometimes more strenuous tactics are used. A witness before the New York Industrial Survey Commission testified: [19] "I have seen fellows thrown down the stairs. I have seen employment office men or clerks and sometimes the boss himself not alone throw them downstairs but finish it on the sidewalk; and a crowd collected and a policeman would come along and scatter the crowd and that is all. Nine times out of ten it was some poor foreigner beaten up by the crook upstairs."

Q. "Do you know why he was beaten up?"

A. "He was trying to get his money back."

A man who applied for work at a Philadelphia clerical agency was asked to deposit $25 as a preliminary fee and

---

[18] R. V. Pikard, How Hotel Jobs Are Sold, *Hotel Management,* January, 1929, p. 35.

[19] As reported in Bulletin of American Association for Labor Legislation, *Employment Agencies Officially Exposed,* p. 5.

was then sent out to what proved to be a wrong address. The second person he was sent to proved to be out of town and he was kept dangling for nearly two months. Ultimately $20 of his deposit was returned but $5 was retained as a service charge and in the meantime the firm had had the use of his money. Thus even when the deposits are ultimately returned, the offices are able to obtain a great deal of their working capital from their clients.

A further difficulty arises when the job upon which the worker is placed turns out to be merely a temporary and not a permanent one. The employment agency has collected its placement fee but the worker has not obtained the long-time employment which he expected. It is, however, very difficult for the applicant to collect any considerable portion of his fee since the agency can always allege that the worker lost the job through his own fault. This may in fact be frequently the case but in many other cases it is not and in these cases the workmen are almost equally helpless.

Thus a woman testified before the New York Industrial Survey Commission that she had paid $18 for a job which lasted for about two weeks. This was one-half of her total wages but the agency would neither refund her money nor give her another position.[20] Another worker testified that he had paid a week's wages for a job which lasted for only a week.[21]

(4) *Collection of Fees Without Performing Commensurate Services.* It is a favorite practice of many private agencies placing office workers to offer to send out circular letters to employers in return for a given fee. The Better Business Bureau of Philadelphia found one man who had paid $50 to the Associa-Trade Service of that city for sending out 500 notices of his abilities to persons who employed his type of labor. The applicant received no reply in three months to the 500 letters which the employment agency

---

[20] *Employment Agencies Officially Exposed,* American Association for Labor Legislation.

[21] *Ibid.,* p. 6.

claimed to have sent out and although he repeatedly asked to be shown a copy of the letter was never able to get the agency to show him one.[22]

Some idea of the carelessness with which such letters are mailed, even when sent, is evidenced by the fact that this same agency sent copies of such a letter advertising the qualifications of a $30 a week stenographer to twelve minor employers of a single company. Although these letters cost the applicant $1.20, "some of the employers of the company to whom the Associa-Grams were sent were dead, not in the employ of the company any longer or persons who had no authority to hire anyone." [23]

(5) *Misrepresentation of Working Conditions.* Mrs. Lillian Sire of the New York Department of Labor has testified that employment agents have frequently sent to summer hotels aliens who are refused their pay at the end of the summer and that the same practice has been followed in the case of men sent to lumber camps.[24] A Philadelphia paper reports the case of 200 men who were brought to that city from various parts of the country to obtain jobs as street railway employees but who were kept idle for two weeks and finally dismissed on the ground that they had been wanted to help break a strike which had finally been settled.[25]

Numerous cases have been reported of workers having been sent to jobs where the actual wages paid were other than those originally represented. This is particularly serious when the workers are hired by the employment agency and sent long distances to the job. The Federal Commission on Industrial Relations states on this point:[26] "Men are told they will get more wages than are actually paid, or that the work will last longer than it actually will, or that there is a boarding-house when there really is an insanitary camp, or that the cost of transportation will be paid when

[22] *Merchandise,* published by Better Business Bureau of Philadelphia, April, 1930, p. 4.
[23] *Ibid.,* p. 4.   [24] *New York Times,* September 12, 1928, p. 26.
[25] *Philadelphia Inquirer,* September 13, 1926.
[26] *Report U. S. Commission on Industrial Relations,* Vol. I (1916), p. 111.

it is to be deducted from the wages. They are not told of other deductions that will be made from wages; they are not informed about strikes that may be on at the places to which they are sent, nor about other important facts which they ought to know."

Some cases with more sinister consequences have been the sending of women as waitresses, hostesses, or chambermaids to places which were really houses of ill-fame and where upon arrival they were expected to lead immoral lives.[27]

It is of course only fair to add that in many of these cases the employment agency is itself unaware that the actual conditions are different from those represented by the employer but even then it is frequently guilty of not taking reasonable pains to be certain that the job to which the applicant is sent is in fact what it was represented to be. In many instances, however, the agencies know fairly well that the real situation is other than that which they state.

(6) *Increasing Fees During Periods of Depression When Applicants Are Most Needy.* Private agencies as business organizations follow the general business practice of altering their charges according to the relationship between the supply of that which they sell and the demand for it. They sell jobs or the opportunity to get jobs. When jobs are few and the applicants for work many and urgent, they can increase their charges. Because a particular job is more important to an unemployed person at such a time than during periods of prosperity when openings are more plentiful, he will pay more for it. The workers thus compete for jobs not only on the basis of their capabilities but also on the basis of how much they can afford to pay the agencies. By raising the fees at such periods of stress, as is a very common practice, the agencies can obtain greater revenue for themselves.[28] This means, however, that

[27] See the *Annual Report of the New York City Committee of Fourteen for 1928* on this point, also *Testimony before New York State Industrial Survey Commission*, p. 5019. For a series of earlier cases see Frances A. Kellor, *Out of Work*, pp. 225-32.

[28] It should of course be remembered that the higher fee per worker is at least in part offset by the reduced number of placements.

not only do the workers pay more for jobs but they do so at a time when, because of unemployment, their incomes are lower and dollars mean more to them than during periods of revival or prosperity. At a period therefore when workers should be particularly aided, the private employment agencies frequently seize the opportunity to increase their financial burdens.

(7) *Selling Jobs to the Highest Bidder.* Allied with the practice of increasing the minimum charges during periods of depression, frequently goes the practice of referring only those workers to jobs who will pay the largest fee over the minimum. This constitutes discrimination between applicants at a given time while the practice discussed under the preceding heading constitutes discrimination as between periods of time.[29]

The abuses of the employment office spring basically from the fact that the workers who apply are generally hard-pressed and need work badly. They are naturally more ignorant of employment opportunities than are the agents who specialize in just such openings. They are willing therefore to accept almost any terms and pay any fee if they can only get a job. This makes it very easy for the more unscrupulous to overcharge and to misserve them. Honorable managers of private exchanges find it difficult to survive and tend to move into other lines of work where the struggle between their conscience and their economic advantage is less severe. The field is gradually left therefore to the less ethical members. They come to dominate it and to set a general level of business practice against which it is difficult for isolated offices to contend.

It should moreover be recognized that even were the private agencies free from such abuses, they would, by the very fact of their uncoördinated multiplicity stand in the way of any very extensive pooling of labor and hence would, so long as they were dominant, prevent the full advantages to be realized from a pooling of jobs and of men.

---

[29] See the opinion of Mr. Justice Stone in *Ribnik* v. *McBride, 277 U. S.*, pp. 366-67.

Because of all of these facts, the existence of fee-taking private agencies has been prohibited in some countries. The evolution of German practice in this respect is noteworthy. Private agencies had been regulated there since the 1860's, and in 1910 a law was passed providing that no further licenses should be issued to such offices unless an absolute need for them could be demonstrated. It was also explicitly provided that the existence of a public employment exchange in the locality was a proof that no such necessity existed.[30] In 1927 the licensing of any additional offices was virtually prohibited and provision was made for all fee-charging private agencies to close their doors by January 1, 1931.[31]

In Canada, four provinces forbid private employment agencies by law, and one other province rigidly restricts their number. In Bulgaria and Rumania private offices are prohibited, while their number is extremely small in Austria, Norway, and Sweden.[32] In Italy the existence of private exchanges was prohibited between 1919 and 1926,[33] and while they are now legal, they have little practical importance. In the other countries of the world, therefore, private employment offices are finding their activities limited by law.

In the United States, the only two states which thus far have sought to abolish the private fee-charging agency have been Washington and Idaho. In 1914, the voters of the state of Washington passed at a referendum a law which prohibited private agencies from collecting fees from the workers. They were, however, left free to collect fees from the employers. The constitutionality of this act was challenged, and the United States Supreme Court in 1917,

[30] *Report on Unemployment,* Prepared for the International Labour Conference, Washington, D. C., 1919, p. 129.

[31] Mollie Ray Carroll, *Unemployment Insurance in Germany,* p. 69.

[32] Manitoba, Alberta, Saskatchewan, and British Columbia prohibit the existence of private fee-charging agencies and Ontario has reduced their number. Cf. Bryce M. Stewart, *The Employment Service of Canada.* (Queens University, Kingston, Ontario, 1919), pp. 8-9.

[33] Unemployment in the United States. Hearings before the Committee on Education and Labor, *United States Senate, 70th Congress, 2d session,* pursuant to S. Res. 219, pp. 170-78.

by a five to four vote, sustained this objection and declared the act unconstitutional.[34] Mr. Justice McReynolds in his majority opinion declared that the exercise of the "police power" by the states was not a justification for destroying "one's right to follow a distinctly useful calling in an upright way." If abuses existed, they could be controlled by regulation. But to deprive a man of the right to pursue such a business was adjudged an infringement of the 14th Amendment since it took property without due process of law.

Mr. Justice Brandeis's dissenting opinion dealt more substantially with the economic realities of the situation. Citing past decisions of the Supreme Court, he argued that "the scope of the police power is not limited to regulation as distinguished from prohibition." If a state considered that an evil could only be prohibited by preventing the practice of a calling, it had the right to do so unless "the measure adopted appears clearly to be arbitrary or unreasonable, or to have no real or substantial relation to the object sought to be obtained." This was a matter of fact, and after marshalling the evidence against the private agencies, Justice Brandeis pointed out that it was legitimate for the people of that state to believe that they should be abolished both because of their flagrant abuses and because this would clear the way for an adequate public system of offices.

Unless and until the Supreme Court reverses itself, however, it will be constitutionally impossible for us in the United States to prohibit outright the existence of fee-charging private agencies.

In 1927, the Supreme Court in the case of *Ribnik v. McBride*[35] still further limited the power of the state to exercise control over the private agencies. Here the majority declared a New Jersey statute to be unconstitutional which limited the maximum fee which could be charged a worker. The argument was that the power of the state to regulate prices was confined only to those industries which, in Sir

---

[34] *Adams* v. *Tanner, 244 U. S.*, p. 590.   [35] *277 U. S.*, p. 350.

Mathew Hale's words were "affected with a public interest." The Court in the case of *Tyson v. Banton* [36] had previously held a New York statute regulating the re-sale price of theater tickets to be unconstitutional on the ground that the brokerage of such tickets was not so affected. Appealing to this decision as a precedent, the majority ruled that to limit the prices charged for the brokerage of jobs was an unjust limitation upon the freedom of the individual and was in violation of the 14th amendment prohibiting the taking of property "without due process of law."

Mr. Justice Stone prepared a robust dissenting opinion which was concurred in by Justices Holmes and Brandeis. Justice Stone declared that in his opinion control by the state over the prices of commodities was justifiable "whenever any combination of circumstances seriously curtails the regulative force of competition so that buyers or sellers are placed at such a disadvantage in the bargaining struggle that a legislature might reasonably anticipate serious consequences to the community as a whole." He then pointed out that the people who dealt with employment agencies were necessitous, and "often dependent on them (the agencies) for opportunity to earn a livelihood, are not free to move from place to place, and are often under exceptional compulsion to accept such terms as the agencies offer." It was not unreasonable, therefore, for the legislature to attempt to protect these weaker parties to the bargain by fixing a minimum price which the stronger could charge, and the Supreme Court should, therefore, abstain from declaring such a measure in violation of the Fourteenth Amendment. As for the precedent of the decision in the case of *Tyson v. Banton,* Mr. Justice Stone said "Ticket brokers and employment brokers are similar in name; in no other respect do they seem alike to me. To overcharge a man for the privilege of hearing the opera is one thing; to control the possibility of his earning a livelihood would appear to be quite another. And I shall not stop to argue that the state has a larger interest in seeing that its workers

[36] *273 U. S.,* p. 418.

find employment without being imposed upon than in seeing that its citizens are entertained." The decisions of the Supreme Court have, however, forced Americans to return in part to their original theory about the relationship of the public to the private employment offices. When public offices were originally opened in this country, they were primarily designed to protect the unemployed against the fees and practices of the private agencies. Then as the possibility of organizing the labor market appealed to many students of the question, it was hoped that it might be possible to give the public offices a virtual monopoly of the placement work by the simple expedient of legislating the private offices out of business. The decisions of the Supreme Court in the Washington and Ribnik cases have stopped this possibility and forced students of the question to turn to the public offices as a means of enforcing control over the private offices by competition which could not be obtained by law.

But, although the Supreme Court has for the time being at least effectively prevented any limitation by the states upon the maximum fees charged by the private agencies, it is still possible for them to regulate the conditions under which these offices are conducted. The majority of opinions in both the Washington and the New Jersey cases explicitly stated that these powers could properly be exercised by the state, although as Mr. Justice Stone pointed out in the Ribnik case, it is somewhat difficult to justify this and at the same time to condemn the control of fees by the state.

It is, however, quite possible that the Supreme Court might approve of legislation designed to limit the number of private fee-charging agencies to those for which there is "a public necessity." This is now the law in Wisconsin, New Jersey, and Minnesota and thus far its constitutionality has never been questioned. In determining the number needed, the total number of private offices in a given industry or locality are considered, as is the adequacy with which the demand is served by the public offices. Since 1913, when Wisconsin adopted such a law, the number of private offices in that state has been reduced from 39 to 10. The Pennsylvania Committee on Unemployment appointed by Governor Pinchot has recommended the adoption of such a policy and defends its constitutionality on the ground that if the state has the right to license, it also has the power not to license. "A license," it declares,[37] "is not a contract nor a vested right. It is in the power of the state to grant or to refuse." A further argument for such a measure could be made on the ground that if the number were not limited, there would be so many competing private agencies as to put severe pressure upon them to take advantage of their strategic superiority over the applicants and practise abuses. The program of regulation, it could be urged, cannot be made fully effective without a restriction of numbers.

It is also possible that the Supreme Court might approve of the regulation or prohibition by the states of registration fees for which no service was rendered since the Ribnik case arose in connection with fees for actual placements. These are now prohibited by South Dakota, Minnesota, and California, and a qualified prohibition of them is recommended by Governor Pinchot's Committee in Pennsylvania.[38]

There are three other main types of private employment agencies besides those seeking profit. These are conducted by: (1) employers' organizations, (2) trade-unions, and (3) philanthropic bodies. In a number of cities groups of employers maintain central employment offices. Examples of these are the offices in Butte which serve the copper

[37] *Report Pennsylvania Committee on Unemployment,* 1931, p. 22.

[38] *Ibid,* pp. 21-24. Other recommendations made by that Committee were (1) enlarging the definition of private agencies so as to include those who solicit jobs for applicants by mail, (2) raising the annual license fees for the private agencies from $100 to $200, and the required bonds from $1000 to $5000, (3) providing that all licenses shall expire at a given date so as to enable the Department of Labor and Industry to survey the situation as a whole and block out a general licensing policy, (4) giving the Department of Labor and Industry the power to revoke a license for cause and not subject it to the delay of first obtaining permission from the courts, (5) making the reasons for revoking a license more explicit, (6) requiring each private office to make a monthly report on the numbers placed and total fees received.

mines,[39] the "Welfare" centers of the carriers on the Great Lakes,[40] and the offices under the auspices of the National Metal Trades Association. The primary purpose in nearly all of these cases is to aid the firms in preventing active unionists from being employed in their establishments. Central records are kept so far as possible on all of the various employees and the active unionists weeded out. In Butte, before a worker's application for work at a specific mine would be considered, it was necessary for him to get a card from the central office authorizing him to apply. These permits, which were called "rustling cards" were denied to those known to be active in union affairs and to those who were "trouble-makers." This practice has been followed by a number of other offices conducted by associations of employers although it is of course not the universal rule.

While such offices can render some services, it would seem highly unsafe from the social point of view to depend upon them since they will inevitably be used to strengthen the hands of the employers in their struggle against unionism.

In the plants and industries which are unionized, such as the building trades, the newspapers, the musicians, teamsters, and men's clothing workers, the chief organized source through which the members are placed is the union. Generally this is done rather informally by the business agent in the course of his other duties. In some cases, of which the most notable example is that of the Amalgamated Clothing Workers of Chicago, more fully organized employment offices have been set up which place the men. Such offices can be of assistance in the unionized trades, but in the nature of the case they cannot aid the non-union workers who form the great bulk of the wage-workers of the country. Placements by the business agents are subject to abuses which, though seldom mentioned, are no less real. It is a great temptation for business agents in giving out

[39] Paul F. Brissenden, The Butte Miners and the Rustling Card System, *American Economic Review*, December, 1920, pp. 755-775.
[40] Paul F. Brissenden, The Employment System of the Great Lakes Carriers, *Bulletin No. 235 of the United States Bureau of Labor Statistics*.

employment opportunities to discriminate against those members of their organization whom they dislike and who are opposed to their policies and to grant instead the first and best opportunities to their friends. It is not difficult for the business agents to do this and the practice is in consequence quite common. The power which the business agent holds over jobs and thus over men contributes indeed towards the building up of his power and helps to protect him against movements from the rank and file to overthrow him. A worker needs to be bold indeed who will openly challenge the power of a man who has such a control over his chances of getting work. It is an unhealthy situation for people who need work to be ever in part at the mercy of those who can use their point of vantage as a means either directly or indirectly of feathering their own nests or of paying off personal scores.

In the various large cities there are generally a number of philanthropic employment offices of which the most important are those conducted by the Y. M. C. A. and Y. W. C. A. These agencies in general do good work and somewhat incomplete reports from the agencies of 21 cities showed total placements in February, 1929, of approximately 5,000.[41] It is probably approximately accurate to estimate the total yearly placements of this group at somewhere around 100,000. It should constantly be borne in mind, however, that just to the degree to which the employment function is diffused among a variety of agencies, good as these may be individually, then to that extent an adequate solution is impeded.

It might, however, be possible to weave the non-profit making private agencies into a public system by inducing them to join a system of central clearances. These agencies could then send lists of jobs unfilled and workers unplaced to the state or district clearance office which would try to fit the applicants who were available into positions elsewhere. This would tie the private agencies up with a co-

---

[41] See Report on Free Employment Bureaus, in the *Report on the Registration of Social Statistics,* Ch. VIII, p. 193.

ordinated system, while at the same time, it would continue to stimulate the interests of private parties in the problem of unemployment and placement, and provide a check on the work of the public offices.

4. SERVICE TO SPECIFIC CLASSES OF HANDICAPPED WORKERS

Among these classes are (a) children and juveniles; (b) the industrially aged; (c) women; (d) the handicapped; and (e) workers in decaying industries or localities.

(a) *Children and Juveniles.* During the last quarter of a century the American public has awakened to the social and individual wastage which so frequently results from turning juveniles loose in the field of industry and letting them find their own way. Their natural tendency is to seek jobs which pay a high initial wage, forgetful of the fact that this is generally an evidence that there is little possibility for a boy or girl in such an industry to become a skilled worker. The tendency is to pass over the jobs which, while initially unattractive, have in them permanent possibilities. Juveniles and their parents are, moreover, often ludicrously unaware of their own capacities and abilities and enter work for which they are manifestly unfit.

To cope with this situation, vocational guidance has developed. Sometimes this has taken the form of separate bureaus but more often it has consisted in having certain persons attached to the public schools who serve as vocational counsellors. These counsellors have performed a valuable service in helping to get the children to choose their work more intelligently.

During the last twelve years part-time continuation schools have developed rapidly. Their growth has been fostered by the Smith-Hughes Act which provided federal aid to the states for vocational education and which specified that part of the federal monies must be spent for this purpose. Seventeen states have passed acts requiring all employed children under certain ages to attend such schools during working hours. The amount of such attendance varies from four hours per week to half-time as in Ohio, and the ages covered from the end of the period of compulsory education to 16, 17, and in some cases 18 years. In this way the school authorities have been able to keep in touch with the juvenile workers and to give them some added training.

But valuable as such work is, it suffers from the fact that there is not a close tie-up with industry. The schools find it very difficult to place the young graduates whom they counsel because they have no general available machinery which they can employ. It is somewhat futile, therefore, for them to counsel unless they can place.

It is impossible, moreover, for the school advisers to counsel and guide the juveniles very effectively unless they have a great deal of first hand information about industry and about the nature of the jobs concerning which they are called upon to advise. The best way of obtaining this essential information for counselling is by participating in the actual work of placement. Vocational guidance and juvenile placement are therefore mutually complementary to each other. It would seem, therefore, to be essential that special branches of the employment exchange should be created, as in England, which would try to place in proper openings the boys and girls who were leaving school.

These divisions of the public employment offices should of course have the fullest coöperative relationship with the public schools so that the students could be receiving vocational information and advice for some time prior to their leaving school.

The effectiveness of this work would be greatly facilitated if the public offices and the approved non-profit making bureaus were alone allowed to place the juveniles. This would bar out the profit-making private agencies and would concentrate the work in the hands of agencies which could coöperate with the schools and which would be planning for the long-run benefit of the juvenile. Such an act would, moreover, undoubtedly be held to be constitutional since children under the age of majority are regarded as wards of the state.

Such an act could also provide that minors who had left one position for any reason must re-register at the public offices before being reëmployed. This would enable the employment offices and school authorities to keep in continuous touch with the children and to work out methods not only of making the continuation school training more vital but also of devising means of training the unemployed juveniles and of preventing them from deteriorating during periods of a prolonged failure to get work. Efforts along this latter line have been made in England during the last decade in the establishment of training centers for the unemployed youths.

Vocational counselling could thus be made a continuous process during the work-life of the young and not primarily confined to the school-period before the children entered industry.

(b) *The Industrially Aged.* Men and women beyond the age of 45 find it much harder nowadays to fit into the industrial world than they did a half century or even a quarter of a century ago. In agriculture, and particularly on the home farm, the worker whose powers are on the down grade can keep himself occupied up to the limit at least of his own capacities. But in manufacturing, transportation, and even in mercantile pursuits this is not so. Modern business works at extremely high pressure and men who are 70 per cent efficient are seldom allowed to exercise even that percentage but are rather ruthlessly weeded out because they cannot attain 100 per cent efficiency. A large part of their talents and abilities is therefore allowed to go to waste. With the pressure which comes from mass production, and with the decline in the numbers employed in manufacturing, many men of 45 years have in recent years been dropped and have found it difficult to get a job again.

In a sensibly conducted society we would not scrap our older men in any such fashion. Since the decline of the death rate is leading to an average prolongation of life, the proportion of the older people in the population will steadily increase in the future until by 1975 it is predicted those of 50 years and over will form 26 per cent of the population instead of 16 per cent as in 1920.[42] This means that the problem of the aged will increase and may become more important than that of the young.

But not only will the proportion of old people increase in the population but, due to the heavier pressure of modern industry, it seems probable that as they reach the ages of 45, 50, and 55 years they will find it increasingly difficult to continue at the specific types of work at which they had been employed during the fullness of their powers. It will then be necessary to find new jobs for them. Part of this transfer can be effected within the concerns which employ them. In some cases, however, it will be necessary to transfer the older workers to other trades and industries and here the employment service can be of great aid. It can and should study various lines of work to determine those for which various types of the older workers are best fitted and by interviews with the employers in these lines should try to cultivate a market for the services of those who have been displaced because of age.

(c) *Women.* The vocational problems of women are peculiar because of the fact that their working lives are generally interrupted by marriage and by the rearing of families. Since they tend, therefore, to be employed in industry for a much shorter period than men, they do not take as much trouble as the latter to learn a skilled trade. In consequence they tend to congregate in unskilled occupations. Because of sex prejudice, it is also difficult for them to gain admittance to a number of occupations for which they are on the whole well-fitted. Among these may be mentioned street-car conductors, barbers, musicians, and a number of other pursuits. Middle-class women are in turn limited in their opportunities to become architects, engi-

---

[42] Thompson and Whelpton, A Nation of Elders in the Making, *American Mercury,* April, 1930, p. 391.

neers, etc. A public employment agency should have a women's division which would be constantly seeking out new positions which women might occupy with credit to themselves. Here again employers should be interviewed and by sending at first exceptionally well-qualified women who would make a good record, broader fields of opportunity could constantly be opened up for them.

Another field of work for women which needs badly to be developed is that of part time occupations. There are many women of the middle-classes who could give a few hours a day of work without detriment to their families and with benefit to themselves. But because they cannot give full-time, it is virtually impossible for them to find any work at all. With the increasing importance of clerical and professional work, on the one hand, and of selling occupations on the other, a number of jobs are developing where attendance throughout the day is not as necessary as where workers must tend costly machines. If these part-time openings are to be adequately developed, however, it will have to be through the efforts of some non-profit making body which will try to interest employers in the possibilities of part-time work by women and which will steadily try to fill with competent applicants the opportunities which may open up. Here again the public offices seem ultimately to be the only logical agency to carry through the work.

(d) *Handicapped Persons.* Men who have once been seriously injured have a difficult time in being placed. Efficient programs of vocational reëducation can do much. But their greater susceptibility to industrial accidents as well as their lessened productivity make employers reluctant to hire them. There is need, therefore, for some agency which will try to place them.

(e) *Workers in Decaying Industries and Localities.* As we have pointed out in our discussion of so-called "technological unemployment," industries and localities frequently decay because of changes in demand, industrial consolidations, and improvements in production which are not balanced by corresponding increases in the quantities demanded. Here it will be necessary for the employment offices to help transfer the men to other lines of work, give advice as to what these other lines should be, and aid the workers to obtain whatever retraining may be necessary to prepare them for these other occupations. By informing the young people about the declining employment opportunities of an industry, they can largely shut off the influx of fresh làbor which frequently makes such a situation very much worse. This will permit the natural wastage of the working force through death, retirement, etc., to, in large part, meet the situation.

The experts attached to the central staff of the service can, after studying the impending improvements in the various industries and approximating the probable elasticities of demand, issue bulletins outlining what industries may be expected to increase and what to decrease in numbers. This information, distributed through the chain of affiliated offices, would help to induce many men in a declining industry to leave of their own free will and thus help to lighten the burden of forced displacements.

Sometimes the turn of industrial events is such that a goodly proportion of the population of a town must be evacuated if they are to find work. Unless some centralized agency is ready to help in this, it will be difficult for all of the individuals to find work. A public employment office under the exclusive direction of the municipality would be reluctant to help workers get out of a city when the consequence would be to decrease land values and diminish the tax-paying capacities of the city. Even state control might not be sufficient to induce this broader policy to be followed. The influence of the national government, both by providing interstate clearance and by giving information about the national labor market, would help distinctly in this direction.

5. The Collection and Distribution of More Adequate Information About the Labor Market

Running through all of our discussion has been the theme of the importance of accumulating and distributing better information about the state of the labor market. The more the real truth is known about the number and types of men and jobs which are available, the more possible it is for men to go into those industries and places where the jobs are most abundant. Vocational counselling for both young and old, and for men and women, is made much more effective if it is based on a thorough knowledge of the labor market.

But in order to obtain this information it is necessary to collect it at its source, namely, from the requests of employers for help and of workers for jobs. This information cannot be collected by investigation agencies. Their questions will be regarded as an extra burden by the employers and they cannot, moreover, reach the workers. It can only be collected by an agency which is actually trying to fill the applications for men and the demands for jobs. The more inclusive this agency, the more adequate will be its information. But the only really adequate agency is necessarily a public one.

The necessity is clear, therefore, for an extensive and coördinated public system of employment offices. It is not enough, however, merely to set up such agencies. It is also necessary to get them fully used. We shall deal with this point more completely in the succeeding pages but it may perhaps be remarked now that, even if it is, in the opinion of the Supreme Court, constitutionally impossible for the states to concentrate employment functions upon the public agencies by abolishing the private offices, it would not be unconstitutional to require that the information, at least about jobs, should be concentrated. Thus the states might (1) require all employers to file with the state offices a report on all the men whom they desire to employ and even perhaps the number actually engaged and (2) require the private employment agencies, as a number of states already do, to report regularly the number of jobs which are listed with them and the number of applicants. Aside from inaccurate reporting by the agencies themselves, the chief source of error in such reports would come from the practice of many companies in asking not one but several employment agencies to refer persons for stated vacancies. There would thus be a distinct tendency for the reports to overstate the number of jobs which were actually vacant. To the degree that workers register at more than one office, there would be double-counting there as well.

The best method, however, of obtaining accurate statistics is by building up an adequate and widely used public employment system and in spite of all the difficulties this can be done.

We shall later discuss the absolute necessity of having a system of public employment offices if unemployment insurance is effectively to be administered. As we shall see, there is no way of determining whether an ostensibly unemployed person is actually seeking work unless there is a central agency where he must register and which takes up the task of helping him to find work at the same time that it casts a watchful eye over him to find out whether he is in fact without employment.

CHAPTER XIX

THE DEVELOPMENT OF PUBLIC EMPLOYMENT OFFICES IN OTHER COUNTRIES

Public employment offices are distinctly the product of the last half-century, and their growth during the last twenty years has been particularly rapid. It is worth while to trace this experience both at home and abroad both for its own sake and for the light which it throws upon current problems.

1. FOREIGN EXPERIENCE IN GENERAL

Although public employment offices had previously been established by local governments in various countries, England was the first to create a national system in 1909. The war and post-war developments speeded up the movement for such offices.

(1) In the first place organized recruiting was found necessary to obtain workers for the essential war industries. Without such orderly means chaos necessarily resulted because of the competition for men among the various industries.

(2) When the armies were demobilized it was equally necessary to have machinery whereby the ex-soldiers might be placed in jobs as speedily and effectively as possible. The task of absorbing nearly twenty million men was difficult enough at best. But to throw these men on their own resources and let them scramble to find their own jobs would have caused untold misery and loss of time.

(3) At the conclusion of the war and during the years which immediately followed, the political and economic power of labor was much greater than it had been before 1914 while in some countries, such as Germany and Aus-

tria, the Socialist parties were in at least nominal control of the government. Even the conservative groups were anxious to make some concessions in order to head off any tendency of the workers to turn to the communists for support and also in order to furnish the Right with plausible arguments that they were the real friends of labor.

(4) The Conference of the International Labor Office, which was held in Washington in 1919, adopted a draft-treaty on the subject of employment exchanges. The second article of this treaty provided that "each member which ratifies this convention shall establish a system of free public employment agencies under the control of a central authority. Committees which shall include representatives of employers and workers shall be appointed to advise on matters concerning the carrying on of these agencies. When public and private free employment agencies exist, steps shall be taken to coördinate the operations of such agencies on a national scale. The operations of the various national systems shall be coördinated by the International Labor Office in agreement with the countries concerned."

This convention still further stimulated the various countries to set such systems into being. By 1929, no less than 24 countries had ratified the treaty and all but The Netherlands had put the necessary legislation into effect. These countries were Austria, Bulgaria, Denmark, Esthonia, Finland, France, Germany, Great Britain, Greece, Hungary, India, Ireland, Italy, Japan, Luxembourg, The Netherlands, Norway, Poland, Roumania, Jugoslavia, South Africa, Sweden, Spain, and Switzerland.

(5) The final force which has operated to create employment exchanges has been the growing adoption of unemployment insurance by various nations. In 1919, eight years after England passed its first act, Italy established compulsory insurance against unemployment for its industrial workers and was followed by Poland. Germany in 1927 put a national system of insurance into force. Russia had already adopted such a plan for its urban workers, and Switzerland had a federal-aided system under which a number

of cantons made such provisions. All of these compulsory and inclusive systems needed employment offices as essential agencies of administration both to determine whether the men were really trying to find work and also to help in the distribution of the benefits. These countries had between them in 1927 approximately 3,000 employment offices.

In countries where the Ghent, or subsidized system of voluntary unemployment insurance is used, the reliance upon the public exchanges might be expected to be less. In Denmark, however, the exchanges are an integral part of the system and they have recently been made such in Belgium.

The growth of public employment offices abroad is indicated by the fact that, whereas in 1911 the total placements of such offices in fourteen countries amounted to approximately 2.8 million workers,[1] of which 1.7 millions were within Germany, by 1921 this number had risen to 8.4 millions or three times as many. By 1927 the placement work had increased still further so that there were 4,017 public employment offices in sixteen countries [2] exclusive of Russia. Since France, Austria, and Italy were not included in this group of countries, it seems safe to estimate that the total number of public exchanges which were then in operation in the capitalistic nations was probably not far from 4,400. It is difficult to determine the total number of placements made by these offices but it seems probable that they amounted to at least 12 millions, or almost five times the number who had been placed sixteen years before. If Russia were included, the total number of offices in 1927 would have been approximately 4,700 and the total placements about 17,000,000.

[1] *International Labour Review,* July, 1922, p. 37. The countries were South Africa, Germany, Belgium, Canada, Denmark, France, Great Britain, Japan, Norway, The Netherlands, Jugoslavia, Sweden, and Switzerland.

[2] Unemployment in the United States; Hearings Before Senate Committee on Education and Labor on S. Res. 219, *70th Congress, 2nd Session;* p. 619. The countries being Czecho-Slovakia, Denmark, Finland, Germany, Great Britain, Hungary, Japan, The Netherlands, Norway, Poland, Rumania, Russia, South Africa, Sweden, Switzerland, Jugoslavia.

2. Employment Exchanges in Great Britain

In 1905 there were only twenty-four non-profit making employment offices in England. The large majority of all these exchanges, however, were primarily designed to help the needy unemployed find relief work and were not serious attempts to organize the labor market on any permanent basis.[3] While the London offices had designated the Westminster bureau as their central clearing house, the ten public offices outside of London were not coördinated.

In 1906 the management of the London offices was separated from the administration of relief work and the exchanges, under the leadership of W. H. Beveridge, were put upon a much more businesslike basis. The growing success of these offices aroused a great deal of public interest and led many to advocate their adoption on a national scale. This movement was strengthened by the report of the Royal Commission on the Poor Laws. That commission, as is well known, divided sharply into two groups: the majority swayed by the individualistic philosophy of Bosanquet, and the minority led by Beatrice Webb with her doctrine of Fabian Collectivism. But widely as these two groups differed on most questions of social policy, they were nevertheless agreed that a national labor exchange should be set up.

The social-reform wing of the Liberal Party, led by Winston Churchill and Lloyd George, was successful in getting the government to sponsor such a measure and a bill introduced by Churchill was passed by Parliament in 1909. Nearly all of the 39 existing agencies were taken over by the Board of Trade and new exchanges were added. By the time the act was put into effect in February, 1910, there were indeed 83 exchanges and two months afterward no less than 214.

The work of the exchanges was increased by the Social Insurance Act of 1911 which extended unemployment insur-

[3] W. H. Beveridge, Employment Exchanges, *Economic Journal,* September, 1907, pp. 66-81.

ance to approximately two and a half million workers in the building, ship-building, iron and steel and machine industries. Unemployed workers in these trades were compelled to register at the employment exchanges, which helped find work for them and paid out benefits. This greatly increased the number of workers who were registered at the exchanges, from 1.9 millions in 1911 to 3.3 millions in 1914, and also necessitated the opening of approximately 900 more branch offices. The number of vacancies filled by the offices also increased from 608,000 in 1911 to 1,067,000 in 1914.

During the war, the employment exchanges performed many invaluable services. They recruited labor in an organized and coherent way for trades connected with the army and for the war industries. In order to check competitive bidding by employers for labor, certain groups of industries were required to hire all labor which came from outside the immediate district through the exchanges. As the unskilled workers were combed out of industry and pushed into the fighting forces, the exchanges helped find women to take their places, to place Belgian refugees, etc. In 1916 the work of the exchanges was still further enlarged by the extension of the unemployment insurance system to 1.5 million more workers in the munitions industries. In the following year a very valuable feature was added in the creation of local advisory committees for most of the exchanges which were composed of representatives of the employers and workers. These committees have been of great assistance not only in the administration of the unemployment insurance acts but also in the conduct of the exchanges themselves.

The demobilization period thrust added burdens upon the offices. Although the program of graduated demobilization was abandoned early in 1919 because of the abundance of employment during that year, the exchanges placed no less than 253,000 non-disabled ex-service men in jobs and by the end of 1920 had induced nearly 24,000 employers to hire 259,000 disabled soldiers and sailors. In addition to all this, the exchanges administered the out-of-work donations granted by the government not only to the demobilized soldiers but also to virtually the entire working population as well. The local employment committees considered indeed approximately 2,500,000 claims for the donation, of which two-thirds were for ex-soldiers and the remainder for civilians. In all the exchanges paid out in such donations approximately $305,000,000 (62.5 million pounds) with an administrative cost of only 7 per cent.

In 1920 the extension of unemployment insurance to all groups of workers, save those in agriculture, domestic service, railroad transportation, and the public service, increased the numbers covered from approximately four to twelve millions.

This in itself threw a still heavier burden upon the exchanges which was greatly intensified by the trade depression which set in almost immediately after the act went into effect and which has continued in Great Britain to a greater or less degree ever since. By virtue of the act, nearly all of the industrial workers have been compelled to register with the exchanges in order to be eligible for benefits. Furthermore for a number of years the local committees were swamped with tasks of determining whether individual claimants who had been unemployed for longer periods than protection was provided for under the law were entitled to "extended benefit."

So much of the energies of the employment exchanges have been absorbed by the administration of unemployment insurance that there have been many who have urged that the two services be divorced in order that the exchanges might be permitted an adequate opportunity to develop their own work. In the opinion of most competent students, however, this separation would be inadvisable both because it would be almost impossible to administer the insurance feature except through the employment exchange and because the provision of compulsory insurance compels all unemployed men to register with the exchanges. These men can, of course, also seek work through other agencies than the public employment exchanges but the latter are at least given centralized information about all of the unemployed and the opportunity of placing all of them if openings for them can be found in industry. This could not happen to the same degree were registration voluntary with the workers.

But the employers, however, are not compelled to place their orders for help exclusively with the public exchanges. They are free to hire at the gate or file their applications for help with private agencies. Nor are they compelled even to notify the exchanges of such positions as are open. There are many, however, who are now urging that this last feature should be changed and that exchanges be furnished with a list of all jobs which the employers are seeking to fill.

Among those who advocate this change in the law is J. B. Seymour, who says in his authoritative book on The British Employment Exchange: [4] "Without such a step, the employment exchanges will have to struggle against many obstructions to their placement work caused by abnormal industrial conditions. The struggles will be costly and the results seem doubtful. The placing work under the existing system may incur the chance of being permanently relegated to a secondary place, whereas the single measure of compulsory notification of vacancies should be sufficient to restore its priority."

The table on the following page, which gives the placements by the exchanges since 1911, shows that there has been no tendency for them to increase.

The number of jobs listed by the employers and the number of workers placed by the exchanges were as a matter of fact slightly less in 1926 than in 1914. It is apparent, therefore, that the exchanges are not gaining ground and that the volume of placements is much below what it should be. If the scope of their work is to be extended appreciably it must be either by some method such as the compulsory registration of available jobs, or by granting

[4] John B. Seymour, *The British Employment Exchange,* pp. 62-63.

TABLE 14

A STATISTICAL MEASURE OF THE PLACEMENT WORK OF THE BRITISH
EMPLOYMENT EXCHANGES 1911–26

YEARS	NUMBERS IN 000's			PER CENT OF	
	Workers Registered	Jobs Registered By Employers	Positions Filled	Positions Filled to Workers Registered	Positions Filled To Jobs Registered
1911	1,966	770	608	31.0	79.0
1912	2,362	1,034	810	34.3	78.3
1913	2,836	1,183	895	31.6	75.6
1914	3,305	1,437	1,087	32.8	75.6
1915	3,047	1,761	1,280	42.0	72.7
1916	3,436	2,017	1,535	44.6	76.0
1917	3,432	1,974	1,536	44.7	77.8
1918	3,594	2,040	1,496	41.8	73.3
1919	5,929	1,909	1,259	21.2	65.9
1920	4,372	1,286	921	21.0	71.6
1921	8,929	986	807	9.0	81.8
1922	8,820	840	697	7.9	83.0
1923	8,775	1,057	894	10.2	84.5
1924	11,263	1,345	1,144	10.1	85.0
1925	12,728	1,481	1,279	10.0	86.4
1926	14,195	1,247	1,083	7.6	86.8

sufficient funds to permit them to solicit business more actively from private employers.

And yet while the work of the exchanges has not grown as rapidly as had been hoped, the fact that they are now filling an appreciably larger proportion of the jobs listed with them by the employers than was the case some years ago is proof that the quality of this work is not a failure but, on the contrary, is probably improving.

Two interesting features of the work of the exchanges have been the attention given to the placing of juveniles and of women. Originally the organized placement of the juveniles was under the joint direction of the exchanges and the local educational authorities. These exchanges for young workers were maintained in a number of localities and much effective work done.[5] The educational authori-

[5] For descriptions of the early work see Keeling, *Labour Exchanges in Relation to Boy and Girl Labour* (1911), and Arthur Greenwood, *Juvenile Labour Exchanges and After Care* (1911).

ties and the exchanges found difficulty, however, in co-operating and in 1921 a committee headed by Lord Chelmsford reported [6] in favor of giving the local educational bodies the power to assume this placement work if they wanted to do so. This change was made in about half of England and of Wales, but London still retained the former system. Scotland, also, with the exception of Edinburgh, maintained the original form of control. In 1927, however, this curiously divided system of control was discontinued and the direction of all of the juvenile employment work was finally lodged in the Ministry of Labour.[7] The work of the exchanges in the counselling, placing, and following up of juveniles has been on the whole increasingly valuable. In 1923 approximately 150,000 boys and girls of from 14 to 18 years were placed by the exchanges and by 1928 this number had risen to 282,000.[8] The percentage of this group in recent years who have been unemployed has, as a matter of fact, been somewhat less than that for the workers as a whole, being in 1925 4.1 per cent, as compared with the average of 11.6 per cent for the insured adults. A particularly worth while feature of the work has been the establishment of Unemployment Centers—of which there were no less than 97 in 1928—for juveniles who were out of work.[9] These centers give training and stimulate recreation which makes the period of unemployment one of development rather than of deterioration for those who attend. It is, however, unfortunate that only about one-fifth of the unemployed boys and girls are taken care of in this fashion.

The exchanges did particularly good work during the war in placing women workers in the various war industries and have since given training to considerable numbers of unemployed women with the primary aim of preparing them for domestic service. The exchanges have, however, not been able in the main to place the most competent

---

[6] *Report on Juvenile Employment*, H. M. Stationery Office (1921).
[7] See Ministry of Labour, *Report of Work of Advisory Committees for Juvenile Employment during 1928* (1929).
[8] *Ibid.*, pp. 20-21.
[9] *Ibid.*, p. 51.

servants who still largely continue to patronize the private employment or "registry offices."

Even the most ardent admirer of the British exchanges must admit, however, that in three important features their work thus far has been seriously defective, namely, (1) in not effectively decasualizing a number of trades; (2) in not providing specialized service for specific trades and industries; (3) in not effectively transferring workers from "depressed areas" and retraining them for new occupations.

High hopes were originally entertained that the employment offices might decasualize longshore work and other overcrowded trades by squeezing out the excess workers, and with a centrally pooled reserve concentrate the available employment upon a smaller number. A number of decasualization plans for various localities were proposed, but of them all, only those dealing with dock labor in Liverpool and ship repairing in South Wales have managed to survive.[10]

Employers have been reluctant to coöperate with the exchanges to reduce the number of workers attached to an industry for two reasons. In the first place, they have been afraid that the diminution in the number of men available for their work would strengthen the bargaining powers of labor and that consequently it was to their own advantage to maintain a labor surplus, while in the second place, the uniform rates of assessment under the unemployment insurance act have placed upon them no financial pressure to decasualize.

The workers have feared decasualization to an almost equal degree. Such a program would necessarily involve the reduction in the numbers attached to an industry and would at least temporarily increase the number of those totally unemployed. It is difficult for any group of men to agree to this because individuals are instinctively afraid that they

---

[10] See Lascelles and Bullock, Dock Labour and Decasualization; *International Labour Review,* April, 1930, pp. 519-39; Seymour, *The British Employment Exchange,* pp. 116-26.

may be among those who will be squeezed out. It is better for them, they think, to be sure of getting partial employment than to run the risk of complete unemployment. This fear of total unemployment becomes very acute in a situation such as England has experienced during the last decade when the volume of unemployment has always been heavy. The result has not only been that few decasualization schemes have been introduced but also that even in those plans which have been adopted, more men have been retained in the labor supply than could be employed on the busiest days. Thus, in Liverpool, the maximum number needed on the docks is apparently 15,000, but the number of men given tallies and licensed to work by the employment exchange has been approximately 20,000 or 5,000 more than are employed at the busiest time. The best that can be said of this plan and that of the South Wales ship repairers is that, were it not for them, the situation would probably have been much worse. For otherwise the great amount of unemployment during the past decade would have caused larger numbers of men to go to the docks which tend to be the first refuge for those "down on their luck."

The second great defect in the record of the employment offices has been their failure to provide specialized placement service. There have been two aspects of this failure. The first is the fact that the staff itself has not had an adequate background for its work. As the committee of the Ministry of Labour on the Work of the Employment Exchanges reported: [11] "The witnesses before us have been practically unanimous in stating that the staff of the Employment Exchanges are lacking in technical knowledge of the industries with which they have to deal."

The second grave aspect of this failure is the fact that the British exchanges are "general" offices without any functional subdivision according to industry. Each official in the employment exchanges will therefore be referring men to a wide variety of crafts and industries and this in

---

[11] *Report of the Committee of Enquiry into the Work of the Employment Exchanges* (Cmd. 1054), 1920, p. 15.

combination with his general lack of industrial knowledge means that he cannot give specialized attention to any one industry.

The result is that it is almost impossible for the clerks to impose tests which will disclose whether a given applicant possesses in fact the skill which he may claim and, therefore, to guarantee the skill and capacities of the applicants who are referred to the employers. This inability in turn prevents the employers from taking a great deal of interest in the exchanges themselves. This indifference on the part of most employers causes them to list a much smaller number of jobs with the exchange than they would if they received better service. The only exchanges in England where a considerable amount of specialized testing and hiring is actually put into effect are the building trades exchange on Tavistock Square, London, and the women's exchange on Marlborough St. of the same city. Here each examiner is skilled in a particular trade, and the result is much more satisfactory.

But what is needed, as a number of witnesses testified before the Committee of Enquiry of the Ministry of Labour, headed by G. N. Barnes,[12] is an extension of this plan and the setting up of many more specialized exchanges and examiners. Only by so doing can they provide that expert service which will encourage employers to utilize the exchanges more fully. And yet, despite the recommendation of the Royal Commission [13] that "the principle of specializing sections within the Exchange should be pressed to its practicable limits," virtually no progress along this line has been made by the Ministry of Labour. It is also probably true that the offices have not shown sufficient activity in soliciting business from employers.

There is still a third way in which the employment machinery has worked somewhat unsatisfactorily. This is the failure to transfer as large sections of the working force

---

[12] *Minutes of Evidence Taken Before Committee of Enquiry Into the Work of Employment Exchanges* (1921) [Cmd. 1140].
[13] [Cmd. 1054], p. 14.

as is advisable from the distressed areas of South Wales, the Northern Counties, and the Clyde to the Midlands and South of England. This reluctance of labor to move is probably due to the local attachments which laborers form and also perhaps in part to the system of Unemployment Insurance which has given to men with families the economic possibility of hanging on in the depressed areas which would otherwise have been impossible. It is, however, true that there has not been enough work in the expanding industries to have absorbed any considerable percentage of the workers from the industries which have fared ill. Nor can employment offices ship men against their will.

But while it is easy to exaggerate the failure upon this score of both unemployment insurance and the exchanges, it is also probable that it would have been possible to have effected a more speedy draining off of workers from the distressed areas had there been a sufficient will to do so.

3. Public Employment Offices in Germany

Public placement began in Germany through the efforts of various voluntary philanthropic societies. Such an office was started in Dresden as early as 1840,[14] while other voluntary societies started similar offices in Stuttgart in 1865, Cologne in 1874, Berlin in 1883, Hanover in 1889, and in other cities at different times.[15] The depression years of 1893 and 1894 caused a number of municipalities to take over a number of offices which had already been started by these private groups but the burden of which had become too heavy for their original supporters. At the same time private groups and municipalities opened additional exchanges where they had not previously existed. By 1899 there were indeed no less than 114 such municipal offices [16] which were of two kinds, namely, (1) those managed and

---

[14] Mollie Ray Carroll, *Unemployment Insurance in Germany*. p. 10. Under the Elberfeld System, poor relief was in the main so administered and the employment offices were generally opened by the same group.

[15] Hearings on H. R. 5783, *64th Congress, 1st Session*, pp. 73-80.

[16] E. L. Bogart, Public Employment Offices in the United States and Germany, *Quarterly Journal of Economics*, Vol. XIX (1900), pp. 341-77.

financed entirely by a given city, (2) those managed by private societies to which the city would make a partial contribution. These were all established by purely local initiative save for those in the State of Württemberg which in 1895 had ordered such offices to be created with the Stuttgart Office serving as the central clearing office. In 1898 a voluntary association of these offices was formed for Germany as a whole with a number of local subdivisions. The movement was still, however, stronger in South than in North Germany.

The growth during the next five years was extraordinarily rapid and in 1904 there were 400 such offices, placing a total of 500,000 persons during the year.[17] At least 150 of these 400 were very vigorous and active. In addition to these public exchanges, an even greater volume of placements was effected by the free private agencies which were of a multitude of types. Thus there were 30 exchanges managed exclusively by employers' associations, and aiming to break down unionism or prevent it from gaining a foothold, which found work for 230,000 employees. Then 2,400 small guild offices, serving in the main the trades still dominated by handicraft, placed 213,000. A full thousand trade union offices in the same year took care of another 120,000. Then 60 offices which were jointly controlled by both employers and employees placed 51,000, while Chambers of Agriculture handled 50,000, and agencies for trade and commerce found jobs for a final 25,000. In all, therefore, 1,239,-000 workers were placed through non-profit making institutions.

The growth continued during the next decade so that by 1912 the placements of the public exchanges had increased to approximately 1,678,000.[18] The employers' associations had in turn found work for 1.2 millions and the unions for 350,000. The total placements for all free agencies, both public and private, amounted to 3.6 millions.

[17] W. H. Beveridge, Public Labour Exchanges in Germany, *Economic Journal*, March, 1908, p. 1.
[18] Hearings on H. R. 5783, *64th Congress, 1st Session*.

In 1910 the German Government passed a law restricting the number of new private fee-charging agencies which could be opened to those cases only where the needs were not met by the public agencies. The public offices were thus given the right of way over the private.

With the coming of the war steps were taken to federate the public exchanges into a more truly national system. A central labor exchange for all of Germany was created in 1914 and in 1918 all of the existing local agencies were turned over to the Federal Office for Economic Demobilization. In 1919 this control was transferred to the Ministry of Labor, and in 1922 a further act established the federal service upon a permanent basis. The organization then effected was on three levels, namely, (1) local, (2) state, (3) national. Existing local agencies were taken over into the system and provisions made for the creation of new offices wherever they might be needed. These local exchanges were to be governed by joint boards composed of a chairman and equal representatives of employers and workers.

The state exchanges were not only to carry on researches into the demand and supply of men and jobs, but they were also given the control over vocational guidance and placement together with the supervision over all private agencies whether or not they charged fees. The state exchanges too were governed by boards although in this instance these boards represented three and not two parties, for in addition to the employers and employees, the local exchanges themselves were given representation.

The National Employment Office was made the seat of final authority and the central statistical source. It was given power to help effect a geographical distribution of labor if that seemed best.

Two other features of this law were also noteworthy. (1) No more private fee-charging agencies were to be licensed and all existing agencies were to be dissolved by the beginning of 1931. (2) The Minister of Labor was given the power to require all employers who were under the health insurance laws to report all vacancies to the nearest labor exchange. Thus far, however, this authorization has not been put into effect.

The effect of all these developments was of course appreciably to increase the activities of the public offices. By 1921 they had come to place no less than 5.2 million workers of whom approximately 3.8 millions were males and 1.4 millions women.[19] The number of applicants for jobs was 6.6 millions and the number of jobs filed by the employers between 6.1 and 6.2 millions. It will be seen that the proportion of the positions which were filled by the offices was extremely high, amounting to 85 per cent of the total number. By 1927 the public agencies were responsible for 89 per cent of all placements made.

In 1927 when the National Unemployment Insurance Act was passed, the system of employment offices was revised. What had previously been a federalized system was now to become a nationalized one. The states were eliminated as administrative units and district offices replaced the former 22 state exchanges. The former 883 local exchanges were nearly all taken over by the new organization which set up 361 local offices. A given local office might, and a number of course did, have one or more branches.

The exchanges were made responsible in the main for the administration of the Unemployment Insurance Act. Insured workers who lose their jobs report to the appropriate exchange and apply for work. Such an unemployed person must present at the same time a form from his employer giving the reason why he does not have a job, and his rate of wages during the preceding three months.

The office immediately tries to place him in one of the positions which has been filed with it. If proper jobs are available in another section of Germany which justify the payment of the railroad fare, the applicants can be referred to those positions and if they refuse to go, they are not regarded as involuntarily unemployed and are not eligible for insurance benefits. Those who are out of work are, moreover, compelled to come back to the exchange every other

[19] *International Labour Review,* July, 1922, Vol. VI, p. 37.

day when the list of available jobs is again gone over until the worker is finally placed. The exchanges try to get the best man for the available places irrespective of other considerations. There is no attempt at "job communism" by placing men according to the length of time which they have been out of work. Comparative efficiency alone is supposed to count. As we shall see in our analysis of the German unemployment insurance scheme,[20] both the exchanges and unemployment insurance are actually administered by joint committees of workers and employers, whose original nominations are made by the unions and the employers' associations. There is thus an attempt to place the employment function in the hands of the two immediately interested parties and for the state, in consequence, to act in a merely supervisory capacity. This practice, by a nation supposedly given to bureaucracy, is an interesting contrast to that followed in Great Britain, where the political state itself carries on the work and is, on the whole, a decidedly superior method.

4. CANADA

The Canadian national service really dates from 1918, although the Canadian Government had begun to study the subject in 1914. At that time (1914) there were only three public employment offices in the country, all of which were located in the Province of Quebec. The abuses of the private employment agencies, which were particularly great in Canada because of the long distances which men traveled to obtain jobs, together with the unemployment of 1914 stimulated the government to take up the matter. The reduction in unemployment effected by the war, and the pressure of other problems led, however, to the side-tracking of this issue for some years. In 1916, however, Ontario, as the result of a report by a special commission on the subject, passed an act authorizing the establishment of public agencies and set up six offices in as many cities, while in 1917

[20] See *post*, Ch. 26.

British Columbia followed suit with a similar law, with Manitoba following in 1918. Alberta and Saskatchewan also passed such an act after the Armistice.[21]

The Ontario Commission, which had utilized much of the data originally collected by the Dominion Government, had suggested in its 1916 report that the Dominion should make financial grants to the provinces which had offices on condition that the latter showed they would conform to standards which the Dominion agency would establish.[22]

The approach of demobilization, coupled with the passage of acts by several provinces providing for the establishment of public offices and for the abolition of private offices in Manitoba, led the Dominion Government again to take up the subject in 1918 and to pass an act creating a federated national system. An initial appropriation of $50,000 was made for the year 1918-19, of $100,000 for the year 1919-20 and of $150,000 for the ensuing years. These sums were to be distributed among the provinces, not in proportion to their population, but according to the ratio which the appropriations of each province for employment exchanges bore to the total expended for this purpose by all the provinces as a whole. There was a provision, however, that in no event should the Dominion grant be more than half the total amount expended by a province.

The Dominion Department of Labor was given a variety of supervisory duties such as [23] "the encouragement of the provincial governments in the establishment of employment offices and clearing houses; the maintenance of interprovincial clearing houses; the promotion of uniformity of methods; the establishment of a system of inspection; the collection and publication of information on employment conditions; supervision of private advertising for labour; the supplying of all forms," etc. Advisory councils of employers and employees were provided for the local, the provincial, and the Dominion services.

---

[21] Bryce M. Stewart, *The Employment Service of Canada* (Queens University, Kingston, Canada), p. 7.

[22] *Report of the Ontario Commission on Unemployment* (p. 916), p. 43.

[23] Stewart, *op. cit.*, pp. 11-12.

The Dominion service was very active in helping to place the returned soldiers and was aided in this work by additional appropriations made for the first two years.[24] There are now 68 offices in the Dominion.

All but the little province of Prince Edward Island have them and their record of work for the last decade shows an average total number of placements of around 400,000 a year.

TABLE 15

PLACEMENT RECORD OF CANADIAN PUBLIC EMPLOYMENT SERVICE[25]
(Number of Placements in 000's)

YEAR	PERMANENT	CASUAL	TOTAL
1920	367	79	446
1921	281	75	356
1922	298	96	394
1923	347	116	463
1924	247	119	366
1925	307	106	413
1926	300	110	410
1927	303	112	415
1928	335	136	470
1929	261	138	398
1930 (first 4 mos) . .	53	47	100

The cost of the service has been approximately $400,000 a year. This means, therefore, that the average cost per placement is approximately $1.00 and that of the total expenses, approximately three-eighths is borne by the Dominion and five-eighths, or nearly twice as much, by the provinces. While the number of placements has necessarily fluctuated with the business cycle, there seems on the whole to have been a pronounced tendency for the number placed in temporary jobs to have increased although no such tendency is observable in the case of the more permanent positions.

[24] An added $30,000 was given for 1918-19 and a further sum of $150,-000 for 1919-20.
[25] *The Labour Gazette,* Canada, June, 1930, p. 701.

This increase in the placements of casuals is at least in part due to the excellent work the service has done in recruiting and mobilizing harvest workers for the provinces of Alberta, Saskatchewan, and Manitoba. Within each province there is a clearing-house to which each office sends a list of the jobs which they do not think they can fill locally and of the men whom they do not think they can place locally. These lists are compiled and copies sent to every office within that particular province. Any individual office which thinks it has laborers who can fill jobs listed by other offices is expected to get in touch with them by telegraph or telephone and try to place its applicants.[26] There are also two inter-provincial clearing offices; one in Ottawa which cares for the Eastern provinces and the other in Winnipeg for the Western. It has been found that about half of the approximate 400,000 workers annually placed in jobs by the service have to buy transportation in order to get to their newly found work. The railroads of the country have granted a reduction of one-quarter to all persons placed who are compelled to travel more than 116 miles. The Canadian employment service also acts as the intermediary with the British Service to place unemployed English workers who are properly qualified in specified jobs which cannot be filled by available Canadians.

The National Advisory Council is composed in an interesting manner. Each province appoints one member while various functional groups also name representatives. Thus the Canadian Manufacturers' Association appoints two members and the Canadian Trades and Labor Congress an equal number. The railways name one as do the Railway Brotherhoods. Two members are appointed by the Canadian Council of Agriculture, and three by the Department of Labor, two of whom must be women.

On the whole the Canadian system can be regarded as a quite successful example of the federal type. Since the

---

[26] Testimony of Bryce M. Stewart, *Unemployment in the United States, Hearings before Senate Committee on Education and Labor on S. Res. 219, 70th Congress, 2nd Session*, p. 151.

prairie provinces and British Columbia prohibit private employment agencies and Ontario and Quebec rigidly restrict their number, the public offices have in fact a virtual monopoly over organized placement.

5. FRANCE

During the latter part of the 19th century, the local *bourses du travail* which were the French analogue of our city central labor unions performed many functions of placement.[27] Their services were limited, however, by the relatively small membership of the French unions, the hostility of most employers, and the growing opposition of the government to the syndicalistic philosophy of the leaders. There was, however, a very efficient employment exchange in Paris in the eighties which as we shall see furnished the inspiration for the first permanent exchanges in the United States.

In 1907 the French Government tried to stimulate the localities to action by requiring that every commune with more than 10,000 inhabitants must establish a free labor exchange. Since the National Government made no grants towards the maintenance of these offices and the full burdens fell upon the communes themselves, the latter were accordingly very reluctant to go to this expense. In 1911 the government tried to meet this situation by granting subsidies to approved communal exchanges. Despite this encouragement, however, there were in 1913 only 27 communes, out of a total of 260,000 with a population of more than 10,000 which had set up such offices,[28] and the total number of placements was only 29,000.

During the war the dislocation of the luxury trades and the inundation of war refugees compelled the National Government to create additional exchanges. A Central Employment Exchange was established in 1914 which in two

[27] See Louis Levine, *The Labour Movement in France;* F. Pelloutier, *Histoire des Bourses du Travail.*
[28] International Labour Office, *The Organization of Employment Insurance and Employment Exchanges in France,* pp. 2-12.

years filled approximately 60,000 places. But it was soon realized that it was necessary to have local offices and, accordingly, a ministerial decree was issued in 1916 giving the 90 departments the same right to subsidies as the municipalities.

This move was successful. The Departments began to organize these exchanges rapidly and by 1921 all but two or three had established such offices. While the placements of the municipal offices remained virtually constant at 45,-000 a year, the placements by the departmental offices increased greatly until by 1925 they formed approximately 95 per cent of the total number placed. The growth in terms of total placements is shown by the following table: [29]

TABLE 16

PLACEMENTS BY FRENCH FREE PUBLIC EMPLOYMENT OFFICES

YEAR	NUMBER OF PLACEMENTS (IN 000's)	YEAR	NUMBER OF PLACEMENTS (IN 000's)
1916	97	1923	1446
1917	173	1924	1512
1918	334	1925	1435
1919	841	1926	1478
1920	1078	1927	1225
1921	1073	1928	1353
1922	1278	1929	1468

Of these placements, those for an indeterminate period of time, or for more than a week, tend to comprise slightly more than half of the total while those for less than a week form the remainder. In 1925, the total expenses of the offices were 5,110,000 francs, of which 1,506,000, or 30 per cent, were paid by the central government in the form of subventions.[30] This was an average cost per placement of 3.6

[29] *Bulletin du Ministère du Travail*, 1925, p. 18; 1926, p. 301; 1927, pp. 58-9; 1928, pp. 72-73; 1929, pp. 58-59; 1930, pp. 78-79.
[30] *Bulletin du Ministère du Travail*, 1928, pp. 55-56. Of the 153 offices, 53, 47 of which were municipal, did not make the minimum of 25 placements a month to entitle them to subventions or failed to comply with other regulations.

francs, which at the existent exchange rates was the approximate equivalent of 16 cents.

The precise scales by which the grants from the central
government are graduated have been changed several times
but in 1928 were as follows for placements of a duration
of a week or more: [31]

TABLE 17

Scale of Grants-in-aid by French Government in Behalf of Free
Public Employment Offices

Percentage Central Grant of Local Expenses	Permanent Placements Monthly in Cities of		
	Less than 50,000	50,000 to 200,000	Over 200,000[1]
0	Less than 25	Less than 50	Less than 100
20	25–100	50–150	100–200
25	101–200	150–300	201–400
30	201–400	301–600	401–800
35	401–800	601–1200	801–1600
40	Over 800	Over 1200	Over 1600 [1]

[1] In cities of over 200,000 a grant of one-tenth of a franc is made for all
short-time placements.

It will be seen from this that the grants are so graduated
as to stimulate the departments and municipalities to increase the scope of their placement work. An initial quantity of placements must be effected before any grants may
be made and this is naturally graduated according to the
size of the city in which the office is located. The relative
proportion of the total expenses which is met by the central
government increases from then on according to the number of more or less permanent placements made.

In France, as in all countries, one finds regional clearing
houses and advisory boards. There are six of such regional
exchanges at Paris, Lisle, Lyons, Marseilles, Toulouse, and
Nantes. Over these regional exchanges is the Central Exchange. Reduced rates are given by the railroads to workers
sent by the exchanges to jobs in other places. Due to the

[31] *Actes Officiels,* published with the *Bulletin.*

compact location of French industry and the French population, however, the amount of movement between localities is much less than in other countries.

Each local and departmental exchange has a managing
committee composed of wage-earners or clerical workers and
of employers. These committees are drawn so far as possible
from those trades and industries which most utilize the
exchanges. The regional offices have committees in a similar
fashion and the central exchange is under the control of
a National Labor Supply Council (Conseil National de la
Main d'Oeuvre). This includes delegates from the appropriate ministries, representatives of Parliament, and representatives of employers' and workers' organizations in the
fields of manufacturing, commerce, and agriculture. These
committees are not merely advisory bodies but are supervisory and exercise general control over the offices.

The National Labor Supply Council as a matter of fact
determines approximately how many foreign workers shall
be admitted to the country and with the aid of the employment offices distributes them to the points of greatest need.
As in Canada, therefore, the national system of employment offices is used to help administer and control the international migration of workers.

In the larger French cities the offices have, as in Germany, specialized their work and have created a number of
trade sections. Thus the Paris exchange which by 1919 was
filling 176,000 jobs a year is subdivided into a very large
number of vocational units covering such groups as (1)
the clothing industries; (2) the employees in hotels, res-
taurants and cafés; (3) barbers; (4) paper and cardboard
industries; (5) domestic servants; (6) laborers; (7) shop
porters. Some of these sections are really autonomous in
their direction and are administered by special committees
composed of representatives of their particular trade or
industry. The staff is selected from either workers or employers in that industry and the work of the section is
therefore directed to the specific needs of an industry in
a fashion which is impossible in the case of a non-special-

ized general office. In some cases, such as the clothing trades, hotel, restaurant and café service, barber, etc., the administration of the sectional employment office is administered according to a collective agreement between the appropriate employers' organizations and the unions.

6. JAPAN

Japan is a country where the system of public offices has developed with extraordinary rapidity during the last decade. In 1920 the public exchanges placed only 63,000 workers. In the following year, an act was passed providing for the creation of local employment exchanges. These can be established either by local initiative or upon the direction of the Minister for Home Affairs. In either event the National Government gives financial aid in the form of a subsidy. Free private agencies can also be set up if the public employment officials give their consent. There were, in 1927, 172 free public agencies and 38 free private offices and in a span of ten months, they received approximately 3 million applications for workers, two and a half million offers of work, and placed no less than 2,365,000 workers in jobs. This was at the rate of approximately 2,900,000 placements a year. It will be seen, therefore, that the Japanese system stands next to the German and Russian in the volume of placements.

Local advisory committees composed of employers and workers have been authorized for the local exchanges and in the larger cities at least of Tokyo, Osaka, Fukuoka, and Nagoya are actually in operation. The power of appointing the members of these commissions rests, however, with the chief magistrates of the localities rather than with groups of employers and employees. The local officials may, however, apparently delegate some of their powers in this matter to special bodies.

Private fee-charging agencies, of whom there are approximately 3,500 in Japan, are compelled to report the number of applications for work and for jobs and the number of placements. During the first ten months of 1927, they were successful in placing 728,000 workers, or at the rate of approximately 900,000 a year. It seems safe to say, therefore, that of the placements which are effected by specialized intermediary agencies, slightly over three-fourths were by the free and one-fourth by the fee-charging agencies.

7. RUSSIA [32]

Prior to 1917, there were virtually no public labor exchanges in Russia. During the Kerensky régime a number were started and, after the Bolshevists assumed power, the hiring of workers through them was made compulsory. During the period of military communism (1919-1921) the offices were given much larger powers in distributing labor.

With the adoption of the new economic policy in 1922, although concerns were still legally supposed to hire their workers through the exchanges, in practice they tended increasingly to engage them directly. In 1925 the legal obligation was removed and the use of exchanges was made purely optional for both workers and employers. The work of the offices declined quite rapidly to a point where the exchanges were filling only about 30 per cent of the vacancies.[33]

The trade unions became alarmed at this decrease in the powers of the offices and, since they are extremely powerful,[34] they succeeded through their collective agreements in getting more and more of the state trusts to hire their men through the offices and to give preference in employment to their own members.

The work of the exchanges has in consequence distinctly increased in recent years. The number of offices rose from 149 in 1924 to 342 in 1929, while the number of applications and placements increased by the numbers shown in Table 18:

[32] See Work for the Unemployed in the U. S. S. R., *International Labour Review,* July, 1930, pp. 46-69.   [33] *Ibid.,* p. 50.
[34] Over 90 per cent of the wage-workers in urban industries are organized in unions.

TABLE 18

WORK OF RUSSIAN EMPLOYMENT EXCHANGES 1925-1929

YEAR	APPLICATIONS FOR WORK (IN 000's)	VACANCIES (IN 000's)	WORKERS PLACED (IN 000's)
1925–26 . . .	2,950	2,015	1,943
1926–27 . . .	3,567	3,498	3,365
1927–28 . . .	3,979	4,981	4,890
1928–29 . . .	3,885	6,658	4,215

The number of placements, therefore, more than doubled during the four years and the percentage of all the workers engaged who were placed through the exchanges rose from 59 in 1926-27 to 73 in 1928-29.[35] In so far as manufacturing was concerned, five-sixths of the workers then were hired through the exchanges.

The exchanges also act as the administrative agencies for the system of unemployment relief [36] and in their management the trades unions play the most important part. The unions, for example, generally nominate the officials who are later designated by the Commissariat of Labor.

8. SUMMARY

The short sketch which has been given of the public employment systems of six countries discloses a wide difference in methods of administration and control. While the first experiments in employment offices have been made in general by municipalities and while in the various countries the work starts by the efforts of local governments, national systems must sooner or later be created. The forms which these take vary widely. England is the example par excellence of a centralized national system which almost sprang into birth as a unit. Germany illustrates a system

[35] *International Labour Review,* July, 1930, p. 54.
[36] See the chapter on Social Insurance in the collection of essays on *Soviet Russia in the Second Decade,* edited by Chase, Dunn and Tugwell, pp. 216-38.

which, starting out upon a city basis, developed organizations for the separate states of the Empire and finally created a nationalized system. Canada, on the other hand, is an excellent illustration of a truly federal system with local authority in the hands of the provinces and with the national government exercising general supervision and control through the device of federal grants-in-aid. The Japanese and French systems are mixtures of localism and national control and in both countries national grants are made towards the support of the local offices.

All of the systems provide for the creation of boards representing workers and employers who assist the various exchanges. The powers of these boards vary—those in Germany being the actual governing bodies while the French committees are also given an important part. In England and Japan, however, these committees are merely advisory. Russia presents the interesting spectacle of a nation where the trade unions in the main dominate the work of the employment exchanges.

In England the exchanges are general placement offices with little specialized attention given to specific trades. In the larger cities of France and Germany on the other hand the offices are subdivided into vocational sections with interviewers who are skilled in the trades for which they are placing.

In England and Germany, which have national systems of unemployment insurance, the employment agencies are the chief agencies for the administration of the benefits and for imposing the test as to whether the applicant is genuinely seeking work.

Finally, all countries, save the smallest, have found that it is necessary to have a number of regional clearing houses instead of merely one national clearing office.

CHAPTER XX

THE DEVELOPMENT OF PUBLIC EMPLOYMENT OFFICES IN THE UNITED STATES

1. Public Employment Offices Prior to 1918

The first permanent public employment offices in the United States were the five established in Ohio by a state law in 1890. The five cities which had these offices were Toledo, Cleveland, Dayton, Cincinnati, and Columbus. In the first year they placed approximately 9,000 workers and by 1899 were placing 15,000. Two-thirds of this number were women for whom work was primarily found in domestic service.[1] In 1894 Seattle, Washington, opened the first municipally initiated and managed office, which by 1899 was placing approximately 18,000 workers a year. New York started two offices in 1897 in the cities of New York and Buffalo respectively, and in 1899 Illinois set up three offices in Chicago. By 1900 there were 15 public offices in operation and by 1905 this number had grown to 37 offices which were located in no less than 15 different states.[2] While most of these were state offices, the example of Seattle had caused a number of other cities in the West, where the demand for rough unskilled labor was great, to establish municipal offices. Among these cities were Tacoma, Spokane, Sacramento, Butte and Great Falls. The movement continued to grow, and in 1912 there were apparently 64 such offices which placed in all approximately 468,000 workers.[3]

---

[1] See Ernest L. Bogart, Public Employment Offices in the United States and Germany, *Quarterly Journal of Economics,* Vol. XIX (1900), pp. 341-77. An office had been opened earlier in San Francisco (1868) but it was not permanent, as had another in New York.

[2] Harrison and Associates, *Public Employment Offices,* p. 624.

[3] E. H. Sutherland, Unemployment and Public Employment Agencies, *Report of the Mayor of Chicago's Commission on Unemployment.*

During these years Wisconsin began to put its offices into a much better condition. Coöperative arrangements were made with several municipalities whereby the latter paid for the rent, light, heating, and janitor service of the offices. This enabled the state appropriations to go farther and enlisted the support of the municipalities without, however, giving them control. Two other important steps were taken.[4] The employment service was put on a merit basis and advisory boards of employers and employees were established. These local boards passed on the local budgets and advised on questions of policy while the Industrial Commission, based on the theory of joint representation, was given general control over the state system. The staff of employees was on the whole well selected and in Milwaukee all of the five officials were finally chosen [5] by "an examining board on which the Industrial Commission, the Civil Service Commission and employers and workers were represented." Promotional opportunities within the service were also provided as a means of providing a real incentive to effort.

The new methods succeeded in greatly increasing the value of the offices. In Milwaukee the number of persons referred to jobs increased in one year from 6,000 to 24,000. In only about half of the cases of those referred to jobs, however, could their placements be, in fact, definitely verified. During the second year the number of persons referred to work increased over the first by about 40 per cent.[6]

The depression of 1914-15 brought a great increase in the number of offices, and in the latter year Dr. Royal Meeker testified that there were then 109 such offices of which 79 were managed by the states and 30 by municipalities. As the state systems began to develop it was but natural that people should begin to consider the desira-

---

[4] W. L. Leiserson, The Theory of Public Employment Offices and the Principles of their Practical Administration, *Political Science Quarterly*, Vol. XXIX (1914), pp. 38-41.   [5] *Ibid.*, p. 39.
[6] Hearings before House Committee on Labor on H. R. 1783, *64th Congress, 1st Session*, p. 48.

bility of a national system. Two bills which were introduced in Congress during the years 1914-15 attracted a considerable amount of attention. One, sponsored by Congressman McDonald of Michigan, proposed to convert the post offices of the country into public employment bureaus,[7] while the second, introduced by Congressman Victor Murdock of Kansas, was drawn up by the research committee of the Progressive Party. In keeping with the principles of the Progressive Party it was framed in terms of a national system rather than a federal system. It provided [8] for the establishment of a bureau of employment in the Department of Labor which would have the power of opening and administering employment offices in various centers of the country. Coöperative agreements could be made with municipalities for the joint operation of these exchanges. There were no provisions, however, for coöperation with the states —it being the intention that the national government should either operate the exchanges directly or coöperate with the cities in doing so. Miss Kellor, in defending this proposal declared,[9] "cities, and not states, are the industrial and commercial units of the country. . . . Federal aid to, and coöperation with, municipal instead of state employment offices will therefore result in greater efficiency." These bills were not even voted on by Congress and had therefore no more than an educational influence.

Several other forces were operating at the same time to arouse a national interest in the program. In 1913 the American Association of Public Employment Offices was formed and has ever since held meetings.[10] The problem of handling harvest labor for the wheat crop in the trans-Mississippi states led also to the organization in 1915 of a National Farm Labor Exchange which tried to route har-

[7] For a critical analysis of this bill see Frances A. Kellor, *Out of Work*, pp. 305-12.
[8] See the hearings on this bill, *H. R. 5783, 64th Congress, 1st Session; H. R. 17017 63rd Congress, 2nd Session.*
[9] Frances A. Kellor, *Out of Work*, p. 516.
[10] See *Bulletins, 192, 220, 311, 337, 355, 400 of the United States Bureau of Labor Statistics.* The name of the organization has been changed to the International Association of Public Employment Offices.

vesters in an orderly fashion in following the grain crop north as it ripened.[11] The Federal Commission on Industrial Relations through William L. Leiserson and Charles B. Barnes prepared a draft plan which called for federal aid to states and localities which would establish such offices and for their standardization and coördination by the National Government. This plan differed from the Murdock bill primarily in the fact that the Federal Government as such was not to operate the exchanges but was instead to subsidize, coöperate with, and regulate those which were started by the states as well as the municipalities.[12]

All of these factors kept the issue of a Federal Service very much to the fore. The Department of Labor had been making a few feeble efforts to grapple with the problem by having the Bureau of Immigration try to place workers and had set up eighteen offices under the direction of this Bureau. They were not, however, very effective.

With the increase of war contracts during the latter part of 1915 and 1916, the surplus of labor gradually diminished and many industries experienced instead considerable difficulty in recruiting an adequate working force. With our entrance into the war, the relative shortage of available labor became acute. Between four and five million men were drawn into the army and navy during the year and a half of our active participation in the struggle. Since the vast majority of these men had previously been employed, there was an urgent necessity for replacing them. In addition, war industries, such as ship-building, munitions, factories, cantonment construction, etc., and their subsidiaries demanded millions of additional workers. There was not enough labor to meet all the demands and employers began to compete against each other for help. The unequal rise in the wage scales in itself induced a great deal of labor turnover as

[11] W. L. Leiserson, The Movement for Public Labor Exchanges, *Journal of Political Economy*, Vol. 23 (1914), p. 713.

[12] The Association of Public Employment Offices had passed a resolution in 1914 declaring that "We do not approve the establishment of local employment offices by the Federal Government." *Bulletin 192 of the United States Bureau of Labor Statistics*, p. 141.

workers would leave lower paid jobs for higher paid ones. In addition, however, many employers followed a deliberate policy of trying to hire workers away from other firms and sent out special labor scouts to round up groups of laborers and bring them back by hook or crook. Many men were being brought from the middle-west to the east at the very time when the other men were being brought from the east to the middle-west.

Such bidding for labor artificially increased labor turnover and led many workers to pay more attention to the possibility of changing jobs than to making good at the job at which they were then employed.

2. The War-Time Federal Employment Service

The employment service within the Bureau of Immigration proved grossly inadequate to deal with the fast-mounting problem of recruiting and stabilizing the necessary labor forces and, therefore, on January 3, 1918, Secretary of Labor Wilson directed that the employment work be taken away from the Bureau of Immigration and that a separate United States Employment Service should be created within the Department of Labor.[13] Mr. John B. Dinsmore, the former solicitor of the Department, but without experience in employment matters, was appointed as the head of the Service.

The Service was really given an impossible task, namely that of handling the labor supply of the country without having any prior organization upon which it could build. It was compelled to set up a nation-wide system with great speed. Existing offices were either taken over by the national service or managed under coöperative relations with the municipalities and the states. New offices were opened rapidly under the direct control of the Federal Service. By May 7, 1918, only four months after the Service was

[13] For the steps leading up to the establishment of such a service and the general problem of creating a labor administration in war-time, see L. C. Marshall, The War Labor Program, *Journal of Political Economy* (1918), Vol. 26, pp. 425-60.

established as a separate and independent branch, the total number of offices amounted to 280 while by the last of August, no less than 560 were in existence. By October 21st this number in turn had increased to 832. At the peak of activities, there were 850 offices in operation. The funds for the fiscal year 1917-18 were provided from a Congressional appropriation of $250,000 plus $825,000 which President Wilson assigned from his general fund for National Security and Defense. The Service was financed during 1918-19 by an appropriation of $5,500,000, a deficiency appropriation of $272,000 and by donations from private sources towards the end of the fiscal year.

The task of selecting a personnel for so rapidly erected and so far flung an organization was difficult enough in itself while in addition, jealousies between state and national authorities were rife because of the necessarily hasty nationalization of the Service.

Since the Service found few competent employment experts in the country, it was only natural that a considerable percentage of the state and local officials should have been drawn from the ranks of organized labor. In many instances these appointees gave efficient service but in some cases, however, they were relatively inefficient and added to the distrust which most employers entertained towards the Service.

The field organization of the Service was subjected to two major changes. The country was at first divided into thirteen districts, each containing from two to five states. In each of these districts there was a District Superintendent with a State Director of Employment in each state. The District Superintendents seemed, however, to interfere with the efficient management of the state offices. They were accordingly gradually eliminated so that the Federal Service could deal directly with the states.

The staff alignment in the central office at Washington was also being constantly changed. It had been originally intended to have two Assistant Directors—one to be in charge of field work and clearance and the other in charge of the specialized divisions in the central office such as Women, Farm Service, Information, Statistics, etc. This was later modified by dropping one of the Assistant Directors and substituting instead a Planning Board, made up of the heads of the various divisions. Finally, five divisions were set up, namely, (1) Control, (2) Field Organization, (3) Clearance, (4) Personnel, and (5) Information. Within each of these divisions there were, in turn, subsections dealing with specific functions.

In June, 1918, President Wilson issued a Presidential Proclamation reviewing the confusion and cross-shipment of workers which resulted from the recruiting of labor by individual establishments and the loss of time and production which was caused by the competitively induced labor turnover. He, therefore, ordered that after August 1st all employers who had more than 100 workers should engage their unskilled laborers through the United States Employment Service. It was understood that if the war continued, and as the Employment Service extended its organization, it would be given the monopoly of placing the skilled workers as well.

The exigencies of the war situation, therefore, compelled the executive to do what the United States Supreme Court had declared that a state could not do—namely, to give at least a partial monopoly in the engagement of labor to the public offices and to bar the private offices from this field. Had the war continued, there is but little doubt that this monopoly would have been made complete by extending it to skilled labor as well.

The Service struggled hard to fulfill the demands for labor which were made upon it. Since the vast majority of the war contracts had been concentrated in the eastern states, there was, in general, a very real deficit of labor in these regions. There was on the other hand a comparative surplus in many of the middle-western states. The Service naturally tried to transfer labor from these localities to meet the needs of the eastern war industries. This move was bitterly resented by the employers of a number of cities who feared that the depletion of their local labor supply would force them to increase wages more than would otherwise be necessary and upon the termination of the war leave them with a smaller force than they would need to carry on ordinary peace-time production. The real estate dealers and merchants of these localities also disapproved of any draining off of population since this would at once lower the price of land and decrease the purchases from local stores. The hostility which this policy aroused has continued in some places to this day and accounts for a portion at least of the opposition to a strong Federal Employment Service. Partially to meet this difficulty, and partially because of the sheer common-sense of the method, the Federal Service set up State Advisory Boards and Community Labor Boards. The State Boards were composed of two employers, two representatives of the employees and the State Director of Employment, who was the chairman. The Community Boards were originally composed of three members, namely, one representative of the workers and employers respectively, and a representative of the employment office. Later two women were added—one from each of the two parties. These boards were not set up until midsummer but by the end of October there were approximately 1400 functioning. They were in many ways the most useful adjunct to the Service but, unfortunately, they did not have long to function before the Armistice came. This changed the whole nature of the employment problem and created a temporary surplus of men in place of the previous deficit.

Despite all the difficulties which the Service faced and the many mistakes which it made, its record during the trying year of 1918 was not discreditable. It received applications for 8.8 million workers and registered in turn 3.2 million applicants. It referred approximately 3.0 million persons to jobs and received reports that 2.4 millions had been finally employed.[14]

[14] E. T. Devine, The Federal Employment Service, *The Survey*, April 5, 1919, pp. 9-17.

The coming of the Armistice aroused grave fears that demobilization would be attended by severe unemployment and the Employment Service began to take steps to meet it. Many urged that demobilization should be gradual and men released according to industrial openings. When this policy was vetoed and demobilization was instead speeded up, there were many prophecies of dire consequences. The industries of the country, however, speedily absorbed the returned soldiers and the transition from a war to a peace basis was made with surprisingly little unemployment. But while the returned soldiers in the main found places in industry through their own efforts, the Employment Service did aid in a large number of instances through 1850 bureaus and through its branches in the various army camps.

By February of 1919, however, the Service had exhausted nearly all its funds and was compelled to appeal to private agencies in a number of cities. At the same time, it sought further appropriations from Congress for the continuation of the service. Secretary Wilson called an employment conference in Washington in April which was attended by representatives of thirty states, by members of the American Federation of Labor and by some progressive employers. It was decided that in the future the Federal Government should not directly operate offices as it had during the World War but that they were instead to be managed and operated by the states. The bill which was drafted provided that the Federal Service was to be made a permanent bureau in the Department of Labor with a Director-General appointed by the President. An annual appropriation of $4,600,000 was asked of which $3,000,000 was to be distributed among the states in proportion to their population on condition that the states would appropriate at least equal sums. The Federal Service in turn was to handle the clearances of labor between states, to inspect the local offices, to outline systems of forms and record-keeping, and to gather information on labor and employment conditions.

The principle of federal aid which was already being used in a number of other services was adopted therefore in place of outright national operation. The bill was introduced in the House by Congressman Nolan of California but met with determined opposition from the National Association of Manufacturers, and from various groups of employers in different parts of the country. They had not opposed a federal service during the war when the chief problem was to obtain men for jobs but now that the problem had shifted to one of obtaining jobs for men, they did not feel any economic necessity for such a service. They attacked the Service on the ground that it had been wasteful and inefficient and charged that it was biased in favor of union labor. They also alleged that the personnel of the Service, itself to a considerable measure recruited from the ranks of union officials, had used its position to help get active unionists jobs in non-union firms with the aim of helping to organize the plants. In addition, the private fee-charging employment agencies joined the opposition to the bill.[15] Congress was itself anxious to reduce the swollen war-time expenditures to the lowest possible figure and the utter absence of a reconstruction program on the part of the government and the absence of President Wilson left the proposal without the support of either a general philosophy or a political leader. The bill was in consequence defeated and Congress instead appropriated only $400,000 for the maintenance of the Federal Service. This, of course, prevented any subsidies from being given to the states and permitted instead only a general staff in Washington.

With this shutting off of funds, the majority of the employment offices were speedily closed.[16] Others were taken over by states and municipalities which in some part entered the breach to make good the loss resulting from the discontinuance of federal appropriations. By the first part of 1920, there were, however, only 269 offices in operation.[17]

[15] E. T. Devine, The Attack on the Federal Employment Service, *Survey,* February 8, 1929, pp. 662-63.
[16] During the entire fiscal year ending June 30, 1919, it is stated that the total placements amounted to 4,254,000. D. H. Smith, *The United States Employment Service,* p. 56.
[17] Harrison, *Public Employment Offices,* p. 624.

The total appropriations for the offices, including the $400,-000 for the Federal Service, was $1,547,000. The state and local appropriations were, therefore, $1,147,000 which was approximately three times the amount expended three years before. Even after taking account of the increases in prices and salaries, this amounted to a substantial increase over the pre-war expenditures.

3. The Decadence of Public Employment Offices— 1920-1930

During the decade from 1920 to 1930 the Federal Employment Service fell into a dry-rot and the state services on the whole went backward. The man appointed to head the Service by President Harding was not a competent administrator and the office has done little constructive work. The chief positive activity which it has carried on has been the work of the Farm Labor Bureau in helping to mobilize and route the forces of harvesters who have been needed in the past to harvest the wheat crop.[18] It has also entered into coöperative arrangements with the states, furnishing forms and the franking privilege as financial inducements for coöperation, and has assigned a number of its staff to certain local offices. These men are not under civil service provisions and are not distinguished for their competence. The various state directors of employment have been automatically made the Federal Directors and thus serve in a double capacity.

From the reports which the state bureaus have made to the Federal Service, the following volume of business seems to have been transacted. The statistical records of the employment offices are, however, quite poor and there is certainly a considerable margin of error in the totals.

[18] For a description of this work see George E. Tucker, Labor and the Grain Harvest, *Proceedings 10th Annual Meeting of the International Association of Public Employment Services*, pp. 70-76; and *Summary of Activities of the Farm Labor Division, United States Employment Service, 1929.*

TABLE 19

Work of Public Employment Offices in the United States 1921–30 [19]

Fiscal Year Ending June 30	Number of Applicants for Work (in 000's)	Number of Jobs Listed by Employers (in 000's)	Number Actually Placed (in 000's)
1921	2434	1888	1398
1922	2875	1810	1459
1923	....	....	....
1924	2756	2201	1807
1925	2664	1877	1610
1926	2728	2092	1791
1927	2441	1992	1688
1928	2259	1607	1413
1929	2333	1772	1534
1930	2346	1518	1346

While this work has of course been done exclusively by the state bureaus, the reports of the United States Employment Service and of the Department of Labor have given the impression that it has been the Federal Service which has borne the brunt of the burden. Thus in the 1928 report of the Secretary of Labor the statement is made [20] that "during the fiscal year ended June 30, 1928, the United States Employment Service in coöperation with the several states placed in employment 1,412,645 men and women."

Since the Service does not, with the exception of the Farm Labor Division, do actual placement work, the chief function which it might perform would be the collection of accurate data on the state of the labor market. In 1921 it did conduct two surveys of unemployment in the months of January and September respectively which covered 182 and 280 cities respectively and during 1921 and 1922 it published data on the numbers employed in a large number of manufacturing enterprises. While there were a number of faults in the methods of collecting these data, they were at

[19] Compiled from the *Annual Report of the Secretary of Labor*, 1928, p. 27; 1927, p. 32; 1926, p. 33; 1925, p. 33; 1924, p. 37; 1922, p. 28. Also Darrell H. Smith, *The United States Employment Service*, p. 61; Monthly Report of Activities, *U. S. Employment Service*, June, 1929, May, 1930, June, 1930.

[20] *Report of Secretary of Labor*, 1928, p. 27.

least useful in showing the changes in employment in the major divisions of manufactures in each of 65 large cities in the country.[21] The Service kept on collecting these statistics for a considerable period of time after the Bureau of Labor Statistics had greatly expanded its employment index and this duplicate collection service caused a considerable amount of irritation and extra work.

During the depression which set in during the latter part of 1929 and continued through 1930, the reports of the United States Employment Service were misleading. Thus in November when the depression was beginning to gather headway, the Service announced in its *Industrial Employment Information Bulletin*,[22] "Movements now under way will have an encouraging effect on industry, which will mean an increase in the volume of employment. All signs are encouraging and better economic conditions should prevail in the immediate future."

As the new year of 1930 opened, the Employment Service issued a forecast for the year embodying the results of a special survey [23] "giving the industrial, agricultural, and general employment prospects for 1930." In the foreword to this report, the Director, Francis I. Jones, declared [24] that "after a careful survey of the business outlook we enter the New Year with optimistic spirit and high hopes and predict that 1930 will measure in volume of business with the preceding year." This was bad enough since every competent student of business knew by this time that 1930 could not equal 1929. But Mr. Jones went so far as to forecast [25] that the automobile industry had the "prospect of a volume of business equal to that of the year just ended, which was the largest in the history of the automobile industry."

[21] For an appraisal of these statistics see Ralph G. Hurlin, The Employment Statistics of the United States Employment Service, *Journal American Statistical Association*, December, 1922 (Vol. XVII), pp. 490-97.

[22] *Industrial Employment Information Bulletin*, November, 1929 (Vol. IX, No. 11), p. 1.

[23] United States Department of Labor, United States Employment Service, *Industrial, Agricultural, and General Employment Prospects for 1930*, p. 23.

[24] *Ibid.*, p. 11.   [25] *Ibid.*

In January, 1930, when the index of employment of the United States Bureau of Labor Statistics covering 4.9 million workers in the principal industries showed a decline of 2.6 per cent from December, 1929,[26] the Employment Service cheerfully and irresponsibly stated,[27] however, that "all reports indicate that an upward swing to employment is in motion."

Despite this display of optimism, however, the index of employment of the Bureau of Labor Statistics fell by one-tenth of one per cent in February,[28] by 1.0 per cent in March[29] and by two-tenths of a per cent in April[30] and by nine-tenths of a per cent in May.[31] In this month the index of employment in manufacturing was indeed 4.6 per cent below where it had been in May of the previous year.[32] The events of these months had a somewhat chastening effect upon the Employment Service. It no longer continued to claim that business would speedily return to the 1929 level but it tried quite desperately to find signs of improvement wherever it could and to minimize or ignore the decline in employment. Thus in February it observed[33] that "business and industry appear to be consolidating the progress made in January for an expected upturn in employment during the spring months." Since business had actually lost ground, the accuracy of this statement could only apply in an Alice-in Wonderland world. During March the Service did grudgingly admit[34] that "there was no great improvement in industrial activity." But the latent hope of the Service found expression in the statement[35] that "all signs" were "pointing to further improvement in the next 30 days." In April, as employment still continued to decline, the Service reluctantly admitted[36] that "the em-

---

[26] *Monthly Labor Review*, March, 1930, p. 149.

[27] *Industrial Employment Information Bulletin*, January, 1930 (Vol. X, No. 1), p. 1.

[28] *Monthly Labor Review*, April, 1930, p. 173.

[29] *Ibid.*, May, 1930, p. 176.   [31] *Ibid.*, July, 1930, p. 173.

[30] *Ibid.*, June, 1930, p. 199.   [32] *Ibid.*, p. 178.

[33] *Industrial Employment Information Bureau*, February, 1930, p. 1.

[34] *Ibid.*, March, 1930, p. 1.   [35] *Ibid.*, March, 1930, p. 1.

[36] *Ibid.*, April, 1930, p. 1.

ployment situation ... can not be described as satisfactory."
But with unquenchable optimism the Service once more
predicted an improvement in the following month and
announced "there are indications that there will be an
improvement in operations and employment in the industrial plants during May."

The truth of the matter is that the representatives of the
Service who sent in qualitative statements of the state of
employment from various sections of the country were in
the main incompetent and ill-informed and neither the
Director nor his assistants showed the slightest ability to
understand what was in fact happening.

The result was that the releases and statements of the
United States Employment Service served only to befuddle
the public mind and to help delude public opinion into
believing that conditions were not bad. So far from giving a
picture of the real state of the labor market, the Service
did the exact opposite.

4. THE ATTEMPTS AT LEGISLATION FOR A GENUINE FEDERAL EMPLOYMENT SERVICE—THE WAGNER BILL

During the decade from 1920 to 1930 periodical efforts
were made to establish a more adequate national employment system. Congressman Nolan regularly reintroduced
the Kenyon-Nolan Bill and after his death it was again
introduced by his widow who succeeded him. While President Harding's conference on Unemployment in 1921 threw
the primary responsibility for caring for unemployment
largely on the local communities,[37] a continuing committee
of that conference on *Business Cycles and Unemployment*
gave "hearty approval" to a national system of employment
bureaus.[38] When Senator Robert F. Wagner of New York
was elected to the Upper House, he took up the Nolan Bill
and pushed it as one of a series of three measures which he

[37] For the recommendations of that conference see *The Survey*, October 22, 1921, p. 109.
[38] *Business Cycles and Unemployment* (National Bureau of Economic
Research), p. XXXI.

was advocating as a preliminary attack by the government upon the problem of unemployment.

The seriousness of the unemployment crisis of 1930 brought the subject to the fore again and in April the Senate Committee on Commerce reported favorably all three of his bills calling respectively for (1) an all-inclusive index of employment and man hours to be collected monthly by the United States Bureau of Labor Statistics; [39] (2) the advance planning of public works and the appropriation of $150,000,000 to help make this effective; [40] (3) the creation of a federal-state employment service.[41]

It is the last of these measures which directly concerns us and which we shall describe. As the bill was introduced by Senator Wagner, an annual appropriation of $4,000,000 was authorized for four years, of which three million was to be allotted to the states according to their relative population with the usual federal aid provision that each state or its subdivision should appropriate at least an equal amount to receive the federal allotment. A state could not, however, shift the full burden upon its localities since it was compelled to pay one-half of the sum which must be put up by the state and local governments together. It was also necessary that the employment system within a state be integrated under state control before federal funds could be received. A state was of course not compelled to accept the act, but if it refused, it was not entitled to receive federal funds. Once under the act, it was however compelled to set up an integrated state service and to submit plans for its operation to the United States Employment Service. If the latter approved of these plans and if upon inspection the state service was found adequate, the allotment was assigned to the state. If the Federal Director refused to certify the plans and the efficiency of the state service, the state could appeal to the Secretary of Labor, but if the latter upheld his subordinate, the funds were to be withheld.

The remaining $1,000,000 was to be expended by the

[39] This was S. 3061.   [40] S. 3059.   [41] S. 3060.

Federal Service itself in conducting clearing houses for labor between states, inspecting the state services, carrying on research and publishing information, setting up a revolving fund for the transportation of workers, and finally in directly conducting offices in states where no state system existed and for one year only in states which refused to come under the act. In order to make possible the efficient administration of the new system, the existing Federal Service was to be disbanded and a new Director-General was to be appointed by the President. The personnel for the Federal work was to be under civil service and it was provided that the Director-General should set up a National Advisory Council composed of equal numbers of employers and workers and that there should be similar councils in each state which accepted the act. It was unfortunate, however, that the bill did not provide that the personnel of the various state services must be under civil service as a prerequisite for receiving federal aid.

The bill did not make any progress until the depression of 1929-30 aroused public and senatorial interest in the measure. By a combination of western Progressives, led by Senator Hiram Johnson of California and Democrats, the bill passed the senate in May by a vote of 34 to 27. The old-guard and the administration Republicans voted almost uniformly against the bill and were led by Senator Bingham of Connecticut. The bill then passed to the lower house where efforts were made to side-track it in the Judiciary Committee. Hearings were finally forced and the bill with some amendments was finally reported on favorably by a vote of 18 to 2 during the closing days of the session. A number of amendments were, however, made to the measure, one of which was an improvement and others of which were not. One of the features of the bill which had been most subject to attack from a constitutional standpoint was that giving the national service the power during one year to open offices in states which refused to come under the Federal Aid Act. This was wisely eliminated. Unfortunately, however, the Service was also deprived of the power to transport workers and with this, by what may have been an inadvertence, the clauses authorizing the Service to establish "uniform standards, policies, and procedures" and pledging it to be "impartial, neutral in labor disputes, and free from political influence." Finally, the committee decreased the salary of the Director-General from $10,000 to $8,500 a year.

The bill was reported out too late for action during the long session by the House and therefore went over to the short session of Congress in December, 1930. While this book was passing through the press, the administration took an attitude of open opposition to the federal aid feature of the Wagner bill and sponsored a substitute measure which did not contain any provision for such aid but which did provide an appropriation of $1,500,000 for establishing interstate clearance and for the setting-up of some offices directly under the administration of the Employment Service. Where state offices were already in existence, the consent of the governor of the state was necessary for the creation of such offices. The House Judiciary Committee then voted to substitute this bill for that of Senator Wagner, but it was defeated on the floor of the House by a vote of 182 to 84. The House then passed the Wagner Bill which went to the President for action.[41a]

The National Association of Manufacturers and the private employment offices were open and vigorous in their opposition to the bill. The motives of the latter group are obvious but those of the former are not at first thought so apparent. Their ostensible ground of opposition which was stressed both by Senator Bingham of Connecticut and by their counsel, Mr. James A. Emery, was on the principle of federal aid. This they asserted is really coercive upon the states and is unconstitutional. Such legalistic objections tend to be at best merely disguises for the real grounds of opposition since the history of constitutional law abun-

---

[41a] For the text of the substitute measure and the accompanying memorandum of Secretary of Labor Doak, see the *United States Daily*, February 19, pp. 1 and 10. President Hoover vetoed the bill on March 7th.

dantly demonstrates that constitutional arguments are generally only the weapons with which group interests contend rather than the motivating cause for their actions. This suspicion is particularly heightened in the present instance both because of the fact that the National Association of Manufacturers itself worked in 1916 for the passage of the Smith-Hughes Bill granting federal aid to the states for vocational education and because the Supreme Court in the leading case of *Massachusetts v. Mellon* (262 U. S. 447) pointed out that under federal aid "nor does the statute require the states to do or yield anything. If Congress enacted it with the ulterior purpose of tempting them to yield, that purpose may be effectively frustrated by the simple expedient of not yielding."

Without pretending to possess any psycho-analytic omniscience, we believe that the real reasons for the opposition of the National Association of Manufacturers, as distinguished from their assigned reasons, are probably as follows: (1) their fear that the offices would be used by the unions to get union organizers into non-union plants, (2) their fear that the offices would decrease the work of the employment bureaus of a number of manufacturers' associations, and (3) their fear that the offices would hasten the coming of compulsory unemployment insurance. The first fear seems to be particularly ill-founded. By the terms of the original bill, the Service was pledged to neutrality in labor disputes and while this clause was inadvertently omitted subsequent to the objections of the manufacturers, it should and doubtless will be restored. Secondly, even if it be thought that the Department of Labor would be biased in favor of labor (which would be difficult to allege against the conduct of that Department during the last ten years), it should be remembered that the Director-General is to be appointed by the President. Furthermore, the employers are to have equal representation on the advisory councils and could in effect prevent any such possibility from developing. Moreover, even were the service to be biased in favor of placing union men, the employers are not compelled to patronize it and are instead completely free to hire their workers at the gate or through any other agency which they choose. The employers by their refusal to deal with the public exchanges could thus keep the latter from abusing their trust. Finally, even if employers ask the public offices to send them applicants, they are not of course obliged to accept them. The individual employer could therefore still maintain a personal blacklist and even if such men were sent to him by the public offices, he could simply decline to give them employment.

The second fear may well spring from the belief that if a free public agency is provided many manufacturers will not be willing to continue to contribute to support exchanges maintained by many employers' associations. This is a perfectly valid reason why the employers' associations themselves should oppose the bill, but it is hardly a cause for opposition by the general public.

Nor will the third fear seem conclusive to any openminded seeker after the best methods of dealing with unemployment. The opponent of unemployment insurance should not refuse to take any step which he knows would lessen the chaos and distress of the labor market merely because of his fear that it would then make it easier to take a second step of which he did not approve. Each issue should be decided on its own merits.

5. The Present Status of Public Employment Offices

According to the United States Employment Service, there were in May, 1930, 218 public employment offices which were coöperating with that service.[42] Upon analysis, however, at least 22 of these offices were not conducted by governmental agencies, but instead by Chambers of Commerce, the Y. W. C. A., the Y. M. C. A., and the American Legion, leaving at the most 196 which were under government auspices. A number of these in turn were very small

[42] *Directory of Public Employment Offices*, May, 1930, 19 pp. Published by the United States Employment Service (1930).

offices where the volume of business was exceedingly slight. In December, 1928, the American Association for Labor Legislation gave the number of public employment offices in the United States as 170 with total state appropriations for that year of $1,204,000.[43] But these statistics did not include the ten municipal offices in the state of Washington, so that there were at that time at least 180 offices which were in fact functioning. It is probable therefore that there are at the present time slightly over that number of active governmental offices. If we include the financial contributions by the municipalities to the work, which were not covered in the study by the Association for Labor Legislation, the total expenditures by other than Federal Government for the year 1928-29 would probably approximate between $1,500,000 and $1,600,000.

While the comparative costs of placement should not be the sole tests as to the relative efficiency of the service in the various states, it is at least one very important criterion and the table on the following page for the latest available years shows the wide differences which exist between the states.

It will thus be seen that placement costs vary widely between the states, ranging from 57 cents in Wisconsin to $2.31 in Pennsylvania. The costs per placement in Wisconsin, California, and New Jersey are approximately only one-quarter of what they are in Massachusetts and Pennsylvania. What then are the causes for these great relative differences? It does not seem to lie in any more rigid system of reporting placements in the high-cost states. Wisconsin for example only reports as placements those for whom it receives definite notice from employers as being actually put to work while New Jersey takes unusual pains to verify its placements. In Pennsylvania, on the other hand, which is the state of highest costs, the record of placements is very loosely made up and is probably something of an overestimate. Were equally accurate records kept therefore, it is probable that the differences between unit costs in Wis-

[43] Financing the Public Employment Service, *American Labor Legislation Review,* December, 1928.

TABLE 20

COMPARATIVE PLACEMENT COSTS OF PUBLIC EMPLOYMENT OFFICES IN
VARIOUS STATES[44]

STATE	YEAR	NUMBER OF OFFICES	TOTAL APPROPRIATIONS STATE AND LOCAL	TOTAL PLACEMENTS	AVERAGE COST PER PLACEMENT
Wisconsin . .	1929	10	$58,081	101,183	$0.57
California . .	1928	10	84,895	144,516	0.59
New Jersey .	1929	7	76,500	120,572	0.63
Ohio . . .	1929	12	155,324	137,538	1.13
Connecticut . .	1928	8	50,000	29,867	1.71
New York . .	1929	11	188,309	100,171	1.88
Illinois . . .	1929–30	20	266,080	135,909	1.96
Massachusetts .	1929	4	68,841	30,157	2.28
Pennsylvania .	1929	13	99,000	41,997	2.31
					(average)
TOTAL . .	....	95	$1,047,030	842,910	$1.24

consin and New Jersey as compared with Pennsylvania
at least would be greater rather than less.

Is the difference then due, as is sometimes claimed, to
differences in the types of labor placed and do the high-
cost states place a greater proportion of skilled labor upon
whom more care must necessarily be expended? One of the
authors when serving as Secretary of the Pennsylvania
Committee on Unemployment collected data on this point

[44] Sources:
  Report Massachusetts Division of Statistics for year 1929, pp. 30–36;
  Report of New York Advisory Committee on Employment Problems,
    Vol. II, pp. 69–72;
  Report Wisconsin Industrial Commission, 1926–28, pp. 28–31, and *Wis-
    consin Labor Market,* January, 1930, pp. 17–25;
  Report Division of State Employment Offices of California, 1926–28,
    pp. 9–17;
  Letter of H. B. Meyers, Chief of Bureau of Statistics and Research,
    Illinois Department of Labor, Oct. 9, 1930;
  Letter of R. J. Eldridge, State Director of Employment for New Jersey;
  *Public Employment Office Appropriations, American Labor Legislation
    Review,* December, 1928. These figures do not include contributions
    by the U. S. Employment Service run by private agencies;
  Letter of George F. Miles, Chief of Public Employment Offices, Depart-
    ment of Industrial Relations, Ohio, September 17, 1930;
  Letter of S. S. Riddle, Director of Bureau of Employment, Pennsylvania,
    September 3, 1930.

which are quite illuminating. The proportions which common, casual, and miscellaneous labor formed of the total placements were found to be as follows for a number of the states: [45]

STATE	YEAR	PERCENTAGE OF COMMON, CASUAL, AND MISCELLANEOUS LABOR OF TOTAL PLACEMENTS
Pennsylvania . .	1929	60
Illinois	1927–28	60
New Jersey[1] . . .	Sept. 1930	51
	July, 1928–July, 1929	57
Ohio[1]	1929–30	82
Massachusetts . .	1928	60
Wisconsin . . .	1929	70
California . . .	1927–28	71% males, 35% females, 64% both.

[1] Males only.

New Jersey, a low cost state, is thus seen to have a slightly lower proportion of the unskilled placements than the high cost states of Pennsylvania, Illinois, and Massachusetts. California and Wisconsin had only 4 and 10 per cent more of their placements unskilled than was the case with these three high cost states despite the fact that their unit costs were only from one-third to one-quarter as much.

It is probable therefore that these differences in cost indicate real, although not necessarily commensurate, differences in efficiency. This conclusion tends to be fortified by a detailed examination of the service in, for example, Pennsylvania and Illinois. In the former state, political power

[45] This table is printed in *Report of Pennsylvania Committee on Unemployment* appointed by Gov.-Elect Pinchot, p. 21. The sources used were: Classified Summary Report for 1929 of the Bureau of Employment, Department of Labor and Industry of Pennsylvania, p. 9; Eleventh Annual Report, Illinois Department of Labor, 1927–28, p. 9; New Jersey Industrial Bulletin, October, 1930, p. 37; Mimeographed report, Department of Industrial Relations, Ohio, July 10, 1930, p. 1; Report Division of Statistics, Department of Labor and Industries of Massachusetts, 1928, p. 21; Telegram from A. J. Altmeyer, Secretary Wisconsin Industrial Commission, January 2, 1931; Report of the State Division of Employment Agencies, California, 1926–27; 1927–28, pp. 61 ff.

has in part dictated the appointments to the service and retention and promotion has not been guaranteed to merit. In Wisconsin, on the other hand, the staff has been under civil service and has been largely protected from politics.

Wisconsin and Ohio are both distinguished not only for the general excellence of their service but also for the coöperation which they have effected between the state and the municipalities. In these states the cities contribute to the support of the state service although not controlling either the personnel or the policies. Unlike Wisconsin, Ohio has not, however, developed advisory boards of employers and workers. This has been partly because the open shop movement in some of the cities has made it difficult to bring employers and workers together and partly because in one of the cities at least, the committee was not found to be helpful. One of the most successful Ohio offices is that at Middletown which is quite generally used by the steel mills and other employers of labor.

In New York the service deteriorated for a number of years but under the energetic direction of Miss Frances Perkins, the Industrial Commissioner for the state, very appreciable improvements have recently been made. Miss Perkins appointed an Advisory Committee on Employment Problems which made a number of important recommendations[46] including a more efficient personnel, a systematic program of clearance between offices, the preparation of a manual of practice, the immediate granting of additional funds, and the improvement of the personnel assigned by the Federal Service. A new chief of the Bureau was appointed. By staff meetings and personal interviews with all the employees of the offices the importance of the work was emphasized and a greater degree of interest on their part obtained. Emergency workers were detailed from other branches of the state department of labor and volunteer workers obtained from Welfare Agencies. After training,

---

[46] *The New York State Employment Service Advisory Committee on Employment Problems,* Vol. II, pp. 14-16.

these workers made over 5,300 field visits to try to enlist the support of employers for the offices. Coöperative arrangements were entered into with the Merchants and Manufacturers' Association of the Bush Terminal Exchange and the state took over the employment problem of this group of enterprises which under normal conditions employed approximately 50,000 workers. A system of daily clearances between the thirty-seven non-fee charging agencies was also introduced and wide-spread information distributed among employers about the bureaus.

The result of all this work was that, although the general unemployment situation was proving worse, the number of orders by employers for men increased from a previous average of approximately 6,000 per month to 7,300 in March; 10,800 for April; 12,400 for May and, although there was a decline in June, the number was over 9,500, which was a more than 50 per cent increase above the average which formerly prevailed.

The number of actual placements also rose during this period from a previous monthly average of slightly less than 5,000 to 5,700 in March, 8,600 in April, 10,400 in May and even with the relapse in June to 7,600. These statistics indicate what can be done in even a short space of time in building up the work of badly run-down offices.

The Laura Spelman Rockefeller Fund is now planning to grant funds to the state of New York to establish in Rochester a demonstration public employment office for a period of years which will be a model and which will try to demonstrate the possibilities in this direction. If a number of such strategic experiment stations could be established in various sections of the country, they would do much to raise by the force of their example, the general level of practice by the offices.

If one visits the public employment offices in the various states, a distinctly unfavorable general impression is received. With a few honorable exceptions, the offices are generally located on dingy streets and are dirty and unattractive. The personnel is underpaid and as the New York

Advisory Committee declared [47] "frequently inert and indifferent." It is generally untrained in placement work and keeps poor records. In most states the men and women in the service owe their appointment and retention to political influence rather than to fitness and many of these appear only irregularly for work. They feel that no one is interested in their work and so pay more attention to their political fences than to the work in hand. As a consequence of all this, with rare exceptions, the work of the office does not command the confidence either of employers or of the better class of workmen. In the main, the placements which the offices make are for unskilled and semi-skilled workers and for casual and domestic labor. Skilled workers in the main depend either upon their own efforts or upon other agencies to place them in work.

The high possibilities which are latent in public employment work are therefore almost totally unrealized in the actual practice of the offices. The American public has in fact started these offices and then has gone off and forgotten about them. Meager financial support is partly responsible for this comparative inefficiency but even with the funds available, the offices could do much better than they do.[48]

[47] *The New York State Employment Service*, Vol. 1. Prepared by the Advisory Committee on Employment Problems appointed by Industrial Commissioner Perkins, New York, 1930, p. 14.

[48] Black as the situation is, there are signs of hope. In Pennsylvania, the efforts of Governor Pinchot and his advisers give promise of a very appreciable improvement in the service while in Illinois, the careful study of the system which is being carried out under the competent direction of Dr. B. M. Squires, the chairman of the Advisory Board of these offices, and Miss Ruth Kellogg should, if accorded sufficient support, put pressure upon the political forces of the state to better matters.

CHAPTER XXI

NEXT STEPS IN THE CREATION OF AN EFFICIENT PUBLIC EMPLOYMENT SERVICE IN THE UNITED STATES

The difficulty with our present public employment offices is not solely a matter of inadequate funds. We need more offices, more workers, and better paid staffs, but even with the money now available, much better work could be done.

If one examines the actual work of employment offices, it becomes quite clear that their comparative success or failure is determined by the attitude which responsible employers assume towards them. It is patent that the offices cannot place men unless the employers will take them. If the employers distrust, or are indifferent towards the offices, then their work will not amount to a great deal. If the employers, moreover, depend on getting their skilled workers by other means and only call upon the public exchanges to recruit their unskilled labor, then the public offices will be limited to the latter group. The quality and quantity of the placements which have been effected, therefore, depend on the attitude of management. The employment offices should seek, therefore, to obtain the confidence and cordial coöperation of the employers, although this does not mean that they should become the partisan agents of the employing class.

The primary way for the offices to gain the confidence of American management is by doing their job better than other agencies are now doing it and thus winning their place in the competition of the market. If this is accepted as the goal, the following features seem to be essential in any program.

1. The quarters of the offices must be clean, commodious

and attractive and permit of the essentials of privacy. Many of the present dingy offices could be rehabilitated by soap and water but there are others which cannot be put into shape by even such necessary treatment as that. The office should not be located in run-down regions of the city and should avoid the sections where cheap lodging houses, homeless men, and private employment offices tend to congregate. For if an office is located in these sections, skilled workers and women will shun it and only the unskilled and the "down and out" will patronize it. Employers, unable to obtain high-class workers, will not use it and the result will be an almost complete degeneration of the service.

Because of the unfortunate political associations which the citizens of most cities come to attach to their city halls, it is probably unwise in general to have the employment office housed there. In some cities, however, such as Cincinnati and Milwaukee, the excellence of the government would remove any such opprobrium.

It is probably best, therefore, if there is only one central office for the city, that it should be located near the chief business district. An office should have separate entrances and waiting rooms for men and women applicants, or if possible either the men's or the women's division might be on the ground floor and the other on the second floor. If both unskilled and skilled labor are handled from the same office it is desirable in turn to subdivide these groups and provide each with a separate waiting room. The office should, moreover, be so arranged as to insure relative privacy between the applicant and the interviewer.

2. **The personnel of the employment service should be competent and really concerned about the success of the work.** Unless this is done, there is no hope for the service.

For a long time the employment offices were the political spoils of trade-union politicians who received these appointments in return for helping to deliver a portion of the vote of organized labor. Beginning in 1906, however, in Massachusetts, civil service laws have spread gradually until in 1924, eleven states had brought the rank and file of their employment office staff under *at least the nominal control of the civil service*.[1] In all save a few of these states, however, the civil service provisions are more nominal than effective.

The first requirement, therefore, for an adequate personnel is that it should be selected under civil service provisions which actually operate. It is not necessary that the employees should be college graduates, but it is essential that they should know their business. It is probable that the best method is to give the candidates both written and oral examinations. In setting these questions, the Civil Service Commission should be aided by the Director of the Service and for the more important state positions representatives of the employers and employees should also be asked to sit on the committee which makes the selection. It is indeed necessary to tie up the responsible groups which patronize the offices with the selection and the work of the personnel in order to resist the efforts of the politicians to have their favorites chosen. The politicians will be extremely active and their influence commonly extends up into civil service commissions. Unless a strong counterbalancing force is mustered to insist on efficiency being made the basis for selection and retention they will almost inevitably win and the service will, in consequence, deteriorate. The strong groups which can be mustered are those which use the exchange, namely, employers and workers. They have an interest in efficiency because it will aid them while inefficiency will be of direct injury. They can, therefore, be depended upon to work for a decent personnel, if their interest is aroused, more than the middle-class public which is not directly concerned with the offices as such. They are also in a better position than anyone else to judge of the qualities which workers in the service need and whether particular applicants do in fact possess them.

Irrespective of the question as to whether the Director

---

[1] Harrison and Associates, *Public Employment Offices* p. 449. The states were Massachusetts, New York, Wisconsin, Illinois, Colorado, Indiana, New Jersey, Ohio, California, Kansas, and Maryland.

of State Employment Service is formally appointed by the governor or by the head of the State Department of Labor, it is also essential that he should in reality be selected by the committee of employers and workers, which as we shall see, is a necessary feature of any state scheme. Unless this is done, the headship of the service will almost inevitably be regarded as a political plum with which to reward the faithful. Once an employee has been appointed, his job should be safe if he gives efficient service. New administrations should not be permitted to change the personnel in order to shake down more jobs from the tree of patronage.

Within the service itself, there should be ample opportunities for promotion. While in the beginning it would probably be necessary because of the present run-down condition of most offices and state bureaus to appoint the major proportion of office managers and state directors from the outside, this should be only a transitional measure. Once a staff has been set up, it should be possible for examiners to rise to the position of branch managers and for the latter to rise to the state directorship. While promotion from within should not be the infallible rule, it should be the presumption.

But if the employment service is to attract the best talent, the positions must also be adequately paid. This is not now the case. Thus in New York, the salary of the State Director is only $4,250 and ten of the twelve superintendents of local offices receive less than $2,600 a year. The highest salary received by any local superintendent is only $3,000.[2]

In the major industrial states of New York, Massachusetts, New Jersey, Pennsylvania, Ohio, Illinois, Wisconsin, Michigan, and California, it is probable that the following salary scale [3] would be able to command men and women of adequate ability. (1) Director of State Service, $6,000-

[2] New York Advisory Committee on Employment Problems, *The New York State Employment Service*, Vol. II, p. 62.
[3] This is similar to but slightly different from that recommended by the New York Advisory Committee.

$7,000, (2) Head of local office in Class A cities, $4,000-$5,000, (3) Head of local office in Class B cities, $3,200-$4,000, (4) in charge of department in local office $2,800-$3,500, (5) Senior Interviewer, $2,400-$2,800. (6) Junior Interviewer $2,000-$2,400. In states where the volume of work would be appreciably less, it should be possible to pay a somewhat lower scale.

In addition to all this, further internal methods of administration are needed to raise efficiency. It is essential that state manuals of practice be developed to guide the staff in the work of placements, the soliciting of employers, the preparation of forms, etc. These should, of course, be revised periodically but each worker should have the current copy to guide him in his work.

Each state director should also make periodical and frequent inspections of the various offices to keep them up to standard and should hold conferences with the members of the staff and the local advisory boards to discuss the local problems. In making the inspections it would be desirable to have the offices rated on a series of qualities rather than judged as a whole. In this way the final rating would be likely to be more accurate and individual offices could be shown in what specific respects they were weak.

3. **The employment offices should regard themselves as business and not as charitable institutions and should therefore refer men to jobs according to their ability and not according to their needs.** It goes without saying that political influence should not sway the employment officials in finding work for men and local politicians should clearly understand that they cannot use the offices to have their favorites given preference. A more subtle temptation, however, is for the officials to find work first for those who are in the greatest need instead of placing first the men of greatest ability. This is not only understandable but springs from generous motives. It is, however, a mistake since it confuses the idea of charity with that of businesslike placement. For employers will be hiring the men on the assumption that they are the best the office can send,

rather than the ones most in need. The employment office will in effect be making the employers use their business for charitable purposes without the latter knowing that they are doing so. Such a policy will be disastrous in the long run for when the employers come to be aware of the practice they will gradually cease to patronize the public offices, and the system will consequently fail. This will be a greater social loss than not placing the needy applicants.

The employment offices need not, however, abandon the needy persons who come to them but whom they cannot place. It is not only their opportunity but their duty to put them in touch with public and private charity. They can, moreover, furnish to these charitable agencies information which will enable the latter more effectively to care for them. The burden of their support will thus be thrown where it belongs, namely, upon charity and not upon industry.

4. **Advisory boards with real powers should be set up for each state system and for each local office which will represent responsible groups of employers, and so far as possible of workers, and which will have a sprinkling of representatives of the general public.** We have seen how essential it is to have advisory commissions representing real and powerful economic interests if the personnel of the offices is to be chosen on the basis of efficiency and protected from political pressure. They are also necessary to help decide major questions of policy, and to get employers and workers to have confidence in and to patronize the service. There will be many issues of a policy-making nature which will come up concerning such issues as the types of labor which an office should specialize in, whether separate sections should be provided for various industries, the policy to be followed in importing labor into the state or locality, the preparation of budgets, and general questions of efficiency and procedure. The final decisions on such matters are much more likely to be intelligent if they are participated in by the groups in a state or locality which are after all the patrons of the service. This will

also check any bureaucratic tendencies which might develop.

These groups, if taken into the major determination of policy, will, moreover, be educated in the actual work and future possibilities of the exchanges. By participating in these activities, they will feel themselves to be a part of the system, and, consequently, they will be promoters of the service. The mere presence of employer representatives on the advisory committees will, moreover, help to reassure their fellow business men that the offices, so far from being hostile to their interests, are in reality designed to coöperate with them in getting a better labor force in a more effective way. They will, therefore, tend to patronize the offices much more than they would were the exchanges to stand alone without a sponsoring or guiding committee. As the members of the advisory committees come to believe in the possibilities of the public offices they can work directly with the groups which they represent and induce them to patronize the offices.

Despite the desirability of having both labor and capital jointly represented on the boards, there will be great difficulty in many places in getting the employers' representatives to meet with those of organized labor. The question squarely presents itself, therefore, as to what should be done in such a case. It is peculiarly essential, as we have seen, for the public employment offices to have the support of most employers. If placing union men on the advisory committees means losing this support and greatly curtailing the placements which the office can make, it would seem wise to waive the union recognition. From the standpoint of the employment offices it is more important that they should be able to place men than that they should have representatives of organized labor on their committees.

But here as everywhere the policy should be a matter of degrees. Though the offices should not wreck their usefulness in the fight for union recognition, they certainly should not surrender control over policy to the more reactionary wing of the employers and should push for as much representation of the interests of the workers as it is possible to obtain under the existing balance of power.

Where it seems thoroughly impracticable to obtain trade-union representation on the local boards, two compromises can be made: (1) Where there are non-union shop committees in the local plants, they can be asked to elect representatives. In this way the workers will be given representation even though from non-union sources. (2) A considerable number of members of the board can be selected from the general public with care exercised to get as independent members as possible. By these methods the employers can probably be prevented from misusing the offices.

In selecting the state advisory boards it will be much easier to have employers sit with representatives of organized labor. Animosities do not run as high on a state as on a local scale. Furthermore, even though the Manufacturers' Association or the Chamber of Commerce of a state might well refuse to elect delegates to a board to which the State Federation of Labor also elected delegates, nevertheless individuals from those organizations who were appointed by the state would be far less likely to refuse to sit with other individuals also appointed by the state, who were officials in the State Federation of Labor. The employers could say with justice that in meeting with individuals, they were not recognizing organizations. In brief, therefore, it should be a cardinal principle of the organization of the state board that members of trade unions should sit on it.

5. As rapidly as possible, the direction of the employment offices should in fact be turned over to the joint boards of employers and workers. We have already stressed the importance of having these joint boards participate actively in the administration of the offices. Ultimately we believe that it will be better if the employers and workers, rather than the state, should actively administer the offices and that the state exercise only general supervision over them. In this way, the groups who are actively interested in placement work would be in charge and the administration would be freed from the often deadening influence of the state. This policy of coöperative management would be worked out not only to cover localities but also for those industrial and trade divisions which, as we shall point out, are ultimately necessary for effective placement work. We believe, in other words, that the German method of administration is more desirable than the English.

The offices should not, however, be turned over to only one of the two parties to administer and should not be surrendered to the employers alone. As long as the employing interests in a locality will refuse to manage an office jointly with the workers, then the state should retain control in order to assure impartiality. It would, furthermore, be a mistake to transfer the offices before the two parties were really interested in the problem and before there was a group who could be depended upon to make the offices a success. For this reason, therefore, it is well to make these joint boards merely advisory at first and then to increase their responsibilities as rapidly as they will assume them.

6. In the case of jobs which are open because of strikes or lockouts, the employment offices should notify the applicants of the facts and allow them to decide whether or not they will take them. The question as to what the policy of the offices should be in times of strikes was much discussed in the early days of the movement. The trade-unions in many places were at first opposed to the offices because they were afraid that they would be used by the employers more easily to recruit strike-breakers. But the unionists came to see that the employers already had very full facilities for recruiting these men and that the public offices could bring a much needed element of publicity into the situation and not allow workers who were ignorant of the true state of affairs to be set to jobs. It was better for them to have offices which were neutral than those which were hostile.

It has come to be an almost universal custom for applicants to be notified where a strike or lockout exists so that they may make their own decision. This preserves the neutrality of the state and at the same time prevents workers being recruited under false pretenses.

Some unionists have contended that the offices should not refer applicants to jobs when the pay is below the going-rate. The proper answer seems to be that the employment offices should not determine what the wage scale should be but merely offer a channel by which the two parties can more easily come together and mutually determine the rate. It follows, therefore, that the offices should inform the applicants of all the jobs which are available, including those which pay less as well as more than the average. The applicant can then decide for himself whether or not he wants to take the job.

7. **The employment offices should actively seek business from employers and should use every legitimate means to induce industry to patronize them.** It is a common failing of the present public employment offices to wait for business to come to them. This is perhaps a natural tendency for most governmental agencies which are removed from the bracing air of competition. It is patent, however, that this is no way in which to build up business. The superintendents of the various local offices should instead be expected to spend a considerable portion of their time in calling upon employers and in trying to get the latter to place orders for men with the public offices. The advantages of the free public office in protecting the employers from the danger of split fees can be pointed out and an appeal made to give the public offices a chance and then judge them on the basis of their comparative service. Special orders for selected groups of men may be solicited as trial ventures if an employer is reluctant to turn over any considerable portion of his hiring work to them.

In the large cities it is probably desirable to have one or more persons especially designated to interview employers and to try to obtain business. When such solicitation has been practiced by the offices it has been repeatedly demonstrated that the volume of placements made by the offices has appreciably increased. Like all other competitive businesses, therefore, the public offices must pay full and alert attention to the problems of marketing and selling their services. A great deal more could also be done in the way of effective advertising through the use of attractive posters, etc. One of the best ways of promoting the service among employers would be for the local offices to designate men who would follow up with the employers the record of the men placed. In this way, they would learn more accurately the needs of the respective businesses and be able to place applicants more effectively. Such a method would as a matter of fact be perhaps the best way of obtaining the confidence of the employers and hence of increasing the orders for jobs.

8. Where the employment offices are still weak and have not reached a commanding position, it is probably better for them to specialize in a particular type of labor, such as the unskilled, instead of scattering their efforts over many industries and crafts. It is of course desirable that the public offices should eventually cover virtually all classes of workers. But it will be necessary for them to grow before they can do this effectively. It is vitally important, therefore, to determine whether from the outset an office should aim at handling all of these types of labor or whether it should in the beginning specialize in a particular type. It is believed that the latter is the better policy. If an office tries to furnish all types of labor to employers it will need to have a specialized staff of workers to test the applicants in the various trades before passing them on to the employers. This will be very expensive and, in terms of the relatively smaller volume of business which the offices will probably do during their early years, will mean a too high cost per placement. If the offices persist in trying to handle all classes of labor but do not sift their applicants in this expert manner then the inevitable result will be that the placement work will be rather badly done and offices will lose the confidence of the employers. The better plan seems, therefore, for a weak office to specialize at the outset in handling unskilled labor which does not require so skilled a staff and by doing a thoroughly effective job with them, come to command the confidence of the employers. When

this is obtained, the office can branch out and take on gradually other types of labor, taking care in the process to go out only for types of labor which it is prepared to handle efficiently.

This is not to say that the offices should turn away individual skilled workmen who will come to them during the early stages for placement. These should be given attention and aid. But the emphasis both in soliciting business and in recruiting workers should be at first to master the problems connected with the placement of one general type of labor, namely, the unskilled. Both employers and workers should, however, realize that the offices do not mean to content themselves forever with placing only that class of labor and that they plan to move onward to include other types as swiftly as possible.

As rapidly as the way opens, therefore, offices should ask the employers to let them recruit certain crafts for them and should take pains to get in touch with the workers of this grade. The offices can thus grow qualitatively as well as quantitatively just to the degree to which their record merits.

9. As placement work is assumed for the more skilled and specialized types of labor, correspondingly specialized sections should be set up in the offices to handle the work. It would be a great mistake if the public service were as in England to maintain only general offices with non-specialized interviewers to handle the placement work for the various crafts and types of work. For if this is done it will not be possible competently to test and select the workers. Specialized sections should instead be set up to care for each major allied group of occupations. These should be in charge of interviewers with practical experience in the occupations for which they are selecting. Advisory committees for these occupations can also be built up. These specialized sections need not be isolated in separate offices but could occupy quarters of their own in the general offices.

In conjunction with its advisory committee, the service

should prepare and utilize adequate job analyses and trade tests which will enable it to know more thoroughly the qualities which a given job requires and the approximate degree to which an applicant possesses these qualifications. It is impossible to do a good job in finding men for positions without knowing what the position demands in the way of skill, etc. This may be known in a general way by a few but it is necessary to centralize the information so that the interviewers may have it at their disposal. It is also necessary that this information should be sharpened and made more precise than is commonly the case. This calls for a fairly careful analysis of the important jobs in terms of the specific trade-skills which are required. For the benefit of the workers it is also necessary to know the probable opportunities for advancement, the general working conditions, and the relative health and accident hazards which may be attached to specific jobs. The United States Bureau of Labor Statistics prepared such a series of job analyses in 1918-19 for the Federal Employment Service, but the virtual disbandment of that service prevented them from being used appreciably. Such analyses should be prepared by the state or federal services with the aid and criticism of the general advisory committees and of specific groups representing the various industries. These analyses should be revised periodically in the light of the additional knowledge about jobs which will continually become available.

The complement to job analysis is the trade test. This is an examination designed to determine the approximate degree of skill at a trade which an applicant really possesses. This is plainly necessary if the office is to make any effort to go beyond the claim of a worker and if it is to do anything but merely pass on all the applicants to the employers. If a rough sifting is to be practiced, then the public offices must provide themselves with a sieve. Trade tests are such a sieve and may be of three kinds: [4] (1) oral,

---

[4] Trade tests were developed in this country during the War by the committee on Classification of Personnel of the Army. See J. C. Chapman, *Trade Tests.*

(2) picture, (3) performance. In the first type a series of questions are prepared for each trade and by the answers of the applicants they will be graded into three or more classes according to the degree of their skill. In the picture tests, the applicant is asked to name, identify, and state the function of various tools, parts, etc., that are peculiar to that trade. The performance test, as its name signifies, calls for the completion of a product from materials and with tools which are furnished.[5] The scales by which all of these tests are graded should be derived from the records which well selected groups of experts, journeymen, and unskilled workers have previously made.

The costliness of these tests is such as to preclude nearly all state services from attempting to frame them. The only body which could adequately carry them out would be the federal service and this along with the preparation of job analyses should be one of the most important research jobs of the federal service. In the preparation of these tests the service can build on the war-time work of the Committee on the Classification of Personnel of the United States Army, the experiments of various industrial psychologists, and the very valuable series of tests for clerical work which have been prepared by the staff of the U. S. Civil Service Commission and the Institute for Public Personnel Efficiency. It is in the interests of efficiency that the giving of these tests, as well as physical examinations and psychological tests, should at as early a date as possible be centralized in the public offices. By keeping the permanent record of the worker on file in the central offices, duplicate examinations of the same worker by various firms could be eliminated. This would reduce the social cost of hiring by a very appreciable margin.

Before the employers will be willing, however, to turn this work over to the public services, it will be necessary for them to demonstrate their ability and impartiality. If and when this is done, many of the employers would be

---

[5] In the case of office workers, such trade tests can be rather easily given.

willing to have them do this work since it would remove a fairly heavy item of expense from their budget and place it upon the shoulders of the state.

10. The offices should not devote much energy to placing handicapped workers such as the crippled, the aged, and women seeking part-time employment until they have built up a record for the efficient placement of normal workers. As we have again and again pointed out, the public employment offices must prove themselves competent in the eyes of industry and in the competition of the market. If employers associate them with charitable work, their possibilities of major efficiency are doomed. They cannot, therefore, devote any very large portion of their energies to trying to find openings for people who for one reason or another cannot give to industry at least average efficiency. For some time at least the placement of these groups should be left to unofficial and charitable groups. When the service has firmly established itself, it can and should take on the placement of these handicapped persons and in the large centers should set up specialized divisions to help care for them.

11. The aid of civic institutions and private philanthropy should be enlisted in building up the service. There are valuable community resources which can be enlisted by the public employment service in its work if it but shows imagination. Thus coöperative arrangements can be entered into with universities and schools of social service in many cities which will give the offices the services of competent and mature students who can, after training, be used to help do some of the necessary office work and to help in the soliciting of employers for orders. The offices should not depend permanently on getting a great deal of unpaid labor in this fashion, but in the initial stages before adequate appropriations are obtained, aid of this sort can be of considerable assistance.

Perhaps even more important is the assistance which the various philanthropic foundations might give by underwriting the expenses of a number of model employment offices in different sections of the country. The Laura Spelman Rockefeller Fund has already made arrangements to finance such an office for a period of years in New York State. If other foundations could help to establish similar bureaus in such states as Pennsylvania, Ohio, Illinois, and California, a number of demonstration centers would be created which would raise the general level of employment practice all over the country.

The public agencies should, moreover, work in the fullest coöperation with the non-profit making private agencies and every effort should be made to get these agencies to agree on the field which each is to cover and to coöperate in a central clearing system.

12. **Each state service should institute and carry out a periodic program of inspection and of ranking the member offices.** It is necessary in employment work, as in hospitals and the army, to keep the offices constantly up to the mark. The best way of doing this is by periodic inspection and by ranking. This will make a local service anxious to do well in order that it may surpass other cities and inject into the service a healthy spirit of striving for excellence. The state services should carry out this inspection during at least the beginning period, and should work out a score-card which will give numerical weights to a number of qualities such as (1) the appearance and arrangement of the office, (2) relation with employers and workers, (3) training and efficiency of office personnel, (4) quality and quantity of placement work including the relation of placements to the size of the community and types of work done, (5) per capita costs of placement, etc.

Each state service of any size should have one competent worker constantly in the field, inspecting the local offices and offering advice in helping them to raise their level of efficiency. These field workers should at the same time interview employers, and promote the extension of the service.

13. **The systems of forms and records should be revised and perfected.** During the pioneer years from 1908 to 1917 the various public offices busied themselves with this prob-

lem. The Massachusetts offices were, in particular, pioneers in this work and developed models which were widely copied. During the last decade, however, little fresh attention has been paid to this subject and the forms and records of most offices remain much as they were a dozen years ago. Fundamentally three sets of records will be needed, namely:

(1) Those dealing with the applications of the employers for help. The fundamental problem here, other than that of getting adequate information with not more than 15 questions is to devise a system which will give the data on the jobs which have been filed according to both occupation and the employers.[6]

(2) Those dealing with the applicant. Here again we find the necessity of connecting the names of the applicants and the jobs for which they apply. Either separate cards can be prepared from the original application, which will be classified occupationally, or the original card itself can be coded and tabbed so that it can be used occupationally. The card should of course provide an opportunity to record what happens to the application. It is well to provide in addition to this a card catalogue listing alphabetically the names of those who have applied along with their occupations, addresses, and telephone numbers. The files of the applicants should be divided into two lists, namely the active and the inactive. Ordinarily the test as to which group a card falls into is that of the period of time since a worker has made application. The length of this period will naturally differ from one type of worker to another. For unskilled labor, two weeks or a month would seem to be long enough, though for the skilled workers three months would not seem to be excessive. If a worker were to be put on the active rôle after this time he would have to return and reapply, but this alphabetical file of former applicants would prevent duplicate forms from being made out.

---

[6] See Harrison and Associates, *Public Employment Offices*, pp. 289-395, for a comprehensive discussion of record keeping.

(3) Those dealing with references of applicants to jobs. Persons who are thus referred should of course be given cards which will introduce them to the employers, and if tests are given, should show their ratings. These persons should be followed up and either the employers or the applicants should inform the office whether or not they have been engaged. On the whole, more complete reports will probably be obtained if the burden of these notifications is placed upon the employers rather than upon the workers. There will inevitably be a considerable number of employers who, in the beginning at least, will not return these cards so that the offices will not know whether or not those referred have actually been placed. These can be followed up tactfully on the telephone and through interviews on the part of the field-agent, an increasing degree of coöperation obtained from the employers. Only those for whom a definite report that they have been engaged has been made, should be counted as placements.

14. **Clearance systems should be established between the various offices within a state and as rapidly as possible between states.** The system of daily clearances of jobs between the offices of the states has largely fallen into disuse. It should be revived, as in New York, by the large industrial states. The surplus of jobs and of workers in separate lines can be telegraphed daily to a central office for the state and a mimeographed bulletin listing these mailed that evening to all the offices. The central office can then have the localities with specific surpluses of men send some of them to localities where there is a deficit. Where there are unfilled jobs care should be taken, however, that no more men should be sent than there are jobs. Some control must then be exercised by the central office over the numbers who are thus recruited for out-of-town work.

It is also desirable to set up interstate clearnance. This is necessary because the labor market is not confined within a state. Thus the immediate market, of which New York is the center, includes parts of both New Jersey and Connecticut as well as the lower part of New York State. The

Chicago market includes not only Northern Illinois but South-western Michigan, North-eastern Indiana, and parts of Wisconsin as well. There are also intersectional movements of labor which need to be directed and controlled. There is a necessity, therefore, for an efficient federal service which will really undertake the work of interstate clearance. It would probably be best to divide the country up into some seven or eight districts and to establish separate clearances within each of these districts with the office at Washington clearing between districts. This of course would be analogous in the clearance of labor to the work of the Federal Reserve Board in the clearance of checks.

15. More funds should be provided for the existing offices and new offices stimulated through the use of the system of federal aid. If the offices are to develop, much more than the present million and a half dollars must be spent upon them. The services need to be greatly strengthened where they do exist and many new offices should be started. Increased state appropriations can do much, but the most hopeful means is federal aid appropriations such as are provided for in the Wagner bill. Such an act would not only add appreciable federal resources, but by requiring that the states and localities must at least duplicate the federal grants, it would greatly increase the state appropriations as well. If the Wagner bill were to be enacted, it would speedily make available annually a minimum total appropriation of 7 million dollars,[7] or approximately four times as much as is now spent.[8]

While many people criticize the principle of federal aid on the ground that it taxes the wealthier states to help support the services of the poorer and also undermines the initiative and autonomy of the states themselves, it seems to the writers to be a most happy reconciliation of the conflicting principles of state autonomy and of nationalism.

[7] *I.e.*, $1,000,000 to be expended directly by the U. S. Employment Service, and $6,000,000 to be spent by the states, one-half of which would be the federal grant of $3,000,000. Some of the states, however, might not accept the federal aid features of the act.

[8] Including the appropriations for the U. S. Employment Service.

The national government, it is true, offers a stimulus to the state governments to undertake the service but the ultimate decision as to whether this shall be done rests with the states. They also carry out the actual administrative work themselves, subject to only general oversight from Washington. The fact that if a federal dollar is wasted a corresponding state dollar will also be wasted induces the states to be much more economical than they would be were they expending only federal funds. The federal aid in turn widens the area of support, sets minimum standards of efficiency, pools the results of research, and in general serves to stimulate the states to greater activity. It is probable, however, that a better method of apportionment could be devised than that on the sole basis of population. A triple system might perhaps be better in which (1) one-third of the total federal grant could be apportioned according to the relative number of gainfully employed wage-earners. This would give additional sums of money to the industrial states and would seem to be fair in view of the fact that they would have more work for each million of the population than agricultural states where the adult population is more fixed. (2) One-third could be divided according to the relative population. In view of the displacement of the agricultural population which is likely to ensue, some use of the population factor is desirable. (3) The remaining third could be distributed among the states in the proportion which their combined state and local appropriations form of such appropriations for the country as a whole. This would be a stimulus upon the states to contribute more than the minimum and thus would increase the total amounts of money available for the work. This last method has been used in Canada with considerable success.

16. **Provision should be made for a reputable private agency to give periodic service in inspecting and ranking the employment services of the various states.** If a federal service is set up similar to that contemplated in the Wagner Bill, it will undoubtedly carry on some service of inspection

in order to determine whether or not a state should receive its allotment. But while the federal service can give some discreet advice, it can do little more than grade the states into the two main divisions of those whose services are acceptable and those which are not.

Even after a federal service has been set up, there will be need, therefore, for some private agency which will be able to inspect and score the various state systems according to some such set of qualities as those which have been previously outlined. The rankings of the states could then be published both in terms of numerical scores and relative position. This would stimulate most of the backward states to improve their status and would lead to a rivalry which would be almost wholly beneficial.

17. When the service has become thoroughly established in a given state, its effectiveness would undoubtedly be increased if employers were compelled to notify the exchanges of all positions which they are seeking to fill. Such a law of course would not compel employers to accept any workers which the public offices might send them and they would still have complete freedom of choice in selecting employees, save for such restrictions as might be imposed by collective agreements. All information about vacant jobs would, however, be centralized and the offices would have complete information about the openings in the labor market. This would be sufficient to show to them large groups of workers who would wish to be put in touch with these openings.

Such a step should, however, come only after the employment offices have abundantly demonstrated their usefulness, have increased the quantity and quality of their placements through the years, and have won the solid support of most employers of labor and of the general public. It should be the capstone of a long and successful development rather than an initial or even an intermediate step.

18. The private employment offices should be more strictly regulated. While it is now constitutionally impossible for a state to prohibit the existence of private employ-

ment offices, it would seem both practicable and desirable for a state to license only that number of offices for which an administrative commission judged there was "a public necessity." In forming such a judgment the commission should take into consideration the adequacy of the public employment offices in the particular region in which the office was to be located. It is believed that such a law might well be held to be constitutional on the ground that if a state has the power to license, it must also have the power to refuse to license. The commission could then use its power to reduce the number of unnecessary and duplicating offices. Such a law has, in fact, been in operation in Wisconsin for a number of years where it has helped to reduce the number of private offices from 39 to 10. Its constitutionality has thus far never been questioned and it would seem to serve as a model which other states would do well to copy.

The regulation of private offices could also be strengthened by requiring higher fees and the posting of a considerable bond as a condition of obtaining a license, by stating in some detail the grounds on which a license may be revalued and giving to the supervisory body the power to revoke such licenses pending a court hearing, by having all licenses expire on a given date so that the whole situation may be canvassed at one time, by requiring adequate reporting by them of placements, and by providing more adequate system of inspection.

19. The Creation of a National Labor Board. Such a board, as Professors Slichter [9] and Leiserson have pointed out, could be of service in helping to transfer labor from decaying industries and localities, in supervising the work of the employment offices and the general policies followed, and in helping to work out an adequate system of vocational guidance and retraining.

[9] See *Bulletin of the Taylor Society,* December, 1930, p. 266.

PART SIX

UNEMPLOYMENT INSURANCE

CHAPTER XXII

VOLUNTARY UNEMPLOYMENT INSURANCE

We have traced elsewhere [1] the attempts of government to alleviate the distress caused by unemployment and turn now to the voluntary efforts of the wage earners to apply the principle of insurance to unemployment. Throughout the nineteenth century fluctuations in employment were sufficiently regular and widespread to create an interest in the possibility of making provision for bad times in periods of good times. Although the principle of insurance was extended to a great variety of risks, no insurance carriers touched the risk of unemployment. The difficulty of determining the actuarial value of the risk and the prevailing view that workers would simulate unemployment were sufficient obstacles.

Trade unions were, however, in a particularly favorable situation. Each union included in its ranks workers with more or less equal chances of unemployment, and members were in an excellent position to check up on the behavior of the unemployed members. In addition many unions performed the functions of employment exchanges, and so had a means of checking up on the willingness of the unemployed to work. They became, therefore, the only agencies which applied the method of mutual insurance against the risk of unemployment. They were impelled no doubt as much by the desire to prevent a nibbling away of the standard wage as by the philanthropic aim of meeting the immediate need of their unemployed members.

As agencies of relief the trade union schemes of unemployment insurance were not unimportant. Thus in Great Britain in 1893 there were some 682,000 members of trade

[1] See, *ante*, pp. 197-204.

unions chiefly in the metal, building, textile, and printing trades who had some form of unemployment insurance. By 1903 the number had increased to nearly a million. The out-of-work benefits these unions paid either in the form of traveling or daily allowance compare favorably with the benefits paid in later years under the state system.[2] Similar provisions for unemployment relief were to be found among the unions of most industrial countries. These were significant especially in Germany, Austria, Belgium, Norway, Sweden, and Denmark. The expenditures for traveling and unemployment benefits formed a varying but substantial proportion of the total expenditures of the unions in these countries.[3]

Even greater importance is to be attached to these trade union methods as pointing the way to the larger compulsory schemes which are now being adopted and for making possible an intermediate stage which, because of its origin, is known as the Ghent system.[4] Under the latter the local or national governments, or both, participate in the voluntary system by granting subventions out of public funds, the objects of which are to encourage the existing schemes, supplement the benefits of these, stimulate other trade unions and voluntary groups of workers to organize additional schemes.

The importancè of the Ghent system—even though in many countries it is still the only form of unemployment insurance—is not to be exaggerated. In spite of the very substantial form of the financial contribution made by the public authorities, the movement has been confined to the organized workers, and has not touched the less skilled workers who do not belong to trade unions. Nor is this limitation likely to be overcome in the future, as workers who do not take the trouble to join trade unions will hardly take the initiative in organizing voluntary unemployment

[2] R. C. Davison, *The Unemployed*, pp. 18-22.
[3] Joseph L. Cohen, *Insurance Against Unemployment*, pp. 75-83.
[4] It is not unimportant to note that in the United States where trade unions have rarely organized unemployment insurance schemes, the public authorities have also been most backward in this regard.

insurance societies. And the trend at present is clearly away from voluntary schemes covering some workers, toward compulsory schemes covering at least the industrial wage earners.

But in spite of its limitations the Ghent system is performing a valuable function in accustoming the community to unemployment insurance, in pointing out the administrative difficulties involved, and in elaborating the necessary machinery for a compulsory system. For the United States it has some additional implications. In the near future we can expect some of the more progressive states to introduce compulsory unemployment insurance. The Federal Government can take a leaf out of the experience of European States and subsidize these state undertakings. In other states single enterprises or groups of enterprises are organizing and will continue, no doubt, to organize smaller schemes for their own employees. In such instances the various states can subsidize these endeavors. Such grants-in-aid have a double function to perform. They will not only encourage the extension of unemployment insurance, but they can also be utilized to establish uniform rules or procedure over the country. It is, therefore, of some importance to review briefly the experiences of some European countries with voluntary insurance against unemployment subsidized by public funds.

For this purpose Belgium and Denmark are fairly typical of the evolution and problems of voluntary insurance. In the former, where government is decentralized, the initiative was taken by the municipalities and later the aid of the national government was superimposed on that of the municipalities. While at first the state participation involved the mere granting of a subsidy to societies which met the conditions imposed by the municipalities, in later years and especially since the war, the national government has become the dominant political agency, and has subordinated the local authorities to its own rules and regulations. But in order to retain the financial assistance of the municipalities and especially their supervision of the local societies, the State encourages the former to continue as members of the local communal or intercommunal institutions which, in the first instance, were organized by the municipalities.

In Denmark, on the other hand, local government is less autonomous than in Belgium, and in consequence the initiative was taken by the national government. At first the municipalities were merely authorized to make subventions to the local societies, but more recently these have been made compulsory. Hence here also, the local authorities are drawn in as agencies of supervision in areas where they are so well qualified to know the possibilities of employment and the extent of need.

In the end therefore unemployment insurance in both countries has developed into a national system. In each it has an additional national character. While at the outset the insurance societies were purely local in character, now by far the most important societies are the national trade unions with branches in the various localities. Another consequence of the important rôle of the national trade unions is that insurance is virtually on an industrial basis— a feature which still has attractions for many.

The participation of the State in the unemployment insurance systems in both countries has made possible a partial solution of difficulties which have since arisen also under the compulsory systems in both Great Britain and Germany. With any limitation of the period during which benefits are paid, some workers will always escape the net of insurance. With benefits low enough to encourage the search for employment, workers with large families find the grants somewhat inadequate. To these must be added the possible exhaustion of the funds for even the limited benefits during periods of prolonged depression. Hence both countries have added emergency funds to meet the above situations.

A more detailed account of the Ghent system of unemployment insurance in Belgium and Denmark is contained in the two succeeding chapters.

CHAPTER XXIII

THE "GHENT" SYSTEM OF UNEMPLOYMENT INSURANCE IN BELGIUM [1]

1. The Development of Subsidized Insurance Before 1914

In 1898 a commission composed of workers, employers, economists, and representatives of the various political parties was appointed by the City Council of Ghent to study ways of relieving distress due to unemployment.[2] This Commission recommended that the city subsidize both the associations of workers having definite provisions for paying out-of-work benefits to their unemployed members and the individual workers who independently provided for unemployment through savings.

In October these recommendations were embodied in a law for a trial period of three years. By this law an administrative commission of ten was set up to determine each month the rate of the subsidy to each society in accordance with (1) the condition of the municipal fund, which was in the main made up of public funds but could be supplemented by private gifts and subscriptions, and (2) the state of unemployment. The subsidy belonged to the individual members of each society and was paid out as an ad-

[1] Antoine Borrel, *La Lutte contre le Chomage*, pp. 189-97; J. Lefort, *L'assurance contre le Chomage*, Vol. 1, pp. 304-47; Joseph L. Cohen, *Insurance Against Unemployment*, pp. 84-91.

[2] An earlier attempt to subsidize voluntary unemployment insurance was made by the Provincial Council of Liége (1897) when 1500 francs were set aside for unemployment insurance societies which had been in existence for at least two years. This was to be distributed one third each in proportion to the number of members in the association, in proportion to the contributions of the members, and in proportion to the benefits paid out. It was not, however, as successful as the Ghent attempt, and by 1907 no more than seven associations with 630 members took advantage of the offer.

dition to the benefits they received from their societies in the form of a percentage on the latter. The various societies paid out the municipal additions and were reimbursed each month, and while they were not limited in the payment of their own benefits, the maximum on which a subsidy could be claimed was a franc per day for sixty days in each year. While in the main each society made its own rules, it could not claim subsidies for benefits paid on account of unemployment resulting from strikes or lockouts, illness, or accidents. As indicated above, the Ghent law aimed to encourage workers who did not belong to associations to make provision for unemployment. An individual unemployed worker could claim a subsidy from the communal fund similar to that paid to members of associations upon proving that he had withdrawn money from a savings account because of unemployment. But few workers actually made such claims, and the scheme has worked only through associations—chiefly trade unions. So promising was the experience of the first years that the surrounding municipalities joined the Ghent Fund and the law was made permanent.[3]

By 1902, 12,239 workers belonged to trade unions affiliated with the Ghent Fund. Of these, 3,250 received benefits for 31,325 days of unemployment or 57,381 francs, of which amount the Ghent Fund contributed 16,161 francs. Five years later the number of workers increased to 17,426 of whom 3,583 received benefits for 36,729 days of unemployment or 65,409 francs, of which amount the Ghent Fund contributed 23,722 francs.

With minor modifications this method of encouraging insurance against unemployment spread throughout Belgium.[4] By 1910 there were twenty-two such communal or

---

[3] A great deal of the success was no doubt due to the fact that Ghent was a strong trade union center, as out of a total working-man population of 36,500, some twenty thousand belonged to trade unions most of which had unemployment insurance provisions.

[4] Thus at Liége the subsidies did not belong to the unemployed workers but to the associations, and individual savers were excluded, while at Verviers a waiting period of three days was established, and benefits for partial unemployment were paid if the worker did not earn one half his usual wage.

intercommunal funds covering fifty municipalities, and by 1914 the number increased to twenty-nine covering one hundred and one municipalities. The membership of the affiliated societies increased to approximately one hundred and twenty-five thousand—still less than one tenth of the industrial wage earners.

Following the example of the municipalities the provincial governments set aside each year various amounts to relieve unemployment. These were either allotted to the Funds in the province or directly to the associations. As the amounts varied from province to province and year to year, and as they were not based on the expenditures for benefits, there is no record to show their importance.

Since 1907 the State has provided an annual subsidy which was distributed to the communal or intercommunal Funds, to the associations affiliated with these, a small amount to associations not affiliated, and a fairly large part to the Bourses du Travail which acted as employment exchanges. In the case of the subsidies to the associations the principle followed was that adopted by the Ghent Fund, and the rules of these associations, which were approved by the various communal or intercommunal Funds, were accepted as adequate for the state subsidies.

Hence during these early years there was no uniform procedure over the entire country, the associations were mainly local in character, and the local authorities played a more important rôle than the national government.

2. The Reorganization of Subsidized Insurance Since the War

During the war years the funds of the various associations were exhausted, and the whole system virtually ceased to function. Temporary relief to the unemployed was provided by the National Committee for Relief and Food Supply which was set up at the very beginning of the war. The activities of the committee lapsed after the Armistice, but not so the need of the unemployed, which, in fact, became much greater. Immediately after the Armistice, over one half of the Belgian workers were without employment, and the essential temporary relief was provided through an Unemployment Relief Fund.

Meanwhile the pre-war unemployment insurance societies were recovering from the destructive effects of the war, and the national government proceeded to utilize these for the substitution of insurance against unemployment for poor relief. In a circular of May 7, 1920, addressed to the presidents of the communal Funds, the Minister of Labor indicated the part which the State was ready to assume in encouraging unemployment insurance.[5] From the first of June to the thirty-first of December, 1920, a daily allowance of 2 fr. 50 was to be paid to members of societies affiliated with communal Funds who became unemployed before completing the required period of eligibility. This was intended to encourage workers to join the societies. To the societies themselves was to be paid a subvention of fifty per cent of the contributions paid in by their members. The individual allowances and the subventions to the local societies not affiliated with national federations were to be paid out through the communal Funds, while local societies affiliated with national federations were to make their claims to the Minister through their national organization. State control was thus introduced over all local societies either through the communal Funds or through the national societies. Communes without Funds were urged to organize them so as not to deprive their residents of the State allowances. To compensate the communal Funds for the additional administrative duties the State undertook to pay one half of their administrative expenses. Finally poor relief was withdrawn from those workers who neglected to join a recognized society.

As a result of these substantial monetary inducements and a propaganda campaign carried on through the provincial and communal authorities the membership increased to approximately 600,000 and the number of communal or

[5] *Revue du Travail*, June 15, 1920, pp. 820-24.

inter-communal Funds to fifty-one covering three hundred communes.[6] This reorganization was effected none too soon, for Belgium, as other countries, was confronted with a great increase in unemployment in the world-wide depression of 1920-21.

Many of the societies exhausted their funds and a large number of workers exhausted their claims to benefits. Additional State aid was provided by the Royal Decree of December 30, 1920, which set up a National Emergency Fund (Fonds National de Crise) which was to come to the assistance of unemployed insured workers who could no longer receive benefits from their associations.[7] At the same time the whole insurance system was unified, and, as the administrative work greatly increased, a special administrative council was created in the Department of Labor to take charge of the Emergency Fund. Subsequent modifications of the first decree retained the Emergency Fund as a permanent feature of the insurance system, and placed its administrative council in charge of the various societies. Under pressure of the central authority the procedure of the societies was unified, one result of which is adequate statistical material on all phases of unemployment insurance.

The Belgian Insurance System is now administered by the National Emergency Fund whose governing body is composed of three members technically qualified to deal with unemployment, three representing the employers, and three representing the workers. This governing board examines the rules of societies applying to the Minister of Labor for recognition, recommends approval or refusal of such recognition, supervises the use of funds granted through it, and hires and discharges its own staff.[8] In addition it may be empowered to authorize loans to facilitate the undertaking of works affording employment to the unemployed.

[6] *Ibid.*, July, 1920, pp. 1015-16.
[7] *Ibid.*, January, 1921, pp. 122-26.
[8] The entire staff is a very modest one and in 1926 consisted of but eight members. See *International Labour Review*, June, 1927, p. 910.

3. The Existing Insurance Societies

There are four types of societies which the worker can join to insure himself against unemployment. (1) The most important is the national associations (Caisses Centrales) with local branches having uniform rates of contributions and benefits. These are under the direct supervision of the Unemployment and Placement Division of the Ministry of Labor. The 34 now in existence are mainly trade union associations whose members must generally join the trade Fund. (2) There are now 140 local societies, not attached to any national organization, under the supervision of the inter-communal Funds. (3) Members of both the above can organize auxiliary societies (Caisses Auxiliares) for the payment of additional benefits. There are now 137 of these. (4) Finally, there are a small number—20—of societies (Caisses Officielles) outside the intercommunal Funds under the direct supervision of the Minister. These are apparently local societies of mixed occupations.[9]

Between the central government and the local societies are the communal and especially intercommunal Funds (Fonds de Chomage) which existed before 1914 but which have since increased in number and importance. Upon being recognized by the State they are delegated the authority of exercising control over the local units in their areas; they verify the involuntary character of unemployment for which benefits are paid; they distribute the state subventions and recover the contributions from the communes upon which the subventions in the case of emergency grants are based. A part of the general expenses is contributed by the State.[10] The national government can thus unify the procedure of the national societies, while the local authorities can unify that of the local societies.

[9] *Revue du Travail*, March, 1930, pp. 418-19.

[10] See *ibid.*, January, 1927, pp. 25-6. The local supervision is made most effective by the fact that Belgium is covered by a network of intercommunal Funds. Thus in 1927 there were seventy-six covering 1,087 communes with a population of approximately six million of whom over six hundred thousand were insured workers. This includes almost all of those insured against unemployment. See *ibid.*, November, 1928, p. 1434.

4. Income of Insurance Societies

The income of the various societies is derived from the contributions of their members, a state subvention of two-thirds of the former amount, and grants from the communes and provinces. The following table shows the income and expenditures of these societies for the most recent years for which data are available:

TABLE 21

Income and Expenditure of Unemployment Insurance Societies
1925–1927
(1000 francs)

Year	1925[1]	1926[2]	1927[2]
Income			
Contributions	12,913	13,611	17,935
Subsidies			
State[3]	5,231	8,114	7,830
Provinces	1,336	618	1,445
Communes	710	574	365
Miscellaneous	749	925	2,230
Total Income	20,939	23,843	29,804
Expenditures			
Benefits	16,157	13,671	23,538
Administrative	2,321	2,296	3,088
Miscellaneous	1,279	1,279	2,651
Total Expenditure	19,757	17,140	29,277

[1] *Revue du Travail*, November, 1927, p. 1520.
[2] *Ibid.*, November, 1928, p. 1436.
[3] The state subsidy has varied from one-half to two-thirds and refers to the contributions of the previous year in each case.

While the State can insist that the contributions be adequate to keep the Funds solvent, within that limitation there are great variations. In 1927 the benefits varied from 55 fr. per member per year among the tobacco workers to 2 fr. 45 among the public service employees. The four largest groups of insured workers paid per capita contributions in 1927 as follows: [11]

Textiles	. 37.50 francs
Metals	. 24.20 "
Mining	. 11.40 "
Mixed Groups	. 35.40 "

The provincial subsidies are paid to the intercommunal Funds, to the societies, and, more rarely, to individual insured members. The amounts shown in the table therefore underestimate the extent of provincial participation. The autonomous character of provincial government makes it impossible to furnish the exact totals which the provinces contribute, but the following figures give a truer picture than those above: [12]

Year	*Amounts Paid out by Provinces (1000 francs)*
1925	. 1,724
1926	. 1,697
1927	. 3,125

The communal participation in unemployment insurance generally takes the form of an addition (majoration) to the benefits paid by the societies. The rates of these vary greatly from one commune to another,[13] and while again it is difficult to give the exact totals, the following figures present a more accurate picture than do those of Table 21:

Year	*Amount paid out on account of communes*[14] *(1000 francs.)*
1924	. 2,804
1925	. 4,601
1926	. 4,595
1927	. 7,292

The communal and provincial assistance is therefore approximately as large as that of the State, and the total com-

[11] *Ibid.*, November, 1928, p. 1438. A large number of the Societies increased the rate of contributions in 1927 so as to bring the benefits up with the increase in the cost of living. *Ibid.*, p. 1434.

[12] *Ibid.*, November, 1928, p. 1434.

[13] For the rates paid in 1924 see, *ibid.*, January, 1927, p. 26.

[14] *Ibid.*, p. 28; November, 1928, p. 1435.

ing from public funds is approximately as large as the amounts paid in by the insured workers. It may also be said that the amount coming from public funds is a larger proportion of the total devoted to insurance than is the case under compulsory insurance in Great Britain.[15] This is even more true if we take into account the payments made out of the Emergency Fund.[16]

5. The Payment of Benefits

As each society pays its own benefits, the rates vary greatly. Thus in 1927 they varied from 78 fr. 50 per insured member per year among the leather workers to 1 fr. 20 among the paper workers.[17] The four largest groups of insured workers paid out the following amounts per insured person in 1927: [18]

Textiles	. 34.50 francs
Metals	. 38.00 "
Mining	. 14.50 "
Mixed Groups	. 52.90 "

Even though the benefit rates can vary, State control involves a certain amount of uniformity in the conditions of benefit payment. No payments can be paid to insured persons who (1) are incapable of work; (2) are on strike or locked out; (3) are unemployed as a direct consequence of strike, if it is proved that the strike was declared in agreement with them, and that they are directly interested in the settlement of the dispute; (4) are unemployed as a direct consequence of a strike to maintain a claim not connected with any trade dispute, and who, individually or as members of any body, give the strikers support calculated

[15] See *post,* p. 41.
[16] The Belgian method of paying a percentage on the contributions of members can be criticized on the basis of need. As the rates of contributions vary between workers, the better paid, who can afford high contributions, get more assistance than the poorer paid workers.
[17] For per capita amounts in 1927 see *Revue du Travail,* November, 1928, p. 1438.
[18] *Ibid.* These do not bring out the varying rates per day which, however, are not available.

to prolong the strike or facilitate its extension; (5) are definitely dismissed from their previous employment and refuse to accept new employment suitable to them under conditions customary in the region. An insured worker who voluntarily leaves his employment can receive no benefits for a month after he has indicated his willingness to work. Before becoming eligible for benefits in the other cases of unemployment the insured workers must be regularly enrolled members and pay contributions for at least a year.

Each society must provide a minimum waiting period of a day per week—the week beginning on Monday. But a further waiting period may be waived in the case of unemployment lasting continuously for six days as long as the worker has not worked more than four days in any one week. It may also be waived in the case of a full week of unemployment alternating with a full working week and, in case of unemployment lasting at least two days during each of the two preceding weeks, from the third week on, until the worker has been employed for more than four days in any one week.

While the benefit rates are fixed by each society they cannot exceed two-thirds of the unemployed workers' wage —this maximum can be raised to three-fourths in the case of the head of a family with at least four children. But any benefits paid by the enterprise of the workers concerned must be deducted from the total amount to which the insured workers are entitled.

Emergency Benefits.[19] It is inevitable that some workers will exhaust their benefits, that the grants will sometimes be inadequate, and that some societies will exhaust their resources. In such cases the National Emergency Fund comes to the assistance of involuntarily unemployed per-

---

[19] The income of the National Emergency Fund from which emergency benefits are paid is derived from state funds and voluntary contributions, but the latter have been unimportant. To obtain emergency benefits, the communes must undertake to repay ten per cent of the expenditures on their residents, and the societies fifteen per cent of the expenditures on their members.

sons who are members of approved societies. To those who have exhausted their claims to benefits, the Emergency Fund undertakes to pay up to 30 daily grants a year.[20] In cases where either the standard or emergency benefits are inadequate, it undertakes to pay family allowances.

The basic grant of the National Emergency Fund for the cases mentioned above is fixed at the rate prescribed by the rules of each unemployment society. But a maximum of 9 francs is fixed for the head of a family or for a person over twenty-five who is single, widowed or divorced and without children, and a maximum of 7 francs for an unmarried person under twenty-five, or for one widowed or divorced and without children, and for a married woman not the head of a family. The family allowances consist of 3 fr. 50 for a wife who does the household work and 3 francs for each child under fourteen and for each child fourteen to sixteen who is attending school or incapable of working.[21]

6. The Extent of Insurance

The following table gives the number of Belgian workers insured against unemployment:

TABLE 22

Total Membership of Unemployment Insurance Societies, 1921–1929[22]

End of Year	Membership	End of Year	Membership
1921	687,660	1926	598,251
1922	704,641	1927	610,889
1923	654,364	1928	628,555
1924	654,580	1929	632,063
1925	606,754	. . . .	. . . .

[20] If a depression exists in a particular industry and it is impossible to employ the unemployed under suitable conditions in another industry, the Minister of Labor upon the recommendation of the governing body of the National Emergency Fund may extend the grants beyond 30 days.

[21] These rates were fixed by the order of March 5, 1929. *Revue du Travail*, March, 1929, p. 488. In previous years they were lower.

[22] *Revue du Travail*, February, 1929, pp. 194-5; March, 1930, p. 418.

The decline between 1922 and 1927 was directly associated with a decline in the membership of trade unions, and since then the numbers insured have remained virtually stationary.[23] The trade union membership as reported to the International Federation of Trade Unions (Amsterdam) on the first of January, 1928, was 530,575.[24] It would appear, therefore, that as far as Belgium was concerned, voluntary insurance against unemployment, even though heavily subsidized out of public funds, is limited by the extent of trade unionism. This leaves a great many workers not insured. The Belgian Census of 1920 reported approximately 3,100,000 as gainfully occupied. If we deduct 500,000 as the approximate number engaged in agriculture and forestry, we have left approximately 2,600,000. This would indicate that only about one-fourth of the workers are insured against unemployment.[25]

A more conservative comparison can also be made. An investigation of October 31, 1926, into industrial establishments (including mines and transportation) with at least ten workers showed that there were approximately 1,177,-000 wage-earners and salaried employees.[26] This would mean that only about one-half of those eligible are insured. For the non-union workers compulsory insurance seems the only way out.

7. THE ADEQUACY OF INSURANCE

In the absence of wage statistics for the insured workers we can make no conclusion as to the adequacy of the grants actually paid. We may, however, inquire as to the extent that unemployment of insured workers is covered by voluntary insurance.

The following table shows the number of days lost by insured workers and the number of these for which benefits were paid:

[23] *Ibid.,* January, 1927, p. 28.
[24] *Ibid.,* August, 1929, p. 1237.
[25] *Annuaire statistique de la Belgique,* 1927-28, p. xxix.
[26] *Ibid.,* p. 187.

TABLE 23

DAYS LOST BY INSURED WORKERS AND DAYS BENEFITED 1921–1929*

YEAR	DAYS LOST (1000)	DAYS BENEFITED (1000)	PERCENTAGE (2) ÷ (1)
	(1)	(2)	(3)
1921	24,101	....	....
1922	9,126	....	....
1923	2,579	....	....
1924	3,157	....	....
1925	4,804	3,114	65
1926	3,698	2,583	70
1927	4,682	3,541	76
1928	3,358	2,338	70
1929	3,556	2,637	74

* *Revue du Travail*, November, 1928, p. 1434; 1928–29 from monthly figures in the same journal.

When to these are added the number of days for which benefits are paid out of the Emergency Fund, it will be seen that voluntary insurance adequately takes care of the amount of unemployment incurred. That the standard benefits are not altogether adequate can be seen indirectly from the expenditures of the Emergency Fund which are shown in the following table:

TABLE 24

PAYMENTS MADE OUT OF THE NATIONAL EMERGENCY FUND, 1921–29*
(1000 francs)

YEAR	BENEFITS	FAMILY ALLOWANCES	TOTAL
1921	101,882	27,022	128,904
1922	31,620	11,903	43,523
1923	3,435	2,467	5,902
1924	1,747	2,425	4,172
1925	4,138	3,794	7,932
1926	4,701	5,723	10,423
1927	5,973	10,606	16,579
1928	4,569	6,683	11,870
1929	4,278	10,002	14,287

* Source 1921–25, *Revue du Travail*, January, 1927, p. 29; 1926, *Ibid.*, November 30, 1927, p. 1521; 1927, 1928, 1929, based on reports published monthly in the same journal.

With the exception of the first two years, which were years of great depression, when it was necessary to make some payments to a great many unemployed workers, a very large proportion of the National Emergency Fund is spent for family allowances. Another interesting feature indicating the attempt made to make the benefits more adequate is the very large proportion which goes to married workers as against single workers. This can be seen from the following table of the number of days for which benefits in the most recent years were paid:

TABLE 25

NUMBER OF DAYS FOR WHICH BENEFITS WERE PAID OUT OF THE EMERGENCY FUND*
(1000 francs)

YEAR	TO SINGLE MEN	TO MARRIED MEN	TOTAL
1927	545	1948	2493
1928	346	1267	1613
1929	242	1151	1393

* Based on monthly reports published in the *Revue du Travail*.

CHAPTER XXIV

THE "GHENT" SYSTEM IN DENMARK [1]

1. The Development of Subsidized Insurance Before 1914

In Denmark as in Belgium many of the trade unions combined mutual insurance with their other functions.[2] And in the same year (1907) that the Belgian state followed the example of its municipalities in encouraging voluntary insurance, the Danish state initiated the payment of subventions to societies providing insurance against unemployment. State rather than municipal initiative in the case of Denmark is to be attributed, in part at least, to the centralized character of the Danish government. But this meant that from the outset unemployment insurance was unified on a national scale.[3]

To obtain the state subsidy [4]—equal to one-third of the contributions paid in by the insured members—each Fund had to be recognized by the Inspector of Unemployment.[5]

[1] Antoine Borrel, *La Lutte contre le Chomage*, pp. 202-5; J. Lefort, *L'Assurance contre le Chomage*, Vol. I, pp. 368-76; Joseph L. Cohen, *Insurance Against Unemployment*, pp. 124-139.

[2] Thus out of 94 federations and local trade unions with a membership of 90,111, in 1904, 83 with a membership of 80,205 made some provision against unemployment. See Cohen, *op. cit.*, pp. 125-26.

[3] The national character of the Danish trade union gave further impetus to centralization of unemployment insurance.

[4] The communes were permitted to pay an additional subsidy of one sixth of their contributions, and assist any of their inhabitants by paying for them not over one-third of their contributions.

[5] The Inspector of Unemployment who had general supervision of unemployment insurance was responsible to the Minister of the Interior. To assist him there was an annual meeting of representatives of the recognized insurance societies, which had the power to make rules for coöperation between the societies, arrange for the transfer of members, and unify the procedure of the societies. In addition it elected a committee of six to advise the Inspector between the annual meetings. Locally, each Fund had a Board of Managers to determine within the state limitations the amount and kind of benefit to be paid.

This involved the acceptance of certain general rules laid down in the law. Each Fund had to have at least fifty members and was limited to a locality or to an industry.

In order to extend insurance beyond the trade union ranks the law provided that the unemployment insurance accounts be kept separate from the other trade union accounts, that the local Funds had to admit every qualified worker in the locality, and the national Funds, every qualified worker attached to the industry. Within the age limits of eighteen to sixty all workers entitled to aid from the official sick funds were eligible to join the unemployment insurance Funds.

Uniform rules for disallowing benefits were provided, and the daily amount of benefit was limited to two-thirds of the average wage in the trade or locality depending on the character of the Fund, but the minimum was fixed at 50 öre and the maximum at two kroner.[6] No unemployed person could receive benefits during the waiting period of six days, which could be increased to fifteen, nor for more than seventy days in a year, and some Funds were authorized to reduce this to fifty days. Before becoming eligible to benefits, the insured worker had to pay contributions for at least twelve months and those having received the maximum number of yearly grants for three years were disqualified until they had again paid contributions for a full financial year.

Societies were rapidly recognized, there being thirty-four in the first year, thirty-seven in the second,[7] and fifty-five in 1913-14. In the first year, 70,449 were insured and in 1913-14, 120,289 were insured. Some 40,000 insured persons received benefits in the latter year for over a million and a quarter days, while the total number of days lost by insured members was over two and one-half million. The same year the receipts were above three million kroner, and the expen-

---

[6] In addition to the daily monetary allowances benefits could be paid also in the form öf traveling allowances, rent, or in kind. These latter are still important. See *post,* p. 398. A form of allowance much opposed by the trade unions was that paid to supplement the income of an unemployed worker who accepted a job at less than the current wage.

[7] It is interesting to know that of 37, 36 were trade unions, while of the 55, 51 were also trade unions, national in scope.

ditures a little over two million kroner. Of the receipts the members contributed about 50 per cent, the State about 33 per cent, and the municipalities the rest.

From the tables at the end of this chapter it will be seen that the voluntary provision against unemployment in Denmark grew steadily as to workers included, receipts, and expenditures. The ordinary benefits and the public subsidies were adequate for the workers insured, and every year there was a substantial balance. And unlike Belgium there was no disorganization of the voluntary insurance system during the war years. But as in Belgium. and in fact as was the case under compulsory insurance in Great Britain, the Danish system was inadequate in the great depression which began in Denmark as early as November, 1917. The extent and variations in the percentages of unemployment as reported by the trade unions, in the succeeding as compared with the earlier years, are set out in Table 29 at the end of this chapter.

2. Recent Developments in Unemployment Insurance

The post-war depression period is interesting because of the varying attempts to provide for the inadequacy of voluntary insurance in a great depression and the reorganized insurance system which emerged out of the various trials.

In the table on the following page are set out the activities of the Insurance Funds in the post-war period.

The increased expenditures in 1917-18 came from the increase in the State subsidy and the increase in membership; the rates of contributions on the average remained at 11 kr. as in 1916-17. In the following year the increase in expenditures again came from the increased state subsidy and the increased membership with the rates of contributions on the average remaining unaltered. In 1919-20 there was a smaller increase in membership but the Funds increased the rates of contributions and levied additional contributions raising the average to 17 kr. The state subsidy was however less than in the previous year but the expendi-

TABLE 26

BENEFITS PAID BY FUNDS, 1917–18 TO 1927–28

YEAR	BENEFITS PAID		EMERGENCY PAYMENTS (1000 kr.)
	Days (1000)	Amount (1000 kr.)	
1917–18	1	6,312	9,556
1918–19	6,920	9,665	37,126
1919–20	3,699	5,673	19,576
1920–21	5,963	17,898	2
1921–22	9,683	30,764	. . . .
1922–23	6,353	19,751	. . . .
1923–24	5,526	17,333	. . . .
1924–25	4,521	14,115	. . . .
1925–26	1	24,824	. . . .
1926–27	1	28,585	. . . .
1927–28	1	28,134	. . . .

[1] Data not available.
[2] For later years see *post,* p. 390.

tures also were less. But during these three years the amounts expended by the State in the emergency grants were much larger than the amounts expended by the societies under the rules as can be seen from the above table. These emergency grants were paid out by the societies either in the form of family allowances to members receiving benefits or in the form of daily benefits and family allowances to members who exhausted their claims under the rules and then were refunded by the state and communes, but chiefly by the former.[8]

In the following years the average rate of contributions was greatly increased reaching 70 kr. per member per year in 1921-22 and then declining to about 50 kr. in 1926-27. The membership declined to 252,072 in 1922-23 and increased slightly during the succeeding years. The expenditures of the societies varied from year to year, but remained at a much higher level than in previous years. As can be

[8] For detailed account of the emergency benefits as paid out by the societies, see the temporary provisions in the law of December, 1919, International Labor office, *Legislative Series, 1920—Den. 1.*

seen from the above table, the increased expenditures did not all imply the indemnification of a correspondingly increased amount of unemployment. For a substantial part of the increased expenditures went to increase the rate of benefits to make them more adequate in view of the rise in the cost of living which took place.

The accounts of the societies, as shown above and in Table 28 at the end of this chapter, do not indicate the total amount spent for unemployment, since, beginning with 1920-21, the emergency benefits were paid not through the societies but through the communal relief agencies.

In the Employment Exchanges and Unemployment Insurance Act of December 22, 1921,[9] while the provision for emergency situations was made a part of the insurance system, the payment of the grants was separated from the work of the societies. An Unemployment Relief Fund was established, the income to be derived from contributions of employers subject to compulsory accident insurance, State grants, and the Unemployment Funds to the extent of 5 per cent of their receipts from contributions. This Fund was to be reserved for periods when the Minister of the Interior declared that exceptional unemployment existed in the country or in a trade, and was then to be used to assist members of recognized societies after they had exhausted the benefits due them under the rules or as a supplement for those receiving benefits who maintained families. Funds could also be used to subsidize relief works and provide courses of instruction for the unemployed.[10]

The amounts expended through the communal relief agencies are shown in the table on the following page. While the amounts expended vary greatly from year to year, they form a substantial addition to the payments made by the societies under their rules, in some years exceeding the latter. As was noted in Belgium, the Danish Emergency Fund is also used to a larger extent to support

[9] International Labour Office, *Legislative Series,* 1921 (Part II), Den. 1.
[10] Benefits to unemployed persons not members of Funds could be paid at the discretion of the communal relief authorities—but at lower rates if they had not availed themselves of the opportunity to join a Fund.

TABLE 27

UNEMPLOYMENT ASSISTANCE RENDERED THROUGH THE COMMUNAL RELIEF
AGENCIES 1919/20–1927/28[11]

YEAR	NUMBER OF UNEMPLOYED ASSISTED		AMOUNT PAID OUT (1000 kr.)
	With Dependents	Without Dependents	
1919–20 .	29,122	9,558	2,473
1920–21 .	50,484	23,823	9,104
1921–22 .	96,044	49,093	54,882
1922–23 .	62,065	29,839	15,018
1923–24 .	37,756	12,429	5,031
1924–25 .	13,350	7,049	1,616
1925–26 .	51,465	22,062	9,865
1926–27 .	66,774	34,374	17,022
1927–28 .	46,290	22,881	7,332

the unemployed who have dependents than for single workers.

The law was revised again in 1924,[12] temporarily in
1926,[13] and again in 1927.[14] We turn now to a brief description of the insurance system as it exists under the law of
1927.

3. THE ADMINISTRATIVE MACHINERY

The separation of the employment exchanges from the
insurance system has long been a source of great weakness.
Some attempts have always been made to establish coöperation between the two in both Belgium and Denmark. In
the latter the next step has been taken and both are under a
single administration.[15] A Directorate in the Ministry of
the Interior has general supervision over the Employment
Exchanges and Unemployment Insurance. Under the Di-

[11] Based on Reports in *Statistisk Aarbog.*
[12] International Labor Office, *Legislative Series,* 1924—Den. 1.
[13] *Ibid., Legislative Series,* 1926—Den. 4.
[14] *Ibid., Legislative Series,* 1927—Den. 3.
[15] This unification was established by the act of December 22, 1921.
See International Labour office, *Legislative Series,* 1921 (Part II), Den. 1,
pp. 1-6.

rector there is an Employment Committee of two sections constituted in the following manner:

(a) The Employment Exchange section which is composed of four employers and four workers chosen by the Minister from the nominations made by the Danish Employers' Associations and the Danish Federation of Trade Unions, has charge of the Employment Exchanges organized by the communes and recognized by the State. The recognized unemployment Funds must report the members applying for benefit to the exchanges, or by agreement can compel their members to register in person at the exchanges, in which case the notification is made by the Exchange to the Fund.[16] Where there are several equally qualified applicants, the exchanges must give preference to insured members.

(b) The Unemployment Insurance section is composed of six delegates chosen by the annual meeting of the representatives of the various unemployment societies, and two members chosen by the Landsting and two by the Folketing, all for a term of six years.[17]

The Employment Committee is an honorary body, with the duties of coördinating the various funds, making rules for their coöperation, including the transfer of members and securing uniformity in their rules regarding admission, contributions, and benefits.

Once a year there is a meeting of delegates from the unemployment societies under the Presidency of the Director. Each recognized fund is entitled to send at least one representative, two if it has over 1,000 members, three if it has not less than 3,000, and one additional representative for each 2,000 members over 3,000. This annual meeting dis-

[16] The extent of the coöperation between the Funds and the Employment Exchanges is indicated by the fact that of the total number registered for jobs in 1927-28, 60,935 presented themselves in person and 383,-517 were referred by the Funds. In the previous year the numbers were 59,890 and 378,157 respectively. See *Statistisk Aarbog*, 1929, p. 121.

[17] In previous years there was a third section on Exceptional Unemployment which supervised the Unemployment Relief Fund. It was abolished in 1927, and its work transferred to the Unemployment Insurance section.

cusses the activities of the funds, lays down general rules for coöperation, and elects the six delegates from its own members to the Unemployment Insurance Section as indicated above.

4. THE INSURANCE FUNDS

Any group of employed workers without means between the ages of 18 and 60 may organize an Unemployment Fund and apply for state recognition. To obtain recognition a Fund must have not less than 100 members, must be set up for one or more specified trades and must cover at least one province. In actual practice the Funds are almost entirely organized by the trade unions, who make membership compulsory, and are, therefore, national in character with local branches. But they must keep the accounts of the Funds separate from the trade union accounts and admit non-union workers to the Funds. In 1927-28 there were 69 of these Funds with 271,695 members.

The income of these Funds is made up of the contributions by members and State and communal subsidies. The annual contributions of members are set by each Fund but must be adequate, in view of the existing experience, with the grants from public moneys to pay the benefits specified in the rules and from an adequate reserve.[18]

Upon state recognition each Fund becomes entitled to a state subsidy, and a communal subsidy. In early years the subsidy was a flat percentage of the contributions paid in. We have pointed out the objections to this method.[19] Denmark has met this objection by graduating the rate of its subsidy in accordance with the annual earnings of the insured workers.

The rates of the subsidy for the state as well as the communes, which have adopted the same procedure, are shown in the following table:

[18] If the Director at any time considers the contributions inadequate he may order an additional levy

[19] See *ante*, p. 379, note 16.

Average Annual Earnings in Insured Trade (Kroner)	Subsidy as a Percentage of the Contributions	
	State	Communal
Up to 1500	40	30
1500 to 2000	35	30
2000 to 2500	30	25
2500 to 3000	25	20
3000 to 3500	20	15
3500 to 4000	15	10
Over 4000	10	5

In the absence of rates of contributions in the various societies it is difficult to say how far this method of basing the percentage on the wage meets the objection of paying a relatively large amount to the higher paid workers. It is to be presumed, however, that the rate of contributions varies directly with the wages received.

When the method of subsidizing voluntary insurance was initiated by the State, the communes were merely authorized to make grants. As we have seen this voluntary grant was actually made year after year. The communal grant was made compulsory in the act of December 22nd, 1919, in the case of unemployment Funds which established special reserves for the payment of extra benefits. In the Act of December 22nd, 1921, communal grants were fixed at 35 per cent of the contributions paid in by their residents and were made compulsory to all Funds. They have remained compulsory since then with the alteration of the basis, as noted above.[20]

5. Benefits

Out of their income the Funds can pay benefits in the form of allowances for traveling or removal, assistance in

[20] Each unemployment Fund submits a report of its operations for the financial year which is examined by the Director and certified for payment out of the public funds concerned. He also submits a statement to each commune showing the amount due which must be paid into the national office and allocated to the various Funds.

rent paying, or daily allowance in cash or in kind. While the extent and character of the benefits paid is to be determined by the governing board of each Fund in each individual case, certain general rules must be observed.

The rate of benefit cannot exceed two-thirds of the average earnings in the trade in case of a trade Fund, while the National Employment Committee fixes the maximum in case of local Funds. But the rate cannot be less than one krone a day, nor more than four for the head of a family, or three for a single person. Each Fund can make rules to withhold payment of benefit for a week in which the insured person works three days or more, and payment must be withheld where the insured person works four days or more. No benefits can be paid for the waiting period or first six days of unemployment, and this waiting period can be increased to 15 days.[21]

The Funds may provide in their rules to pay benefits for partial unemployment, but only if the hours of work are reduced by more than a third, and providing it is arranged that it is financially advantageous for the worker concerned to procure work rather than receive benefits.

With respect to Funds including a large number of seasonal workers, the Minister of the Interior, after consulting the Employment Committee, can order the suspension of benefit payment during the periods of customary unemployment, or until after unemployment has lasted more than fifteen days, either to all members or to the seasonal workers involved. On the other hand in trades where short periods of unemployment usually follow each other at frequent intervals, the waiting period may be waived.

There are, of course, the usual exclusions from the payment of benefits to those taking part in strikes or lockouts, those unemployed because of sickness, and those having left work on insufficient grounds or because of drunkenness or quarrelsome behavior and those in receipt of poor relief,

---

[21] To encourage the search for temporary employment, the waiting period is not exacted more than once every two months, if employment during this period is temporary, *i.e.*, under three weeks.

old age pensions, or invalidity pensions. A more stringent condition than even that recently introduced in Great Britain is that unemployed workers cannot refuse work and receive benefits, even though the wages offered are less than those previously received, providing the wages offered are not below the wages paid for corresponding work in the occupation or locality involved.

In addition to these requirements an insured worker does not become eligible for benefits until he has been employed and paid his contributions for at least ten months during the two preceding years. But this additional requirement may be suspended in the event of exceptional unemployment prevailing in the trade or having prevailed for twelve months in the two preceding years. The number of days for which benefits are to be paid are to be specified in the rules of each Fund, but it cannot be less than seventy. And a member receiving the maximum number of daily benefits, for a period not exceeding four years is disqualified until he has paid contributions for twelve consecutive months and has been employed for twenty-six weeks in these twelve months.

6. EMERGENCY MEASURES

In addition to the ordinary operations indicated above each Fund is authorized to constitute an emergency fund (Krisefond) made of separate contributions which cannot be less than twenty per cent of the ordinary contributions, but which can be suspended when a sufficient reserve is built up. The State and communes are to supplement these as they do the regular contributions. There is one other source of income. The Central Unemployment Fund contributes an amount not to exceed twenty-five per cent of the members' contributions to the emergency funds but limited to four-fifths of the Central Unemployment Fund's own receipts from interest during the financial year for which the grant is made.

It will be recalled that this Central Fund was first set up

in 1921 [22] and that it handled the emergency payments either through the Funds or through the communal relief agencies. Its income is derived from contributions of employers of three kroner per year for each insured person employed. These are collected by the approved accident insurance societies and handed over to the Fund. As soon as a reserve of twelve million kroner is established the employers' contributions are suspended. In addition to the grants to Emergency Funds of the various societies the Central Unemployment Fund can be used to subsidise relief works and vocational classes, and to grant loans to recognized Funds to enable them to discharge their liabilities.

The emergency funds of the societies are to be used in periods of exceptional unemployment [23] to pay benefits to those who have drawn the maximum allowance under the rules. These cannot exceed two-thirds of the ordinary benefits or seventy days in the course of twelve consecutive months.

As a result of the post-war experience, there is now a definite means of assisting Funds which exhaust their income, and an attempt made to encourage the workers to provide for emergency situations. A significant step has also been taken to draw the employers into the insurance system even though only for the emergency situations. How adequately these provisions will take care of exceptional unemployment remains yet to be seen.

7. THE EXTENT OF INSURANCE

The activities of the Funds since 1907 indicate fairly conclusively that the Danish insurance system is sufficiently

[22] Before 1927 it was a distinct unit under the control of one of the three sections—now abolished—of the Employment Committee. Its governing body now consists of the Director as chairman, two employers selected by the Minister of the Interior on the recommendation of the Danish Employers' Association, and one representative of the Unemployment Insurance Funds selected by the Unemployment Insurance Section.

[23] The act of 1927 has detailed provisions for the statistical methods of determining when exceptional unemployment exists.

well established to provide against normal unemployment of those workers insured. But, as in the case of Belgium, we may ask how many workers are excluded from insurance. The membership of the Funds and Trade Unions is set out in Table 29 at the end of this chapter. A study of that table will reveal the similarity in movement. Up to 1920 the trade union membership increased steadily and with it membership in the Funds. Then there was a marked decline in both and since 1924 there has been a slow increase in both. This would indicate that in spite of the effort to open the Funds to non-union workers, voluntary insurance in Denmark is limited by the extent of trade unionism.

In March, 1928, there were approximately 272,000 insured workers and approximately 314,000 workers in trade unions. But according to the census of 1921 there were approximately 990,000 wage earners and salaried workers. If we deduct those attached to agriculture, the professions, public service, and domestic service, there will be left approximately 440,000.[24] We can also compare the numbers insured with the census of manufactures and trade for July, 1925, which reported approximately 454,000 employed. But aside from industrial enterprises which showed approximately 270,000 employees, there was no separation of employers from employed. On the other hand, there were not included agricultural workers, domestic and public servants.[25] If we take 500,000 as the approximate number eligible to unemployment insurance, the Danish system has drawn in only slightly more than one-half of those eligible.

[24] *Statistisk Aarbog,* pp. 14-19. These deductions are excessive as at least public servants and agricultural workers belong to trade unions and are insured against unemployment.

[25] *Ibid.,* pp. 50-62.

TABLE 28

RECEIPTS AND EXPENDITURES OF UNEMPLOYMENT INSURANCE FUNDS IN DENMARK, 1907–8 TO 1927–28 [1]

(1000 Kr.)

	1907–8	1908–9	1909–10	1910–11	1911–12	1912–13	1913–14	1914–15	1915–16	1916–17
RECEIPTS										
Ordinary Contributions	180	848	1,091	1,200	1,305	1,408	1,517	1,548	1,694	1,981
Extra Contributions	12	213	16	29	....	....	29	110	1	2
Subventions [2]										
State	....	150	576	682	771	823	891	987	1,097	913
Communal	....	85	252	311	339	374	414	449	491	523
Miscellaneous [3]	21	39	35	53	61	87	123	158	178	219
TOTAL	213	1,335	1,970	2,275	2,476	2,692	2,974	3,252	3,461	3,638
EXPENDITURES										
Daily Benefits	206	1,243	1,406	1,668	1,627	1,551	1,823	2,688	2,019	1,869
Other Assistance [4]	10	93	68	59	76	97	127	111	116	109
Administration	22	112	184	209	226	240	269	279	314	381
Emergency	....	....	....	....	....	....	....	....	66	123
TOTAL	238	1,448	1,658	1,936	1,929	1,888	2,219	3,078	2,515	2,482

[1] Based on Annual Reports in the *Statistisk Aarbog.*
[2] The subventions are in each case based on the contributions of the previous year.
[3] Including receipts from non-benefit receiving members, gifts, interest, etc.
[4] Allowances for traveling, removal, payments in kind, and aid at Christmas time.

TABLE 28 (*Continued*)

	1917–18	1918–19	1919–20	1920–21	1921–22	1922–23	1923–24	1924–25	1925–26	1926–27	1927–28
RECEIPTS											
Ordinary Contributions	2,406	3,260	4,593	7,747	8,856	8,655	9,428	1,706	11,414	12,344	14,336
Extra Contributions	2	14	860	1,277	9,250	7,022	2,790	543	43	2,186	6,676
Subventions [2]											
State	3,189	4,773	2,406	4,403	4,512	9,053	7,836	6,109	3,937	4,010	5,094
Communal	735	902	1,021	1,258	2,147	4,542	3,236	4,911	4,447	3,609	3,572
Miscellaneous [3]	273	276	391	455	2,240	574	723	945	1,082	837	754
TOTAL	6,605	9,225	9,271	15,140	27,005	29,845	24,013	23,215	20,924	22,986	30,432
EXPENDITURES											
Daily Benefits	6,170	9,463	5,435	17,253	29,454	19,402	16,997	13,813	24,362	27,718	27,579
Other Assistance [4]	142	202	237	644	1,309	350	336	302	462	866[5]	555
Administration	540	864	1,344	1,567	1,420	1,510	1,376	1,387	1,568	1,573	1,856
Emergency	144	208	282	480	457	428	485	....	....	....	....
TOTAL	6,996	10,737	7,299	19,945	32,641	21,690	19,194	15,502	26,392	30,157	29,990

[5] Includes 317, as emergency grants according to law of 1926.

TABLE 29

MEMBERSHIP OF TRADE UNIONS, UNEMPLOYMENT INSURANCE FUNDS, AND
EXTENT OF UNEMPLOYMENT IN DENMARK, 1908–1928[1]

YEAR	TRADE UNION MEMBERSHIP[2] (1000)	UNEMPLOYMENT INSURANCE FUNDS[3]	NUMBER OF INSURED WORKERS[3] (1000)	PERCENTAGE OF UNEMPLOYMENT[4]
1908	117	34	70	
1909	120	44	84	
1910	123	48	95	10.7
1911	128	51	105	9.5
1912	139	53	111	7.6
1913	153	55	120	7.5
1914	156	55	131	9.9
1915	174	57	140	7.7
1916	189	60	159	4.9
1917	219	59	177	9.2
1918	316	62	221	17.4
1919	348	66	297	10.7
1920	355	65	313	6.1
1921	321	65	284	19.7
1922	307	66	262	19.3
1923	296	66	252	12.7
1924	305	67	256	10.7
1925	307	67	265	14.7
1926	310	67	270	20.7
1927	314	68	274	22.5
1928	315	69	272	18.5

[1] Based on Reports in *Statistisk Aarbog*.
[2] At the end of each year, except after 1924 when the reports refer to the end of March.
[3] On the last day in March of each year indicated.
[4] Based on the number unemployed at the end of each month, and the average number of organized workers on which the reports are based.

CHAPTER XXV

UNEMPLOYMENT INSURANCE IN GREAT BRITAIN

1. Introduction

We have briefly traced elsewhere the prevailing intellectual view of unemployment in Great Britain during the nineteenth century, the belief in the need of a work-test to prevent unemployment, the attempts to solve the problem on this false basis, the utter failure of such attempts, and finally the laudable efforts of many of the trade unions to make rational provision for periods of unemployment.[1]

It is significant to point out that a state system of compulsory insurance had few whole-hearted supporters in these years. The trade unions were jealous of their own schemes, the result of years of effort, and were wary lest these be submerged in a national system. Like other groups, they were too absorbed in their own problems to pay much attention to the masses of workers who were not in the trade unions, and for whom the risk of unemployment was much greater. The rising Labor Party was not then an ardent advocate of unemployment insurance. Instead, it concentrated its efforts—as far as unemployment was concerned—in the demand for "Work not Doles," *i.e.,* a demand for the extension of the Unemployed Workmen Act, which was then voluntary. It is also significant to recall that the Minority Report of the Poor Law Commission—due perhaps to the trade union bias of the Webbs—did not propose a compulsory insurance system. Instead it advocated the encouragement and extension of the Ghent System with a state subsidy of 50 per cent to trade unions paying out-of-work benefits. The actual advent of unemployment insurance was, therefore, the more remarkable in the face of the half-hearted support of experts and workers.

[1] See *ante,* pp. 197-201.

2. The First Step

The case for public employment exchanges was quite different. The trade unions, it is true, were sceptical; there was a threat to vested interests. But both the Minority and Majority Reports of the Poor Law Commission advocated the establishment of a system of state controlled employment exchanges. The former actually proposed the compulsory notification of vacancies by both employers and employees "so far as discontinuous or casual employments were concerned." [2] Beveridge's vigorous arguments were not without converts.[3] But strange as it may now appear, it is Mr. Davison's opinion that "Without the impulsive energy of Mr. Churchill, who was the Liberal Minister in charge of the Labour Exchanges Bill, it might never have reached the Statute Book. 'One hundred new Labour Exchanges,' he is reported to have said, 'would be less costly, and more valuable to the nation than one new battleship,' and this statement was prophetic." [4]

The Labour Exchanges Act of 1909 (as we have pointed out) set up a system of employment exchanges under the control of the Board of Trade, and it began operations in January, 1910, under the direction of Mr. W. H. Beveridge. In addition to its aims of adjusting the demand and supply of labor, and the gathering of better unemployment statistics, another objective was kept in view: "To lay the substructure of a scheme of unemployment insurance, i.e., to set up local offices which could apply a test of genuine unemployment by reference to the unsatisfied demand for particular kinds of labor known to exist at that time." [5]

Against some hostility and much scepticism the employment exchanges gradually established themselves in all the industrial centers. Their placement work which was not large—during the first two years there were no more than a million registrations a year—their attempts to break down hostility, and their special efforts to deal with the

---

[2] R. C. Davison, *The Unemployed*, p. 69.
[3] W. H. Beveridge, *Unemployment*, Ch. IX.
[4] Davison, *op. cit.*, p. 68.   [5] *Ibid.*, p. 70.

problem of new additions to the labor supply and casual labor need not detain us. Our especial interest at this point is the machinery which was elaborated for the subsequent establishment of unemployment insurance.

3. The Second Step [6]

In the face of great indifference, approximately two million British workers were insured against unemployment in 1911. To quote Mr. Davison: "The Unemployment Insurance Scheme of 1911 was an almost unsolicited and spontaneous venture on the part of the Board of Trade. Mr. Lloyd George used all his fighting powers to carry the unpopular National Insurance Bill and, as Part II of that Bill, the tentative Unemployment Insurance Scheme crept on to the Statute Book under the shelter of its more conspicuous twin." [7] Now that compulsory unemployment insurance has won its spurs in other countries, we may fail to realize what a significant step this was, and how markedly it broke with the traditions of the past.

As an experimental scheme insurance was limited in scope, including slightly over two million people in the industries which were most exposed to cyclical and seasonal fluctuations—Building, Construction of Works, Ship-building Engineering, Construction of Vehicles, Iron Foundry, and certain kinds of Saw-milling. It is to be noted that in those branches of these industries which were organized the workers had had some experience with their own unemployment contributions and benefits.

The burden of financing this insurance was placed on the workers, the employers, and the State, the first two paying contributions of 2½ d. per week each, and the last, 1½ d. per week.[8] Each insured worker obtained an unemployment book from the local exchange which was valid for one insurance year—July to July—and lodged it with the em-

---

[6] *National Insurance Act, 1911. (Part II—Unemployment Insurance).*
[7] Davison, *op. cit.,* pp. 74-5.
[8] For boys and girls under 18 years of age the rate was 1 d. for the worker and employer, respectively, 2/3 d. for the State.

ployer whose duty it was to make a deduction from the weekly wages and affix stamps for his own and the worker's contribution.

When an insured worker became unemployed, he registered at the local employment exchanges, deposited his unemployment book, and continued signing the register daily. Upon proving to the Insurance Officer that his unemployment was involuntary,[9] his claim to benefits was allowed providing he had paid in ten weekly contributions.[10] Then after a waiting period of six days, if the exchange could not provide suitable employment, the insured worker was entitled to a weekly benefit of 7 s. in the case of a man and 6 s. in the case of a woman, and half rates for boys and girls under 18. But he could draw no more than one week's benefit for each five contributions and no more than fifteen weeks' benefit in any one year. When a claim was exhausted the worker was left to shift for himself or apply to the poor law authorities, since there was no provision for emergency benefits as in later years.

The Act came into force in the middle of 1912, but no benefits were paid for six weeks, thus allowing the accumulation of a reserve fund. In the first two years no great enthusiasm was evoked by the Act due chiefly to the low percentage of unemployment, which was 2.1% in 1913 and 3.3% in 1914. Only once since 1875 had the percentage been lower, and that was in 1899 when it was 2.0%.[11] But this and the low benefits paid placed the fund for the time being on a secure financial basis.

The war years are of no consequence for unemployment insurance. There was virtually no involuntary unemploy-

[9] Decisions of the Insurance Officer could be taken to the local court of referees, consisting of a chairman appointed by the Board of Trade and two other members, taken in rotation from panels of employers and workers. The Insurance Officer or the association through which the worker claimed benefit, but not the individual insured person, could appeal a decision to the Umpire whose word was final. The body of "case law" thus built up was regarded as binding on both the insurance officers and courts of referees.

[10] This rule was substituted in 1914 for the previous rule which required that the insured person had worked at least twenty-six weeks in the preceding 5 years.   [11] Pigou, *Industrial Fluctuations*, pp. 353-4.

ment, and the fund went on collecting the contributions from week to week and augmenting the reserve. The employment exchanges became entirely agencies of placement, the need for which was very great in view of the extensive industrial shifts which were essential.

4. THE FIRST EXTENSION OF INSURANCE [12]

Before the war was over it was apparent that the cessation of the war industries and the transferring of the workers to other occupations would involve a certain amount of unemployment. In anticipation of this event the insurance scheme was extended in 1916 to all munition workers—virtually all workers on war supplies. This extension resulted in four million insured workers by the end of 1919 instead of the original two million. As it turned out, this extension was a financial advantage to the Insurance Fund. As a great many of the war workers were women, they dropped out of work subject to insurance.[13] The men also who lost their war jobs did not in the main fall back on the insurance fund, for they were provided for out of the more generous allowances of the government in the form of the out-of-work donations.[14]

[12] National Insurance (Part II—Munition Workers) Act. 1916.
[13] The number of women workers insured which reached 1,293,000 in 1917-18 dropped to 609,000 in 1919-20. Ministry of Labour, Report on National Unemployment Insurance to July, 1923, p. 25.
[14] The annual amounts paid out in benefits can be seen from the following table for Great Britain and Ireland:

Period	Benefits Paid (1000£)
January 15, 1913–July 12, 1913	208
July 13, 1913–July 18, 1914	531
July 19, 1914–July 17, 1915	419
July 18, 1915–July 15, 1916	79
July 16, 1916–July 14, 1917	34
July 15, 1917–July 13, 1918	86
July 14, 1918–July 12, 1919	153
July 13, 1919–July 17, 1920	1,009

In 1918–1919 the rate of unemployment was approximately 5.3% and the small amount paid out can be accounted for by the fact that most insured workers preferred out-of-work donations as already noted.   In the following year the out-of-work donations were paid only for the first five months to civilian workers and for the entire year to ex-service men or the amount of benefits would have been larger than it was. Ibid., pp. 30–31.   For a discussion of out-of-work donations see post, pp. 408–9.

The features of unemployment insurance discussed above have been retained—with some modifications—to this day. There were, however, a number of provisions in the 1911 Act designed to reduce the volume of unemployment. While they have since been abandoned, there is still sufficient belief in the efficacy of such preventive measures to warrant a brief review of them. Even though the results are not conclusive, they point out at least the inherent difficulties involved.

(1) A refund of one-third of the employer's contribution was provided for each worker continuously employed during the year.[15] These refunds were not extended to the war workers included in the Insurance Act of 1916, and were abolished in 1920. During the years the provision was in force, the refunds amounted to approximately £100,000 per annum. There was little justification for the view that the refunds were an adequate inducement to employers to stabilize their employment, while to the insurance system they were a considerable financial burden.[16]

(2) Refunds equal to the contributions paid were provided for those employers who, during periods of depression in their own enterprises or in the industry, kept their workers on short time and paid both their own and the worker's contributions without making any deduction from the worker's wages. But this often meant that in times of good trade a small subsidy was paid to firms who were in difficulties even though the whole industry was working full time.[17]

(3) To discourage casual employment the rate of contributions for periods of work of less than three days was 1 d. per day, which was higher than the daily rate on a weekly

---

[15] In 1914 the refund was changed to a flat rate of 3 s. per annum, and "continuous" was defined as the payment of 45 weekly contributions during the year. *National Insurance (Part II Amendment) Act. 1914.*

[16] Ministry of Labour, *Report no Unemployment Insurance to July, 1923*, pp. 35-6.

[17] In 1914 an attempt was made to remove this difficulty by substituting the exemption of both employers and workers from the payment of contributions, but only if the entire branch of the trade was depressed. But as there was little short time work during the war, and as it was abolished in 1920, there was no opportunity to test the effectiveness of these refunds.

basis. This too was abolished in 1920.[18] The abolition of this provision, and also of the two above, was due not only to their doubtful effectiveness, but to the cost and administrative difficulties of checking claims and making refunds.

Two other provisions directed to encourage voluntary unemployment insurance are worth noting. (1) A subsidy of one-sixth the amount paid out by any trade union, whether in an insured trade or not, in the form of benefits to unemployed members was provided in the Act of 1911. As payments in excess of 12 s. per week were excluded, this proved a great difficulty in checking claims, especially in the case of members receiving more than this maximum. In 1914 the limitation was removed with the provision that, where the rates exceeded 17 s. per week, the subsidy was subject to a reduction at the discretion of the Board of Trade. In the years this provision was in force the total amount paid out was only £283,307. The extension of insurance in 1920 left no need for voluntary insurance, and the provision was abolished.[19] (2) Trade unions in insured trades which provided unemployment benefits to their members could make arrangements to pay out the state benefits. They could then claim a refund of three-fourths of the amount paid out, but this refund was to be equal to the amount which the workers would have received by direct application to the exchanges. It meant, therefore, that the trade unions had to pay higher rates of benefits, i.e., 9s. 4d. in order to get back the 7 s. By 1920 there were 92 associations with 1,345,900 members who made such arrangements.[20] This provision was retained in the 1920 Act and associations other than trade unions were included. While there was much opposition to this modification on the part of the Labor Party, the condition that associations had to prove their ability to ascertain wage rates and working conditions of all their members and provide the services of

---

[18] It can be said, however, that the provision of the 1920 Act, making the first employer of a casual worker pay the contributions for the entire week, is even more effective.

[19] Ministry of Labour, *Report on Unemployment Insurance to July, 1923*, pp. 38-41.   [20] *Ibid.*, pp. 31-2.

employment exchanges meant that few associations other than trade unions qualified.[21]

5. Out-of-Work Donations

As early as 1915 the government made plans for the payment of out-of-work donations to all those who had served with the Forces during the war, as a means of tiding them over the transition period from military service to civil occupations. While few foresaw the debacle of 1920-21, there was a general realization before the Armistice that the end of the war would involve temporary dislocations of the labor market. As only about one-third of the workers were covered by the insurance system, it was decided to include all civilian workers over fifteen subject to health insurance —this included agricultural and domestic workers—under the plan elaborated for ex-service men. Payment of donations began on December 5th, 1918, and were to be continued for 26 weeks—later increased to 39 during the first twelve months for ex-service men, and for 13 weeks—later increased to 26—for civilians. The rates in both cases were 29 s. for men, 25 s. for women, 6 s. for the first child, and 3 s. for each additional child and half rates for boys and girls under eighteen years of age. One year after the Act was introduced, the rates were scaled down to 20 s. and 15 s. for men and women respectively, in the case of ex-service men and women, but donations were continued for another 50 weeks until March 31, 1921. A similar reduction in the rates for civilian workers was effected six months after the Act was introduced, but with continued allowances for children as above. These latter donations terminated on November 24th, 1919.[22] Out-of-work donation policies were given to applicants at the employment exchanges, and claims for donations were paid under conditions similar to those under the then existing unemployment insurance

---

[21] See Morley, *Unemployment Relief in Great Britain,* pp. 39-41.

[22] Ministry of Labour, *Report on National Unemployment Insurance to July, 1923,* pp. 41-9.

scheme. The local employment committees as well as the insurance officers and courts of referees were utilized to pass on claims.

In the eighteen months during which donations were paid, the government spent sixty-two million pounds, of which forty million went to ex-service men and twenty-two million to civilian workers. As there was no time to make adequate preparation for the payment of donations to the greatly increased number of workers, the actual work was carried on under great pressure, the staffs were inadequate and inexperienced, and there was much complaint of abuses of the system, especially during the earlier months. While it is always difficult to *prove* abuses, a Committee of Inquiry summarizing the evidence concluded that "When account is taken of the difficulties with which the Department had to contend the process of adopting additional safeguards in order to eliminate abuse of the scheme was carried out on the whole as speedily as could reasonably be expected." [23]

The outstanding criticism of the two years after the war is not so much whether the out-of-work donations were well administered, but rather of the delay in extending insurance. These two years were ones of great economic activity and little unemployment, and if, in addition to paying out-of-work donations, the government had introduced the extension of insurance in 1918 instead of at the end of 1920, a substantial reserve would have been accumulated for the collapse of 1921.[24] Early extension was not without its advocates. As early as February, 1918, one of the committees in the Ministry of Reconstruction urged that "unless a scheme of general insurance is devised and launched at the earliest possible date, it may be impossible to avoid the disastrous chaos of unorganized and improvised methods of

[23] *Ibid.,* p. 49.
[24] It should be recalled that by the end of 1920 the limited insurance system had built up a reserve of twenty-two million pounds—due in part at least to the fact that after the Armistice the insured workers paid in contributions but claimed no benefits as the rates of the donations were much higher than those of benefits.

relieving distress." [25] Similarly the Labor Party urged the adoption of a systematic plan as early as 1917.[26] It cannot be said, however, that there was any widespread realization of the economic consequences of the end of the war. In fact there was probably a general belief that full employment would continue.[27]

After the Armistice, opinion gradually changed. The trade unions favored a general extension of unemployment insurance, providing the funds came from the Treasury, while the employers favored an extension providing the funds came out of joint contributions as in the past. The National Industrial Conference called by Mr. Lloyd George in February, 1919, unanimously approved a general extension of insurance and divided only on the contributory principles. Even then there was no great haste to enact the recommendations into law. A bill was not introduced into Parliament until December, 1919, and was not passed until August, 1920, to take effect in November of that year. Hence when the extension was actually effected, England, in common with the other countries, was entering the great economic debacle of 1920-21. To a discussion of the 1920 extension of insurance we turn in the next section.

6. The Post-War Extension of Insurance

The Act of 1920 [28] superseded all previous Acts and became the basis of all subsequent legislation. Insurance was thereby extended to cover eleven and three-quarter million employed persons of 16 and over; the chief exclusions were

---

[25] Morley, *Unemployment Relief in Great Britain*, p. 27.

[26] *Ibid.*, p. 27, note 1. On the other hand the Ministry of Labour reports that industrial opinion generally was opposed to the extension of insurance at the time. See its *Report on National Unemployment Insurance to July, 1923*, p. 6.

[27] A curious illustration of this view is the case of the boot and shoe industry which was included under the Insurance Act of 1916, but which succeeded in getting itself out, because, as it was argued, "the trade had not suffered in the past and would not suffer in the future from an amount of unemployment sufficient to justify its inclusion in the scheme." See R. C. Davison, *The Unemployed*, p. 52.

[28] *Unemployment Insurance Act, 1920.*

of agricultural workers, domestic servants, and certain permanent employees in public service and on the railways.[29] Four classes were retained and the contributions increased to 10 d. per man, 8 1/6 d. per woman, 5⅓ d. per boy, and 4½ d. per girl. The former method of collection was retained, and the payment of benefits was, in the main, on the same conditions as formerly. The waiting period was reduced to but three days, later extended to six. The benefits were increased to 15 s. per week to men, 12 s. to women, and half rates to boys and girls.[30]

The 1920 extension of insurance was formulated under the assumption that the pre-war average of unemployment would prevail in the succeeding years. Had that been the case the rates of contributions would have been adequate to tide the workers over between jobs.[31] But the period of depression set in even before the 1920 Act went into effect and in 1921 the percentage of unemployment rose to seventeen per cent, a figure known in the United States but not in Great Britain. In the years since 1921 the average amount of unemployment has been over ten per cent which is approximately twice as high as the pre-war average.[32]

In this new situation the restrictions of the 1920 Act could not be adhered to without causing great hardship to the unemployed. Not only did the average period of unemployment increase, but thousands of workers who became unemployed did not even begin to make contributions, while thousands of others had so few contributions that the one-in-six rule would have rendered the assistance given them insignificant.

It was at first hoped that the depression which set in at the end of 1920 was but temporary, but as the numbers of

[29] Certain other exemptions for pensioners and dependent persons were provided, for whom, however, the employer had to pay his contributions.

[30] The increase in benefits was much overdue because of the increase in the cost of living. The first change in the rates of benefits since 1911 was made by the *National Insurance (Unemployment) Act, 1919,* when the rates were increased to 11 s. for men and women 18 and over, with half rates for boys and girls 17 to 18.

[31] In 1913 and 1914 less than one per cent of the benefit claimants had reached the maximum of fifteen weeks. Davison, *op. cit.,* p. 99.

[32] See *ante,* Ch. 3.

the unemployed increased month after month, the government was faced with two alternatives. It could revert to the out-of-work donations and pay the bill out of the Treasury or make a departure from the restrictions which had proved their merit in the pre-war period, extend the payment of benefits, and thus pass the major portion of the cost directly onto the workers and employers. It decided on the latter policy, motivated, as Mr. Davison suggests, by the reluctance of the Treasury to shoulder the financial burden, by the existence of the large reserve in the unemployment fund, and by the existence of the adequate administrative machinery in the employment exchanges.[33]

But no government was willing to acknowledge the more or less permanent nature of the depression and reorganize the insurance system upon a ten per cent average of unemployment. Hence the framework of the 1920 Act was retained as an ideal to be attained year after year, and the immediate needs of the unemployed were provided by continuous extensions of benefits, met immediately out of public credits, ultimately to be repaid out of contributions.

In point of fact the hope that a trade revival would make possible a return to the scheme set up in 1920 has proved futile, and the continued depression in coal, shipbuilding, engineering, and textiles, due in part to important technological changes, in part to financial policies followed, and in part to post-war international barriers, has prevented the return to this day. To quote Mr. Davison: "The original fabric of the scheme was retained, and a large proportion of claimants drew benefit only within the statutory conditions, but it was by means of the emergency provisions that the greater part of the unemployment up to the year 1928 was relieved. *Most of the claims were to uncovenanted (extended) rather than to covenated (standard) benefit, and although the actual amounts paid out in the two kinds of benefits have never been shown separately, it is safe to say that the largest drain on the fund was due to uncovenanted benefits.*"[34] We now turn to the frequent changes in

[33] Davison, *op. cit.,* pp. 102-5.   [34] *Ibid.,* p. 107.

these years, which undermined the contributory basis of the insurance system, by the progressive extension of the period in which benefits were paid, by the softening of the requirements for benefit claims, and finally by the elimination of the arithmetical relationship between weeks of contributions and weeks of benefits.

7. The Payment of Benefits, 1921-27

The first extension of benefits [35] was introduced in March, 1921,[36] which provided for two special periods (March 3, 1921, to November 2, 1921; and November 3, 1921, to July 2, 1922) of thirty-five weeks each, during which the fifteen weeks' rule was temporarily suspended. During each of these periods a maximum of 16 weeks' benefit could be paid.

Before the end of the first period a second act was passed which made further [37] extetnsions. It authorized the Minister of Labour at his discretion to extend payments of benefits up to twenty-two weeks in each period, to waive the one-in-six rule, and to refer claims for uncovenated benefits to the local employment committees [38] instead of to the insurance officers.

There was thus introduced a second kind of benefit with but a tenuous relationship to contributions paid. Hence between 1921 and 1927 [39] there were two distinct forms of

[35] The Act of 1920 contained a temporary provision for the first twelve months, by which eight weeks' benefit could be paid after 4 weeks' contributions. A further temporary measure was provided in December, 1920, so that any person who was engaged in insurable employment during ten weeks since December 31, 1919, or during four weeks since July 4, 1920, could receive eight weeks' benefit up to March 31, 1921.

[36] *The Unemployment Insurance Act, 1921.*

[37] *Ibid. (No. 2) Act, 1921.*

[38] The employment committees composed of equal numbers of representatives of employers and workers in the district covered by an employment exchange were first attached to the exchanges in 1917 to advise them on the purely industrial problems of placement. The chairman was appointed by the Ministry of Labour. When the work of passing, first, on out-of-work donation claims and, later, on uncovenanted benefit claims was turned over to them, the committees worked through sub-committees which were popularly known as "Rotas" or Rota Committees. For an evaluation of their work, see Davison, *op. cit.*, pp. 122-25 and Morley, *op. cit.*, pp. 101-2.

[39] *The Unemployment Insurance Act, 1922,* as amended by *The Unem-*

benefit. For both the claimant had to satisfy the first statutory condition of thirty contributions at any time or eight in the two preceding insurance years.[40] If the claimant could show twenty contributions since the beginning of the last preceding insurance year his claim was considered for standard benefits. If he exhausted his claim or did not qualify, he became eligible to uncovenanted—renamed "extended" in 1924—benefits, which were decided not by the insurance officers, but by the local employment committees. In addition to the statutory requirements for standard benefits the claimant for extended benefits had to satisfy four other conditions: (1) that he was normally in insurable work and would normally seek his job in such work, (2) that such work would normally be available for him, (3) that in view of the opportunities prevailing he had had a reasonable amount of employment during the two preceding years, and (4) that he was making every reasonable effort to obtain employment.

While it is true that these extended benefits were not a statutory right of the insured person, but a privileged grant made at the discretion of the Minister of Labour when he deemed it "expedient in the public interest" to do so, in actual fact as far as the attitude of the workers and a large body of public opinion was concerned, there was little to distinguish the two forms of benefit.[41]

ployment Insurance (No. 2) Act, 1922, and the *Unemployment Insurance Act, 1923,* provided a third and fourth special period (April 5, 1922—November 1, 1922, and November 2, 1922—October 17, 1923) during which a maximum of 22 weeks and 44 weeks of benefits respectively was authorized. The last named Act as amended by the Act of 1924 established an insurance year—October 18, 1923, to October 18, 1924—during which a maximum of 41 weeks' benefit was authorized. During each of these periods there were gaps provided of varying intervals during which the unemployed were thrown on the poor-law authorities, but the Labor Government abolished these gaps and by the *Unemployment Insurance (No. 2) Act of 1924,* made the payment of benefits continuous and unlimited.

[40] It will be recalled that the statutory requirement under the 1920 Act was twelve contributions preceding the claim. The second Act of 1924 changed this to thirty contributions within the preceding two to three years. But this was intended for normal times and the above conditions have been continuously substituted.

[41] Under his discretionary power the Minister of Labour excluded from extended benefits (1) single persons living with relatives to whom they could reasonably look for support, (2) married women whose husbands

One of the shortcomings of the Act of 1920 was that, in keeping with the policy of flat contributions, there was no provision for the greater need of men or women with dependents. When the benefit rates, which were increased in March, 1921, were reduced to the 1920 level in July, 1921, the complaints resulting from this need increased. What it meant actually was that a large number of the unemployed had recourse to the poor law authorities to supplement their income from benefits. Precedent for allowances was established by the out-of-work donations of 1919 and 1920, and the heavy expenditures involved in the extension of benefits militated against an increase in the rate of benefits. Hence in November, 1921, it was decided to introduce dependents' allowances as a temporary measure and to levy a separate contribution for them.[42] The rates were 5 s. for a dependent wife or husband and 1 s. for each child. These allowances were made a permanent part of the insurance system in 1922 and the rates for children were increased to 2 s. in 1924.

So much for the official regulations regarding the payment of benefits. There were also administrative changes, which tended on the whole to restrict the payment of benefits. Thus, to quote Mr. Davison, "It seems clear, however, that in the year 1925, quite independent of any changes in legislation there was a tightening up of benefit administration, and this affected claimants to standard as much as claimants to extended benefit." [43] Statistical evidence is not easily available, but in 1924, 267,579 claims—chiefly for standard benefit—were disallowed by the Chief Insurance Officer and 47,907 by the Courts of Referees on appeal; in 1925 the numbers were 442,000 and 90,026 respectively.[44]

were employed and received sufficient income, (3) married men whose wives were employed and received sufficient income, (4) short-time workers who received sufficient income, and (5) certain classes of aliens. The Labor Government took away the discretionary power and made extended benefits a right of the insured worker. But the discretionary power was restored in 1925. See *Report of the Unemployment Insurance Committee, Vol. I* (1927), p. 17.

[42] *Unemployed Workers' Dependents (Temporary Provision) Act, 1921.*
[43] Davison, *op. cit.*, pp. 117-18.   [44] *Ibid.*, p. 118.

The chief ground for disallowance turned on "not genuinely seeking work." It should be recalled that registration at the Exchanges was no longer adequate and very often personal search for work was required. Similarly a large number of claims to extended benefits were disallowed on the ground of "not making reasonable efforts to obtain employment."

There were, of course, substantial differences in the strictness with which claims were scrutinized from district to district. In the depressed areas where no new industries developed to take the place of the old ones and where, as a result, unemployment often lasted for two years or more, it was useless to insist on a "reasonable period of employment" in the preceding two years. Nor would it have been of any point to insist on a personal search for work when it was well known that jobs were not available. But in London and the South of England, the districts in which the new industries sprang up, stricter standards were established and personal search for work often made a condition of allowing claims.[45]

8. CONTRIBUTIONS

The various changes in the rates of contributions up to the Act of 1927 are set out in table 30 on the opposite page. The increase in the aggregate contributions for men in 1920 from 6⅔ d. to 10 d. was less than the increase in the rate of benefits. The further increase in the rate of benefits, and the extension of these in March, 1921, left the contributions wholly inadequate.[46] First to go was the reserve which had been built up by the limited insurance system, which was exhausted by the middle of 1921. But even the reduction of benefits in July, 1921, to the 1920 level and the increase in contributions first to 1s. 6¾ d. per man and, as a result of dependents' allowances, to 2s. 1¾d. left the income inadequate. The difference in each year was made up

[45] See Davison, op. cit., pp. 120-21.
[46] The act of March, 1921, also increased the rates of contributions, but not to take effect until July, 1921, when, however, they were again changed.

TABLE 30

RATES OF CONTRIBUTION 1911-1927

DATE	MEN			WOMEN		
	Employer	Worker	State	Employer	Worker	State
	d.	d.	d.	d.	d.	d.
1911	2½	2½	1⅔	2½	2½	1⅔
1920	4	4	2	3½	3	1⅔
1921 (July) . .	8	7	3¾	7	6	3¼
1921 (Nov.) . .	10	9	6¾	8	7	5¼
1926	8	7	6			

DATE	BOYS			GIRLS		
	Employer	Worker	State	Employer	Worker	State
	d.	d.	d.	d.	d.	d.
1911	1	1	⅔	1	1	⅔
1920	2	2	1⅓	2	1½	1
1921 (July) . .	4	3½	1⅞	3½	3	1⅝
1921 (Nov.) . .	5	4½	3⅞	4½	4	3⅝
1926						

by public credits, so that by July, 1920, the Treasury had advanced at interest, twenty-three million pounds.[47]

When the insurance system was first introduced the workers and employers paid equal shares and the State provided one-third of the contributions of both. Since 1921 the workers have had a slight advantage over the employers, but the State contribution has been reduced to one-fourth. Now whether the State should make any contributions and how large these should be, has to be decided in each country separately upon a multiplicity of factors. But something can be said in favor of an increased rather than diminished state share in England during these years. In fairness to those workers who had accumulated the reserve by 1920 the State should have assumed a greater share than it did in the extension of insurance. There is

[47] To anticipate later events, on September 27, 1930, the insurance system was in debt to the Treasury to the extent of fifty million pounds. See *Ministry of Labour Gazette,* October, 1930, p. 380.

also some evidence that some workers and employers have been paying more than their share. There can be no quarrel with the fact that under an insurance system the regularly employed workers and their employers must pay for the irregularly employed workers and their employers, providing the risk of unemployment is uniform. It is well known that this latter condition is not fulfilled and an "investigation made in 1926 revealed that over a period of five years, only 52 per cent of the insured who had paid contributions had at any time drawn benefit." [48] This would argue for a differentiation of the contribution rates among workers, which in practice is difficult to work out. A state subsidy makes up in part the disadvantages to the steadily employed workers, and the fact that the 48 per cent of the workers had to pay for the extended benefit as well lends support to the argument that the state share should have been increased during these years.

9. THE BLANESBURGH COMMITTEE

By 1925 there was a great deal of dissatisfaction with the existing unemployment insurance practices. There were those who wanted benefits to all and there were those who wanted the numbers receiving benefits greatly reduced. There were accusations of fraud and pauperization. [49] As

[48] See Davison, op. cit., p. 108.

[49] In spite of the oft-repeated accusations of fraud and abuse of benefit administration, little evidence has ever been adduced to support them. Nine separate investigations have been made since 1920, and all have failed to detect evidence for such accusations. The ninth investigation carried out in 1925 considered 192,480 claims in 78 local offices. Of these a sample of 51,959 was selected for analysis. The results showed that the investigators suspected only 83 cases of fraud. They further doubted the validity of 8,900 cases in which benefits were allowed. Of these 6,468 were for extended benefits and doubt arose over the indefinite issues of whether the claimants had had "a reasonable period of employment within the last two years" and whether they were making "reasonable efforts to obtain employment," issues over which there is much room for difference of opinion. That there are attempts to obtain benefits under false pretenses none will deny. But there is no reason to suspect that many are successful. Thus in 1925 there were 11,413 cases suspected of fraud, 1964 were prosecuted and 1844 convicted, of which 468 received prison sentences. Report of the Unemployment Insurance Committee, 1927, Vol. I, pp. 18-23.

the Blanesburgh Committee wrote later, "In dealing with these problems there is room for acute divergence of opinion, and the principles, the administration, 'the alleged deficiencies, excesses, and ulterior consequence of the present system had, before our inquiry began, become a topic of far-reaching comment and keen criticism." [50]

A committee was therefore appointed with the general reference: *To consider in the light of experience gained in the working of the Unemployment Insurance Scheme, what changes in the Scheme, if any, ought to be made.* The coal strike delayed the report until January, 1927.

The chief point of contention was the desirability of the dual system of relief which had replaced the system of 1920. The committee was therefore confronted with two alternatives. There were some who advocated a strict insurance system "under which contributors received benefits bearing some proportion of their own payments." In such an event there would be no room for extended benefits, and unless the needs of many unemployed workers were callously disregarded, some modification of the Poor Law support would be entailed. The other alternative, advocated in the main by those who were in favor of a non-contributory system, was a "provision of benefit for all genuinely unemployed people, no matter how long they are unemployed, provided they are genuine in the sense already indicated." Under this second alternative there would also be but one form of benefit, but there would be no need for any other. In this event either the contributions would have to be greatly increased, or the state share greatly increased, or both. The Committee recommended neither of these alternatives and decided "to steer a middle course." [51]

While the Committee recommended but one form of benefit, it suggested a statutory condition of 30 contributions within the previous two years at each three monthly review which would have disbarred many who were then receiving extended benefits. It felt that some mechanical test was desirable, that the one-in-six rule was too strict,

---

[50] *Ibid.,* p. **7.**   [51] *Ibid.,* pp. 28-31,

and that its proposal would provide for all who were genuinely unemployed. As to those unable to get 15 weeks' work out of 52 the Committee argued, "It will be conceded that in the generality of cases, persons with so poor a record of employment could scarcely claim still to be in the insured field; that there is grave doubt as to the genuineness of their search of work; and that the exclusion of such individuals is only fair to the general body of insured contributors." [52] Whatever the merits of this argument in a normal situation, it certainly is not applicable to the economic conditions which prevailed in Great Britain before and since the Blanesburgh Report. A sample analysis of April, 1927, showed that as many as 13.8 per cent of those who were then claiming benefits had less than 30 contributions in the two previous years, and in some industries the percentage was much higher. At this rate the Blanesburgh condition would have excluded some 130,000 out of every million applying for benefit. And by no stretch of the imagination could these 130,000 be all set aside with the remark that they were not genuinely seeking work.[53]

After reviewing the merits of contributions in proportion to income received, the Committee approved the existing method with slight modifications by the addition of two new classes, young men and young women. The English objection to contributions according to income is based on administrative difficulties. On the other hand it has always been felt that benefits adequate for adults might lead to idleness on the part of younger persons with smaller incomes. The former division into four classes was an attempt to avert the situation and the Committee carried this one step further. The lower contributions of these two new classes would also lighten their burden, while the lower benefits would be a distinct economy to the system. The rates proposed are set out below:

	d.		d.
Men	5	Young Women (18 to 22) . .	3
Women	3½	Boys (16 to 18)	2½
Young Men (18 to 21) . . .	4	Girls (16 to 18)	2

[52] *Ibid.*, p. 41.   [53] Davison, *op. cit.*, p. 143.

As a temporary measure to extinguish the debt which then amounted to over 20 million pounds the Committee recommended an additional contribution of 1d. in the case of men and young men and ½d. in the case of the others. The state contribution was to be slightly less than one-third of the total.

In fixing these contributions and the benefits [54] the Committee was guided by the Report of the Government Actuary who wrote that "Taking the broad view of the problem to which I am limited by the actual conditions, I am led to conclude that in arranging the finance of the permanent scheme, it would be advisable to provide for a rate of unemployment of six per cent, on the average, throughout the whole of the period commonly regarded as a 'trade cycle.' " [55] This, as we now know, has so far proved a vain hope.

As there was to be but one form of benefits, the Committee recommended the abolition of the Rota Committees in so far as benefits were concerned, and the passing of all claims through the Insurance Officer, the Court of Referees, and the Umpire.

Since the Committee reviewed the entire insurance system it will be best to indicate its other important recommendations in the description of the new Insurance Act in which they were embodied.

10. THE ACT OF 1927 [56]

In fixing contributions, the government disregarded the recommendations of the Blanesburgh Committee and left the contributions unchanged except for the two new classes which were incorporated in the Act. The suggested benefit

---

[54] The recommended rates of benefits were 17 s. and 15 s. for men and women respectively, 10 s. and 8 s. for young men and young women—18 to 21—respectively, and 6 s. and 5 s. for boys and girls—16 to 18—respectively, with dependents' allowances of 7 s. for one adult dependent and 2 s. for children under 14.

[55] *Report of the Unemployment Insurance Committee, 1927*, Vol. I, p. 89.

[56] This act did not go into effect until April, 1928.

rates were adopted except that for the two new classes six subdivisions were created. The rates of contributions and benefits are set out below:

CLASS	EMPLOYER'S CONTRIBUTION	WORKER'S CONTRIBUTION	STATE CONTRIBUTION	TOTAL	WEEKLY BENEFITS
	d.	d.	d.	d.	s.
Men (21 to 65)[1]	8	7	6	21	17
Women (21 to 65)[1]	7	6	4½	17½	15
Young Men (20 to 21) (19 to 20) (18 to 19)	7	6	5¼	18¼	14 12 10
Young Women (20 to 21) (19 to 20) (18 to 19)	6	5	3¾	14¾	12 10 8
Boys (16 to 18)	4	3½	3	10½	6
Girls (16 to 18)	3½	3	2¼	8¾	5
Adult Dependent					7
Dependent Children . . .					2

[1] The age limit of 65 is now established as since January 2, 1928, persons over 65 become eligible for a state pension. But employers still pay their contributions for workers over 65.

The recommendation of the Blanesburgh Committee providing for but one kind of benefit was adopted, so that all claims are now decided by the Insurance Officer, with appeals to the Court of Referees and the Umpire. The Court of Referees must now review all cases involving the payment of benefit for thirteen weeks during a period not exceeding six months.

The statutory conditions for the receipt of benefit are (1) that 30 contributions have been paid during the two years preceding the claim, (2) that the claim has been made in the prescribed manner and the claimant has proved continuous unemployment since the date of his application (3) that the claimant is capable and willing to work (4) that the claimant is "genuinely seeking work" and unable to obtain "suitable employment" and (5) that, if required, the claimant has attended an approved course of instruction.

The first statutory condition was not to, go into effect until April, 1929, and insured persons unable to fulfill it were eligible for benefits under the following conditions:

1. The claimant can show eight contributions during the two years previous to the claim of benefit, or thirty contributions at any time; and

2. The claimant is normally in insurable employment, will normally seek to obtain his livelihood in it; and

3. During the previous two years the claimant has been employed to such an extent as was reasonable having regard to all the circumstances of the case and in particular to the opportunities for obtaining insurable employment during that period.[57]

Since registration at the Employment Exchange is no longer adequate, the interpretation of "genuinely seeking work" has proved and will continue to prove a difficult matter. The Blanesburgh Committee grappled with the problem and recommended a statutory definition which would take account of the following conditions: (1) Period or periods of unemployment, (2) Qualifications, experience or training in the particular occupation, (3) Record of previous employment, (4) Prospect of becoming reëmployed in the previous or usual occupations, (5) Efforts to obtain employment which claimant has a reasonable chance of obtaining.[58]

The payment of benefits to workers who refuse employment in an occupation other than their own has long been a standing criticism of insurance since it may interfere with the mobility of labor. But how long a claimant may stand

---

[57] These transitory conditions were extended first to April, 1930, and again to April, 1931, and the cost of the extension is borne by the Exchequer. The last condition noted above has been repealed. See *The Ministry of Labour Gazette*, November, 1929, p. 399.

[58] While these conditions were not made part of the law, they have for some time been considered by the Umpire and Courts of Referees. See Appendix 3 of the *Report of the Unemployment Insurance Committee* (1927), Vol. 1, pp. 93-6, where terms of a decision by the Umpire in 1926 are set forth.

out for employment in his own occupation is difficult to determine. The 1927 Act laid down the following principles:

After the lapse of such an interval after the date on which an insured contributor becomes unemployed as, in the circumstances of the case, is reasonable, employment shall not be deemed to be unsuitable by reason only that it is employment of a kind other than employment in the usual occupation of the insured contributor, if it is employment at a rate of wage not lower, and on conditions not less favorable, than those generally observed by agreement between associations of employers and of employees, or failing such agreement, than those generally recognized by good employees. This, however, still leaves the issue to the judgment of the persons deciding the claims.

In an economy where occupations are interrelated, it has always been difficult to decide when workers unemployed because of a trade dispute should not receive benefits. In the coal strike of 1926 the Umpire had disqualified many from benefits because other members of the grade or class to which they belonged were helping in the dispute, even though the other members were not employed in the same premises or district.[59] The 1927 Act made further interpretation less strict, and workers are disqualified from benefits only if directly interested in a dispute unless "other members" of their class or grade employed in the same premises as themselves participate in the strike.[60]

There is still much dissatisfaction with the British Unemployment Insurance System.[61] But there are few, if any,

---

[59] See Davison, *op. cit.*, p. 154.

[60] Another amendment introduced in 1927 is the abolition of the right of industries to contract out of the general scheme. In 1919 it was expected that many industries—especially those not subject to great unemployment—would set up their own schemes and thus not be subject to the high contribution rates. Only the Insurance and Banking Industry have actually contracted out. The depression of 1921 led to the abandonment of the projected schemes, and in 1923 no further schemes were allowed until the Fund had discharged its debt. The 1927 Act permanently removes the possibility of such separate schemes, except that the two in existence are permitted to continue.

[61] See Beveridge, Unemployment, *The Political Quarterly*, July, September, 1930, pp. 326-50.

who advocate a return to the Poor-Law Principles of the nineteenth century. None but a person with a strong class bias has accused unemployment insurance of fostering a distaste for work and a preference for benefits among the British workers.

But there are some grounds for believing that the insurance system strengthens the resistance of the trade unions against wage cuts which might otherwise take place and reduce the volume of unemployment, and that the payment of benefits for partial unemployment tends to increase the practice of it.[62] Thus Professor Cannan suggests a lengthening of the waiting period which would at once discourage partial unemployment and provide larger funds for the more serious cases of long-time unemployment.[63]

But it is clear that for a prolonged period of unemployment as obtains in Great Britain, maintenance is not enough, to use Mr. Davison's phrase. Not only must the Employment Exchanges return more vigorously to the problem of adjusting the labor market, but until such times as normal economic influences empty the depressed areas, great efforts must be directed to training the new additions to the labor supply away from blind alley occupations and to retraining the skilled and semi-skilled workers for occu-

---

[62] The effect of insurance on wage rates can only be discussed from a theoretical standpoint. See A. C. Pigou, Wage Theory and Unemployment, *Economic Journal*, September, 1927. But it has been asserted again and again that the treatment of three days of unemployment within six consecutive days or two periods of unemployment of at least three days each separated by a period of not more than ten weeks' work as continuous unemployment, and the payment of benefits in such cases has led to organized short time and hence immobility in the labor market. See for example, the *Report of the Blanesburgh Committee*, p. 62, and Henry Clay, *The Post-War Unemployment Problem*, p. 118. While there is no mention of the industry in which this has taken place, it is generally understood that the cotton trades are the chief culprits. It is worth noting, however, that for some time before the insurance system was introduced, "*the working of short time during depression has become a regular practise organized and advised by the employers' associations.*" W. H. Beveridge, *Unemployment*, p. 221. Mr. Beveridge emphasizes the point that while this practice was followed in many trades and industries, it was in the *cotton and coal trades* that the practice was on an organized basis.

[63] Cannan, The Problem of Unemployment, *Economic Journal*, March, 1930, pp. 45-55.

pations in which they have a possibility of employment.[64] It is equally important to remove those who verge on the unemployable class from the insurance funds in order to lighten the direct burden that now falls on employment.

[64] For an evaluation of the limited scale upon which this has been carried out, see Davison, *op. cit.*, pp. 154-156; 217-257.

CHAPTER XXVI

UNEMPLOYMENT INSURANCE IN GERMANY

1. Introduction

The absence of unemployment insurance in Germany until very recently is all the more marked because of the other highly developed forms of social insurance. The trade union and Socialist organizations continuously demanded an ultimate compulsory scheme, and immediate state and municipal aid to voluntary insurance funds. But even this latter form made but little progress except in some of the smaller cities.[1]

The dislocation due to the war, the poverty of the German people, the violently fluctuating character of unemployment with financial instability, and the revolutionary spirit made some form of relief imperative. Hence from 1918 to 1927 there followed an array of orders and counter-orders, calling upon the municipalities and states, private and public enterprises to provide relief for the unemployed. We have noted elsewhere [2] the elaborate schemes of relief works which were provided out of public funds to create employment. Even the law of 1923 which provided a fund contributed in the main by workers and employers was not divorced from the principles of need and the work-test. Not only did this satisfy none of the groups, but the whole process proved inadequate and in the end Germany was forced to abandon the dogmas of poor relief and follow the path marked out some two decades earlier by Great Britain.

As the German scheme is the only one on a par with that of Great Britain, and as it is sufficiently differentiated from the latter, it warrants a full description of its provisions and

[1] Joseph L. Cohen, *Insurance Against Unemployment,* pp. 140-152.
[2] *Ibid.,* pp. 294-99.

an analysis of the experiences during the short period it has prevailed.

2. The Unemployment Insurance System Established by the Act of 1927 [3]

About seventeen million workers were included in the unemployment insurance system. While the exceptions from unemployment insurance were very similar to those of Great Britain, the striking difference was the inclusion of about a million of the less regularly employed agricultural workers.[4] The larger part of the agricultural workers were, however, excluded. These included owners or tenants who worked on hire on neighboring farms but, in general, lived on the proceeds of their land; agricultural laborers on a yearly or indefinite contract who got six months notice (they come under the law six months before the end of their employment); domestic servants in agriculture because of the unusually favorable labor market. Others excluded were workers in inland or coastal fisheries having a share in the catch and certain forestry workers. In the urban centers all apprentices under a two year contract were excluded but came under the law six months prior to the termination of their apprenticeship. Domestic workers earning more than 3600 marks were excluded as were salaried workers, mercantile and clerical employees, theatrical employees, education and public welfare employees, and crews of German seagoing ships earning over 6000 marks. Casual laborers working on jobs lasting less than a week could be exempted from unemployment insurance by petition if they worked less than 26 weeks in the year. This means that about four-fifths of the wage and small salary earners were included in the scheme. With their dependents of about 13 millions they constitute about 50 per cent of the total German population.[5]

[3] International Labour Office, *Legislative Series, 1927—Germany 5.*
[4] R. C. Davison, Unemployment Relief in Germany, *Economic Journal,* March, 1930, p. 142.
[5] Carroll, *Unemployment Insurance in Germany,* p. 115.

The entire burden of financing unemployment insurance and the employment exchanges was placed upon the workers and employers. The government was to participate only in times of great unemployment with loans, when the contributions were inadequate, and to provide for emergency relief, which was to be contributed in the ratio of ⅘ from the federal government and ⅕ from local authorities. In actual practice, as we shall see, the federal government has had to assume a great deal of the burden.

The contributions, unlike those in Great Britain, were fixed as a percentage of the representative wage in each class,[6] to be paid in equal parts by the workers and employers.[7] The employer deducts the workers' share from the pay and forwards it along with his own contribution to the local sickness insurance agency, thus avoiding any great extra expense in collection. These contributions are then transmitted to the District Employment Offices, and are considered as composed of two parts, one to provide for the expenses of the district office and to pay the benefits of the local offices in the district and the other to pay the expenses of the national office and to provide a National Fund to take care of 600,000 unemployed workers for three months. The maximum rate was fixed at 3 per cent and was established as the initial rate until such a fund was accumulated. Reductions could then be made in each district after it showed an excess of income over expenditure for three consecutive months. The reduction by districts was intended to encourage local economies. Any district not having sufficient income could obtain grants from the national reserve. No reduction for an industry or enterprise within a district was permitted.

Benefits. The Act of 1927 provided for two distinct forms of benefits: (1) standard benefits paid out of the contribu-

---

[6] See *post*, p. 433, for wage classes established.

[7] In fixing contributions and benefits according to the income of the workers, Germany has carried the English differentiation of the insured workers into men and women, adult and juvenile to its logical conclusion. The step was undoubtedly facilitated by the classification in the sickness insurance system which although different from that adopted for unemployment insurance, provided the necessary experience.

tions of workers and employers and (2) emergency benefits paid out of state and municipal funds.

Standard Benefits. Rights to standard benefits were based on three qualifications. (1) Persons must be able and willing to work, (2) they must acquire eligibility, (3) they must not have exhausted their claims.

(1) A person able to work is "one capable of earning, in an employment suited to his strength and ability which can reasonably be assigned to him in view of his training and previous occupation, at least one-third of the sum usually earned" by persons with similar training in the same neighborhood.[8] But to encourage the search for work in other occupations, there was a provision that after an unemployed person had received aid for nine weeks,—the period might be extended—or "during a period of unemployment customary in his occupation," he could not refuse a job because of his training or previous employment unless its performance would be seriously disadvantageous to his career.

In order to receive benefits a person had to prove involuntary unemployment. However, he might justifiably refuse to accept employment (1) for which the standard wage was not paid; (2) which had become open on account of strikes or lockouts (only for the duration of the strike or lockout); (3) where the conditions of the job were physically or morally objectionable; (4) where the support of dependants was not adequately provided for.[9] Those who refused to accept a position without sufficient reason, even though it was away from home, were denied benefits for four weeks, (this period might be reduced to two weeks), as were those who left their positions without sufficient reason or because

[8] An insured person receiving pecuniary sick benefit, pecuniary maternity benefit, or substitute benefits which take the place of these payments, was excluded from unemployment benefits. This is in marked contrast to the practice in England.

[9] A further condition was set in the case of unemployed persons under 21 "in respect of whom the conditions for vocational retraining or further vocational training are not fulfilled, and of unemployed persons who receive emergency benefit." In these cases benefit could "be made conditional on the performance of work insofar as opportunity exists for same." This refers to employment on relief works. See *post*, p. 439.

of their behavior, and those who refused to undergo vocational training. Those out of work because of strikes or lockouts were not entitled to benefits, but "where the unemployment is caused indirectly by a strike or lockout, especially outside of the establishment, occupational group or place of employment or residence of the unemployed, benefit shall be paid if the refusal of support would be an undue hardship." [10]

(2) No insured person became eligible to receive standard benefits until he had worked in an occupation subject to unemployment insurance for at least 26 weeks in the preceding twelve months. But exceptions were made for employment in certain occupations for temporary work, care in institutions by order of authorities, sickness or childbirth by an extension of the qualifying period to three years.

(3) The law authorized the payment of standard benefits for a period not exceeding 26 weeks. [11] After this eligibility must be once again established. [12] A waiting period of 7 days from the day of registration of unemployment was provided during which no benefits could be paid. But suspension of

[10] Whether an undue hardship is involved was to be decided by the management committee of the District Employment Office or by the executive of the Reichsanstalt in case of a strike extending beyond the District.

The definition of "undue hardship" has proved difficult. It has since been agreed that no "undue hardship" is caused by indirect unemployment resulting from a strike within Germany, if it lasts for less than fourteen days; if the persons unemployed stand to gain directly by the dispute; if the payment of benefits may exert an influence on the result; if the unemployment is the result of a strike or lockout in the same establishment, unless it is due to a strike or lockout of salaried employees or foremen, in which case the local labor office can decide the issue; if unemployment results from the failure of the supply of electricity, gas, water, or intermediate goods as a result of a strike or lockout. Carroll, *op. cit.*, p. 98.

[11] Workers in receipt of standard benefits are also maintained in other forms of social insurance. This has proved quite a drain on the insurance fund. During the first year these took about eight per cent of the total expenditure. Carroll, *op. cit.*, p. 84.

[12] The governing body of the Reichsanstalt could extend the maximum duration of benefit beyond the 26 weeks but not for more than 39 weeks if the labor market was particularly unfavorable. This extension could be limited to particular occupations or districts and the power to extend could be delegated to management committees of State Employment Offices.

the waiting period was authorized in the following cases: (1) employment lasting less than 6 weeks, (2) short time employment lasting less than a fortnight during which remuneration is reduced by at least one-third, (3) incapacity for work for at least one week, (4) detention in an institution for at least a week by order of a public authority. In other cases the governing body of the Reichsanstalt was authorized to reduce the waiting period to three days and prolong it in case of unemployment customary in the trade. The latter was designed especially to encourage the search for temporary work on the part of seasonal workers.

Benefits as well as contributions were fixed on the basis of the wage class in which the unemployed person finds himself. The eleven classes into which all persons were divided and the rates of standard benefits are shown in Table 31 on the opposite page.

On the surface this appears to be in great contrast with the practice in Great Britain where contributions and benefits are not based on the wages received. But the differences are not as great as they appear, "since Class I presumably includes only apprentices and Classes II to IV only a small number of unskilled women and youthful workers.[13] These first four classes are, therefore, comparable with the class of women and youths in Great Britain who pay lower contributions and receive lower rates of benefits than the adult male workers.[14] While the contributions are on the basis of a fixed percentage of the unit wage, the benefits are on the basis of a declining percentage through the seventh class, but an increasing absolute amount throughout all classes. The justification for such distinctions can be made not on the basis of risk, but of need. The lower paid groups can ill afford large weekly contributions. But as they live very near the minimum of subsistence, they are given a very large percentage of their weekly wages. The higher wage classes are, on the other hand, accustomed to a very high

[13] Wunderlich, German Unemployment Insurance, *Quarterly Journal of Economics*, February, 1928, p. 299.

[14] For the wage distribution of the recipients of standard benefits see Table 34 at the end of the chapter.

TABLE 31

WAGE CLASSES AND RATES OF STANDARD BENEFITS WITH ALLOWANCES FOR DEPENDENTS

Wage Class	Wage Range (Marks)	Unit Wage (Marks)	Principal Weekly Benefit Percentage of Unit Wage	Principal Weekly Benefit Marks	One Person %	One Person Marks	Two Persons %	Two Persons Marks	Three Persons %	Three Persons Marks	Four Persons %	Four Persons Marks	Five or More Persons %	Five or More Persons Marks
I	0 –10	8	75	6.00	80	6.40	80	6.40	80	6.40	80	6.40	80	6.40
II	10.1–14	12	65	7.80	70	8.40	75	9.00	80	9.60	80	9.60	80	9.60
III	14.1–18	16	55	8.80	60	9.60	65	10.40	70	11.20	75	12.00	75	12.00
IV	18.1–24	21	47	9.87	52	10.92	57	11.97	62	13.02	67	14.07	72	15.12
V	24.1–30	27	40	10.80	45	12.15	50	13.50	55	14.85	60	16.20	65	17.55
VI	30.1–36	33	40	13.20	45	14.85	50	16.50	55	18.15	60	19.80	65	21.45
VII	36.1–42	39	37.5	14.63	42.5	16.58	47.5	18.53	52.5	20.48	57.5	22.43	62.5	24.38
VIII	42.1–48	45	35	15.75	40	18.00	45	20.25	50	22.50	55	24.75	60	27.00
IX	48.1–54	51	35	17.85	40	20.40	45	22.95	50	25.50	55	28.05	60	30.60
X	54.1–60	57	35	19.95	40	22.80	45	25.65	50	28.50	55	31.35	60	34.20
XI	60.1 and over	63	35	22.05	40	25.20	45	28.35	50	31.50	55	34.65	60	37.80

standard of living. If they are not to be reduced to the level of the lower wage groups they must receive a higher absolute income.

In addition the governing body of the Reichsanstalt, with the consent of the Federal Minister of Labor was authorized to pay benefits for partial unemployment to employees engaged in an employment liable to insurance who, during any calendar week, failed to complete the number of hours work customary owing to shortage of work and who, consequently, suffered wage reductions. The benefit could not be higher than unemployment benefit which the employee would receive if unemployed, and with the remuneration could not exceed five-sixths of the full remuneration.

Emergency Benefits. The second form of benefits authorized in the law of 1927 was the granting of emergency benefits to unemployed workers who, in addition to being able and willing to work, were also in *necessitous circumstances,* if (1) they could not show twenty-six contributions but had been employed in an insurable employment for at least thirteen weeks in the previous year or (2) they exhausted their claims to standard benefits. The emergency benefits could be granted at the discretion of the Minister of Labor "when the situation in the labor market persistently remains particularly unfavorable," and could be limited to particular districts or occupations.[15] These benefits are similar to the non-covenanted benefits provided in Great Britain after the war, and can be made conditional on the acceptance of employment on public works.

Administration. The general administrative features of the German system are the unification of employment exchanges with unemployment insurance,[16] the national char-

---

[15] See *post*, pp. 450-53, for the actual administration of emergency benefits.

[16] From the point of view of placement some objections can be raised against this unification. Not only does the administration of insurance add to the burden of the exchanges, but it is often asserted that there is a tendency to subordinate the proper allocation of workers to mere finding of jobs to avoid paying benefits. From the point of view of insurance administration this unification is all to the good. For a description of the Employment Exchanges see *ante*, pp. 304-5.

acter of the system, the control by the economic interests concerned, and the subordination but retention of the local and provincial political authorities. The control by workers and employers was a logical step to the general agreement that these should assume the entire financial burden; it also satisfied the objections of those who were afraid of "political and bureaucratic pressure." [17]

To administer both the employment exchanges and unemployment insurance there was created the Federal Public Corporation (Reichsanstalt) for Employment Exchanges and Unemployment Insurance. It was divided into three sections, the Central Office, the District Employment Offices, and the Local Employment Offices. Each of these sections has an administrative body whose position is honorary, a staff to perform the regular work, and a court of referees to pass on decisions. General supervision over the entire system is exercised by the Federal Minister of Labor.[18]

Local Employment Offices. Every commune must be in some local labor office of which 361 have been created.[19] Each local office is administered by a committee of management, composed of a chairman or vice chairman and equal representation from employers, employees, and public bodies. The number is fixed by the committee of management of the district office having jurisdiction, but it cannot be less than five. The representatives of the employers and employees are appointed by the chairman of the district labor office from nominations by the "economic associations of employers and employees." The representatives of the public bodies are appointed by the "joint communal supervising authority on the nomination of the executive of the communes concerned." The chairmen and permanent vice-chairmen of the local labor offices are appointed by the

[17] See Wunderlich, *op. cit.,* p. 283.

[18] In his office there is a small department composed of civil servants to enable him to carry out his supervision, and deal with legal and legislative measures.

[19] Carroll, *op. cit.,* p. 60. The Executive of the Reichsanstalt in agreement with the supreme state authority has charge of the boundaries and numbers of both district and local offices.

Executive of the Reichsanstalt after hearing the committee of management of the office concerned. This authority of appointment may be delegated to the local chairman who appoints the other permanent officials.

In the local office are concentrated the work of providing employment, instituting vocational guidance, and paying unemployment insurance benefits. It may also take measures leading to the prevention and combating of unemployment, by paying traveling benefits, assisting workers in new occupations until full earnings are attained, and, if so delegated, the promotion of relief works.

An unemployed person applies for benefit to the local office.[20] He must bring with him evidence of being in an insured employment, the amount of his remuneration during the last three months, the reason for termination of employment, and essential family circumstances. Upon request an employer must issue a certificate regarding employment and earnings upon termination of employment. The chairman of the local office makes the decision on the application for unemployment benefit. Actual payment of the benefit is effected in the local office unless delegated to the communes and federations of communes in the district.

District Employment Offices. The number of district offices is not specified in the Act, but thirteen have been created. As there are 18 German states, the district offices overlap the political state boundaries. Each district office is administered by a Committee of Management consisting of a chairman and representatives of employers, employees, and public bodies in equal numbers. The Executive of the Reichsanstalt can fix the actual number, but at not less than seven, and appoints the representatives of the employers and employees from nominations of the economic associations of employers and employees. The supreme state authority appoints the representatives of public bodies, taking into account representatives of the state and communes. The chairmen and permanent vice-chairmen of the District

----

[20] During the receipt of benefits he must register with the local employment exchange at least three times a week.

Employment Offices are appointed by the President of the Reich after consultation with the Executive of the Reichsanstalt and the supreme state authority and have the rights and duties of federal officials. The Executive of the Reichsanstalt appoints the rest of the permanent staff in each state office after consulting the committee of management of that office.

The state offices supervise the activities of the local offices, direct the transfer of workers from one district to another, and are charged with the promotion of relief works to create employment and act as distributing agencies for the funds collected in their districts.

The Central Office. The Reichsanstalt has two administrative bodies—a governing body and the Executive. The governing body consists of the president or one of the vice-presidents of the Reichsanstalt (who is chairman) and at least ten representatives each of employers, employees, and public bodies.[21] The representatives of employers are elected by the employers' division and those of employees by the employees' division of the Federal Economic Council, while the Minister of Labor appoints the representatives of the public bodies on the recommendation of the Federal Council. The Executive consists of the president or one of the vice-presidents of the Reichsanstalt, as chairman, and five representatives each of employers, employees, and public bodies.[22] They are all appointed by the Minister of Labor from separate lists of candidates drawn up by the three groups on the governing body, in the order in which they are submitted. The president and permanent vice-president of the Reichsanstalt are appointed by the President of the Reich and have the rights and duties of federal offi-

---

[21] The actual number, which must be equal for the three groups, is fixed by the rules made by the governing body itself. It is further specified that the representatives of employers and employees shall include representatives of agriculture and forestry, those of employees at least two salaried employees, and those of public bodies at least two "who by profession take cognizance of communal interests."

[22] These are to "include at least one employers' representative and one employees' representative in agriculture and forestry" and one "who by profession takes cognizance of communal interests."

cials. The other members of the permanent staff in the central office are appointed by the Executive under private contract.[23]

Courts of Appeal. Courts of appeal are attached to each of the three divisions. In the local office the court of appeals consists of the chairman or vice-chairman of the employment office and one employers' and one employees' representative from the committee of management. To this court are taken the appeals against the decisions of the chairman of the local employment office. Such appeals must be made within two weeks.

From the local courts appeals may be made by the unemployed person, the chairman, or any of the representatives on the management committee of the local office to the court attached to the district office.[24] This court consists of a chairman who is a member of the superior insurance office in the district in which the headquarters of the state employment office are situated and one employers' and one employees' representative from among those belonging to the superior insurance office. In case of emergency benefit no appeal may be taken to this court, unless the lower court does not adopt its decision unanimously.

The court of final appeals is attached to the Federal Insurance Office, the office for all types of social insurance. This court consists of a chairman, a permanent member of the Federal Insurance Office or a member of the Reichsanstalt, both appointed by the Minister of Labor, an additional judicial officer, and one representative each from

---

[23] To provide smaller administrative groups than those specified in the Act there is permitted the appointment of executive committees by the administrative committees of the local and district offices to which duties not prohibited in the act may be delegated. To safeguard particular interests there is a provision for the creation of trade and salaried employees' departments in the local and district offices where necessary and definite instruction for the creation of a Department of Agriculture and Forestry and one for salaried employees in the central office. In all cases equality of representation is retained. Women are represented on all administrative bodies, and provisions are included to insure genuine representations from all groups. No paid official of the Reichsanstalt can serve as a representative of any group. The honorary officers serve for a period of five years.

[24] There may be more than one court of appeal in a district.

employers and employees. The judicial officer is nominated by the Minister of Labor from the judges of the labor courts. The two representatives are drawn "from among the non-permanent members of the Federal Insurance Office." The courts may refer cases to this final court if the Federal Insurance Office has not yet published a decision on the general principles to be followed, and they must refer such cases if they dissent from the published decision.

In addition to these courts, there are provisions for appeals from the decisions of the chairman, in cases other than benefits, to the local committee of management, from it and from the chairman of the State Employment Office to the management committee of the latter, from the latter to the Executive of the Reichsanstalt, and from it to the governing body.

Preventive Measures. One feature of the Act of 1927 is the provision for measures to prevent unemployment. While not important from a quantitative point of view, the provision is of some interest as a means of bolstering up the test of willingness to work and making effective the transfer of workers from one locality to another and from one industry to another.

The local employment exchanges were authorized to pay expenses to a job in another locality and to pay allowances to the family of the absent worker. They might provide working outfits to those in need, and make allowances for a period not exceeding eight weeks to a person entering a new industry where full remuneration is not attained until some skill is acquired. They might also establish or assist existing centers for vocational training and retraining.

The committee of management of the District Employment Office might make loans or subsidies to productive relief works which provide employment to those eligible to standard benefits. Similarly grants might be made from the emergency fund contributed by the Reich and the local authorities for similar works providing employment to those entitled to emergency benefits. Both of these forms of expenditure were under the supervision of the Reichsanstalt. In addition the Federal Minister of Labor might also make grants out of state funds for such public works. As a rule these were to be matched by the states in which the grants were expended. Wages on these undertakings were to be the same as those locally customary, and while the state office was to fix the maximum period of remuneration, the conditions of work were to be the same as those under free contracts.

3. ·THE UNEMPLOYMENT INSURANCE SYSTEM, 1927-1930

When the law of 1927 was formulated, it was estimated that the average monthly receipts with the maximum contribution rate of 3 per cent would be equal to 49 million marks, and the cost of maintaining an unemployed worker was estimated at 70 marks. The estimated income would, therefore, have carried approximately 700,000 workers each month.[25] Neither of these forecasts was correct but both erred in the same direction. As can be seen from Table 34 at the end of the chapter the average monthly income during 1928 was 852 million marks and the average per capita expenditure was approximately 86 marks.[26] This meant therefore that another 100,000 unemployed workers could be assisted out of the revenues. During the first year of insurance—to October, 1928—a slightly larger number of workers were actually assisted and expenditures exceeded income by the small amount of 14 million marks. The Reichsanstalt had, however, started with a reserve of over 100 million marks so that it ended its first year with a reserve of 89 million marks, which in November, 1928, was increased to 109 million marks.

[25] *Reichsarbeitsblatt*, No. 24, 1929, Part I, p. 205. No attempt was made to estimate the average amount of unemployment over a trade cycle. The period during which the insurance system has functioned is too short for such an analysis. But an examination of the chart of unemployed persons assisted through national unemployment relief or insurance, or employment on public works, presented by Dr. Carroll in her book on *Unemployment Insurance in Germany*, p. 12, for the period of December, 1918-December, 1928, will indicate that the insurance system of 1927 was introduced just before a period of depression.

[26] Reichsarbeitsblatt, No. 24, 1929, Part I, p. 205.

The winter of 1928-29 brought out clearly the significance of seasonal variation in unemployment. In the months of January, February, and March the numbers in receipt of standard benefits averaged over a million. The framers of the original law, not unaware of this problem of seasonal unemployment, provided three ways of dealing with it. (1) Workers could not refuse employment elsewhere during periods of unemployment customary in the occupation although unemployed for less than nine weeks. (2) The governing body of the Reichsanstalt was authorized to fix the maximum duration of benefits differently for 'workers in occupations or industries with customary recurrence of unemployment. (3) The governing body could lengthen the waiting period in such occupations or industries. But only the third was put into effect and that by the decree of December 2, 1927, which was valid until March 31, 1928.[27] It did not, however, prove a significant differentiation between seasonal and non-seasonal workers in receipt of benefits. The winter of 1928-29, much severer than usual, brought into clear relief the consequences of seasonal unemployment on the insurance funds. In February of 1929 the numbers receiving benefits increased to 2,368,000 and did not fall below a million until May of that year.

In anticipation of the heavy winter unemployment there was introduced by the Act of 24th December, 1928, and orders based on it,[28] a special form of benefit as a temporary measure. The new regulations were confined to those occupations in which regularly recurring unemployment was usual—chiefly the out-door occupations of agriculture, forestry, building, stone-quarrying, brick-making, and railway maintenance. In the months of December to March inclusive, workers in these listed occupations who qualified for standard benefits were to receive only six weeks' benefits, after which they were entitled to special benefits (Sonder-unterstützung) the cost of which was to be met by the Exchequer ($\frac{4}{5}$) and the Reichsanstalt ($\frac{1}{5}$). These benefits

[27] Ibid., No. 35, 1927, Part I, p. 548.
[28] Ibid., No. 36, 1928, Part I, pp. 281-5.

were to be paid on the same rates and conditions as were the emergency benefits, which meant that the worker had to prove necessitous circumstances.[29]

The control of these expenditures for seasonal benefits remained entirely in the hands of the unemployment insurance authorities. This combination of public funds with the regular insurance funds can only be explained as a financial device on the part of the State to make an outright grant to the Reichsanstalt and differentiate between seasonal and non-seasonal workers.

TABLE 32

DATA SHOWING PROPORTION OF SEASONAL WORKERS TO ALL WORKERS
RECEIVING BENEFITS

(thousands)

DATE	NUMBER RECEIVING SPECIAL SEASONAL BENEFITS[1] (1)	TOTAL NUMBER OF SEASONAL WORKERS RECEIVING STANDARD BENEFITS[2] (2)	TOTAL NUMBER RECEIVING STANDARD BENEFITS[3] (3)	PERCENTAGE 2 ÷ 3 (4)
January 15 .	128	1006	2046	49.2
January 31 .	566	1156	2288	50.5
February 15	805	1269	2356	53.8
February 28	942	1300	2461	52.8
March 15 .	885	1095	2325	47.1

[1] *Statistische Beilage zum Reichsarbeitsblatt*, No. 4, 1930.
[2] *Reichsarbeitsblatt*, No. 12, 1930, Part II, p. 175.
[3] Based on monthly reports in the *Statistische Beilage zum Reichsarbeitsblatt*.

The numbers who were assisted in this way are included in the numbers receiving standard benefits as shown in Table 33 at the end of this chapter. They have, however, been published separately and are set out above along with the total number of seasonal workers who were in receipt either of the special benefits or standard benefits and the total number receiving standard benefits. The largest single group of workers consisted of those in the building trades,

[29] These grants, however, counted for only one-half toward the total number of weeks for which standard benefits could be paid.

who on February 28th, for example, constituted about two-thirds of those receiving special seasonal benefits, while another three hundred and fifty thousand in the same trades were at the same time in receipt of standard benefits. The above table indicates the great extent of seasonal unemployment which on the average was responsible for about fifty per cent of the total number receiving benefits. And even though the Exchequer assumed such a substantial part of the financial burden due to seasonal unemployment,[30] the total amount of unemployment in seasonal and non-seasonal occupations was so large that the Reichsanstalt on the first of June, 1929, had a deficit of approximately 265 million marks. In the months following, the numbers in receipt of benefits did not fall below 700,000 and the income was but slightly in excess of the expenditures. Hence the Reichsanstalt ended its second year with a deficit of some 250 million marks. If to this be added the reserve of 109 million and the expenditures by the Reich for special benefits of 105 million, we have a total excess of expenditures over income of 464 million marks during the second year.

While it was generally agreed that the winter of 1928-29 was exceptional, nevertheless the conclusion of the previous winter, that the funds were not adequate to meet the winter unemployment, was strengthened. In fact some discussion has arisen as to whether the seasonal workers should be included at all in unemployment insurance. Thus to quote Dr. Carroll: "The Unemployment Insurance System had been designed for persons whose loss of work was unexpected, infrequent and of short duration. The funds were being used up for regularly recurring and prolonged idleness."[31] It cannot be that the framers of the German Unemployment Insurance System were unaware of the existence of seasonal variation in unemployment. We have already noted the limited way in which provision against it

[30] It paid out approximately 105 million marks. See Table 34 at the end of this chapter. When the amending act was introduced the estimated expenditure was about 35 million marks.

[31] Carroll, *op. cit.*, pp. 98-99.

was made. It is, of course, well known that the German trade unions were against any differentiation between seasonal and non-seasonal workers. It may also be that the last three years have witnessed seasonal variation greater than is usual, which would give only temporary importance to the problem. It should be noted that statistical regularity itself is one of the characteristics which make insurance against unemployment possible. There are, however, three considerations which Dr. Carroll also notes, which differentiate the problem of insuring seasonal workers from that of insuring non-seasonal workers. (1) On *a priori* grounds the risk of insuring seasonal workers on the same conditions as non-seasonal workers is a bad one. This was brought out most clearly by an investigation into the industrial history of those in receipt of benefits on March 15, 1929. Thus in the year previous to the claim for benefits, 17.2 per cent of those in seasonal occupations were employed continuously while 33.8 per cent of those in non-seasonal occupations were so employed. Similarly in the previous year 47.6 per cent of the seasonal workers received benefits while only 23.8 per cent of the non-seasonal workers received benefits.[32] (2) The regular occurrence of seasonal unemployment makes possible an adjustment of the wage structure, and the payment of benefits during seasonal unemployment will put seasonal workers at an advantage. (3) The payment of benefits during seasonal unemployment keeps the labor force intact and hence discourages rather than encourages stabilization. In fact workers may actually refuse to search for temporary employment. Not only is there no inducement to do so, but the fear of being put in a lower wage class and receiving lower rates of benefits should he again lose employment will actually deter the seasonal worker from searching for temporary work. The last two considerations are the less important. The same forces which raise the wages of seasonal workers to allow for lost time, will lower them as soon as insurance becomes a permanent feature of the economic system. The problem of

[32] *Reichsarbeitsblatt,* Nos. 21 and 24, 1929.

immobility can be cared for by adequate safeguards in defining willingness to work, and fixing the benefit rates so that it is to the advantage of the seasonal worker to search for temporary employment. The employment exchanges, the provision of benefits for partial unemployment, and the limitation of the period during which a seasonal worker can refuse employment in another occupation or place can be so administered as to get around the factor working for immobility. The most serious consideration is, therefore, the first, which can only be solved—aside from excluding seasonal workers from the insurance system—by a differentiation in the rates of contribution, or in the rates and duration of benefits, or in both. Only the latter has so far been utilized and to a limited extent so that the solution is but a partial one.

In the summer of 1929 it was generally recognized that even with a continuation of the special seasonal benefits coming mainly out of the Exchequer funds, the heavy winter unemployment of that year could not be met by the income of the Reichsanstalt. But the continuation of the special seasonal benefits was most unlikely because of the financial difficulties of the Reich. In addition there were widespread charges of abuses in the administration of benefits. The trade unions were in the main in favor of increasing the contributions and retaining the existing rates of benefits, while the employers were in favor of reducing the rates of benefits.

There was first undertaken an elaborate statistical investigation into the industrial history of those receiving benefits on the 15th of March, 1929, to which we have already referred and which has been published in the *Reichsarbeitblatt*. Then a committee of experts "known to some as the 'German Blanesburgh' Committee was appointed with the twofold object of finding an acceptable way out of the financial deadlock and of examining the very widespread charges of abuse of the benefit rules under the scheme." [33] The Committee made its report in August,

[33] Davison, *op. cit.*, p. 146.

1929, and recommended reforms both in the law and procedure, and a temporary increase in the rate of contributions to three and a half per cent.[34] While these recommendations were in the main embodied into an amending act, as a result of considerable opposition, the proposal to increase contributions was dropped because of the fear that it would endanger the permanent reforms on which there was general agreement.

The bill was finally passed as the Act of October 12, 1929, to take effect on November 1, 1929.[35] Its chief features consisted of a stricter definition of unemployment and employment, changes in the waiting period, and an attempted solution of seasonal unemployment. The new definition of unemployment was directed to make it more difficult for small tradesmen, farmers, innkeepers, and the like to qualify for benefits, and to make it impossible for the unemployable to qualify for benefits by petty employment—i.e., employment at less than eight marks per week. The period of employment necessary for qualification was more strictly defined so that work of less than 24 hours in a calendar week or 4 hours a day can count for only ½ toward the qualifying period, and periods of illness which were formerly included were omitted from the period. Another modification of the qualifying period was made by the division of all claims to benefit into first claims and all others, and instead of the period of 26 weeks in the previous year for all workers, those making their first claim since the Act of 1927 must show at least fifty-two weeks in insurable employment during the preceding two years—which may be extended to three years. For the other claimants the original period of 26 weeks in the preceding year was retained.

Slight changes in the wage classes were also made. The wage on which the contributions and benefits are paid is to be determined by the average earnings in the preceding 26 weeks instead of three months; the benefits in the lowest

34 *Reichsarbeitsblatt*, No. 24, 1929, Part I, pp. 205-9.
35 International Labour Office, *Legislative Series, 1929, Germany—5.*

wage classes can no longer exceed the wages received, and the benefits of workers receiving their grants in a locality other than the one in which they were employed, must be adjusted to the local wages paid. The last was designed especially for rural workers losing employment in the cities and then returning to their rural homes where wages may be lower than in the cities.

The original waiting period established by the Act of 1927 was 7 days with a few exceptions later made in seasonal occupations. The new waiting period is more flexible, being 14 days for minors under twenty-one who form part of another household and can make no claims for dependents' allowances, three days for those who can claim dependents' allowances for four or more, and seven days for all others.

As a temporary measure until the end of March, 1931, the special seasonal benefits of the previous winter were incorporated in the Act but the funds were to come out of the ordinary income of the Reichsanstalt. For these benefits the rates in the wage classes VII to XI were reduced to the level of the emergency benefits, so as to encourage seasonal workers to search for temporary employment.

The economies which would be introduced were estimated at approximately 92 million marks a year, and important as they are, with the advent of the depression of 1929-30, they have proved but a slight check to the deficit which has since accumulated.

To the problem of seasonal unemployment there was superimposed the unemployment resulting from the depression, in consequence of which the number of recipients of standard benefits in the summer of 1929 was higher than in the previous summer and in the following winter and summer greatly exceeded the previous averages. While the average number of recipients of standard benefits was 867,000 in 1928, 1,276,000 in 1929, it reached 1,824,000 in the nine months of 1930.

There was first an increase in the rate of contributions to 3½ per cent as from the first of January, to the 30th of

June, 1930.[36] This, however, was quite inadequate to meet the mounting expenditures. It became apparent that unless the Reich was in a position and willing to make further loans, additional reforms would have to be introduced. The political situation made any new legislation impossible and it was not until the end of July that the President under authority of Article 48 of the German constitution, issued the new legislative measure.[37]

This new Act increased the revenue of the Reichsanstalt by raising the rate of contributions to 4½ per cent, by a State grant of 184 million marks for the financial year 1930, and by an addition of five per cent of the expenditures for emergency benefits to cover the cost of administering these. At the same time it was specified that, if in spite of the new reforms the expenditures exceeded income, the Reich would contribute one-half the excess and the balance would have to be raised by a further increase in contributions or decrease in benefits.

The other sections of the Act were further extensions of the provisions in the Law of October, 1929, directed to economize the resources of the Reichsanstalt. Unemployed workers were excluded from benefits if they had families to maintain them; the exclusion of petty employment from insurance was made more strict; the penalties for voluntarily leaving employment, or refusal to accept new employment were increased; a stricter interpretation was placed on "employment" for the qualifying part; and the waiting period was fixed at 14 days for those without claims for dependents, 7 days for those with one to three claims inclusive, and 3 days for those with four or more claims. A new departure was established in the payment of standard benefits according to duration of employment as well as income. Workers in classes VII to XI inclusive were to receive the benefits specified for their respective classes only if they had been employed in an insurable occupation for at least 52 weeks previous to the first claim for benefits. Otherwise

---

[36] *Reichsarbeitsblatt*, No. 36, 1929, Part I, p. 297.
[37] *Ibid.*, No. 22, 1930, Part I, pp. 150-2.

the rates were reduced to those of lower classes. The element of need was also introduced in two provisions. The first specified that unless the unemployed worker had a claim for dependents' allowance for two or more, the income of a wife exceeding 35 marks a week was to be taken into account in the payment of benefits. The second provision specified that in the case of those in Classes VII to XI inclusive receiving benefits jointly with a wife and having no claims for dependents' allowances, the benefits of the one receiving the smaller rate should be cut in two.

One other provision worth noting is that which made the way clear for variation in rates of contributions for enterprises or groups of enterprises where workers are subject to greater unemployment than the average. The Reichsanstalt and the Minister of Labor were authorized to fix the groups, the amount, and duration of additional contributions. While such measures have not yet been put into practice, the way has been cleared for handling the problem of seasonal unemployment from the side of contributions.

In spite of the economies and increased contributions, the great increase in the numbers unemployed created a deficit of 933.3 million marks by the end of August of this year.[38]

Any arbitrary fixation of the period during which standard benefits are paid needs to be investigated as to adequacy. We can see this by looking into the actual duration of benefits, and in the case of Germany, into the payment of emergency benefits. The facts regarding the duration of benefits are set out in Table 33. On the basis of the experience during the first year when of the total number receiving benefits, 64.5 per cent received them for less than 13 weeks, Dr. Carroll has argued that "The evidence bears out the contention of those who say that the present

---

[38] Since then there has been a further increase in contributions to 6½ per cent as from October 6, 1930. *Reichsarbeitsblatt*, No. 28, 1930, Part I, p. 208. The loans for 1928-29 to the extent of 623.0 million marks have been canceled and in accordance with the emergency legislation the Reich has made grants of 184 and 50 million marks which still leaves a deficit of 76.4 million marks. *Reichsarbeitsblatt*, No. 30, 1930, Part II, p. 477.

26 weeks' provision is ample to care for most of the really insurable cases and therefore represents the acceptable maximum duration of eligibility." [39] Now it is difficult to say just what "insurable" signifies. But it can hardly be claimed that 26 weeks is more insurable than say, 36 weeks. That aside, it must be admitted that in the case of Germany a maximum of 26 weeks excludes substantial numbers in no way differentiated from those unemployed for shorter periods. In fact the first year, which was one of relatively little unemployment, underestimates the numbers. As the seasonal element predominated the average period of unemployment tended to be short. Since the depression, as can be seen from Table 34, the percentage of the numbers receiving benefits for less than 13 weeks has declined, indicating, of course, a lengthening of the average period of unemployment.

The other way of examining the adequacy of the 26 weeks' maximum is to analyze the numbers in receipt of emergency benefits. In Table 36 these are subdivided into those who did not fulfill the requirements and hence did not become eligible to benefits and those who exhausted their claims.

In the early months, as is to be expected, the numbers not meeting the requirements greatly exceeded the numbers who exhausted their claims. Also through the month of June the numbers underestimate those receiving benefits for longer than 26 weeks as in the transitional period benefits were paid up to 52 weeks in the form of standard benefits.[40] Nor do these figures tell the entire story as eligibility to emergency benefits has varied.[41] But the consequences of the 26 weeks' rule are shown by the increasing numbers who received emergency benefits as the depression developed.[42]

We are not suggesting that our analysis justifies a lengthening of the maximum period, but simply that the rule

[39] *Op. cit.*, p. 85.   [40] See note 2 to Table 3 on p. 463.
[41] See *post*, pp. 451-
[42] The numbers receiving emergency benefits by no means indicate the total number excluded by the 26 weeks' rule. Data published for the period

excludes a substantial number of workers who are involuntarily unemployed, because of the changing fortunes of the labor market, and that they cannot be dismissed as being not insurable. It may be that there is some justification for separating these employed for longer periods and imposing special conditions for the receipt of benefits as was done in Great Britain and as is now done in Germany.

The changes in the numbers receiving emergency benefits can only be understood in the light of the administrative changes which have taken place. In the Act of 1927 the emergency benefits were intended for times when the labor market remained persistently unfavorable. They were to be discretionary grants authorized by the Federal Minister of Labor. The fact that the unemployed worker had to prove necessitous circumstances, placed the emergency benfits half-way between standard benefits and poor relief. The first Ministerial Decree of the 28th September, 1927,[43] limited the payment of emergency benefits to twenty-six weeks and reduced the rates of wage classes VI and VII to the standard benefit rate of VI, classes VIII and IX to VII, and classes X and XI to VIII. Two groups of workers were admitted to emergency benefits: (1) workers who did not qualify but had worked at least 13 weeks in the previous year in an insurable employment and (2) workers in market gardening, metal and engineering, clothing, wood-working, leather trades, and salaried workers who exhausted their claims to standard benefits.

The above decree was valid until the end of March, 1929, when as a result of the improved situation in the labor market, emergency benefits were limited to the above classes for workers who either did not qualify but had worked thirteen weeks as above, or had exhausted their claims.[44] At the same time the Minister authorized an extension to

---

July 15, 1929, to August 15, 1930, indicate that of the numbers excluded from standard benefits because they have exhausted their claims only about one-third are carried over into the emergency benefit system. See *Reichsarbeitsblatt*, No. 25, 1930, Part II, p. 403.

[43] *Reichsarbeitsblatt*, No. 28, 1927, Part I, pp. 441-2.

[44] *Ibid.*, No. 10, 1928, Part I, pp. 93, 95-6.

39 weeks for workers over forty. In two subsequent decrees, as a result of the end of the transitional period during which workers received standard benefits for longer periods than 26 weeks, the duration of emergency benefits was increased to 39 weeks and for workers over forty there was authorized an extension to 52 weeks.[45] The administrative authorities of the Reichsanstalt were also authorized to admit certain additional classes whose employment possibilities were unfavorable.

One of the ways of meeting the consequences of the heavy seasonal unemployment of the winter of 1928-29 and of the general depression which developed, would have been by an extension of the duration of standard benefits as authorized in the law. The financial situation of the Reichsanstalt made such a course impossible and hence the Decree of the 25th of February, 1929,[46] admitted to emergency benefits all occupations except those enumerated—chiefly coal mining, chemicals, and those covered by seasonal benefits.

The summer improvement in the labor market and the hope that this would continue led the Minister to revert to the previous system of admitting a stated number of occupations—chiefly glass-working, metals and engineering, leather, wood-working, clothing, theatrical workers, and salaried workers—to emergency benefits, and authorizing the Presidents of the District Employment Offices to admit workers in other occupations as the need arose. Workers under twenty-one and workers in seasonal trades during the seasonal period were excluded, and the duration of benefits was limited to 39 weeks with an authorized extension to 52 weeks in the case of workers over forty.[47] The hopes for an improved labor market proved vain hopes, and in point of fact there was a worsening of the labor market. In consequence the number receiving emergency benefits which averaged 176,000 in 1929, increased steadily until

[45] *Ibid.*, No. 24, 1928, Part I, pp. 223-4; No. 25, 1928, Part I, p. 227.
[46] *Ibid.*, No. 6, 1929, Part I, pp. 37-9.
[47] *Ibid.*, No. 19, 1929, Part I, pp. 161-3.

by August there were 422,000. Unfortunately, however, the Reich itself had financial difficulties and the Minister, therefore, had to restrict again the payment of emergency benefits.[48] The great need necessitated the admission of all workers. But the lack of funds led to a reduction in rates of emergency benefits, a stricter regard for other incomes of the unemployed and their need, the exclusion of certain groups—agriculture, domestic service, and workers under twenty-one. In localities with less than 10,000 inhabitants the District Labor Offices were given authority to determine the classes of workers which would be admitted. Also only workers who have exhausted their claims are now eligible to emergency benefits. The duration of these is now limited to 32 weeks, except that for workers over 40 an extension to 45 weeks is authorized.

The chief point of contention is, of course, that since the granting of emergency benefits hinges on the determination of necessitous circumstances, the agencies administering poor relief are in a better situation to ascertain the facts and such work should not be thrown on the labor offices.[49] We have noted, however, that only slight distinctions can be made between workers receiving benefits for the maximum period and those unemployed for longer intervals, and we think there is justification for removing from poor relief as many able-bodied workers who are involuntarily unemployed as is possible with the available finances.

When the insurance system was introduced much was expected from the utilization of value-creating relief work to reduce the amount of unemployment.[50] The numbers who were thus assisted (Notstandsarbeiter) are set out in Table 33 in columns 6 and 7. As the bulk of the work consists of construction—road-building and mending, maintenance of parks, etc.—the numbers vary greatly during the year. Also although at the end of the war Germany was much

---

[48] *Ibid.*, No. 29 1930 Part I, pp. 219-22.
[49] Cf. Dr. Philipp Beifiegel, Die Neuregelung der Krisenfürsorge, *Reichsarbeitsblatt*, No. 30, 1930, Part II, pp. 455-59.
[50] For a full discussion of value-creating relief work, see Carroll, *op cit.*, Chs. IV and IX.

behind in public construction work, that need has been met, and it has been increasingly difficult to find suitable work which would not be otherwise carried on. In consequence the number of relief workers has greatly declined as can be seen from the Table just referred to. If we make comparisons with 1927 this decline is brought out even more markedly. In March, 1927, there were 177,244 workers employed on relief works which was 10.7 per cent of the total number in receipt of standard and emergency benefits. The percentage was as high as 19.2 per cent in August, 1927, while in recent months the percentage has been below two per cent.[51]

Closely allied to the relief workers are the *Pflichtarbeiter* whose numbers also are set out in Table 30. The object of Pflichtarbeit was quite distinct from relief works, as it was intended for juveniles under 21 who were eligible to standard benefits, and workers who were out of work for long periods of time and were receiving emergency benefits. The goal was not so much the provision of employment and the accomplishment of work, but rather the provision of a work test and the protection of the morale and skill of the workers. It has, however, proved most difficult to find work which is both interesting and instructive and which would not otherwise be done.

One other form of assistance not included in the statistics covered so far is that given during partial unemployment. The numbers who were so assisted are set out in Table 36. Since the depression the numbers have greatly increased and the same criticism made in England, that benefits for partial unemployment lead to organized short time and immobility, have been made in Germany, and with as little evidence to support these criticisms.

[51] See *Reichsarbeitsblatt*, No. 27, 1930, Part II, pp. 425-6.

STATISTICAL TABLES

TABLE 33

NUMBER OF GERMAN WORKERS RECEIVING ASSISTANCE DURING UNEMPLOYMENT, OCTOBER, 1927 — AUGUST, 1930[1]

(thousands)

MONTH	NUMBER OF INSURED WORKERS[2] (1)	RECIPIENTS OF			(4) ÷ (2) + (3) (5)	RELIEF WORKERS		TOTAL (2) + (3) + (6) + (7) (8)	PFLICHTARBEITER[4]	
		Standard Benefits[3] (2)	Emergency Benefits[3] (3)	Dependents Allowances[3] (4)		Standard Benefits[3] (6)	Emergency Benefits[3] (7)		Standard Benefits (9)	Emergency Benefits (10)
1927										
October	16,061	342	114	501	1.1	50.9	20.9	528	...	...
November	15,952	446	130	596	1.0	43.0	17.7	637	...	...
December	15,499	874	177	1,227	1.2	28.0	11.2	1,090	8.7	9.1
Average	15,837	554	140	775	...	40.6	16.6	752	...	...
1928										
January	14,887	1,297	218	1,948	1.3	24.3	8.9	1,549	17.6	11.7
February	14,917	1,287	215	1,794	1.2	43.6	14.2	1,560	18.1	12.2
March	15,198	1,150	208	1,688	1.2	57.2	17.7	1,433	15.3	11.4
April	16,034	862	181	1,173	1.1	67.7	20.3	1,130	10.3	8.8
May	16,394	667	146	807	1.0	69.2	20.9	903	6.1	5.7
June	16,481	621	124	709	1.0	64.9	18.5	828	5.1	4.1
July	16,331	585	95	597	.9	58.8	15.4	754	4.7	2.6
August	16,459	569	81	576	.9	54.1	12.8	717	4.6	2.2
September	16,539	576	83	591	.9	51.3	11.3	722	4.8	2.0
October	16,539	614	90	630	.9	46.1	9.4	759	4.8	1.9
November	16,123	835	100	868	.9	41.3	8.0	985	4.8	1.9
December	15,319	1,344	117	1,409	1.0	31.4	5.5	1,498	7.2	1.8
Average	15,935	867	138	1,066	...	50.8	13.6	1,070	8.6	5.5

456

1929										
January	15,039	2,012	137	2,288	1.1	15.5	2.8	2,168	....	2.0
February	14,491	2,368	154	2,718	1.1	6.0	1.2	2,529	6.1	1.7
March	15,035	2,228	177	2,713	1.1	15.5	2.5	2,423	4.6	1.7
April	16,223	1,502	196	1,704	1.0	54.7	9.1	1,762	5.2	2.0
May	16,704	954	200	1,020	.9	87.8	14.0	1,256	2.8	1.9
June	16,878	759	205	814	.8	87.5	14.9	1,066	1.7	1.6
July	16,793	718	184	757	.8	72.5	13.8	989	1.4	1.7
August	16,811	718	155	723	.8	58.9	11.8	943	1.4	1.5
September	16,738	737	159	749	.8	48.6	10.2	955	1.3	1.2
October	16,656	807	166	818	.9	41.1	8.1	1,023	1.5	1.5
November	16,307	1,035	179	1,084	.9	34.7	6.4	1,255	2.0	1.4
December	15,358	1,469	197	1,523	.9	24.9	4.1	1,696	2.6	1.4
Average	16,086	1,276	176	1,409	....	45.6	8.2	1,505	2.8	1.6
1930										
January	14,912	2,034	230	2,228	1.0	16.8	2.5	2,283	3.8	1.2
February	14,550	2,312	265	2,492	1.0	16.5	2.3	2,596	4.1	1.3
March	14,669	2,237	286	2,442	1.0	21.9	2.8	2,547	4.1	1.3
April	15,146	1,883	304	2,032	.9	27.8	3.5	2,219	4.4	1.6
May	15,379	1,643	326	1,766	.9	30.5	4.2	2,004	3.0	1.5
June	15,310	1,507	352	1,630	.9	30.8	4.8	1,895	2.6	1.4
July	15,126	1,476	382	1,587	.9	29.6	6.0	1,894	2.1	1.5
August	14,917	1,499	422	1,639	.9	26.7	7.1	1,954	2.1	1.6
Average	15,000	1,824	321	1,977	....	25.1	4.2	2,174	3.3	1.4

[1] Based on reports in the *Reichsarbeitsblatt* and *Statistische Beilage zum Reichsarbeitsblatt*, December, 1927 – September, 1930.

[2] Excluding workers in receipt of benefits — columns (2) and (3).

[3] Average of the number receiving benefits at the end of the previous month, the middle and end of the month in question.

[4] Included in columns (2) and (3).

TABLE 34

INCOME AND EXPENDITURE OF UNEMPLOYMENT INSURANCE FUND, OCTOBER 1927–AUGUST, 1930[1]

(Million Marks)

MONTH	TOTAL INCOME[2]	EXPENDITURES				MONTHLY BALANCE	EMER-GENCY BENEFITS[4]
		Adminis-tration	Benefits	Measures to Pre-vent Un-employ-ment	Total[3]		
	(1)	(2)	(3)	(4)	(5)	(6)	(7)
1927							
October	59.2	5.5	19.9	1.7	27.0	32.2	7.8
November	66.6	5.1	29.4	2.6	37.1	29.5	10.1
December	70.6	7.1	73.1	2.1	82.3	− 11.7	15.2
TOTAL	196.4	17.7	122.4	6.4	146.4		33.1
1928							
January	67.8	7.3	106.1	1.6	115.1	− 47.3	16.1
February	64.3	6.8	99.8	2.1	108.7	− 44.4	15.6
March .	70.2	7.4	101.3	4.1	112.8	− 42.6	10.9
April .	67.1	6.7	64.4	4.1	75.2	− 8.1	19.8
May .	57.6	6.5	50.7	3.1	60.2	7.3	11.1
June .	72.9	5.7	48.7	3.6	59.0	13.9	10.2
July .	72.2	7.0	42.3	3.3	52.6	19.6	7.5
August .	76.8	6.5	44.5	3.8	54.8	22.0	7.0
September	73.1	7.9	45.5	4.3	57.8	15.5	7.4
October	78.1	6.7	45.3	3.0	55.0	23.1	7.3
November	74.8	6.9	66.7	3.0	76.6	− 1.8	8.1
December	66.8	7.3	104.3	2.3	113.9	− 47.1	9.1
TOTAL	851.7	83.7	819.6	38.3	941.7		130.1
1929							
January	76.9	8.3	161.9	2.6	174.4	− 97.5	10.9
February	61.5	8.5	121.6	2.2	142.5	− 81.0	11.2
March [5] .	77.8	14.7	143.0	5.3	177.2	− 99.4	17.1
April .	54.1	7.6	93.5	.8	102.1	− 48.0	13.1
May .	68.3	7.9	79.0	1.8	88.8	− 20.5	16.1
June .	70.9	8.1	58.6	3.2	69.9	1.0	15.3
July .	78.8	8.9	58.0	5.0	71.9	6.9	15.2
August .	78.9	7.8	60.3	4.1	72.2	6.7	13.1
September	75.3	8.4	57.2	4.1	69.7	5.6	12.3
October	82.0	8.7	66.9	3.9	79.6	2.4	13.5
November	77.4	9.4	82.0	3.1	94.5	− 17.1	14.0
December	72.5	9.7	110.1	3.9	123.7	− 51.2	14.9
TOTAL	874.4	108.2	1092.1	40.0	1266.5		166.6

458

TABLE 34 (*Continued*)

Month	Total Income (1)	Expenditures				Monthly Balance (6)	Emergency Benefits[4] (7)
		Administration (2)	Benefits (3)	Measures to Prevent Unemployment (4)	Total[3] (5)		
1930							
January	78.2	10.2	163.5	2.6	176.3	− 98.1	18.6
February	71.8	10.4	163.9	2.9	177.1	− 105.3	18.9
March .	80.1	10.6	172.5	2.8	185.9	− 105.8	21.4
April .	72.1	8.7	134.3	.7	143.7	− 71.6	20.4
May .	80.6	8.8	139.3	2.1	150.2	− 69.6	25.6
June .	76.1	8.6	116.4	1.8	126.8	− 50.7	25.1
July .	83.0	9.4	119.8	2.2	131.5	− 48.5	29.5
August .	79.3	8.9	117.4	2.0	128.4	− 49.1[6]	31.6
Total	621.2	75.6	1127.1	17.1	1219.9		191.1

[1] Based on monthly reports in the *Reichsarbeitsblatt*, December, 1927–September, 1930.

[2] Predominantly from contributions of employers and workers, but including a small amount — about two million marks each month — from miscellaneous sources, but excluding sums granted for emergency benefits and subsidies for value creating relief works.

[3] The differences between the totals and constituent expenditures from January to May, 1929, are accounted for by the one-fifth of the seasonal benefits which was paid by the Reichsanstalt. See note 4.

[4] The funds for emergency allowances come from the Reich and municipalities. In addition to these emergency benefits the following amounts were contributed by the Reich for seasonal benefits in the months indicated:

Month		Million Marks
January	1929 .	5.9
February	"	40.7
March	"	57.0
April	"	.8
May	"	.5
June	"	.2
July	"	.1
		105.2

These amounts represent in each case ⅕ of the total amount spent for the special seasonal benefits, as another ⅕ was contributed by the Reichsanstalt and is included in column (5) above.

[5] Including the corrections for previous months published as a supplement to the March account. See *Reichsarbeitsblatt*, No. 21, 1929, Part II, pp. 308–9.

[6] The deficit on August 31, 1930, was 933.3 million marks. Of this amount the Reich cancelled the loans of 1928/29 to the extent of 623.0 million marks and in accordance with the emergency legislation made grants of 50 and 184 million marks which gave a total of 857.0 leaving a minus balance of 76.4. *Reichsarbeitsblatt*, No. 30, 1930, Part 2, p. 477.

TABLE 35

NUMBER OF WORKERS IN RECEIPT OF EMERGENCY BENEFITS NOVEMBER 1927–SEPTEMBER, 1930[1]

(thousands)

DATE (15th of Month)	TOTAL (1)	NUMBER NOT MEETING REQUIREMENTS (2)	NUMBER WHO EXHAUSTED CLAIMS (3)
1927			
November	126	38	88
December	172	86	86
Average	149	62	87
1928			
January	228	144	84
February	216	147	68
March	212	147	65
April	182	123	59
May	143	89	54
June	126	70	55
July	90	48	41
August	81	35	46
September	82	31	51
October	90	31	59
November	99	33	67
December	117	37	80
Average	139	78	61
1929			
January	138	41	97
February	154	44	110
March	177	47	130
April	198	49	150
May	199	46	153
June	206	47	159
July	192	43	148
August	154	35	119
September	159	36	123
October	165	35	130
November	178	36	142
December	194	42	152
Average	176	42	134

[1] *Statistische Beilage zum Reichsarbeitsblatt*, December, 1927–October, 1930. The total numbers shown here differ from those of Table 33 as the former refer to a single day in the month, and the latter are averages of three days.

TABLE 35 (*Continued*)

Date (15th of Month)	Total (1)	Number Not Meeting Requirements (2)	Number Who Exhausted Claims (3)
1930			
January	230	51	180
February	267	57	210
March	286	66	221
April	302	61	241
May	323	64	259
June	353	67	286
July	380	68	312
August	421	72	349
September	459	76	383
Average	336	65	271

TABLE 36

Number of Workers Receiving Benefits for Partial Unemployment
January, 1928–June, 1930[1]

1928		1929		1930	
Week Ending	Number	Week Ending	Number	Week Ending	Number
January 28 .	6,010	January 26 .	26,357	January 25 .	53,977
February 25 .	6,278	February 23	30,797	February 22	67,975
March 31 .	7,196	March 23 .	31,112	March 29 .	80,687
April 28 . .	8,205	April 27 .	30,511	April 12 .	78,962
May 26 . .	8,532	May 18 . .	31,753	May 24 . .	90,945
June 30 . .	14,942	June 22 . .	29,247	June 28 .	98,416
July 28 . .	16,359	July 27 . .	30,373		
August 25 .	21,015	August 31 .	35,643		
September 29	16,488	September 28	37,696		
October 27 .	12,532	October 26 .	36,939		
November 17	14,563	November 30	38,711		
December 22	18,941	December 21	32,466		

[1] *Reichsarbeitsblatt*, December, 1927–October, 1930.

TABLE 37

DISTRIBUTION OF RECIPIENTS OF STANDARD BENEFITS ACCORDING TO
PERIODS FOR WHICH BENEFITS WERE RECEIVED[1]

DATE (15th of Month)	PERCENTAGE OF TOTAL RECEIVING BENEFITS FOR SPECIFIED NUMBER OF WEEKS[2]	
	0 — 13.0 Weeks (1)	13.1 — 26.0 Weeks (2)
1927·	%	%
November	61.3	20.1
December	78.1	12.8
Average	69.7	16.5
1928		
January[3]	. . . .	. . . .
February	78.2	16.6
March	63.0	31.8
April	51.2	42.4
May	55.8	38.0
June	59.0	35.3
July	63.8	36.2
August	64.6	3ᴜ.4
September	64.0	36.0
October	64.8	35.2
November	69.5	30.5
December	75.6	24.4
Average	64.5	32.9
1929		
January[3]	. . . .	. . . .
February[3]	. . . .	. . . .
March[3]	. . . .	. . . .
April[3]	. . . .	. . . .
May	51.7	48.3
June	53.4	46.6
July	56.7	43.3
August	58.3	41.7
September	58.5	41.5
October	59.6	40.4
November	64.0	36.0
December	68.1	31.9
Average	58.8	41.2

TABLE 37 (*Continued*)

Date (15th of Month)	Percentage of Total Receiving Benefits for Specified Number of Weeks[2]	
	0 — 13.0 Weeks (1)	13.1 — 26.0 Weeks (2)
1930	%	%
January	70.5	29.5
February	66.8	33.2
March	59.2	40.8
April	50.2	49.8
May	49.2	50.8
June	50.5	49.5
July	51.8	48.2
August	52.4	47.6
September	52.4	47.6
Average	55.9	44.1

[1] *Statistische Beilage zum Reichsarbeitsblatt,* December, 1927–October, 1930.
[2] The differences in the percentages shown and 100% through June, 1929, are accounted for by the transitional measures which authorized the payment of standard benefits up through 52 weeks.
[3] Data not published.

TABLE 38

Wage Classification of Recipients of Standard Benefits

(Number in each wage class as a percentage of the total number receiving benefits on the fifteenth of each month.)

Wage Class	I	II	III	IV	V	VI	VII	VIII	IX	X	XI
1928											
January	1.4	2.6	4.4	9.2	13.0	15.9	15.5	14.1	9.8	6.7	7.4
February	1.7	3.1	4.1	10.0	13.8	16.1	15.1	13.3	9.3	6.1	6.6
March	1.7	3.0	5.0	10.1	13.7	16.0	15.1	13.2	9.2	6.2	6.8
April	1.9	3.0	5.0	10.8	13.9	16.0	14.9	12.8	8.9	6.0	6.8
May	2.3	3.4	5.3	11.2	13.9	15.7	14.3	12.2	8.7	5.9	7.1
June	2.4	3.5	5.6	11.8	14.2	15.3	13.9	11.7	8.5	5.9	7.2
July	2.6	3.7	5.9	12.4	14.5	15.0	13.5	11.3	8.5	5.8	6.8
August	2.6	3.6	5.6	12.0	14.2	15.0	13.6	11.5	8.8	6.1	7.0
September	2.5	3.4	5.4	11.6	13.8	15.2	13.8	11.8	9.2	6.2	7.0
October	2.1	3.1	4.8	10.7	13.1	15.0	14.2	12.3	9.9	6.9	7.9
November	1.8	2.9	4.7	10.1	12.5	14.7	14.3	12.9	10.3	7.3	8.5
December	1.9	3.2	5.2	10.2	12.2	14.4	14.2	12.8	10.1	7.2	8.6

463

CHAPTER XXVII

UNEMPLOYMENT INSURANCE IN THE UNITED STATES

Since no state in this country has passed an unemployment insurance law, such plans as exist are purely voluntary. There are three varieties of these plans, namely, (1) Union, (2) Employers, and (3) Joint.

1. Union Benefit Plans [1]

The benefit schemes which are financed and managed by the unions are found primarily in the printing trades where 23 locals with a total membership in 1928 of approximately 29,000 had such plans. In addition, there were nine locals of bakery workers who paid unemployment benefits. There were four small locals of lace workers, one local of the brewery workers, and one of the wood-carvers which also had some form of benefit. Three very small internationals, the German-American Typographical Union, the United Wall Paper Crafts, and the Diamond Workers also provide such benefits. Two more internationals, the Cigar Makers and Lithographers once had out-of-work benefits but have discontinued them, the former dropping its plan in 1920 and the latter in 1923. The plan of the cigar makers was abandoned as was their general benefit system because of increasing average age of their members and the inroads made by machine methods of rolling cigars.

[1] For the information on these plans see American Federation of Labor, *Unions Provide Against Unemployment* (Washington, 1929), pp. 109; Bryce M. Stewart, *Unemployment Benefits in the United States*, a study prepared under the auspices of the Industrial Relations Counsellors, Inc., and published by them. Some of this material was published in Unemployment in the United States, *op. cit.*, pp. 422-29. See also John B. Andrews, chapter on Trade-Union Unemployment Funds, in *Business Cycles and Unemployment*, pp. 293-301.

In all, Dr. Bryce M. Stewart estimates that in 1928 the number of workers covered in the exclusively union plans was 35,000.[2] The most liberal of these plans are the nine sponsored by locals of the Photoengravers, a union of very skilled and highly paid workers. The benefits provided by these locals range from $30 a week in Chicago to $12 a week in Cleveland and Cincinnati. The waiting period is, in general, two weeks and the period of benefit ranges from 26 weeks in Chicago and Boston to 12 weeks in Minneapolis and Cincinnati. The average annual cost per member is $16 in New York and (including sick benefits) $33.50 in Chicago. In the smaller cities the per capita cost ranges from $2.00 to $7.50.

The two largest local unions which pay unemployment benefits are Typographical Union No. 6 of New York City and Pressmen's Union No. 51 of the same city. The former, which now has a membership of over 10,000, has had a long history of out-of-work benefits. It has changed several times from levying special assessments in periods of business depression to protect its members against current unemployment to a regularized plan of fixed assessments. Since 1916 it has assessed its membership one-half of one per cent of their earnings for half of the year. After $10,000 is deducted each year for the benefit of the School for Apprentices, the remainder goes into the fund. The benefits are graduated according to the length of membership in the local. Those who have been members for less than two years receive but $8.00 a week while those who have been members for four years or more receive the full $14.00. There are two intervening groups which are paid $10.00 and $12.00 respectively. After a waiting period of one week, benefits can be paid during the summer slack season from June 15 to September 15 for a period not to exceed seven weeks. On an average approximately 4 per cent of the members have claimed benefits for an average duration of nearly 3 weeks. In 1927 and 1928, however, the percentage of mem-

[2] See *Unemployment Benefits in the United States.*

bers paid was larger and the duration of their unemployment longer than the previous average.

The New York Printing Pressmen's local, with a membership of about 3,500, has paid unemployment benefits of $12.00 a week since 1927. In 1928, 501 members or approximately one-seventh of the total, drew benefits for an average period of 5 weeks and an average amount of $49.00. The cost per member of the union was thus a little over $7.

A number of locals in the Bakers' Union have paid unemployment benefits for long periods of time. The Buffalo local has, for example, had such a plan for over forty years, while St. Louis began to make payments in 1920. New York followed in 1920, and subsequently a number of other locals. St. Louis plan is fairly typical and provides that those who have been members of the union for at least three years (after a waiting period of two weeks) receive benefits of $7 a week up to a maximum in any one year of $70. These are also confined to the slack period which, in this case, is from Christmas to the end of March. During 1927, 149 of the 1,190 members received benefits amounting on the average to $56.78, or an average cost per member of about $7.

The most striking impression gained from the trade union plans is that of the meagerness of the experience. Whereas out-of-work benefits were very frequently paid by the English unions from 1850 and 1875 on,[3] at present only slightly over 1 per cent of the membership of the American Federation of Labor is in unions which grant such benefits.

2. Employers' Plans

At the time when the General Electric Company announced its plan in the summer of 1930, there were 11 companies with a total of 11,200 employees which had their own plans of unemployment compensation. These firms were as follows:

[3] See S. & B. Webb, *History of Trade Unionism*.

Firm	Date Plan Formed	Approximate Number of Employees in 1928	
		Total	Eligible
1. Dennison Mfg. Co.	1916	2,790	2,308
2. Columbia Conserve Co. . . .	1917	155	98
3. Dutchess Bleachery	1919	488	441
4. United Diamond Works . . .	1921	100	100
5. Crocker-McElwain Co.	1920	742	316
6. John A. Manning Co.	1920	516	466
7. S. C. Johnson Co.	1922	359	300
8. Leeds and Northrup	1923	921	800
9. Procter and Gamble			
Ivorydale	1923	2,607	2,058
Port Ivory	1923	1,468	1,123
10. Brown and Bailey	1927	154	120
11. Consolidated Water-Power and Paper Co.	1929	900	700
Total	. . . .	11,200	8,830

Two of these plans, those of the Columbia Conserve Company and the Proctor and Gamble Company, are really systems of guaranteed employment. The former, which is well known for its progressive policies and which has been managed and is now primarily owned by its workers, puts workers who are chosen by their fellows on an annual salary and guarantees them that amount for as long as they are retained or not demoted. Procter and Gamble, on the other hand, as we have pointed out, guarantees 48 weeks of work to those who have been employed for over six months and have bought stock in the company. This amount of employment has always been furnished and the payments have been infinitesimal.

Of the plans providing unemployment insurance rather than guaranteed employment, those of the Dennison Com-

[4] We are indebted to the Industrial Relations Counsellors, Dr. Bryce Stewart and Miss Mary Gilson, for permission to use this material. The Rockland Finishing Co. and the American Cast Iron Pipe Co. once had such plans but have abandoned them.

pany, the Dutchess Bleachery, Crocker-McElwain, and Leeds and Northrup, are perhaps the best known and should be briefly analyzed. By 1916 the Dennison Company had been fairly successful in regularizing its production. It then decided to accumulate a reserve with which to pay unemployment benefits and during the next four years laid aside a total of $140,000 for this purpose. The plan went formally into effect in 1920 and provided protection not only against a complete lack of work because of lay-offs but also against diminished earnings which resulted from transfers to other jobs. In the case of complete lay-offs, the workers without dependents receive 60 per cent of their average earnings during the preceding six months while those with dependents receive 80 per cent of this average.

These provisions apply to cases of temporary lay-offs where the workers are to be reëmployed. In those cases where the lay-off is permanent because the force is being reduced in size, either a two weeks' advance notice is given or a dismissal wage equal to two weeks' pay. The feature of the plan which has caused most discussion inside the plant is that which provides that, when a worker is transferred to a new job where his earnings are less than before, the difference shall be met from the unemployment insurance fund. Up to the end of 1928, the total amount which had been paid out in benefits was $83,502, or approximately three-tenths of one per cent of the total payroll during the nine-year period. It is understood, however, that the depression period of 1929-30 caused a very severe burden upon the fund and decreased it greatly.

Two other closely associated plans have been those of the Dutchess Bleachery Company [5] and the Rockland Finishing Company, which are both owned by the well-known firm of Deering-Milliken and which under the inspiration of Mr. Harold Hatch, the Vice-President of Deering-Milliken, established unemployment insurance in 1920. The funds for these benefits are built up after (1) 6 per cent

[5] See Ben M. Selekman, *Sharing Management with Workers;* James Myers, *Representative Government in Industry.*

has been earned on the capital stock of the company and (2) a further 6 per cent has been set up as a reserve fund to provide for the payment of dividends in years when they are not earned. The maximum amount which was to be available in the unemployment insurance fund was $85,-000—a sum approximately equal to the 6 per cent on capital which was the annual prior payment to the stockholders. The benefits provided protection against short-time as well as against complete unemployment. The plan originally provided that if a worker who had been employed for more than 12 months was furnished with less than 48 hours of work a week he should be paid one-half of the earnings which he lost. This would mean, for example, that if a worker were employed for 24 hours, he would receive his regular pay for this time plus an unemployment benefit equal to 12 hours' earnings on the twenty-four hours which were lost.

The plan was instituted during a period in which profits had been high and unemployment low. The depression of 1920-21 made inroads upon the fund and cut down the profits very greatly. In order to limit its liability, the company felt obliged in 1922 to provide that, if and when the fund fell below $50,000, the payment of unemployment benefits should begin only when the hours worked per week fell below 35. It was provided, however, that in no event should the workers receive less than 24 hours' pay, or half-time. Thus if a worker were employed for 24 hours, he would under these circumstances be paid for 29½ hours and not for 36 as under the former arrangement. If he were not employed at all, he would, however, receive 24 hours' pay.

During the decade which has elapsed since the plan was put into operation, the Dutchess Bleachery Company has experienced many of the same economic difficulties which the whole northern textile industry has suffered. Since surplus earnings over the amount set aside for capital have seldom been made, the fund has had few replenishments and in consequence, like the Dennison fund, has shown a gradual tendency to exhaust itself. By 1928 it had fallen to approximately $19,000 after a total of approximately $68,-000 had been paid out in benefits. It is also true that the fact that those who have been employed for less than a year are not eligible for benefits, permits the company to reduce the size of its force somewhat without attendant cost.

The plan of the Rockland Finishing Company was virtually identical with that of the Dutchess Bleachery. The depression of 1920-21 necessitated paying out slightly over $99,000 in benefits and virtually ate up the original contribution of $100,000 to the fund. The continuance of the depression in the textile industry finally caused the company to discontinue the plan in 1923, having paid out in benefits during its life slightly over $106,000 or 2.6 per cent of the payroll during the period the system was in effect.

The plan of the United Diamond Works, which is the only non-union plant in that trade, is an informal one. When the plant is shut down the company pays 25 per cent of their wages to all male manual workers who have been employed for over six months and 20 per cent to all women manual workers. Those in supervisory positions are paid a larger percentage. This plan was probably in part adopted because of the fact that the Diamond Workers Union pays unemployment benefits. It was perhaps felt necessary to provide somewhat similar benefits in order to remove this inducement for their workers to join the union.

The Leeds-Northrup Company of Philadelphia furnishes the next most notable illustration of an employer's plan. The firm deposits 2 per cent of the weekly amount paid out in wages until a reserve is built which with accumulated interest amounts to twice the maximum payroll during the preceding year. Further contributions stop when this point is reached but are resumed whenever the benefits paid deplete the balance below this amount. Employees without dependents, who are laid off, receive 50 per cent of their usual earnings, while those with dependents receive 75 per cent. Losses from part-time or from transfer are protected to the same degree as complete lay-offs, namely in the ratio of one-half and three-quarters respectively of the loss in earnings which has been suffered.

There is no waiting period but the length of time for which benefits are paid is graduated according to the amount of time the worker has spent with the company. Those who have been employed for three months are, for example, eligible for three weeks' benefit a year, while those who have been employed for over 5 years are eligible for twenty-six weeks' benefit. Up to the end of 1928 the company had paid out in benefits approximately $39,000 or three-tenths of one per cent of its total payroll during the four and a quarter years in which it had been in effect.

The most recent employees' plan for unemployment insurance is that announced by the General Electric Company, which has now been adopted by nearly all of its works. Each works is treated as a unit and, when 60 per cent of the workers there have agreed to become members of the plan, it goes into effect. The members then contribute 1 per cent of their previous average earnings for so long as they are earning more than half pay and these sums are matched with equal contributions on the part of the company.

The benefits do not provide protection against men who are permanently laid off because of a reduction in the size of the force but they do protect the workers who, though they are to be retained, may be temporarily laid off. Because of the fact that the business of the General Electric has been quite steadily increasing, any reduction in the working force is, for the present at least, fairly remote. For the first two weeks of unemployment no benefits are paid. After that they amount to 50 per cent of the average full-time earnings but are not to exceed $20.00 a week for not more than 10 weeks during the year. The maximum amount which an unemployed worker can obtain in a year will then be $200.00. There is a provision that, under certain conditions to be worked out later, benefits may be paid for short-time whenever a worker is employed for less than half-time. A small part of the fund can also be used to make loans to especially needy cases, but which are not to exceed $200.00 to any person and which are to be repaid by subsequent deductions from his earnings.

Another interesting feature of the plan is that when the expenditures from the fund "amount to 100 per cent or more of the average normal weekly receipts" the company is to declare an emergency. "Normal" contributions from the contributory members cease at this point and instead *all* of the employees, whether members or not, who are employed for more than half-time are assessed 1 per cent. This includes all the supervisory staff of the particular works from the general manager down. In addition, the overhead administrative and sales force of the company, which is not attached to any particular works, will be assessed that fraction of a per cent of their salaries which the payroll of the particular works forms of the total payroll for all the works. Thus if the emergency should be declared at the Schenectady plant and if the amount paid out in wages and salaries by this plant was 25 per cent of the total wages and salaries in all the plants, then the general executive, engineering, and sales force would be assessed a quarter of one per cent of their salary. This would have the direct effect of making the higher officials share in the burdens of the manual workers and of offering a slight stimulus to the sales force to get more business in order to lessen the deductions from their own salaries.

While all of the workers will thus be liable for assessments during these periods of emergency, the benefits will be paid only to those who have already become members and have agreed to have 1 per cent deducted from their earnings. By January, 1931, the plan had obtained the necessary 60 per cent vote in nearly all of the plants and approximately 38,000 workers were formally under the system. Since the remaining manual workers are liable for emergency assessments but not eligible for benefits, it is expected that the majority of this group will sooner or later elect to come under the plan.

Even with this most promising addition, however, it

must be confessed that progress on the part of employers in voluntarily installing unemployment compensation plans has been disappointingly slow. The total number of employees covered, even with the General Electric workers, is only approximately 47,000 or about one-sixth of one per cent of the wage earners or salaried workers who might be expected to be eligible for such protection. The total sums paid out in unemployment benefits up to the end of 1928 by private firms was only $330,590,[6] which in turn was only one-half of one per cent of the payroll during the period. The General Electric payments will of course greatly increase this amount but the total will still be comparatively small as compared with the need.

The scope of voluntary company plans in England, which provide additional benefits to those given under the unemployment insurance act, is greater than in the United States. Miss Mary Gilson found that 13 English companies employing in all approximately 62,000 eligible workers had installed such additional schemes.[7] This was over seven times the numbers who were then protected by employers' plans in the United States. Even now with the General Electric plan, there are more workers in such voluntary plans in England while in proportion to the population the disparity is still greater. The absence of compulsory unemployment insurance in this country cannot, therefore, be said to have encouraged more voluntary initiative on the part of employers in furnishing such protection than has the compulsory system of Great Britain.

3. JOINT PLANS OF EMPLOYERS AND UNIONS

There are a number of cases where unemployment insurance has been provided by collective agreements between

[6] Data furnished by the Industrial Relations Counsellors, Inc.
[7] Mary B. Gilson and E. J. Riches, Employers Additional Unemployment Benefit Schemes in Great Britain, *International Labour Review*, Mar. 1930, pp. 9-47. The chief firms which put these plans into effect are the Quaker "Model Employers" of the Cadbury, Rountree, and Frye cocoa firms and Lever Bros.

unions and employers. The most notable illustrations of this kind are: (1) the agreements negotiated by the Amalgamated Clothing Workers in the men's clothing markets of Chicago, New York, and Rochester; (2) the 40-week guarantee in the women's clothing industry of Cleveland, Ohio, by the manufacturers to the International Ladies' Garment Workers, and (3) the recent national agreement in the full-fashioned hosiery industry between the manufacturers with "union shops" and the Full Fashioned Hosiery Workers. The following table lists these joint plans and a number of others of less importance:

TABLE 39

UNEMPLOYMENT INSURANCE PLANS PROVIDED FOR BY JOINT AGREEMENT

INDUSTRY	DATE OF ESTABLISHMENT	NUMBER OF WORKERS COVERED
1. Wall Paper	1894	450
2. Women's Clothing:		
Cleveland	1921	1,100
New York	. . . .	. . . .
Cloaks and Suits	1924	. . . .
Dresses	1925	. . . .
3. Men's Clothing		
Chicago	1923	15,000
Rochester	1928	10,000
New York	1928	30,000
4. Lace	. . . .	400
5. Hats and Caps		
Cloth Hats	. . . .	2,000
United Hatters	. . . .	500
6. Cleaning and Dyeing		
Chicago	. . . .	2,100
St. Louis	. . . .	450
7. Full Fashioned Hosiery	1930	7,000
Total Number of Workers Covered	. . . .	69,100

The Chicago plan was put into effect in 1923 when a general increase of 10 per cent in wages was being obtained in other markets. In order to get the system started, the union in Chicago agreed to accept an increase of only 7 per cent provided the employers would contribute 1½ per cent of the payroll to an unemployment insurance fund which was to be matched by an equal contribution of the workers. The workers thus really paid the employers' contribution in the form of a 1½ per cent smaller increase in wage costs than would otherwise have occurred. In 1928 the employers' share was raised to 3 per cent which was, of course, the precise amount by which the 1923 increase in the base rate fell below the general increase in other markets.

In the system of benefits which was set up it was provided that the year should be divided into two seasons, namely, May—October and April—November. A waiting period equal to one week of unemployment (44 hours) was required in each season before the worker was eligible for benefits. These benefits were to be 40 per cent of the full-time wages of the worker but were not to exceed $20 a week nor to run for more than 2½ weeks in each season, or a total of 5 weeks during the year.[8]

The question of compensation for short-time gave rise to some interesting provisions. The union has insisted upon and has obtained the equal sharing of work among the members of a shop. This made unemployment more a matter of part-time than of complete unemployment. The union consequently struggled to obtain and finally secured payment for short-time as an integral part of the plan. After a total of 44 hours which were lost during a season from part-time, the partially employed workers became eligible for benefits but with the added proviso that the first four hours of part-time in each week would not be compensable. The benefits on any further time which was lost in this fashion were to be 40 per cent of the hourly wages, but in no week were the earnings and unemployment benefits to exceed $50. In 1925, benefits were paid for only those hours of short-time below 36 per week. Since then all short-time has been recognized as subject to compensation.

---

[8] For the provisions of the original agreement see *Agreement between Clothing Manufacturers of Chicago and Amalgamated Clothing Workers of America Establishing Unemployment Insurance Fund*, 1923, 11 pp.

A number of further administrative issues arose as to whether the fund was to be on a market or establishment basis and how the unemployment was to be computed and paid. The union naturally wanted the fund to be a general one for the market as a whole since in this way any unexpended balance, which a particular factory would otherwise have, would be merged into the pool for the industry as a whole and would be available for the workers in other establishments where unemployment was high and where otherwise the funds would have been exhausted by the claims for benefits. The employers, however, and particularly those with comparatively steady employment, wanted to make the company the unit. In this way, firms whose contributions exceed the claims for benefit made by their workers would be able to retain this balance for themselves. The manufacturers finally won their way and separate establishment funds were set up for the manufacturing house. In the case of the sub-manufacturers who took work on contract from the manufacturers, it was, however, provided that the contributions should be pooled in a market fund which would protect equally all those who worked for subcontractors. In practice, to lessen administrative difficulties, all the firms have chosen the same persons to serve as trustees, and these meeting with the representatives of the union and the neutral chairman act simultaneously in this capacity for all the firms. The rules are therefore uniform between firms.

An efficient employment office has been found to be an essential feature of the plan. Up to 1922 the union office had not been efficient and the manufacturers wanted to take over the employment function completely. To head off this possibility, the union engaged Bryce M. Stewart, then director of the employment service of Canada, as the director of this office, and he speedily put affairs on a much more business-like basis. The office was furnished with copies of the payrolls of each firm and used these to make the proper entries on the record card for each worker of the amounts of time worked and pay received. It was not a difficult task then to compute twice a year how much employment benefit each worker was to receive. If the amount of claims on any particular fund exceeded the money available, then the claims were scaled down proportionately. The checks once made out were distributed to the workers by the business agents of the union. This method was adopted as a means of building up the prestige of the officials of the organization and of the union itself.

In 1928, when the contributions of the employers to the fund were raised to 3 per cent, which made a total payment of $4\frac{1}{2}$ per cent, the length of the benefit period was also increased by one-half or up to a total of $7\frac{1}{2}$ weeks during the year. A further proviso was added—that any unpaid fraction of this might be cumulated from year to year. In order to protect the funds the proportion of the earnings which is paid out in benefits has been lowered from 40 to 30 per cent. No benefits were paid out until the fund had been in operation for a year, and during the six years that followed, the fund paid out approximately a total of five and a half million dollars, with administrative costs approximately equal to 6 per cent of contributions.

The New York and Rochester plans were established in 1928 and have the following differences from the older Chicago system: (1) the employers alone contribute to the fund—the amount of their contributions being $1\frac{1}{2}$ per cent; (2) the New York fund is on a market rather than an establishment basis, although the Rochester funds are for specific establishments; (3) the rules governing the payment of benefits are not as precise as under the Chicago system and these are distributed upon more or less of an individual basis according to the need of the applicant. This has been brought about largely because of the inadequacy of the available resources and the desire to avert as much hardship as possible. It has, however, caused the system at times to partake more of the nature of poor relief than of insurance and has caused the unions and the Board of Trustees a great deal of embarrassment in deciding just which individuals are to be given relief and how much they are to receive. One lesson from these experiments is that it is highly desirable that every plan should be as automatic as possible in its administration. By the fall of 1930, a total of $455,000 had been paid out by the New York fund and approximately $114,000 by the Rochester fund.

The Cleveland guarantee plan was instituted in the unionized branch of the women's clothing industry of that city in 1921, when the Board of Referees, in putting into effect a 15 per cent wage reduction and the establishment of production standards in the factories, ruled that the employers should in return guarantee to their employees 40 weeks of work a year. Although this was increased in 1922 to 41 weeks, it was subsequently reduced to 40 weeks. Each firm agrees to pay one-half of the wages which regular workers may lose from failure on the part of the firm to offer the full 40 weeks of employment and, as a guarantee, posts currently a bond equal to 10 per cent of the wage bill.

In practice most of the firms have been able to furnish the full amount of employment. During the nine years from 1921 to 1929 inclusive, the total amount of benefits paid out was slightly over $186,000. This was, however, a very relative charge upon the industry, averaging slightly less than one-half of one per cent of the total wages bill in the three years of 1927-29 and less than one-tenth of one per cent of the total sales of the firms concerned. In recent years, moreover, the majority of the firms have not found it necessary to make any payments at all. By far the major portions of the benefits have been paid by comparatively few firms and particularly by those who produce carefully tailored garments in the face of the fact that increasingly less importance has been attached to these qualities by the consumers.

It is, however, doubtless true that the employment guarantee has somewhat limited the ability of the manufacturer to train a sufficient number of workers for the peak periods. They have naturally been reluctant to take on permanently workers to whom they must guarantee 40 weeks of work.

To help meet this situation, the employers are permitted to take on peak workers up to 20 per cent of their force for not more than 8 weeks a season, and on occasion even these provisions have been liberalized. But to take on workers who can be employed for so few weeks tends to be costly and some of the firms are inclined instead to rely upon outside sub-contracting shops to meet their peaks.

These outside shops, run by sub-contractors, were originally under the employment guarantee. Because of the fact, however, that the orders for women's garments, and more particularly for coats, were sharply peaked in the spring and fall, it became evident that these workers could not be guaranteed as much employment as 40 weeks. The guarantee was then removed from the outside shops and the manufacturers then increasingly used these shops to meet their peak loads. The employment guarantee which did operate to stabilize employment within the factories therefore probably did make employment in the outside shops somewhat less steady. The union now found itself composed of two groups, namely the inside workers, forming two-thirds of the total, who were guaranteed 40 weeks of work and whose yearly incomes compared very favorably with those in other industries, and the outside workers, who comprised the remaining third, and who were fortunate if they average 24 or 26 weeks of work a year. An attempt to protect the outside workers was made in 1928, when it was ruled that both the firms and the sub-contractors should pay a 1 per cent assessment upon their payrolls and that the funds should be used to relieve the workers in the outside shops. These amounts have, however, been grossly inadequate to meet the claims of the outside workers and have in practice been distributed as a form of poor relief.

Unemployment insurance funds were also started in the women's garment industry and in the fur trades of New York City. The Communist faction got control of these organizations in 1926 and 1927 and helped to precipitate strikes which resulted in the discontinuance of the funds. One of the most interesting agreements is that recently negotiated by the Union of Full Fashioned Hosiery Workers with manufacturers producing about 40 per cent of the product. The union, in return for agreeing to a reduction in wages and an increase in the number of machines which a worker would tend, obtained the complete union shop and a provision for unemployment insurance. For the first year the manufacturers pay 1 per cent of their payroll to furnish protection against unemployment to their workers and after that the union's contribution is to be one-half that of the employers. The precise rules of the plan as to whether it is to be on an establishment or market basis, to provide for part-time as well as complete unemployment, etc., are in the process of being worked out. The scope of the program, however, has been recently reduced because of the refusal of a number of manufacturers to make the payments for unemployment although accepting the wage-reduction and the extension in the standard day's work.

4. Legislative Attempts to Obtain Unemployment Insurance in the United States

The first unemployment insurance bill was introduced in the Massachusetts Legislature in 1916 and was modeled upon the English system in that it called for contributions by all three parties, namely employers, workers, and the state. This bill failed to make any headway, although a committee was appointed to investigate social insurance in general. The next development came from Wisconsin, and owed its impetus to Professor John R. Commons. Professor Commons was struck by the pressure which workmen's compensation had placed upon employers to reduce accidents in order to reduce premium payments. He came to believe that if unemployment were made a burden upon the employers they would seek in a similar fashion to reduce it.

Stressing therefore the idea of prevention, he advanced the theory that the sole cost should be thrown upon the employer, and at his instance such a bill was introduced into the Wisconsin legislature by Senator Huber. The bill provided for a maximum payment of $1 a day for the involuntarily unemployed after a waiting period of three days, up to a maximum of 13 weeks a year. The maximum which a worker could obtain would therefore be $91 a year. The employers were in turn to insure themselves for the first year in a state-wide insurance company, which was to be formed for the purpose, and after that in any other mutual insurance company which might be formed. These mutuals were, however, to turn over 10 per cent of their receipts to the state to meet the expense of administering the act and of maintaining the system of free public employment offices, which were recognized as being essential in determining whether or not a person was actually unemployed.

It was provided that the premium rates were to be varied between industries according to the relative amount of unemployment which characterized them and that individual employers within these industries were to have their rates graduated according to their experience.

The bill attracted a great deal of attention but in 1921 was voted down by the Wisconsin Senate by 19 to 10. It was reintroduced in 1923, with a number of amendments, among which was a permission to commercial companies to carry the insurance. It was, however, again defeated and, although introduced in both the 1925 and 1927 sessions, was defeated both times. In 1925 the vote in the Senate was 20 to 12, while in 1927 the vote in the House was 66 to 20.

Professor Commons defended the bill on the ground that not only would it make employers try to reduce seasonal unemployment by producing to stock and developing fillers, but that it would lessen cyclical fluctuations as well. He argued, for example, that banks would restrain individual companies from over-expanding in periods of prosperity if the firms were to be liable up to $90 for every workman whom they took on who would later be laid off.

Aside from the question as to whether the employers should bear the full costs of unemployment insurance and whether such payments could be expected to prevent unemployment, which we shall discuss later, there were two further defects in Professor Commons' plan: (1) the control of the insurance agencies was given completely to the employers and to private interests, and also (2) the administration of the insurance agencies was divorced from that of the employment bureaus. The inevitable result of this would have been that the insurance bodies would have resisted claims strenuously in their efforts to keep down costs and that a great deal of friction would have developed because of the separation of the placement and paying agency from the insuring bodies. This latter feature is one of the weakest features of the British Health Insurance Act and it would be unfortunate to embody it within any system of unemployment insurance in this country.

The present depression has revived the interest in unemployment insurance and bills are pending in a number of states. The three main types of bills are those providing for: (1) contributions by the employers and the state, as is advocated by the Socialist Party, (2) exclusive contributions by the employers with the state paying the cost of administration, as provided in the draft bill of the American Association for Labor Legislation, (3) joint contributions by employers and workers. A number of state groups which have studied the problem have come to feel that the last is the most desirable form and bills with these provisions have been introduced in Ohio, Michigan, and California.[10]

Summary. Taken in their entirety, the trade-union, employers, and joint employment benefit plans at present include approximately 151,000 workers distributed as follows:

[10] For a more detailed description of the content of these various sets of proposals see Paul H. Douglas, American Plans of Unemployment Insurance, *Survey Graphic*, February, 1931, pp. 484-86. Copies of the bills may be obtained from tht Consumers League of Ohio, 341 Engineers Building, Cleveland; the American Association for Labor Legislation, 131 East 23rd St., New York City; the National Socialist Party, 2653 West Washington St., Chicago, and the Conference for Progressive Labor Action, 104 Fifth Avenue, New York City.

Plans	Approximate Number of Workers Covered
Union	34,700
Employers	47,000
Joint	69,500
TOTAL	151,200

This number is approximately one-half of one per cent of the gainfully employed wage and salaried workers. Since it has taken a decade for even this number to be covered, it would seem that while such ventures are extremely valuable, both as experiment stations and to get the public mind interested in the subject, we cannot rely upon voluntary efforts if substantial progress is to be made in furnishing any adequate protection to the workers.

CHAPTER XXVIII

THE CASE FOR UNEMPLOYMENT INSURANCE AND A PROPOSED PLAN FOR THE UNITED STATES

1. The Case for Unemployment Insurance

At present the only two defenses which protect the unemployed worker in the United States from want are his savings and charity. If the worker is married and unskilled, or if though skilled, he has several dependents, it will be difficult for him to accumulate substantial reserves from his own earnings. If he is both unskilled and has dependents, it will be almost impossible for him to have such savings.

If the period of unemployment is protracted, as it is likely to be when cyclical and technological causes are at work, then the families are commonly forced to undergo the most severe types of privation. Even when the unemployed do not suffer from actual cold and hunger, their previous standard of living will be seriously reduced and many of their families will suffer losses which will never be fully repaired.

Thus the average starting rate for unskilled labor in July, 1930, was 43.1 cents an hour.[1] If the unskilled were therefore to work for 10 hours a day, their maximum daily earnings would be $4.31, and if they worked 306 days during the year, their maximum yearly earnings would be $1316. But in practice, the average, even without complete unemployment, is less than this. For not all of the unskilled are in occupations with a 10 hour day and there is a considerable amount of broken time within employment which this class of labor necessarily suffers. It is virtually impossible to expect that an unskilled worker receiving $25.00 a week

[1] *Monthly Labor Review,* November, 1930, p. 187.

or less and who has a wife or more dependents to support can make any appreciable savings. Unemployment of even a few weeks' duration would generally exhaust his reserves. The skilled workers, of course, fare better, but in view of the fact that the average yearly earnings of the employed non-agricultural wage and salaried workers in 1928 was only $1504 or $29 a week,[2] the general surplus available for saving is not large among the majority of the American workers.

The only protection which we are now able to afford to these persons is through charity. This is grossly defective in that it is humiliating, inadequate, and uncertain. There should be some better way of helping to take care of good workmen and their families than by doling out niggardly quantities of relief in such a manner as to lower the self-respect of the applicant. There is indeed a certain grim irony in the fact that in a country where the dominant economic and political classes have for a decade prided themselves on the supposed fact that we did not have the "dole," which they confusedly thought the European systems of unemployment insurance to be, the only social protection against the losses of unemployment should be the real dole of public and private charity.

Our discussion of the various causes of unemployment has shown that, despite all the efforts to reduce its volume, a very considerable amount can be expected to continue for the predictable future. But if we cannot greatly stabilize employment we can and should stabilize the incomes of the workers to a far greater extent than is now the case. The only practicable method of accomplishing this is by the method of insurance, whereby, while workmen are employed, pooled reserves may be built up which will be paid out as benefits to those who are unemployed through no fault of their own.

This practice is indeed now employed by nearly all well-managed enterprises so far as their investors are concerned.

[2] Douglas and Jennison, *The Movement of Money and Real Earnings in the United States, 1926-1928*, p. 27.

It was formerly accepted business practice for corporations during periods of prosperity to distribute virtually all of their net earnings to their stockholders. When the periods of depression came and net earnings were either low or non-existent, there were but scanty funds to distribute as dividends. The cash income of those investors who bought stock fluctuated therefore widely. During the last fifteen years, however, well-managed enterprises have changed their policy and now lay aside a portion of their net earnings in good times. These reserves are then used to meet dividend payments in periods when the current net earnings are low. In this way the cash incomes of the American middle and upper economic classes have been greatly stabilized and their lives rendered far more secure. Thus, according to the Standard Statistics Company, the total amount paid out in interest and dividends in 1930 by reporting American corporations was 8.0 billions of dollars as compared with 7.6 billions in 1929.[3] In other words, despite the adverse business conditions, the cash income of the investors in these corporations was actually 5 per cent more than it had been during the preceding year. It is of course probable that investors in smaller corporations did not fare so well and it is doubtful whether the reserve funds of the larger corporations can maintain this rate of payment during 1931. But a very large degree of stability has been achieved for investors.

In contrast with this, however, has been the appreciable decline in the income of the wage-earners during the period of depression, both because of unemployment and part-time. The Standard Statistics Company has, for example, estimated that the total income of wage and salaried workers in industries other than agriculture shrank from 44.6 billions of dollars in 1929 to 35.75 billions in 1930, or by a decline of 8.85 billions of dollars.[4] We are inclined to believe that this somewhat overstates the actual decrease

---

[3] *Statistical Bulletin*, Standard Statistics Company, November 15, 1930; January 1931, p. 15.

[4] *Standard Trade and Securities, General Section* (issued by the Standard Statistics Co.), October 15, 1930, pp. 1-3.

but there has, beyond doubt, been a very great shrinkage.

It would seem to us only logical that in some way the same type of protection which is now provided for investors should be extended to workers. Such a method would be the farthest removed from the real "dole" which we now have and would be as self-respecting as fire or life insurance or any other method of providing financial protection against great risk through the accumulation of pooled reserves.

Such a program would, moreover, contribute towards the stabilization of industry itself. Dollars of purchasing power would be transferred from periods of prosperity, when demand is brisk and men are employed, to periods of depression, when men are unemployed and the monetary demand is apparently unable to take all the goods off the market at their cost prices. By putting more purchasing power into the hands of consumers in these periods, more goods will be purchased than would otherwise be the case, with the result that the cumulative decline of production would be at least in part arrested. It should be frankly recognized, however, that the program of handling the reserves would need to be carefully worked out. If all of the premiums were invested in government bonds during periods of prosperity, they might, by indirectly diverting purchasing power from consumers' goods to the investment market, contribute to a still further expansion of fixed capital, or to a heightened increase in the prices of securities. It would seem desirable therefore to impound a portion of the premiums received during the initial period of prosperity in the form of cash reserves and place them in a type of sub-Treasury system. In this way, they could be used to neutralize the possible expansion which the investment of the remainder in bonds might cause. It should also be borne in mind that the slight checking of the purchase of consumers' goods during the later periods of the upswing in business would lead to a greater diminution in the rate of increase in producers' goods and hence would diminish the virulence of one of the major causes of business fluctuations.

During periods of depression, the unemployment reserve funds, in coöperation with the banking structure, could use the accumulated bonds as security for expanding the amount of bank credit.[5] This would then be paid out in the form of benefits and would constitute a net addition to the stock of monetary purchasing power. It is precisely this, as we have pointed out, which is needed in a period of depression to slacken the rate of decrease in the price level by increasing the demand for consumers' goods. This increase in the demand for consumers' goods above what it otherwise would be, would in turn prevent the rate of decline in producers' goods from proceeding as rapidly and would probably have a greater indirect than direct effect.

During the succeeding period of prosperity, the loans contracted on the basis of the bonds as security could be retired from the surplus of receipts over expenditures. A quantity of bonds sufficient to meet the excess of expenditures over receipts during depression periods would therefore be accumulated as a permanent asset upon which loans could again be obtained during the succeeding depressions.

These stabilizing influences would be especially marked in the case of real estate and of all products customarily sold upon the installment plan. There has been a concerted movement in most of the industrial cities of the country during the last decade to get the workers to buy their homes. This program has worked well as long as the workmen were employed and could meet their payments. But when they lose their jobs, they are customarily unable to continue these payments. In a large percentage of the cases, this failure has meant the loss of virtually all the part payments as well, and with this, the sweeping away of savings. The real estate dealers in turn have been compelled to take back property which they thought had been finally trans-

---

[5] This could either be through renewals of the 15 day loans which the Federal Reserve Banks can make to member banks upon such security or by altering the Federal Reserve Act to permit bonds held by the unemployment insurance funds to serve as security for longer loans.

ferred. As long indeed as the jobs and income of the workers are so uncertain as they are, it is probably unwise for the unskilled and semi-skilled to attempt to buy their homes. The real estate industry cannot hope, therefore, to be really stabilized unless the worker's income is at least partially stabilized during the periods of unemployment. What is true of real estate is of course in some degree also true of such industries as radios, the cheaper grades of furniture, and many other articles which are sold on the installment plan.

There is still another way in which such an insurance system could be made to exercise a stabilizing influence, that is by the method of varying the employer's contributions in part according to the relative quantity of unemployment in his particular industry or firm. Thus industries with a comparatively high volume of unemployment, such as women's clothing, and iron and steel, would pay premiums which might be two or three times the average while others where employment was relatively steady, such as flour-milling, would pay appreciably less than the average. Within any given industry, moreover, the employers might be divided into several categories, with rates which varied according to the unemployment rates of each firm. These rates would originally be set for industries according to the extent of their seasonal and cyclical fluctuations in the past. They could then be revised according to experience and so adjusted for individual firms.[6] In this way an added incentive would be offered to both individual business and industries to stabilize themselves to the fullest extent practicable because, by so doing, they would reduce their premium charges. It is not certain how appreciable this added stimulus would be and it is probable that its efficacy has in the past been somewhat overstressed by advocates of unemployment insurance. There are already strong financial incentives to regularize and it may be argued that a saving of some 2 per cent on the payroll would not be decisive.

[6] The development of automatic electric computing machines should make this a comparatively manageable affair

The indirect influence of such a payment in calling attention to the losses from irregularity of operations might, however, be more important than the stimulus of the direct saving on premiums alone. While the major portion of such a stimulus would probably be to reduce seasonal fluctuations, it might also serve to restrain slightly undue cyclical expansion.

If past experience is any guide, it is idle to expect that any considerable proportion of the workers can find adequate protection through the voluntary adoption of such insurance plans by employers. For, as we have seen in our last chapter, a decade of experimentation has brought less than one per cent of the workers within the scope of such voluntary plans. Individual businesses will, moreover, always be very reluctant to adopt such proposals which will impose an appreciable added expense and thus place them at a competitive disadvantage in comparison with other companies.

The only way in which the creation of such unemployment reserves can be generalized is then by state action which will be mandatory upon industry and which will protect those firms which wish to adopt such measures from the competitive pressure exercised by their less conscientious rivals. But we should like to make clear from the very outset that state action to compel industry to set aside these reserves does not and, in our opinion, should not mean actual administration by the state of the system itself.

2. A Proposed Plan.

We turn therefore to a discussion of the features which we think any such program of insurance should embody.

1. The scope of the act should include all manual workers in industries other than agriculture employed by employers who have three or more workmen on their payrolls and all clerical workers whose full-time salary is less than $2,000 a year.

2. We prefer *joint contributions by workers and employ-*

ers to throwing the entire burden upon the employers, as has been urged by so eminent an authority as Dr. John R. Commons and is now favored by the American Association for Labor Legislation. In the first place, if the entire cost is thrust upon the employers, legislatures, because of their natural reluctance to put the enterprises of their states at a competitive disadvantage with those of others, will try to cut down on the burden by rigidly restricting the amount of benefits and their maximum duration. It will, therefore, be extremely difficult to provide adequate benefits unless both parties contribute to the support of the plan. Secondly, if the employers bear the cost, they will naturally claim the privilege of administering the mutual insurance companies the Commons plan provides. This, as we have pointed out in the preceding chapter, will inevitably create discord in the administration of the act since these companies will naturally try to reduce claims by contesting as many as possible. It is important that the workers should have an equal share in the administration of the funds. We also believe that, if the workmen contribute to the fund, they will take more of an interest in it and both they and the general public will not regard the benefits as a "dole" but rather as sums towards which they have made a self-respecting contribution. It is believed that contribution by the workers will make them more anxious to prevent abuses and to reduce unjust claims to a minimum, since the depletion of the fund by such claims will be a wastage of their contributions as well as those of the employers.

There are some who believe that the entire cost of the system should be borne by the state and others who urge that at least a portion should be. The former emphasize the reduction in administrative costs and records which would result and the ability of the state to distribute the burden through income and inheritance taxes among those best able to bear it instead of burdening workers and perhaps ultimately consumers with it. Such payments would seem, however, to the American public to be doles and to be outside the limits of political possibility. It would also remove the effect which such a system might have in stimulating industry to reduce unemployment. In our opinion it is better that the states themselves should not bear a portion of the cost of the standard benefits but should make this instead a charge upon industry and the workers. It should be recognized, however, that there will be a number of workers who will exhaust their claims to standard benefits but who, because of technological or cyclical causes, are not able to find employment. To throw these workers immediately upon poor relief will be regarded generally as a heartless act and in practice such a group will tend to be carried for a time on emergency benefits. We believe that this cost should not be saddled upon industry and is a proper charge upon the state. The state could and, in our opinion, should also bear the cost of administration of the system and of running the public employment exchanges.

3. The administration of the funds should be put in the hands of a joint board representing the accredited organizations of workers and employers, with a chairman representing the state. Industry itself, in other words, should administer the fund rather than the state. The state chairman could break deadlocks and exercise the functions of an auditor but not seek to dominate the administration. In order to be eligible for federal grants-in-aid, the state funds should be given official status but this is consistent with assigning its actual administration to such a functional body.

4. The work of the public employment offices should of course be integrated with the insurance fund and should be managed by the same body.

5. The premium rates between industries and firms should, as we have urged, be varied according to the relative amount of unemployment characterizing them.

6. Benefits should be paid primarily only to those laid off because of lack of work and not to those discharged for just cause or who quit voluntarily.

7. Benefits should only be paid to those who are customarily employed in industry and who have been employed

for wages for at least 32 weeks during the two preceding years. These standard benefits should not be paid for more than 16 weeks in any year. The unemployed will be expected to register at the nearest public employment office immediately upon being unemployed but no benefits will be paid for the first two weeks after registration. There should, moreover, be at least four contributions for each worker for every week of benefit paid.

8. The applicant cannot decline work at his trade in his locality at the going rate of wages (if there is no strike) and still continue to draw benefits. After a reasonable period of time he may be required, as jobs open, to go to other localities or take up other trades on penalty of being dropped from the benefit roll. Every effort should be made, in other words, to prevent the benefits from freezing labor in decaying industries or localities.

A worker should not of course be paid for unemployment directly due to strikes or lockouts but he should not, on the other hand, be dropped from the benefit roll because of a refusal to take work where such a strike or lockout is in progress. The system, in other words, should be neutral in the case of industrial disputes.

9. The benefits should always be appreciably less than the wages the worker could earn at his work. We favor, instead of crude flat-rate benefits, graduating the payments roughly in some proportion to the full-time weekly earnings of the worker but with the percentage decreasing as the income increases. Thus there might be some eight groups with the workers in the lowest group receiving 50 per cent of the midpoint of their group limits as benefits and with the best paid groups receiving approximately 30 per cent of a given wage in their group. The benefits would, therefore, increase as the income increased, but at a diminishing rate. As the administration of the system became more routinized we believe the system would be improved by the addition of very modest additional benefits for dependent children of the unemployed.

10. While it is probably administratively impossible and

undesirable to pay for all underemployment within employment, nevertheless when these lay-offs amount to whole days, these may be counted to the credit of the workers if reported by them to the exchanges. Another way of dealing with this problem is that of paying benefits on all time lost under 75 per cent of the standard week. This is provided in the Ohio bill, which more than any other conforms to the standards which we have suggested.

11. We believe that the system would be improved if the state were given the power to require that all workers receiving benefits be required to receive either general or vocational training during these periods. The period of unemployment might then be transformed into one of positive development and the transfer of employees from decaying industries and localities facilitated.[7]

3. Some Objections to Unemployment Insurance Considered.

1. *It is feared that the payment of benefits will in reality constitute "doles" and will undermine the independence of the wage-workers.* Here it should be pointed out that such benefits would not partake as much of the nature of doles as does the present method of granting relief from public and private charity. Moreover, if the workers contribute, such a charge will most certainly not be true while it is only proper that industry and the consumers should pay part of the burden caused by seasonal, cyclical, and technological changes from which the worker suffers but over which he has no control.

2. *It is feared that the benefits to the unemployed will cause them not to seek employment but instead to remain idle and that thus the result of any such measure would be to make the situation worse rather than better.* This danger can and should be prevented under any proper law by pro-

---

[7] For a discussion of some of the problems involved in this retraining, see the symposium sponsored by the American Association for Adult Education, *Unemployment and Adult Education.*

visions which we have already outlined but which we ask
the reader again to notice: (a) The benefits would be paid
only to those who have been laid off because of lack of work
and not to those who were discharged for cause or who
voluntarily left without just cause. (b) A waiting period of
from one to two weeks would be required before the payment of benefits begins. (c) Each unemployed person would
register at the nearest public employment office which
should seek to get work for him. Any person who refused
work in his trade or locality where there was no strike or
lockout, at the going rate of wages should not receive any
benefit, and after a reasonable period of time if he refused
work in other localities or industries, he should not receive
benefits. (d) The benefits would always be appreciably less
than the wages the worker could secure if employed. (e) The
benefits would only be paid for a limited number of weeks
in any year and should be limited to one week of benefits
for every four or five weeks for which premiums were paid
for or by the worker.

3. *It is feared that the imposition of such burden upon
industry in one state would place it at a competitive disadvantage in comparison with similar industries in other
states.* This is, of course, an objection to all social legislation by the states under our Federal form of government.
The previous adoption of workmen's compensation laws
was not, however, found to be a serious burden upon the
pioneering states and it should not be forgotten that such
a program would bring with it many savings as well. It
would stimulate the industry of the state in question to
regularize and thus effect economies, and it would also
lessen the burden upon employers of contributing to charity. Any pressure of inter-state competition can, moreover,
be greatly lessened by a coöperative movement on the part
of the chief industrial states to enact such laws. A program
of Federal grants-in-aid to the states adopting such measures would, moreover, greatly stimulate other states to
enact similar laws and thus lessen the pressure upon the
pioneers. Such Federal aid can hardly precede the passage

by some states of unemployment insurance laws but it can help to generalize the system.

4. *It is feared that many employers would take advantage of the payment of unemployment insurance to lay men off who, if no other support were available, would otherwise be retained.* It is urged that employers are sometimes reluctant to drop workmen whom they would like to let go for inefficiency, but whom they retain because of their reluctance to thrust men who do not possess reserves into the harsh rigors of unemployment. If these workmen are given some protection through unemployment insurance, it is alleged that the conscience of the employer will be assuaged and they will more readily drop the workers in question.

In dealing with this objection, we should bear in mind a number of considerations: (a) that large groups of workers such as those on the railroads and in various public utilities, etc., are employed on the seniority basis and hence are immune to such possible dangers of discrimination; (b) that it is not certain whether any very large group of employers now act in such a manner as that stated, or retain any considerable number of men whom they would fundamentally like to drop; (c) that as more workers are laid off, the higher will be the premium rates of that employer with the result that a direct penalty will be imposed for such acts.

The danger of alleging that a worker is discharged when he is in reality laid-off can be checked both by an adequate administrative system which will probe such cases and by determining whether or not he is replaced. If the size of the working force be decreased, it is quite clear that such an ostensible dismissal would in reality be a lay-off.

5. *It is feared that the payment of unemployment benefits would prevent downward readjustments of wages which at times might be necessary and thus stand in the way of industrial recovery.* The fact that unemployed workmen can refuse to accept work at less than the standard rate and still continue to draw benefits will, if the experience of

Great Britain and Germany is any guide, lessen the pressure upon workmen to accept lower wages as a condition of obtaining employment and will thus operate to keep up wage-rates. During periods of business depression, this may operate to put industries producing for the foreign market at somewhat of a disadvantage as compared with nations which do not have such systems, and if profit margins are reduced in industries producing for the home market, may discourage activity in these lines as well. But it should be noted here that the two other chief industrial nations, England and Germany, already have such systems and that this is also true of Italy, Poland, and Russia and France, while a large percentage of the workers in Belgium, Denmark and Switzerland are similarly protected.

6. *It is feared that since there is inadequate statistical information concerning the extent of unemployment in the United States, it will be impossible to fix accurate actuarial rates of contributions.* Two replies can be made to this: (a) that after the system has been in operation for a time, a body of adequate experience will be developed upon which the rates can be readjusted, (b) that studies by Hart [8] the National Bureau of Economic Research,[9] and by one of the authors [10] (although admittedly based upon inadequate data) indicate an average volume of unemployment through the years in manufacturing, mining, transportation, and construction of somewhere between 8 and 10 per cent. If a two weeks' waiting period is imposed and if the average benefits are fixed at approximately 40 per cent of the earnings, the average cost for these industries would seem to be somewhere between 3 and 4 per cent of the payroll. The inclusion of mercantile trade and the public utilities would in turn somewhat reduce this figure.

[8] Hornell Hart, *Fluctuations in Unemployment in Cities of the United States,* 1902-1917.
[9] *Recent Economic Changes,* Vol. II, pp. 469-78.
[10] Douglas, *Real Wages in the United States,* pp. 403-460.

BIBLIOGRAPHICAL NOTE

The references which are listed below are merely those which it is believed will be of especial interest to general students and to readers. There are a number of very excellent bibliographies on various aspects of unemployment which can be utilized by those who wish to do more detailed work in the various fields. Among these are (1) *Bibliography of Unemployment,* International Labour Office (1930), 217 pp. (2) *Bibliography on Unemployment Compensation,* 1891-1927, 117 pp., and a supplementary bibliography on the same subject for 1928-29, 36 pp. Industrial Relations Counselors, Inc. (3) *List of References on Public Employment Agencies,* Library of Congress, 1919, 10 pp. (4) *List of References on Utilization of Public Works,* Library of Congress, 1922, 14 pp.

Further articles on the problem can be found in the *International Labour Review,* the British *Ministry of Labour Gazette,* the French *Bulletin du Ministère du Travail,* the Belgian *Revue du Travail,* the German *Reichsarbeitsblatt* and in this country the *Monthly Labor Review,* the *Survey,* and the *American Labor Legislation Review.*

1. *General.*

Pigou, *Unemployment* (1913).

Clay, *The Post-War Unemployment Problem* (1929).

Beveridge, *Unemployment; a Problem of Industry* (1911). New edition, 1930.

United States Senate Committee on Education and Labor. *Unemployment in the United States;* Hearings 70th Congress, 2nd Session pursuant to S. Res. 219 (1929).

Bowley, Clay, Rowntree, etc. *The Third Winter of Unemployment* (1923) and *Is Unemployment Inevitable?* (1929).

2. *Effects of Unemployment.*

Calkins, *Some Folks Won't Work* (1930).

Hall, *Case Studies of Unemployment* (1931).

Klein, *The Burden of Unemployment* (1923).

Lundberg, *Unemployment and Child Welfare*, Bulletin 125 of the United States Children's Bureau (1923).

3. *Seasonal Unemployment.*

Feldman, *The Regularization of Employment* (1925).

Lewisohn, Draper, Commons and Lescohier, *Can Business Prevent Unemployment?* (1925).

Smith, *Reducing Seasonal Unemployment* (1931).

Report New York Committee on the Stabilization of Industry (1930), 96 pp.

Chamber of Commerce of the United States, *Balancing Production and Employment Through Management Control* (1930).

4. *Technological Unemployment and the Fear of Over-production.*

Hobson, *Rationalization and Unemployment* (1930) and *The Economics of Unemployment* (1922).

Martin, *The Limited Market* (1926).

Gregory, Rationalization and Technological Unemployment, *Economic Journal*, December 1930, pp. 551-67.

Foster and Catchings, *Profits.*

Lubin, *The Absorption of the Unemployed by American Industry* (1929).

Myers, Occupational Readjustment of Displaced Skilled Workers, *Journal Political Economy*, August, 1929, pp. 473-89.

Barnett, *Chapters on Machinery and Labor* (1926).

5. *Cyclical Unemployment and Price Stabilization.*

Mitchell, *Business Cycles*, 1913, and Volume I of the revision of the same (1927).

Snyder, *Business Cycles and Business Measurements*, 1927.

Thorpe, *Business Annals* (1927).

Wagemann, *Economic Rhythm* (1930).

Clark, Business Acceleration and the Law of Demand, *Journal of Political Economy*, 1916, pp. 217-235, and *Economics of Overhead Costs* (1923).

Hawtrey, *Currency and Credit* (3rd edition) (1928).

Pigou, *Industrial Fluctuations* (1927).

Keynes, *A Tract on Monetary Reform* (1923); *A Treatise on Money*, 2 vols. (1930).

Fisher, *Stabilizing the Dollar* (1921).

Edie, *Money, Bank Credit, and Prices* (1928).

Robertson, *Banking Policy and the Price Level.*

Interim Report of the Gold Delegation of the Financial Committee of the League of Nations (1930).

6. *Public Works.*

Wolman, *Planning and Control of Public Works* (1930).

Dickinson, Public Construction and Cyclical Unemployment, *Annals of the American Academy of Social and Political Science,* Vol. CXXXIX.

Foster and Catchings, *The Road to Plenty* (1928).

Bielschowsky, Business Fluctuations and Public Works, *Quarterly Journal of Economics,* February 1930, pp. 286-319.

Webb, *The Public Organization of the Labour Market* (1909).

7. *Public and Private Employment Offices.*

Harrison and Associates, *Public Employment Offices* (1924).

Lescohier, *The Labor Market* (1919).

Seymour, *The British Labor Exchange* (1928).

Report Committee of Enquiry into the Work of the Employment Exchange (cmd. 1054) (1920); *Minutes of Evidence* (cmd. 1140) (1921).

8. *Unemployment Insurance.*

Stewart, *Unemployment Benefits in the United States* (1930).

Davison, *The Unemployed* (1929).

Gilson, *British Unemployment Insurance* (1931).

Ministry of Labour (Great Britain), *Report on National Unemployment Insurance to July 1923.*

Report of the Unemployment Insurance Committee (Blanesburgh Committee) (1927), 2 vols.

Carrol, *Unemployment Insurance in Germany,* 2nd edit. (1930).

Cohen, *Insurance Against Unemployment* (1921).

International Labour Office, *Unemployment Insurance* (1925).

Lefort, *L'Assurance contre le Chômage* (1913).

INDEX

Aftalion, A., 179
Australia, seasonal variations in employment, 35; sources of statistics, 44; trade union percentages of unemployment, 36, 37.
Austria, private employment offices, 274

Baker, Elizabeth F., 140
Barnes, Charles B., 320
Barnes, G. N., 300
Barnett, George E., 148
Belgium, days benefited, 383, 384; days lost, 383; Fonds de Chômage, 376; Fonds National de Crise, 375; income and expenditures of societies, 377; number of insured workers, 381; partial unemployment, 35; payments from National Emergency Fund, 383; postwar average of unemployment, 35; seasonal variations in employment, 38 ff.; sources of unemployment statistics, 43; trade union percentage of unemployment, 36, 37; types of existing insurance societies, 376; voluntary unemployment insurance, 369, 371 ff.
Benefits, emergency in Belgium, 380, 383, 384; in Denmark, 388, 395; in Germany, 434, 452, 460; in Great Britain, 404, 412; extended, 294, 415; seasonal in Germany, 444, 447; standard in Belgium, 379; in Denmark, 388, 390, 393 ff.; in Germany, 429, 433, 449; in Great Britain, 404, 405n, 411, 413; in the United States, 465 ff., 492 ff.
Beveridge, Sir William H., 41, 258, 292, 402.
Bielschowsky, Georg, 220.
Bingham, Senator, 333, 334.
Birth Control, 162.
Blanesburgh Committee, 418, 422, 423.
Bowley, A. L., 192, 205, 211.

Bulgaria, private employment offices, 274.
Business Cycles, current theories of, 178 ff.; discription of phases of, 169 ff.; direct regulation of, 231 ff.; indirect regulation of, 235 ff.; individual enterprise and, 222 ff.; influence upon employment conditions, 162, 163, 167 ff.

Calkins, Clinch, 64.
Canada, placement record of public employment service, 307; private employment offices, 274, 305; public employment offices, 305; sources of unemployment statistics, 44; trade union percentages of unemployment, 36, 37.
Cannan, E., 425.
Carroll, Mollie Ray, 201n, 203, 204, 274n, 443, 444, 449.
Cassel, Gustav, 184.
Charity, 485.
Census of unemployment in the United States, Bureau of Census 1890, 1900, 1910, 6, 7; 1930, 5, 6, 9 ff.; Jan. 1931, 23; Bureau of Labor 1901, 30; 1915, 7, 31; Local, 7.
Churchill, Winston, 292, 402.
Clague, Ewan, 147, 149.
Clark, J. M., 175.
Commons, John R., 480, 481, 482, 491.
Contributions, in Belgium, 378; in Germany, 429; in Great Britain, 403, 416, 417; in the United States, 465 ff., 482, 490; rates of, 388, 411, 417, 420, 422, 447, 448, 492; refunds to employers, 406.
Courts of Appeal, in Germany, 438.
Costs, comparative of placement in various states, 338; of placement of labor, 337 ff.; of public works in Great Britain, 200; regularization, 109 ff.; unemployment, 64 ff., 67 ff.
Couzens, Senator, 153.

SOCIAL PROBLEMS
AND
SOCIAL POLICY:
The American Experience

An Arno Press Collection

Bachman, George W. and Lewis Meriam. **The Issue of Compulsory Health Insurance.** 1948

Bishop, Ernest S. **The Narcotic Drug Problem.** 1920

Bosworth, Louise Marion. **The Living Wage of Women Workers.** 1911

[Brace, Emma, editor]. **The Life of Charles Loring Brace.** 1894

Brown, Esther Lucile. **Social Work as a Profession.** 4th Edition. 1942

Brown, Roy M. **Public Poor Relief in North Carolina.** 1928

Browning, Grace. **Rural Public Welfare.** 1941

Bruce, Isabel Campbell and Edith Eickhoff. **The Michigan Poor Law.** 1936

Burns, Eveline M. **Social Security and Public Policy.** 1956

Cahn, Frances and Valeska Bary. **Welfare Activities of Federal, State, and Local Governments in California, 1850-1934.** 1936

Campbell, Persia. **The Consumer Interest.** 1949

Davies, Stanley Powell. **Social Control of the Mentally Deficient.** 1930

Devine, Edward T. **The Spirit of Social Work.** 1911

Douglas, Paul H. and Aaron Director. **The Problem of Unemployment.** 1931

Eaton, Allen in Collaboration with Shelby M. Harrison. **A Bibliography of Social Surveys.** 1930

Epstein, Abraham. **The Challenge of the Aged.** 1928

Falk, I[sidore] S., Margaret C. Klem, and Nathan Sinai. **The Incidence of Illness and the Receipt and Costs of Medical Care Among Representative Families.** 1933

Fisher, Irving. **National Vitality, its Wastes and Conservation.** 1909

Freund, Ernst. **The Police Power:** Public Policy and Constitutional Rights. 1904

Gladden, Washington. **Applied Christianity:** Moral Aspects of Social Questions. 1886

Hartley, Isaac Smithson, editor. **Memorial of Robert Milham Hartley.** 1882

Hollander, Jacob H. **The Abolition of Poverty.** 1914

Kane, H[arry] H[ubbell]. **Opium-Smoking in America and China.** 1882

Klebaner, Benjamin Joseph. **Public Poor Relief in America, 1790-1860.** 1951

Knapp, Samuel L. **The Life of Thomas Eddy.** 1834

Lawrence, Charles. **History of the Philadelphia Almshouses and Hospitals from the Beginning of the Eighteenth to the Ending of the Nineteenth Centuries.** 1905

[Massachusetts Commission on the Cost of Living]. **Report of the Commission on the Cost of Living.** 1910

[Massachusetts Commission on Old Age Pensions, Annuities and Insurance]. **Report of the Commission on Old Age Pensions, Annuities and Insurance.** 1910

[New York State Commission to Investigate Provision for the Mentally Deficient]. **Report of the State Commission to Investigate Provision for the Mentally Deficient.** 1915

[Parker, Florence E., Estelle M. Stewart, and Mary Conymgton, compilers]. **Care of Aged Persons in the United States.** 1929

Pollock, Horatio M., editor. **Family Care of Mental Patients.** 1936

Pollock, Horatio M. **Mental Disease and Social Welfare.** 1941

Powell, Aaron M., editor. **The National Purity Congress;** Its Papers, Addresses, Portraits. 1896

The President's Commission on the Health Needs of the Nation. **Building America's Health.** [1952]. Five vols. in two

Prostitution in America: Three Investigations, 1902-1914. 1975

Rubinow, I[saac] M. **The Quest for Security.** 1934

Shaffer, Alice, Mary Wysor Keefer, and Sophonisba P. Breckinridge. **The Indiana Poor Law.** 1936

Shattuck, Lemuel. **Report to the Committee of the City Council Appointed to Obtain the Census of Boston for the Year 1845.** 1846

The State and Public Welfare in Nineteenth-Century America: Five Investigations, 1833-1877. 1975

Stewart, Estelle M. **The Cost of American Almshouses.** 1925

Taylor, Graham. **Pioneering on Social Frontiers.** 1930

[United States Senate Committee on Education and Labor]. **Report of the Committee of the Senate Upon the Relations Between Labor and Capital.** 1885. Four vols.

Walton, Robert P. **Marihuana, America's New Drug Problem.** 1938

Williams, Edward Huntington. **Opiate Addiction.** 1922

Williams, Pierce assisted by Isabel C. Chamberlain. **The Purchase of Medical Care Through Fixed Periodic Payment.** 1932

Willoughby, W[estal] W[oodbury]. **Opium as an International Problem.** 1925

Wisner, Elizabeth. **Public Welfare Administration in Louisiana.** 1930